Contents

Prologue

Culture X? Who is Culture X? We all are. And while the adult population in our country has *become* Culture X, the young people in our society are being taught to be without a cultural identity. The confounding messages of a diminishing cultural heritage are embedded in the explicit and implicit messages sent both from the schools young people attend and the greater community in which they live.

Is this a problem? It is if there exists a desire for a nation to perpetuate itself along some common set of values and ideals. If that is not the case, then there is no problem other than the ultimate demise of the nation as it is replaced by a new and incidental cultural identity. But if the nation wishes to survive, to prosper, then it is indeed a problem.

Is there any evidence of cultural confusion? If you have ever heard a stylized version of "The Star Spangled Banner" sung at a civic or sporting event, then you have experienced the quiet chipping away of a national cultural identity. If you or people you know refer to their own identity as a hybrid American (for example, African-American, Asian-American, German-American, or—as my father would say—Bronx-American), then you have witnessed the subtle supplanting of one cultural identity with another. But be aware that we are not talking about denying one's heritage! Heritage is an inalienable facet of one's personal identity. We are, however, speaking of our national *cultural* identity, which is, by definition, a matter of our group identity rather than a personal one.

Are the schools to blame for a decline in cultural identity? In our opinion, no. The schools respond to what the society at large wants. The problem lies in not knowing what society's members want. And that's what this book is all about; as a nation, as a society, we need to make some decisions about who we are, where we are going, and where we want to go. The schools may then more effectively guide the intellectual and cultural development of succeeding generations.

Ultimately, it is a question of vision—not the vision of the authors of this book, mind you. Instead, it is a matter of a shared vision for a multiethnic society. One might think of it as phase 2 of the American Revolution, and much of it will occur in school.

I

WHO ARE WE?

1

Wrestling with the Beast

The great enemy of the truth is very often not the lie—deliberate, contrived and dishonest—but the myth—persistent, persuasive and unrealistic.

—John F. Kennedy, Yale Commencement Address, 1962

Perhaps you are a parent with children in school, or you have a child who will shortly begin school. It could be the case that you are a student who is considering a career in education as a teacher or administrator. In any case, you may well be concerned about what looms ahead in this great enterprise we know as education.

The term *education* is a noun with at least two distinct meanings. In one sense, it may refer to an individual's accumulated experiences—whether obtained formally (as in that which the teacher teaches in the classroom) or informally (as in "my time in politics was a real education"). In another sense, it may refer to an institution of society charged with the task of seeing that particular experiences, information, and skills are passed on to a new generation. This second sense, *education as an institution*, is our focus here.

IMAGES OF EDUCATION

Education as an institution might conjure up images of children in classrooms, adolescents meandering through hallways, high school students recognizing the rudiments of their adult identities, and of course yellow school buses and red apples for the teacher. But education goes beyond that. One may think of sons and daughters leaving home to live on campus at a college or university or of graduate students working through the day and taking classes at night. It includes technical schools and adult education courses. At its highest levels, education seeks to broaden one's thinking while also imposing greater and greater specificity to a course of study. Though a colleague once remarked that education is the process by which people learn more and more about less and less until they know everything about nothing, it *is* an institution that prepares its constituents to live and work in society. It stands

3

ready to help people expand their understanding. For any society that values its culture, an effective institution of formal education is integral to social prosperity.

But the mention of education can also bring to mind images of a society conflicted. Issues such as sex education, evolution and creationism, and prayer in schools still remain as volatile topics facing school boards and the communities they serve. Though these are viable matters, they are also issues that have been debated for decades. Few other enterprises could exist for so long when questions of fundamental importance are only "temporarily" resolved, or perhaps simply left unresolved. And pertinent though these issues may be to the education of children, they are almost benign events by comparison to many other occurrences in contemporary schools.

Twenty years ago, the "bomb scare" became more frequent in schools than its predecessor, the false fire alarm. At that time, threats of bombs in schools were typically phoned in by the perpetrator. Yet, now we see that it is the students who bring the guns and bombs to school. For years the complaint has been made about students bringing weapons to school because the *having* of weapons greatly increases the possibility for the *using* of weapons. The nuance that we face today is that weapons are being brought for the specific purpose of mass injury, even death, to make some sort of social or individual statement.

The sad irony is that those students who bring weapons to school "for protection" are proving to be prophetic. At this time, an incident of armed violence in the schools has not yet escalated into a gunfight between students as some protect themselves from the actions of others. However, with all of the elements in place, can such a situation be very far off? What will be the legal ramifications when children exchange gunfire in a public institution with *compulsory* attendance? And keep in mind that the new millennium began with a six-year-old shooting another six-year-old *at* school *in* the classroom. It is one thing to say that a few isolated incidents in high school have been sensationalized, but it is hard to ignore something that spans all grade levels across the entire country. This is not to say that children are "bad" but rather that something is definitely amiss on a larger scale.

We may well ask why events such as these are associated with school at all. Are these the issues that should come to mind when we think of what schools are all about? Firearms, explosives, litigation over the trivial, as well as litigation against schools over forces and factors beyond their control, are all issues that beg the question, how does a *school* prevent these things from happening? And still, we haven't even gotten to consider the implied purpose of schools: education.

The frightening conclusion is that the notion that "kids have changed" coerces us into accepting what we find. Indeed, a prominent thinker in education has noted, "Children today are tyrants. They contradict their parents, gobble their food, and tyrannize their teachers." This attitude among children, with which most of us can certainly identify, demands our attention. Yet, when we look at the bigger picture and consider that the thinker quoted above was the Greek philosopher Socrates, who lived between 469 BC and 399 BC, it becomes obvious that "kids have changed" might not be the most viable explanation for the situation.

*   *   *

Despite the presence of security guards and metal detectors, the schools are not all gloom and doom. The public schools account for the whereabouts of nearly one-fifth of the entire U.S. population on any given school day. The vast majority of these chil-dren leave the house and come home without having brought a weapon along or hav-ing had one brandished in their face. And it is fairly safe to say that most school-age children do not feel threatened (that is, that their life is on the line) by going to school. So, why is any of this an issue? After all, it could just be the fact that those few sensa-tional stories of tragedy are what make it to the newscasts.

Unfortunately, the academic statistics that compare U.S. students to those of other nations indicate that something indeed is wrong. The United States is trailing the world leaders in educational achievement, and trailing badly. The latest figures available (2003) found that U.S. fourth graders were performing above the interna-tional average in both science and mathematics. Pretty good, right? Unless you keep in mind that above the average does not necessarily mean very far above the aver-age. In fact, the report of the National Center for Education Statistics (NCES) groups countries into three categories: those with scores significantly higher than the United States, those with scores not significantly different from the United States, and those with scores significantly below those of the United States. To that end, the results show that countries with average scores in mathematics not significantly dif-ferent from the United States were Malaysia, Latvia, the Russian Federation, the Slo-vak Republic, Australia, Lithuania, Sweden, Scotland, Israel, and New Zealand. Those countries with average scores *significantly higher* were Singapore, Korea, Japan, Hong Kong SAR, Chinese Taipei, Belgium-Flemish, Estonia, Hungary, and the Netherlands (NCES, 2005). That's the good news. The bad news is that, relatively speaking, our fourth graders were doing *better* than our eighth and twelfth graders as compared to their international peers.

When faced with information such as this, along with the headline-grabbing stories, we are compelled to search for answers, for reasons, for explanations. Here's a key point to keep in mind throughout our search: Though circumstances change, the prob-lem is not new. Though there are good schools, it is nonetheless the case that thou-sands of children attend class in dilapidated buildings, without the proper materials and equipment for the task, and in environments in many ways not at all conducive to learning—at least not to learning what is intended.

The "Failure of the Schools" Syndrome

Eventually, someone in politics—or, as is the fashion in good economic times, some-one in business—makes the complaint that these things happen because students fail to get an education in school: If only we would do this or that in a "businesslike" way, it would all change. Business wants better workers; government wants better citizens—preferably citizens who will vote for the party that was in office when they became such good citizens. Parents want better children, and teachers want better students. To that end, some states are advocating "courtesy" laws, which dictate the conventions of eti-quette that students will exercise in their interactions with teachers and other adults: courtesy laws to bring an end to school shootings. Certainly, we all hope to sit down to the celebration banquet when such an effort proves to be a resounding success. But whether character education (once considered the foundation of education, once con-sidered taboo, now resurgent) is the panacea for the troubles facing the public school remains to be seen. In the meantime, it might be worthwhile to look at the *entire issue* of education in considerably greater detail.

The fact is that students *do* receive an education in school. It is the process, content, and quality of the educational outcomes that have given rise to more than just serious concern. Some would go so far as to say that education, public education in particular, is failing. If this is true and we keep in mind that school is often referred to as a microcosm of the society (a microcosm that includes about 50 million of the nearly 260 million American citizens [NCES, 1999], a fairly large microcosm, perhaps even a "mediumcosm"), then the failure of public education may signal a much greater social collapse to come. What if, instead of taking the perspective of "failure," we take the perspective of examining what is being taught, why, how, to whom, and by whom. Perhaps, as a result, substantive changes can be made to yield the sort of outcomes that we, as a society, would prefer.

A Political Exercise for the People

It is important to recognize at the outset that of all the institutions that have arisen through the progress of our society and culture, education continues more or less as a grand experiment. "Experiment" perhaps is not the correct word, and "grand" might only apply in terms of scale. In fact, were education an *experiment*, there would be considerably more focus, structure, and control of its development. There would be more credence given to the data collected about its successes and failures, as well as a more rigorous academically based and discipline-directed interpretation of the data.

Ironically, a vast amount of research is continually pursued on virtually all aspects of education. Due largely to the particular nature of the institution of education—flaws in its defining characteristics—research becomes topic for debate rather than prescriptive information for use in *systematically* accomplishing a predetermined goal or for *systemically* changing the institution to operate in different ways. And it must also be admitted, even by those of us in higher education, that much of what is carried out as educational research amounts to little more than academic busywork that remains on library shelves and keeps the tertiary level of the institution in business.

Politically, the popularity of education as a campaign platform plank (a plank typically devoid of a practical plan) results in the institution of education being a pervasive social issue that can be bent and twisted to local and regional wishes and ideas with fantastic ease. Elections at the district, county, state, and national levels can all impact upon education. One might expect with this ready accessibility that education would be an institution operating from highly detailed plans tailored to very specific needs. One might anticipate the establishment of clear objectives that elicit strong support within the community. It might be assumed that the political players in the enterprise of education would bring to their constituents crystallized plans for accomplishing the most noble of goals.

Contrary to the expectation, and even contrary to the volumes upon volumes of regulation and procedural policy that govern education, the institution remains vague. The goals remain obscure. The intended outcomes of twelve years of education are not readily identified. After all, there are expectations for *these* children, different expectations for *those* children, and still other expectations for still more stratifications of the enrollees at any public school. Politics and politicians, unfortunately, do not offer real solutions.

In defense of those seeking elected office, it might be said that to offer real solutions during a campaign is counterproductive for there is always someone ready to disagree.

But what does that leave us when election decisions must be made? Perhaps you have heard candidates for superintendent, legislator, or even president affirm that in terms of education they are "advocates of children." Yet, really, how many candidates would make the claim that they are *not* advocates of children? Where is the plan beyond the platitude? Goals 2000, an admirable example of the desire to improve education, is also an excellent example of politics in education. Written in 1994, Goals 2000: The Educate America Act (HR 1804) listed eight goals:

By the year 2000,

1. all children in America will start school ready to learn,
2. the high school graduation rate will increase to at least 90 percent,
3. all students will leave grades 4, 8, and 12 having demonstrated competency over challenging subject matter including English, mathematics, science, foreign languages, civics and government, economics, arts, history, and geography, and every school in America will ensure that all students learn to use their minds well, so they may be prepared for responsible citizenship, further learning, and productive employment in our Nation's modern economy,
4. the Nation's teaching force will have access to programs for the continued improvement of their professional skills and the opportunity to acquire the knowledge and skills needed to instruct and prepare all American students for the next century,
5. United States students will be first in the world in mathematics and science achievement,
6. every adult American will be literate and will possess the knowledge and skills necessary to compete in a global economy and exercise the rights and responsibilities of citizenship,
7. every school in the United States will be free of drugs, violence, and the unauthorized presence of firearms and alcohol and will offer a disciplined environment conducive to learning,
8. every school will promote partnerships that will increase parental involvement and participation in promoting the social, emotional, and academic growth of children.

(HR 1804, Educate America Act, Title I, Sec. 102, 1994)

These, of course, are good words, inspiring words, but the year 2000 has come and gone. American students are not first in the world in science and mathematics. Not all Americans are literate. And the schools are certainly not free of violence.

As a political function within the community, education can be more readily affected by people at the local level (sometimes by one, sometimes by more) than any other institution of our society. Almost as if granted to the public as a political exercise with which to dabble, each generation makes its own mark on the institution. That mark takes on a national demeanor due to the mobility of Americans even though by Constitutional omission education is a responsibility of the individual states. This ready accessibility (local, state, or national) is not characteristic to an equal degree of other aspects of our social system. Within other governmental endeavors, older generations eventually give way to younger generations, and longtime legislators ultimately yield to newer candidates and changing constituencies. But even in these situations, elected officials must appeal to a wide range of voters representing multiple generations. Legislation that will pass through the U.S. Congress must accommodate an entire nation. Not so with the local public school: It is much more responsive to local thinking and to local pressure. That responsiveness, however, is a double-edged sword if ever the metaphor was appropriate.

It is no wonder that education undergoes continual change, a process that is typically referred to as "reform." Indeed, we are still asking questions about learning that have been asked for well over a hundred years. It should be expected, given the ease with which this particular system can be augmented, adjusted, and altered, that each generation will make the same cry, "Education must be reformed!" Yet, with all of the input, with all of the money, with all of the advances in our understanding of how people learn, with the development of learning systems and strategies, with the technological progress that facilitates rapid interpersonal communication, as a society we are still wringing our hands and trying to decide what's *wrong* with the institution of education. Why? At least one reason may be found in *the myth of reform*.

The Myth of Reforming the Institution of Education

There is indeed a host of issues that must be confronted in wrestling with this leviathan we call education. It is, however, the *myth* of reform that must be confronted squarely and with an attitude of reconceptualizing our perspective. We refer to a myth of reform because efforts in this regard have gone on for so long that people tend to believe that changes, substantive changes that alter the character of the institution, actually occur at some point. But how much really changes?

If it should be the case in your area that a brand-new school building is going up, take a look at it. What has changed from the classrooms of the mid-1800s? Likely you will find that the plan is still for large rooms that will accommodate as many as three dozen students and one teacher. There will probably be some sort of writing board affixed to the wall at the front of the room. If it's a "high-tech" school, the boards will be whiteboards on which will be used dry-erase or water-soluble markers. Chalk and some sort of blackboard are still the standard, however, in schools from kindergarten through higher education. Perhaps the school will use individual student desks, perhaps small tables. There will probably be a teacher's desk. Perhaps the class will be wired for computer use. Chances are just as good that it will not be.

What real *innovations* will you find? Keep in mind that it is now nearly one hundred years since the world went from a twelve-second flight on the sands at Kitty Hawk to airliners carrying hundreds of people at a time. Where are the comparable innovations in education? Medicine, space flight, communications, and *weapons of war* have undergone phenomenal development. What of education? Many schools now use photocopying machines as opposed to the old purple-ink mimeograph machines. Remember those? That's progress, but not much.

Moving to a discussion of curriculum and teaching practice, a realistic accounting indicates that reforms come and go. Though the following example is a satirical look at math education, it illustrates the characteristic of education to be influenced by changing social imperatives from generation to generation. The poignancy of satire, remember, is in its relationship to the truth of the matter.

1960s Arithmetic Test: "A logger cuts and sells a truckload of lumber for $100. His cost of production is four-fifths of that amount. What is his profit?"

1970s New-Math Test: "A logger exchanges Set (L) of lumber for Set (M) of money. The cardinality of Set (M) is 100. The Set (C) of production costs contains 20 fewer points. What is the cardinality of Set (P) of profits?"

1980s "Dumbed Down" Version: "A logger cuts and sells a truckload of lumber for $100. His cost is $80, his profit is $20. Find and circle the number 20."

1990s Version: "An unenlightened logger cuts down a beautiful stand of 100 trees in order to make a $20 profit. Write an essay explaining how you feel about this as a way to make money. Topic for discussion: How did the forest birds and squirrels feel?" ("Illustration Digest," 1996, 82)

Within any generation it can be expected that there will be at least one "back-to-basics" movement (the Chapter 11 Bankruptcy version of educational reform) and that on either side of that initiative is some form of "new and different" educational intervention. Yet, even "back to basics" is now seen as reform. It becomes obvious that something else must be at work within the institution if not only the new interventions fail (or at least fail to meet the expectations within the anticipated time frame) but the system reverts to *old interventions* that at one time or another were also considered to have failed. And so, we use the term *myth*, for it is a widely held, but false belief that reform is actually taking place.

The primary lesson from the parade of educational-reform efforts, efforts that any individual who was raised on K–12 education in the United States has experienced, is that the *fundamental problem* with education is that education is *fundamentally an institution*. This becomes an issue because, as will be discussed at length in chapter 3, an institution will not tolerate substantive reform. Institutions resist true reform because such change threatens to *redefine* the institution itself, in which case the old institution would cease to exist. Fortunately for us, rather than making the efforts to improve education more difficult, this situation actually clears things up quite a bit because it points clearly to the direction that needs to be taken. To effect the changes that seem to be required, education as an institution cannot be reformed; it must be rebuilt. In stronger terms, though this is not as scary as it might sound, education must be *revolutionized*.

Did You Say "Revolution"?

Mention the word "revolution" and raised eyebrows, startled looks, and requests to repeat what you've said often follow. That seems curious in our country, given its own distant (all two hundred plus years) and recent history with the many changes that have occurred. There are some "wise sayings" that might help to explain this attitude: *There is only one constant—things change* (note: institutions don't really change, they "adjust"); *everybody wants change, just not right now; change is a good thing, especially quarters* (just kidding); and perhaps most telling of all, *the more things change, the more they stay the same.* Somehow, it just seems difficult to fit the notion of "revolution" into the same category with "change" in a comfortable way.

It may also be the case that people are more comfortable talking about revolutions (and their ensuing changes) in the past tense. Not many folks have a lot of trouble with the idea of the Industrial Revolution, or the electronic age ushered in by the development of the transistor, or the generation-to-generation "revolutions" in music. Living on the far side of any revolution isn't so bad, particularly if the revolution turned out pretty well. Once the old has been replaced with the new, we can all see the advantages of having made the change—and life is good. However, staring the need to make a significant change right in the eye is a very different matter, even with a wealth of rational reasons backing the cause. So, perhaps we need to discuss this whole "revolution" idea just a bit more.

It should be admitted that, as is the case with so many terms, some of the things we talk about as "revolutions" really aren't. What is a revolution? A revolution is the process through which, by virtue of some *imperative* for change, one thing is replaced with something significantly different from that which previously existed. For example, the Industrial Revolution mentioned above replaced agriculture as the economic basis of many societies. It did not replace agriculture, but it replaced it as the core economic force.

The microwave oven, on the other hand, did not revolutionize cooking—cooking is still defined in the same way as "preparing foods by heating." Microwave energy is just a different way of providing heat. So, it *radically changed* cooking (for many of us), but it was not a revolution. Conventional ovens are still standard in homes and restaurants.

Compact disks offered a radical change in how music was stored for playback. The form in which the information is stored and the means by which that information is translated back into sound are substantively different from the record player technology many of us can recall. Those of you with children are aware that youngsters today may only know what record players are from pictures in books or in old movies. But was it a revolution, other than a marketing revolution? Not really. Though the technology changed, there was no *imperative* for change. With technological progress came new capabilities, and those capabilities fostered change. Change and substantive redefinition by revolution are two very different dimensions of a dynamic process.

It seems, then, that the real intimidator in this whole process is recognizing the imperative and then being the *initiator* of that change. This is particularly true when formulating and verbalizing an ideology is necessitated. That's serious stuff. When we speak of ideology, for some reason, mention of instigating a revolution still engenders the idea of bloody conflict, mass destruction, and eradication of all that once was pure and noble in a perfect world. Yet, for our purposes, let's set aside visions of rappelling down the side of the gymnasium or storming the steps of your state capitol building. The revolution that we are looking for in education does not require razing all of the elementary school buildings across the country, burning books at a community bonfire, or exiling the principal of your hometown school. Quite to the contrary, we are *advocates* of the more than five million teachers and administrators in the United States, more than three-quarters of that number being in public education (NCES, 1999). We recognize the efforts of the legions of support staff who work to deliver our system of public education. Certainly, there is room for improvement, as with any organized concern. But let this particular message be clear in these early stages of our discussion of educational revolution: *The school is not the enemy*. Rather, we see the school as responsive to the expressed desires of the society at large. It is the society itself that is not clear about its own desires. Therefore, our task is to consider who we are as a society, understand what part education plays in the perpetuation and progress of that society, and look at ways in which to make that happen. The revolution is in the *reconceptualization of what an institution of education should be*. From there, we can consider (1) how it might be accomplished, and (2) since it must be recognized that substantive change takes time, how to maximize children's experiences in the old institution in the meantime.

Summary

As you might expect, revolutionizing a school or anything else is an interactive endeavor. People can't just read a book "about" the idea and then it happens. So, what you have here is a workbook for revolutionizing the institution. There are important questions for you to consider. We won't be checking up on you, but if you're using this book as part of a course, somebody might be. If you are using this book as a concerned parent, you'll be checked up on every time you look at your children. So, be honest with yourself. At the very least, you will become more aware of an institution that on any given day directly involves well over fifty million Americans and indirectly involves tens of millions more. This is a big topic.

WHAT TO EXPECT IN THIS BOOK

This book will not tell you what to think, but it will give you things to think about. It will not tell you what to do, but it will provide some ideas for how we might begin. It will not identify the individuals who will lead a revolution in education, but it will invite you to be an active participant.

Throughout the chapters, you will be provided with opportunities to engage in an activity, typically a reflective activity that will ask for *your* thinking. After all, in any discussion the most flattering question that can be asked of you is, what do you think? When you are prepared to engage in the discussion, you will immediately transition from bystander to participant. Our hope and intent is that this book will prepare you to be a participant in the reconceptualization, the revolutionizing, of school. Activity 1.1 is your opportunity to begin.

FINAL THOUGHTS

Without doubt, the sheer size of the educational institution is enough to make many people decide that things are not so bad after all. It would certainly be *easier* to leave things as they are. One peculiar characteristic of the institution that contributes to this

---

Activity 1.1.
WHAT IS YOUR PERCEPTION OF SCHOOL?

1. In just a brief paragraph, describe what comes to your mind when someone mentions "school." You can describe it in terms of whatever characteristics are most important to you (e.g., academic, social, athletic, career preparation, etc.). Write quickly, and remember that no one else has to see this, so spelling, grammar, and syntax are not important. Just get your thoughts down on paper.
2. Now take a look at your paragraph. Have you said anything about culture? About what it means to be American? *Based on the paragraph you wrote*, what would you say was the main purpose of school for you? What, in your opinion, is the main purpose of school today?

view is a deceptive fluidity to the whole enterprise. Children move from grade level to grade level on a regular basis. Parents are most concerned with the system only while their children are involved with it. Terms of political office are much shorter than the thirteen years spanning K–12 education, and so administrations and emphases change frequently, relative to the time it takes to complete the public school curriculum. Considered on these fractional planes, it may indeed be easier to just let things continue as they are—we might even rationalize that it is a self-correcting system.

However, the message of this chapter has been that the problems seen with education are much more pervasive than disagreements with teaching strategies and the provision of special services. Institutions take on the character of the social forces that will enable institutional survival. So, we must look closely at that character. What we find now is a society that has consistently been losing its sense of identity. That confusion manifests itself in terms of what is taught and why it is taught.

If schools were a business, management would invoke the luxury of shutting it down and retooling before the corporation faced bankruptcy. But education today includes over fourteen thousand school districts and nearly ninety thousand schools. Shutting down and reorganizing is not so easily accomplished. And so, it is a simple matter to say that it is just *too big* to change. Instead, we need to take the perspective that it is *so big*, it *must* be changed.

The distinguished news broadcaster John Chancellor once noted in remarks about Earth Day efforts that talk of saving the planet really misses the mark. The planet, he indicated, did quite well before we arrived, and no doubt will do just fine after we have wiped ourselves from the face of the earth. What we are really talking about, he concluded, is saving ourselves. What we see in the schools is the symptom rather than the problem. With a vision toward the future, the schools can be the instrument through which solutions are implemented. So, essentially, we see that "saving the schools" is actually a matter of saving the society—of saving ourselves.

Is this doable? The fact that it may have been easier to face these issues and make changes in years gone by is no longer of consequence. What is pertinent is the notion that there will not be a better time than now to put all of our human, fiscal, and social resources to work. With so much information available, it is time for *the age of problem solving* to begin. And so, let's wrestle with the beast!

2

The American Culture

If democracy has a moral and ideal meaning, it is that a social return be demanded from all and that opportunity for development of distinctive capacities be afforded all.

—John Dewey

On the first day of class, a number of things happen in a particular "Introduction to Education" course taught by a particular professor. First is the practice of having the students introduce themselves by stating their names and sharing a little background information, followed by a similar introduction of the professor if anybody should happen to ask. Following this is a point-by-point discussion of the syllabus, detailing the topics, the expectations, the tentative schedule, and, of course, the policy regarding absences. Throughout the ordeal, an attempt is made to incorporate an element of humor, along with the establishment of high expectations and an emphasis on the implicit requirement for "power thinking" that will pervade the semester.

Oftentimes, depending on how willing the students are to engage in dialogue, these first tasks will take up the majority of a typical class period. Then, as the students start sensing that not much more will take place on this first day of class, the professor asks a question. It is one of those simple questions that most anybody should be able to answer. It is not an involved, multipart question. In fact, the eventual request is that it be answered in one sentence. It is not one of those questions that sends students scurrying back to the recesses of their long-removed high school days to recall information that some teacher said they would need to know someday. And that's a good thing because "Introduction to Education" is also taught to evening classes of adult learners who have been away from high school for many years.

No, the question is none of these dastardly things. It requires only that the student has grown up in the United States. Actually, it does not even require that, for it is often the case that the students who have the least trouble formulating a response are those from other countries. Rather, it is a mere five words followed by the appropriate punctuation of an interrogatory clause, twenty-nine characters actually, the spaces and question mark included. Two words are capitalized when it is written out. All in all, a much shorter question than "What do you want to have for lunch?" Yet, for some reason, it causes reactions of consternation, of frustration, of dubious regard for its value. The question: *What is the American culture?*

WHAT IS THE AMERICAN CULTURE? PART I

What *is* the American culture? Students in the class often say the culture is baseball, apple pie, and hot dogs. When asked whether that means that it is accurate for someone to describe him- or herself as a baseball or an apple pie, the response is usually something to the effect of the American culture being "everything." After several minutes of trying to find out how "everything" might be narrowed down to "everything American," an additional criterion is added to the question to avoid allowing the answer to fill up several volumes of descriptors. The challenge is restated this way: "In one sentence, define the American culture."

The task presented is to identify in just one sentence, albeit a long sentence with plenty of obscure punctuation if students like, that which makes us uniquely American. For people who have lived all of their young lives in the United States, how difficult a task could this possibly be? Apparently it is quite difficult, for having realized that attempts at satisfying the professor by saying that the American culture is "everything" will not suffice, the approach taken next is to say that it cannot be defined. All are in agreement that there is an American culture, yet it is something that is beyond putting into words. How can it be, they are asked, that something we all agree exists cannot be defined? And so, the semester begins.

We offer this brief insight into a contemporary college classroom because these young people represent the success stories of our system of education. These are the students who achieved the required SAT scores, accumulated the recommendations, and participated in the extracurricular activities. These are the students who got the grades and made their way into college. Of any of the graduates of K–12 education, these are the people who we might expect would be able to consider, conceptualize, and verbalize a reasonable answer to the question.

In their defense, the difficulty is by no means confined to college students: Ask adults, ask high school students, ask professors or politicians, and likely the results will be the same. Americans have a very difficult time describing what makes them American other than geographic location and some sort of documentation of citizenship. Despite a lifetime of living the American life, many people have a very difficult time putting into words a description of what constitutes Americanness. Yet, for better or for worse, "American" does indeed mean something around the world.

The Chinese word for America is *Mei Guo* (pronounced "may gwah"). The literal translation is "beautiful country." While one of the authors of this book was teaching in China, there were times when, upon hearing the term *Mei Guo*, it was clear that it had been said in a very friendly way and other instances when it was most obviously uttered with a sneering element of derision. Whether or not students in "Introduction to Education" can verbalize what it means to be American, others in the world have some very definite ideas of what it means (the grammar is correct, by the way, for the question is concerned with what it means to be American rather than "an" American—one among many).

We believe that students *are* capable of formulating an answer to the question; they just haven't been challenged to think on such levels. Paradoxically, the difficulty students have with answering this particular question both supports and refutes Hirsch's (1988) perspective that students have suffered from what might be called noncontextual education, that is, that the curriculum has become caught up with "basics," or with critical thinking, or perhaps with problem solving, though without any *context* for working with these skills and processes. There is no cultural background information provided for use with the basic skills, or the critical thinking, or the problems being solved. Therefore, it is understandable that students cannot answer the question. In school they have learned rules, skills, and heuristics but have not learned the cultural underpinnings for which those skills and so forth were intended as facilitators of communication.

The paradox comes into play vis-à-vis the notion that even if school is an exercise in acculturation (and this is a current topic of debate in our society), understanding the American culture does not require *attendance at school*; rather, it requires *exposure to the culture*. And so, it might be argued that given an abundance of contextual matter to consider (i.e., a lifetime of cultural experiences), without the "skills" of critical, creative, and problem-solving thinking, the bits and pieces of the big picture fail to get assembled in a meaningful way. Paradox or otherwise, most disturbing is the degree to which students resist resolving, or even *refuse* to resolve, a question that takes more than finding the appropriate underlined phrase in a textbook.

How did you define the American culture? Did you begin writing one thing and then make changes as you went along? Did you want to give up and just move on? The students in the "Introduction to Education" class eventually found that there was no escaping this question for it became the foundation of all that was done in the class from the study of educational philosophies, to questions of the role of education in society, to the responsibilities of teachers, and, of course, to the question of curriculum, that is, determining what the schools should be teaching. Even so, it is difficult to impress upon these young minds fresh from the high school routine of memorize, repeat, and forget that knowing who you are is critically important when determining how to become who you want to be. This foundation is equally essential whether the question is of self-concept or cultural identity.

As we continue to work with this topic, there are a couple of things that would facilitate your own consideration of the question. First, it would be helpful to have several definitions to consider along with your own. A second item that works very well with the first is that it would be good for you to have first-hand experience with the way people react to being asked this question. So, write out the challenge on a couple of pieces of paper and then give them to several of your friends. Keep in mind that you are asking for opinions and so should not pass judgment on the responses you get. Also, there is no doubt that people often feel ill at ease when confronted with a question that they

Activity 2.1.
DEFINING THE AMERICAN CULTURE

Take the challenge yourself. Without discussing the issue with anyone else, write out your response to the prompt "In one sentence, define the American culture."

You can make the sentence as long as you like, but confine yourself to just one sentence. Remember, at this point you are *defining* the American culture, not *describing* it.

Activity 2.2.
SURVEYING OTHER PERSPECTIVES

This won't be as difficult as Activity 2.1. For this activity, write out the challenge on several pieces of paper. Select five individuals to approach with the challenge. Try to find people of different backgrounds or perspectives. For instance, if there's a middle school or high school student that you know, it would be good to get his or her opinion so that you can compare it with those of older folks.

It is very important for you to remember that you are soliciting opinions and are not evaluating responses! If at some point you want to discuss the topic with any of your volunteers, do so only after they have given you a response to the prompt, and even then be open minded and accepting of their opinions.

Take a look at the five responses. Compare them with your definition.

1. What common elements do you see among the six definitions?
2. What differences of perspective can you find?
3. What patterns can you identify based on the backgrounds of the people you have asked to do this?
4. Do you feel as though your definition needs to be refined? If so, do so!

---

think they should be able to answer but then find they are not so sure about. It's fine to go on *Jeopardy* and not be able to name the tallest mountain in the United States, but not knowing who you are hits a whole lot closer to home.

You should not feel badly if this task has been more difficult than you had expected. It is likely, however, that if you did write your own definition and then asked others to define the American culture, you have generated some interesting discussions. Even so, at this point you may be asking why it is important to define the culture. After all, whether or not Americans can explain their culture, it still exists. Correct? Oh no, another question; they're starting to pile up!

WHY IS IT IMPORTANT TO DEFINE THE CULTURE?

We do not have a long history to fall back on in terms of identifying ourselves. Despite the accomplishments of two hundred years or so, our youth as a nation is at a distinct disadvantage compared to many other cultures that extend back for many millennia. It is not entirely metaphorical to say that a culture as young as ours still feels the pain suffered by the various constituencies that have struggled for recognition within the greater identity of a nation. The freshness of the wounds and the recency of successes make a discussion of what the culture is, what it should be, and what it is becoming an especially delicate enterprise.

This becomes even more important in terms of the American culture because, like it or not, there *is* a picture that can be described. Yet, a description is all that is required to put us on the trail toward a suitable definition. That is, it is simply a matter of describing those things that make Americans uniquely American. Unlike the question of revolution that was raised in chapter 1, there is no need here to delineate a new ideology. We need not formulate a philosophy for the ages. All of that is in place, and it is simply our task to verbalize it in a statement of what constitutes our culture.

This new question, however, asks why it is *important* to define our culture—and that does involve extensive philosophical, sociological, and ideological concerns. Why is it important to know who we are as a people? What point does it serve to know? And if known, what purpose might it serve? Certainly most people reading this book could present the argument that they have lived their entire lives not being able to define our culture, so what makes it important now?

The question is indeed important if you have any concern about the condition of public education. It is equally important if at any time in the recent past you have lamented the lack of legitimate choices available in political campaigns. It's even important if you watch those "lowest-rate" telephone commercials on TV and simply have to ask yourself who's telling the truth and who isn't. For better or worse, cultural identity establishes parameters and expectations and imposes limitations on the unquestioned acceptance and use of information.

As we become increasingly isolated from our cultural identity, the culture itself assumes less and less obligation to maintain any constancy of character. For example, as is the case with burgeoning technology, users of technology find themselves at the mercy of machines they don't understand—and have little hope of ever understanding (Ebert & Ebert, 1998). The infamous Y2K frenzy of the late 1990s is testament to this phenomenon. Similarly, people find themselves faced with ethical questions arising from new technology and the realization that they are ill prepared to answer those questions (Ebert & Ebert, 1998). Charlie Chaplin's film *Modern Times* (1936) demonstrates that the possibility of people being "driven by the machine" is not a new concern. Allowing technology or the culture, both of which are dynamic entities, to evolve unabated and misunderstood is to relinquish decision-making responsibility within those processes. In essence, if people cannot define their culture, the culture will ultimately define them. We see this happening when Americans find themselves unwelcome in other countries by other cultures and when members of other cultures pursue terrorist acts on American soil.

Interestingly enough, despite the Industrial Revolution, technological development, and the dominance of electronic media and machinery, the United States is—and always has been—primarily about people. From the moment "foreigners" first arrived in North America, the new culture that began to evolve was one of multiethnic coexistence. (We say "multiethnic" because the current craze over "multiculturalism" is a contradiction in terms when offered as the American culture being *multicultural*. We will take this point up in greater detail in the discussion of defining "culture.") Even amid the ethnically exclusionary practices of the nouveau Americans and Native Americans hundreds of years ago, the culture of each group was impacted upon by the culture of the other group, and thus a new culture was being synthesized. Despite the influx of peoples of varying nationalities and the unfortunate pattern of negative racial discrimination in our history, the United States came into being and has struggled as an infant culture with a constituency of diverse cultural backgrounds.

The Constitution remains a document that made little *stated* distinction by race or cultural heritage. For the purposes of determining representation and taxation, Article I, Section 2 refers to "free persons, the exclusion of Indians not subject to taxes, and three fifths of all other persons." Those counted as three-fifths of a person were, ostensibly, slaves. However, given the fact that women and children are not mentioned, and as easy as it would have been to have stated that slaves (or any given ethnic group) would be counted as three-fifths of a person, one can speculate as to why no explicit disqualification is presented pertaining to race, culture, or religion in the eight articles of the Constitution or in the first ten amendments, the Bill of Rights, ratified two years later. Whether the framers of the Constitution were myopic or visionary in the language that they used could long remain debatable, but the text as written provides the cornerstone for a multiethnic culture. If anything is to be considered uniquely American, it is the degree to which our society embodies a diversity of cultural heritages.

For the Purpose of Perpetuation

Knowing who we are as a culture is critically important as it regards perpetuation. We and our culture are here now and cannot be anything other than what we are at this time. However, if for any reason we believe the culture should be perpetuated, then we need to know (1) what we wish to perpetuate, and (2) how we will accomplish that task. Item (1) takes us back to the question of defining the American culture. We can find this notion addressed in the preamble to the Constitution in which the authors succinctly stated that the ideas contained within were presented to "secure the Blessings of Liberty to ourselves *and our Posterity.*" Thus, they saw the agreement offered for ratification as worthy of being handed down to future generations. Item (2), of course, takes us back to the institution of education and its responsibility to the society. These two concerns, the *what* and *how* of perpetuating the culture, are the first two divisions of the representation shown in figure 2.1.

What to Perpetuate

An advantage of youthful exuberance is the capacity for change. So, the comparatively few years that our American culture has existed offers the opportunity not only to examine who we are as a culture but to entertain our desires as well. And so, as we consider the question of *what* to perpetuate, our concern will be with the subheadings on the left side of the chart: "Identity" and "Aspirations."

Some might argue that deciding how to perpetuate a culture is one thing, but *designing* a culture is beyond the realm of reason, and so a consideration of aspirations is a frivolous exercise. Certainly, this constitutes an interesting philosophical concern. However, our attempt here is simply to acknowledge that when considering who we

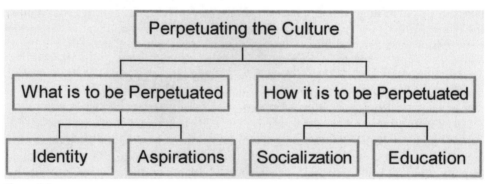

Figure 2.1.

are, a logical extension is a consideration of who we would like to be. This is not to suggest a controlled cultural evolution, as Skinner dabbled with in his work *Walden Two*. Rather, it is to acknowledge that without being bound to several thousand years of cultural heritage, it is possible at this point to consider issues that will impact our own posterity.

Though anthropologists such as White (1975) argue that "man does not and cannot control his culture or direct its course" (8), it is nonetheless the case that the culture of a people emerges from human activity. From the standpoint that culture is the *result* of the activities of a society, it would be correct to say that it cannot be controlled or directed. However, because it *is* the result of such activities, activities in which people can choose to engage, it is possible to have an impact on what would ultimately emerge as culture. That's what the American Revolution was all about. And in that regard, we might agree that a consideration of aspirations is not only worthwhile in the context of cultural identity but also representative of the highest intellectual capabilities of humankind: an ability to conduct ourselves in a manner that considers the future consequences of our actions.

Identity Anthropologists generally suggest that it takes about one hundred years for an idea to become part of the fabric of culture. That is, for some notion to transcend the level of being a "fad," or characteristic of just a generation, it will have to remain intact for at least a century, long enough for previous generations to have vanished while the characteristic remains. If that is the case, we are still very much in our formative years. Our identity is tied closely to events of a mere two hundred years and to the way in which we and our ancestors have dealt with those events. Issues such as equality of civil rights and the emphasis placed on education, issues that are each just into their second century of controversy, only now have sufficient background to be coalesced in our diverse and multifaceted society. However, the events that have contributed to this resolution, recent though they may be, are the rudiments of our current culture. And issues that arise as technology extends our capabilities (e.g., colonization of space and biological cloning) make an understanding of our cultural values imperative.

In the consideration of values, it is often the case that people wish to think of our culture within the context of the many cultures from which our social constituents have descended, taking a multicultural approach, so to speak. However, we must keep in mind that our cultural identity as Americans is based on our actions and beliefs as a people who can be subsumed under one particular national heading, regardless of our diverse heritages. The question of *culture versus heritage* is another matter, and it will be addressed in a subsequent section of this chapter.

We return, then, to the task of finding those descriptors of our beliefs and actions that make us uniquely American. Inasmuch as our society arose from revolution, it is not surprising to find that our brief history is a turbulent one, particularly with regard to questions of human relations, civil equity, and a series of other problems and issues that understandably could only arise as the evolution of the society proceeded. We make these remarks simply to reinforce the notion that for all the wondrous things that have been accomplished by this nation, the actual picture of our culture is going to include many elements that represent struggle and strife at the hands of our own people and as the result of our own oft-befuddled social conscience. For these reasons, with full awareness of our identity as a culture, the possibility of addressing our aspirations places each of us in a position to make decisions that may one day be seen as pivotal points in our cultural history.

Aspirations   It needs to be made clear at this point that when we speak of aspirations for the culture, we are not talking about replacing our form of government or making adjustments to the ethnic constituency of the society. These are fundamental aspects of who we are as a people. However, how the United States should relate to the rest of the world in terms of its political power, military capability, humanitarian responsibility, or capitalist enterprise are questions that could be considered. Should the youth of our country be required to serve in some sort of civil or military service for a period of so many years? What can be done to bridge the ethnic divide that continues to pervade our society? How do we select national goals and prioritize national efforts? These are just a few of the questions that a multiethnic society not only needs to consider but about which it can articulate policies and draw plans. Our aspirations will ultimately impact upon our cultural identity. To consider these aspirations, we need to consider who we are. The question is fundamental.

How the Culture Is to Be Perpetuated

As indicated previously, the question of how to perpetuate the culture is directly involved with the institution of education. Within this context, at least two major considerations can be identified, each of which will be a function of the way the culture is defined.

The *social ramifications* of education are primarily concerned with the identified goals of the institution. That is, as a society, what are those goals that we expect our system of public schooling to accomplish? These issues are properly considered outside of the institution for they provide the prescriptive information from which the institution will address the *instructional ramifications* of designing a curriculum and identifying instructional strategies. In other words, society sets the goals, and the institution of public education determines what to teach and how to teach it that those goals may be met.

That the schools should be accountable to the society at large for meeting those goals is an obvious and reasonable expectation. However, it must also be understood that the society is responsible for setting goals that can be maintained for more than several years, thus enabling the schools to plan for and reach those marks. The developed habit, however, is to continually change the goals from administration to administration, generation to generation. Given that circumstance, it is understandable that the schools, ever trying to shift gears and meet new and different expectations, are doomed to failure.

One response to this predicament has been to "water down" lofty goals to make them more achievable. Such an effort is eventually followed by a concern that the goals are too low and need to be raised. Chapters 3 through 5 will take a detailed look at the schools as they are and as they could be, but it must be acknowledged here that the society at large has a primary responsibility that it thus far has failed to meet: It is our responsibility as a society, as a culture, to determine what the goals are for education. This cannot be done unless we know who we are as a culture. And so, we find ourselves again asking, what is the American culture?

Defining "Culture"

It is possible that a confounding variable in putting together this definition is that many people are not really clear about what "culture" means, regardless of how it per-

---

Activity 2.3.
DEFINING "CULTURE"

Now don't go running to your nearest dictionary for this activity. Anyone can look up a definition of culture!

Instead, take a moment to write out what comes to mind when you think of the term *culture*. What does it encompass? What elements are actually *culture* rather than just *perspective*? And to what degree does pop culture influence what you think of as the culture of a society?

The good news here is that you need not confine yourself to one sentence.

---

tains to a specified people. So, let's spend some time with that issue in order to disentangle our approach to the greater task.

The Components of Culture

How did you define *culture*? Does it become obvious that even the generic term can be confusing? Finding a description of culture that we can work with will make our primary task considerably more manageable. Figure 2.2 provides an expanded version of our earlier representation of the issues involved in the perpetuation of a culture. The six categories listed beneath the heading "Identity" are not provided as the only categories worth considering, or even necessarily the "best" categories to use, but they do offer some guidelines for developing a consideration of what culture is all about. Did any of these show up in your definition of culture?

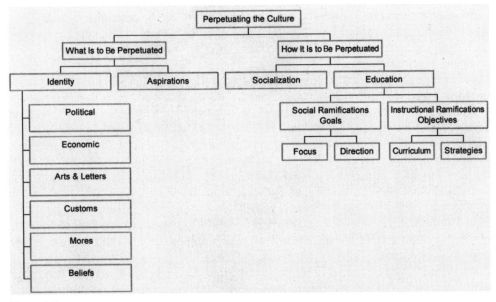

Figure 2.2.

Keep in mind that the terms that fall into each of these categories constitute *descriptions* of our culture rather than counting as a definition. For instance, way back at the beginning of this chapter, we mentioned that students would say the American culture is "baseball, hot dogs, and apple pie." Each of those terms represents a description of something they considered to be "American." The items did not define the culture; they provided examples of what one might see if they were to look at a picture labeled "The American Culture."

This distinction between descriptions and definitions is not at all superficial. In fact, the inclination of people to define their culture in a descriptive and superficial way is testament to the fact that our system of education is not turning out thinkers. The tendency in these situations is to look to the obvious in the hopes that the listener will be persuaded to accept the response. Students very often try answering questions in class with a response couched as a question. So, while it is worthwhile to take the time here to find descriptors of the American persona in terms of each of these categories, do not be lulled into the idea that the description is the definition.

The category of "Government" is fairly self-explanatory. Though a culture can certainly evolve through many forms of government, at any one point in time, it is characterized by one such system for establishing and enforcing the "rules" of the society. In our case, the Constitution guarantees to the states a republican form of government based on the democratic principle of consent by the governed.

In terms of "Economics," we utilize a capitalistic system of free enterprise. However, just as governmental systems can change, economic systems can change as well. There are those who would argue that while we are capitalists as a nation, the majority of the capital is held and controlled by comparatively few of the citizens. The degree to which this distinction is valid or important in the defining of our culture will be left up to you. It is the nature of this task, however, to find that many of those principles we consider to be obvious and easily recognized may actually be much more obscure than feels comfortable. In fact, it is these issues in particular that make defining the culture such an important endeavor.

Another aspect to be considered is the basis upon which the economic system operates. For example, some cultures are agriculturally based, others industrially based, others technologically based. And then, of course, there's the United States. What is the basis of our economic system?

We include the category of "Arts & Letters" with the intent that you consider it in its broadest possible sense. It is here that you would list those activities that our society seems to value in terms of expressing human capability and appreciating beauty in its various incarnations. This would include things that have originated outside the culture as well as here. For example, many musical forms are practiced and enjoyed in the United States, though very few can be said to have originated here. On the other hand, some of the major sports that are played around the world (such as baseball and basketball) and are part of the fabric of our society did originate in this country.

"Customs" refers to a society's usual way of behaving or acting. Some cultures are reserved and quiet, others excitable. Some are considered conservative in their expression of ideas or emotions; others are considered ebullient, perhaps even to the point of being considered crass.

We include "Mores" in this list to the degree that *customs* refers to ways of behaving, while *mores* refers to moral principles that guide that behavior. For example, though some societies might consider the behavior of our culture to be, shall we say, "crude" in some respects, it is not necessarily the case that the principles guiding that behavior are intended to offend others. People in one country might say that the mores (guiding moral principles) of the United States are imperialistic as evidenced by its custom (way of acting) of keeping warships in the vicinity of skirmishes between independent nations. What *moral principles* would you say underlie the behaviors of Americans?

A most difficult category to consider with regard to the American culture is certainly that of "Beliefs." This is where we discuss the source of our trust and confidence, particularly in things unseen. It is here that we consider the *what* and *why* of those things we accept as true. Despite our colonial heritage and even the inscriptions on our currency, it is a gross oversimplification to categorize our culture as representing a particular system of religious belief. Our high tolerance for religious diversity—spanning the spectrum from the notion that there is no divine being to the notion that such a being exists in all things—makes it most difficult to determine what we, as a culture, believe. In fact, it may be easier to address this category in terms of what the culture *does not* believe: Although as individuals we may believe strongly in any one of many religious explanations, as a culture we do not believe it is necessary that we all accept one sacred explanation of our existence.

We do not need to tell you how delicate these considerations are. Without doubt, there are many who would say that while it is not necessary for everyone to share our particular beliefs, those who don't are wrong. And who knows? That may be the case. As a culture, however, we can coexist and prosper, even with the phenomenal diversity of such beliefs. So, delicate though the task may be to identify who we are, it is still something that can be done. And in the doing, we may well expect that considerable insight will be one of the results. Take a moment to consider what descriptors of American behavior you would include in each category. You might even ask some friends to help!

Activity 2.4.
DESCRIBING THE AMERICAN CULTURE

This is probably what you wanted to do back in Activity 2.1. In this activity, however, we are specifically trying to broaden the focus rather than narrow it down. For each of the six categories listed below, identify several examples of each as they are manifested in the American culture. You may find that for some categories you can think of many examples, while for others it's a strain to come up with more than two or three. Why do you suppose that is? Would it be because there are only a few examples or because you haven't thought much about that aspect of culture before? Also, if you find that you come up with examples that are difficult to fit into one of the six categories, just add a new category!

- government
- economics
- arts and letters
- customs
- mores
- beliefs

Metaphors for a Diverse Culture

Even with the categories of cultural components that have been discussed, it can be difficult to list those things most pertinent to a description of what it is to be American. It is also true that when we return to the challenge of defining in one sentence what the American culture is, it won't be appropriate to simply write out a long list of items separated by commas. After all, though James Naismith developed the game of basketball on a chilly Massachusetts day in 1891, not all Americans would include "basketball" in a statement of who they are, culturally or otherwise. So, as you tackle the problem of describing our culture, it may be useful to discuss some of the metaphors that have been used to conceptualize the "big picture" of the American condition.

The Melting Pot   The period of 1820 to 1920 was one in which America wrestled mightily with the overwhelming desire of people from other countries to emigrate in favor of a new life in the United States. Laws were written and rewritten (and some, thankfully, repealed) to control the influx, which at one point reached as many as a million people per year. Quotas were established, and exclusions were enforced. Yet, through the early part of this century up to and including the years following World War I, it can be seen that people came to America *to become Americans*. The metaphor was that the United States was a cultural melting pot: many cultures combined (and continue to combine) to form something new. That new culture, though often changing—evolving—was distinctly different from the cultures that went into the mix. More importantly, becoming an American meant relinquishing one's prior culture to an appreciable degree to become a part of this new culture. There was a time when becoming acculturated was a good thing.

The Salad Bowl   More recently, particularly in the latter half of the twentieth century and with great acceleration in the last twenty-five years, the metaphor has changed as the Constitution of the United States has been interpreted in light of many unique and clearly unanticipated circumstances. For whatever sociological reason (far too involved for us to pursue here), the emerging cultural conscience shifted from the desire to *be* American in favor of being of another culture *in* America. The "salad bowl" metaphor came into vogue, and the social psychology of multiculturalism was born. In the salad bowl, the various ingredients do not lose their individual identity as a result of being mixed with the other ingredients. All are contained in one bowl and presumably have an identity as a particular sort of salad, but individual "cultures" are preserved. The salad bowl is the repository of hyphenated Americans: African-Americans, Irish-Americans, Asian-Americans, and on and on. The movement to preserve non-American cultural identity is obvious in the public schools, where virtually all subjects can be taught from a multicultural perspective: multicultural science, multicultural math, and so forth. Yet, there still has to be some bond other than simple geography that enables this bowl to hold its constituents together. Somehow, the bowl is "American."

The Fog   A third metaphor, however, may categorize our cultural identity as the twenty-first century begins. That is, the American culture can be thought of as a fog. It is evident that discrete components exist within the mist, but the fog distorts the nature of the interrelationship between them. Those components then lose their distinguishing characteristics, and it becomes very difficult to articulate just how the components interact as one culture. Navigating through the fog becomes increasingly dangerous as the various constituencies demand greater autonomy. This further obscures the common bonds between components. But worst of all, in a fog the wind is not swirling, and the subsequent complacency lulls us into thinking that dangers obscured are not dangers at all.

The melting pot idea points to some sort of common bond. The salad bowl exacerbates our differences. The fog emphasizes our inability to describe what is essentially right before us.

The Illusion of Multiculturalism

Which of the three metaphors presented is the best or most desirable is not the issue. In each case, they represent a picture of the culture as it existed at a particular time. Whether being melted down to form a new culture is better or worse than maintaining an identifiable "foreign culture" operating in another culture remains debatable. (This is not a question of "indigenous" culture versus "alien" culture. We say "foreign" only in terms of the fact that the each culture necessarily has discrete characteristics.) However, the degree to which various factions seek to maintain their separate distinctiveness can only serve to divide the larger culture. A philosophy of "separate but equal" is, by its own terms, culturally divisive.

Multicultural versus Multiethnic   Often the students in the education class that we mentioned at the beginning of this chapter seize upon this idea that the culture of the United States is actually many cultures living together. Therefore, they argue, ours is a multicultural society and cannot be defined any more precisely than that. Yet, despite the best arguments of sociologists, anthropologists, and even college students in "Introduction to Education" (all of whose arguments tend toward the historical or esoteric rather than having prescriptive value), the notion remains that *a culture* cannot be *multicultural*. Despite the best efforts of any group to maintain cultural purity, if they practice that culture within the context of another and away from where the culture "naturally" exists, a change is made, however slight, that yields a new culture. This is acknowledged every time someone describes his or her cultural identity with a hyphen. If one is not entirely of the prehyphen culture and not entirely of the posthyphen culture, he or she must be a member of some other culture that subsumes both descriptors. Thus, the hybrid culture is neither "X" nor "American" but something else. For better or worse, we are witnessing the evolution of Culture X. More than just a generation, America's emerging Culture X can neither articulate its cultural ideology nor embrace a common heritage. Educating Culture X in a manner that fosters collaboration as well as the perpetuation of the "American culture," a task still expected of our schools, is becoming increasingly problematic.

Culture versus Heritage   A necessary condition for becoming a member of a culture, other than one's ancestry, is that the individual relinquish his or her previous culture. No doubt that statement will anger many readers. However, continue on, for there is more to the issue. Think back to the discussion of the components of culture: We listed items such as mores (guiding principles), beliefs (that which we accept as true), and customs (usual ways of behaving). For an individual to live and work as a contributing member of one culture, it is necessary that he or she do so in accord with the mores, customs, and beliefs of that culture, following the law of the land being an obvious requirement. To do this necessitates giving up one's previous culture, a decision that is made to enjoy the benefits of a chosen culture. *However, it does not require that the individual give up his or her heritage.* And therein lays the distinction.

One's heritage cannot be separated from one's identity. Heritage, as Thomas Jefferson might have phrased it, is an inalienable aspect of any individual's persona. Recognition, even celebration, of heritage is not detrimental to the cohesiveness of a culture for it does not preclude the individual from being committed to the ideals of the chosen culture. In fact, that same recognition and celebration can be among the strongest components of a cultural tapestry as the best of each culture contributes to the strength of the commonly held culture.

Our culture, therefore, can be *multiethnic.* Our culture can be the result of combining people of many cultures around *a common cause and underlying ideal.* It can be representative of people who bring heritages of vastly differing circumstances. But the inescapable fact is that when they are all combined, *one culture* that contains all of these ingredients in a unique combination is what remains. To proceed as if individual cultures with their own beliefs, customs, and mores can function independently (let alone autonomously) within another culture is to embrace the murky cultural metaphor of the deepening fog.

Summary

There is no doubt that this discussion is a difficult one to conceptualize and resolve. In the paragraphs since the heading "Why Is It Important to Define the Culture?" appeared, many notions have been brought up that can easily make people feel uneasy. So, let's review for just a moment.

We began this portion of the chapter by saying that defining the culture becomes especially important if we want to perpetuate who we are. Perpetuation, it was noted, requires attention to two concerns: what we want to perpetuate and how to go about it. From there we discussed the subheadings that could be identified. In terms of what to perpetuate, it seemed important to identify the culture and to consider what our aspirations are for the continuation of that culture. With regard to how to perpetuate, we looked briefly at the social ramifications and the instructional ramifications that would be involved. Things were going pretty well.

However, defining the word "culture" seemed to bring up some new difficulties. To make this a bit clearer, we listed six components of culture: government, economics, arts and letters, customs, mores, and beliefs. Each of these categories could be repeated for a discussion of our aspirations once the descriptors of our identity have been found. Some of our descriptors might remain, whereas others may be in need of some reconsideration. Still, it seems, filling in those categories can be pretty tough going, and so we moved to a discussion of cultural metaphors to make the big picture just a bit more understandable.

Our discussion of the melting pot, the salad bowl, and the fog ultimately led to a consideration of the confounding notion of a culture being "multicultural." Our intent at this point was to demonstrate that while multiculturalism is indeed a popular buzzword, it is actually a divisive perspective with regard to establishing, maintaining, and perpetuating one national culture. It must be remembered that living in the United States is a choice that people freely make. Specifically because of this, the American culture is an appropriate forum for considering the idea that people must relinquish a prior culture, *though not their heritage,* to live in a culture different from their native culture. The willingness to surrender the former culture but to *celebrate one's heritage as part of the new culture* is one of the unique strengths of what we eventually may define as the American culture.

These are very big issues not to be taken lightly. In terms of establishing an institution of public education, these issues are of staggering importance. So, just reading about them is not enough. You need some time to think them over. You might even want to ask some other folks about it. Do so, and reflect upon what you hear. Consider whether or not you want your children to be referred to as "Culture X."

WHAT IS THE AMERICAN CULTURE? PART II

As you might expect, the chances of any two readers of this book coming up with identical lists of cultural descriptors are very slim. However, as more and more individuals develop such lists, patterns of overlap will start to appear. We might see repetition of specific items or ideas, for instance that the United States is a "democracy" (although "republic" is more accurate, as in "to the Republic, for which it stands"). We might also expect to see broader concepts emerging as we consider greater numbers of lists. Perhaps you wrote down that Americans believe in God. A friend of yours (if you have any left after asking all of these questions) may have written that Americans acknowledge the existence of a supreme being, though they are not necessarily in agreement about the "particulars." Still another respondent may have indicated that a formalized religious doctrine is not necessary to be an American. From these three differing responses, we can surmise that a consideration of religion plays some part in what it means to be American—not to say that one religion is preferred over another but simply that there is significance given to the question of religion from an American perspective.

Acknowledging these differences is part of identifying the fundamental aspects of our culture. So, it is necessary to look at the items on your list and on others' lists in an attempt to find the themes that recur. We need to find the expressions of those themes that can more or less describe each of us and exclude none of us. It's not getting any easier, is it? Don't let that bother you. If you have come this far, you are obviously capable of finding a definition with which you can be comfortable. So, let's push on!

Activity 2.5.
A REDEFINITION OF THE AMERICAN CULTURE

Before pushing on to the next discussion, take a moment to review your definition of the American culture. You may also want to review those that you solicited from friends (or former friends, as the case may be).

1. Do you see any need to revise your definition? If so, do so.
2. Based on what has been discussed thus far and what you found from asking others about the American culture, would you say that people are pretty clear about what it means to be American, or is there some ambiguity about it?
3. How might people gain a better understanding of their culture?

Toward a More Formalized Definition

Perhaps we should reiterate that there is no need to flip to the end of the chapter to find "the" definition of the American culture. In fact, what you will find at the end of the chapter is one last request that you write out your own final (for the time being) definition. It would be thoroughly presumptuous of us to try to tell you what the culture is. Instead, we need to work through this together.

Keeping your own list of cultural identifiers in mind, consider the definition below. This one was compiled by a class of "traditional" college freshman. They were traditional in that they were enrolled full-time in the day program of a four-year college. With only one or two exceptions, all were first-semester freshman still with vivid memories of their high school graduation ceremonies.

> The American culture is a young, mobile republic that is a composite of nationalities and ethnicities who traditionally remain identifiably separated by race, socioeconomic status, and cultural differences, who maintain the freedom and rights set forth in the U.S. Constitution, coexisting with a high tolerance for diversity, operating a system of free enterprise whose market has far-reaching effects on the world economy, striving to be a world leader and protector of the world with predominantly altruistic intentions, and who are characterized by regional differences and an ever-changing popular culture.

Yes, freshmen do tend to be enamored of words, and many cart around little dictionaries. On the other hand, they made a good effort at packing a lot of emotion, both positive and negative, into their definition. What elements of the six categories of cultural identity, if any, can you find in their definition? And what overlap, if any, do you find with your own definition?

You should be able to find references to government, economics, behaviors, and the mores that guide those behaviors. Less obvious are references to the "Arts & Letters" category or even specific customs that characterize Americans. You also might notice that in an effort to look at the culture as honestly as possible, they acknowledge that a significant feature of our culture is to remain separated by race, socioeconomic status, and cultural differences. In fact, it is only in reference to this aspect of who we are that the idea of "tradition" is expressed. To their credit, they admit that our attitude of being a world leader is not necessarily as selfless as we might wish it to be. Rather, as they say, our intentions are "predominantly altruistic."

There are two other facets of this definition that are particularly worth noting. One is that rather than trying to coalesce the regional differences that exist in the United States into common themes, they instead chose to say that the common theme is that those differences *do exist* within the culture. This is interesting, to say the least, for it points to one of the great paradoxes of our culture: As a nation, Americans are extremely tolerant of differences, yet as individuals, we struggle to maintain those differences, sometimes to frightening extremes. That such a paradox exists didn't seem to bother the students; after all, the question was to define the culture, not to solve its problems.

It should also be mentioned that this definition characterizes the culture as dynamic to the point of being "ever changing." Sociologically speaking, cultures don't change generation to generation, but the students were adamant that living in the 1990s and living in the 1940s or 1950s were substantially different experiences. This idea of a constantly changing culture supported the notion of "pop culture" and made those generational differences acceptable. No amount of fast-talking from the professor could get them to stand back far enough to see culture as a bigger picture. The question arises, of course, as to whether an inclination to look at the *personal picture* rather than the *big picture* is a characteristic of American culture.

Here's another version of a student-generated definition. This one was written by adult students attending evening classes. See what similarities and differences you can find with the definition provided by the younger students, as well as with your own.

> The American culture is based on the amendable Constitution of the United States, which allows for the continuing reinterpretation of federal law by virtue of the U.S. Supreme Court; allows for a free enterprise system; provides its citizens with protection under the confines of the law as established by the Constitution of the United States and similarly takes responsibility for the protection of human rights around the world; possesses a high tolerance for diversity; and provides opportunities for all citizens to pursue happiness and fulfillment according to their individual desires.

The older students obviously had a greater concern for the establishment and following of laws than the younger students. This seems curious given the fact that the younger students had just left a level of the American experience that for thirteen years had been preaching to them about conformity and following rules. There is little argument that college is often a liberating experience, but still one has to wonder if there was a problem either with the message or with its delivery. By the way, why was it always so important that we walk single file on the right side of the hallway in school? Did anybody every really get run over walking down the hall?

In any case, we do find that both definitions point to the Constitution as underlying who we are as a culture, and both mention a high tolerance for diversity. The second definition also mentions that Americans are provided the opportunity to pursue "happiness and fulfillment according to their *individual* desires." Sounds like another paradox coming to the surface.

In fact, both definitions point to a concern that is difficult to resolve. Examine your own lists. Do you see a prevalence of opposites? For instance, the descriptors found by the younger students led to a definition referring to the American culture as a *composite* of nationalities and ethnicities that remain *identifiably separate* by race and cultural differences. The second definition talks about the *commonality* of the law and the protection of rights around the world but ends with an emphasis on *individual* desires. Is the American culture one that seeks "the best of both worlds," so to speak? Does your list, or do others you have seen, indicate that Americans are English speaking, though without an "official" language? Or maybe you've noticed that we just can't latch on to that whole "metric" idea, yet our currency is handled in metric denominations. Or perhaps you included our penchant for discussing the environmental dangers of burning fossil fuels—maybe even with a cell phone and stuck in rush hour traffic (with only one or two people in each car).

We are a culture whose constituents seek *stability* (economic, family, career) but have a tradition of fostering *change*. We advocate *competition* but tell our children that *it's how you play the game that counts*. We champion an ethic of *hard work* and persistence, yet sponsor lotteries into which people pay huge amounts of money for the *chance* of winning the million-dollar prize. In school we teach *democracy* in a decidedly *undemocratic* venue. Corporal punishment is still a *consequence* in many classrooms where teachers argue against the use of *violence* in the resolution of conflict.

And the institution of education itself, which gobbles up billions of dollars annually, is a matter of state's rights according to the Constitution, but because of *omission*, not *inclusion*. Could it be the case that "paradox" is the most basic theme of the American culture?

It is likely, as you look over your lists, that the description of the American culture becomes increasingly confused by the opposing themes that emerge. In fact, the more enjoyable task may be examining lists of cultural descriptors and identifying the paradoxes. Remember, a paradox is not a question of either/or, right/wrong, or good/bad; instead, it's the occurrence of two individually acceptable views that seem to be mutually exclusive. Talk about a complex culture!

Our culture, by virtue of the Constitution, can well be expected to generate paradoxical situations. We are a nation, yet we have a high regard for the rights of the individual. Therefore, whenever the greatest good for the greatest number impinges on the greatest good for an individual, fertile ground exists for raising a paradox. Initially, of course, we refer to this as an exception; paradox only comes into play when the exception becomes a sort of "subrule" to the rule. However, there are several dangers inherent in all of this.

When the cultural identity is strong vis-à-vis the underlying principles and common goals of the society, paradox can be tolerated because it is played out according to those basic principles. However, we *know* things as individuals, not as nations. "Collective conscience" is a nice phrase and perhaps even an enviable goal, but conscience and thinking are characteristic of the individual. Nations seek to bind people together through shared agreement regarding ideas, not by virtue of making all people think the same thoughts. People are more likely, as individuals, to be aware of the "subrules" because they encounter these in their personal lives. They are the referent by which people balance the "shoulds and oughts" of behavior with their wants and desires. Eventually, the subrule becomes the colloquialism, and the original rule is little known. No doubt you are familiar with the phrase "the exception becomes the rule." As the exceptions move further and further from the original rule, or idea, the cultural metaphor of the fog becomes increasingly accurate. What is the underlying idea? Ask yourself whether you can articulate the ideals of the Constitution of the United States and its amendments. Ask your friends and colleagues. Ask children in middle school and high school. Some will be able to recite the preamble to you, so be prepared to ask what it *means*.

When cultural identity is obscured and people no longer share common goals, paradox begins to move beyond acceptable parameters. The unabated loss of cultural cohesion and of national goals pushes the limits of exceptions to the rule. Paradox then becomes *hypocrisy*. Such situations feign the virtue of the underlying principles they wish to represent. For instance, the individual who screams his message of religious repentance, or of social collapse, or of inside stock market information at the top of his lungs to no one in particular while standing on a street corner wishes to invoke his right to free speech. Though technically the right is his, the hypocrisy is the notion that one individual's rights are granted even at the expense of another's (those who don't want to be disturbed in this case). Organizations protecting *victims rights* grew out of paradox (the equal protection of the rights of the accused) turned hypocrisy (the dismissal of charges based on "technicalities"). Companies and public institutions that cannot hire and fire employees based on merit (or lack thereof) is another example. A welfare system supporting generations of families is another. *Yet, it is here that we seem to find Culture X.*

Paradox governed by reasoned principles is in essence a form of tolerance. It is an admission that all situations cannot be anticipated and that due consideration needs to be paid to individual circumstances. As isolated incidents, these are, as we have said, exceptions to the rule. Extended to a huge constituency (e.g., a nation), they become paradoxical though not necessarily irrational. Tolerance of paradox devoid of the underlying shared principles is a haphazard exercise that obscures cultural identity and often borders on the absurd. When what was once a shared vision becomes a collection of special-interest visions, cultural cohesion begins to fail. And when the absurd becomes the norm, then we have real trouble. Can you think of any examples?

Synthesizing an Operational Definition

As we have said, the capacity for generating "acceptable" paradox is to be expected in a social system such as ours, that is, in seeking the greatest good for the greatest number while protecting the rights of the individual. And in that regard, ours is a unique cultural environment. Combined with an acceptance of diversity, the two (paradox and diversity) provide an environment conducive to inquiry, discovery, and development. We call all of this *innovation*. That strand of innovation further describes the culture, for we possess a penchant for testing limits and exploring what heretofore has been left unexplored. Perhaps this is a function of our cultural youth, but in any event an inclination toward innovation (perhaps mischief?) is clearly at the root of who we are, or once were.

To this point, we have recognized that some degree of acceptance of varying heritages (diversity) is fundamental to defining the American culture. We have also found that it can be possible for opposing themes (paradox) to exist within our culture in positive ways if we don't lose sight of our fundamental values. We've indicated that the acceptance of diversity and accommodation of paradox are fuel for the fire of innovation. Those are some pretty substantial themes for a culture. So, let's try once again to see if we might find a statement that accommodates all of those diverse items on your list and also encompasses these foundational elements. Keep in mind that the goal is to find an operational definition of our culture that we might let its underlying principles guide educational endeavors.

> The American culture is a multiethnic republic existing with a high degree of tolerance for and acceptance of the expression of practical and ideological endeavor by virtue of a proclivity toward innovation; it functions in an environment intended to offer opportunities for the individual to pursue his or her own economic, social, and intellectual potential in the context of shared principles; and it seeks the greatest good for the greatest number while zealously protecting the civil and spiritual rights of the individual.

In this definition we try to accommodate each of the six categories of cultural descriptors, though you may have to look to find them. Obviously, government is addressed by the term *republic*. Economics is specifically addressed in terms of individuals having the opportunity to reach their own economic potential. In fact, that term *opportunity* is of key importance. In our culture, protection under the law is guaranteed, but achievement is a matter of seizing the opportunities provided; the culture does not "owe" anyone a job, or an education, or a swimming pool. As a culture, we do owe everybody the opportunity to achieve those things they wish to achieve (within the confines of the law).

You might also see that customs are addressed in this definition in terms of our culture being "multiethnic." As we said earlier in this chapter, the ability to celebrate a diversity of heritage is a virtue, or at the very least a strength. Mores are acknowledged in that the guiding principle of the culture is to find the greatest good for the greatest number while protecting the rights of the individual. Beliefs are accommodated in that the republic seeks to protect the civil and spiritual rights of each person. This can also be found in the meaning behind the phrase "tolerance for and acceptance of the expression of practical and ideological endeavor by virtue of a proclivity toward innovation." Though this speaks most specifically to the category of "Arts & Letters," the tolerance and acceptance of ideological differences accounts for the very broad spectrum of thoughts subsumed under the heading "Beliefs." In particular, however, this phrase gives credence to our cultural nature as people willing to question what we know and to see the world from new perspectives. In fact, a reading of the Constitution will reveal that the founders of our nation recognized the merit of original thinking and its value to the society: We typically refer to it as copyright and patents, both of which have limits (see the Constitution of the United States, Article I, Section 8).

You might look again to your list of descriptors and determine whether there is anything that is conspicuously absent or specifically excluded by this definition. Otherwise, do you think it might work as an operational definition of the American culture? What adjustments would you recommend?

FINAL THOUGHTS

Defining the American culture has proven to be a difficult exercise. That difficulty should, in itself, indicate to you how far we have removed ourselves from understanding our own identity. If you have not started to do so already, when you read a newspaper or watch programs on television, consider what has been discussed in this chapter. It is easy to let questions such as these fall into the "out of sight, out of mind" category. Education (and public education in particular), however, is such a huge enterprise that by the time problems show up, the extent of those problems pervades the whole of the institution. And that's where we find ourselves today.

The three fundamental elements of the American culture (reasoned paradox, acceptance of diverse heritage, and proclivity for innovation), along with the six categories of cultural descriptors, provide a template for addressing all of the other components of the diagram presented in figure 2.2. We can perpetuate our culture and provide some direction in terms of our cultural aspirations if we have defined the culture before making decisions.

Throughout this chapter, the point has been made that it is not our intent to provide you with *the* definition of the culture. Our goal was to begin the discussion. You need to consider how the culture can be defined and to engage others in the discussion as well. In particular, you should ask this question of the principal at your local school. You should attend a meeting of your local school board and ask the members of the board to define the culture for you. As a concerned citizen, as a parent, you should expect that the people entrusted with administering any formal system of education in

---

Activity 2.6.
YOUR FINAL THOUGHTS

This is it! Having considered the entire chapter and talked to a number of other folks, rewrite your response to the prompt, "In one sentence, define the American culture."

---

the United States should be able to tell you how their school fosters the development of informed, competent citizens. But by now, you should not be surprised if they have considerable trouble doing so.

Since this book must necessarily be written without the benefit of your particular perspective on the American culture, we will proceed using the operational definition derived in this chapter. That does not mean that you must do so. If you are in agreement with what has been said here, great. If you feel the definition needs elaboration or additional considerations, add them in. The remainder of this book requires a definition, but it does not have to be ours; it has to be yours. We encourage you to write out one more version of the American culture (for now) and refer to it as you continue with this book. Do not hesitate to make changes as new ideas come to mind. And by all means, do not hesitate to ask for other perspectives from people you encounter.

If this final version matches your first version, that's great! If you have made changes along the way, that's great too.

Keep your final version handy as you consider the chapters about designing a new curriculum. What is taught in the schools should be derived from the statement of what it means to be American.

Two more final thoughts: First, congratulations for working your way through this very difficult and abstract discussion. And second, just in case anybody asks, Mt. McKinley is the tallest mountain in the United States, but it was kind of a trick question since it is way up there in Alaska.

3

The Institution of Education

Pushing harder and harder on familiar solutions, while fundamental problems persist or worsen, is . . . what we often call the "what we need here is a bigger hammer" syndrome.

—Peter Senge

In the first chapter, we discussed the myth of educational reform. We drew the conclusion that the *fundamental* problem with education is that education is *fundamentally* an institution. We didn't spend a lot of time on the topic of institutions but promised to return to it in a later chapter (this one). In chapter 2, we turned to a discussion of the American culture, and you probably noticed that the term *institution* showed up quite a bit. There's good reason for that. Institutions arise in cultures that wish to *perpetuate* themselves. They are the mechanism by which a culture maintains its values and disseminates those values to another generation. Institutions exist by virtue of a *collective cultural conscience*.

Given all of that, you might begin to wonder just what an institution is. Where do they come from? Do you suppose John Adams and Thomas Jefferson were sitting around a colonial-Philadelphia Starbucks one afternoon in 1776, when one of the two said, "You know, there's just got to be some way around this taxation without representation deal," to which the other replied, "Sure, why couldn't we institute some sort of system in which the government derives its just powers from the consent of the governed?" Okay, it probably didn't happen quite this way. But nonetheless, institutions (within governments, for example) do arise from *the ideas that people hold in common*. As counter to traditional thinking as this may sound (i.e., that institutions are big dreary buildings from which bureaucracy is meted out), institutions are actually the dynamic manifestation of a culture that has found an *identity* through its shared ideals and so wishes to sustain itself through time.

You should notice some familiar themes already: perpetuation, cultural identity, and survival. Since all three of these are embodied in institutions, and education is considered to be an institution, now would seem to be a good time to consider this whole idea of "institutionality" in greater detail. From there we can look more closely at education in particular, and along the way, we may even dispel a myth or two.

INSTITUTIONS AS THE COLLECTIVE CONSCIENCE

No matter what opinion one might have about institutions—that they are bland, slow to change, or nonresponsive—the fact is that they can exist only by virtue of people. Unlike a tree, or a lake, or an expanse of wildflowers, institutions result when people formally organize their widely held ideas. Take away the people, and you eliminate the institution. This means that if we have a disagreement with the functioning of any given institution, we must look *inward* to find the source of that dissatisfaction.

Schemas That Grow Up

In terms of cognitive psychology, it is often suggested that much of our mental functioning is based upon *schemas*. Schemas are general representations of how something is done or what one expects to happen based upon accumulated experiences. For instance, you have likely gone out to eat at a restaurant on an occasion or two during your life, and having done so, you have "constructed" a schema for what is generally expected during such an experience. If you take a moment, as the following exercise suggests, to outline what happens when you dine out, you will be graphically representing a schema. Go ahead; see what a schema looks like. Write it out.

After listing the steps, go back through the schema to see how you might assimilate different dining experiences based on the general schema. For instance, going to a fast-food restaurant will typically mean reading from a single menu that hangs above the order counter, whereas going to a swanky sort of place may involve being handed a printed menu for you to read from.

As you review your schema, you'll probably find that no matter where you go to eat, there are some general expectations. For instance, going out to eat means leaving your home to go somewhere else. You will enter the restaurant, sometimes wait to be seated, sometimes be seated by virtue of a reservation, and sometimes select your own seat, but in any case there will be a component that gets you to a seat. Likely a waiter or waitress will bring you a menu from which you will select the meal you prefer. You will then wait for the food to be prepared, after which you'll consume the meal, and after

---

Activity 3.1.
SCHEMAS

This activity is intended to show you the generic schemas that you construct for different events in your life. For this particular example, try listing the common steps that are involved in going out to eat. By "common," we mean those things that would apply to virtually any dining out situation. For example, leaving your home to go somewhere else would be one of the steps: It doesn't matter where you are going, but if you are going out to eat, you will be leaving your home.

that, you will be presented with a bill. Having paid the bill (perhaps including a tip), you will depart. All of these generic steps will occur even though there may be slight differences from one dining experience to the next. But what we have described here is the general *schema* for what one expects when going out to eat. Small changes to all of this are no problem (e.g., fast-food establishments make you pay before being served). Big changes, however, may require a greater adjustment to your schema.

How big a change is a big change? The work of Jean Piaget in the first half of the twentieth century suggests two mechanisms for changing schemas: assimilation and accommodation. *Assimilation* is what we do when small changes are necessary to an existing schema. For example, standing at a McDonald's counter and selecting your meal from a large overhead menu is a small change to make in an existing schema. Being responsible for clearing your table and throwing away the "dinnerware" is a small change in a schema. Those particular cost-saving moves have worked with relative success simply because they did not challenge people to make a significant change to their dining schemas. In fact, the vast majority of what we do as adults each day involves making assimilations. If you've ever had the feeling of being in a rut, it is because there is nothing happening in your life that requires anything more than minor assimilations to your schemas. Schemas help maintain our cognitive balance (known as "equilibration"), and assimilations are easy and not intimidating adjustments. There is comfort and safety in a familiar schema.

A major change in a schema or the construction of an entirely new schema requires the mechanism of *accommodation*. Have you ever gone bungee jumping? For most of us, that would require a very significant change or even a brand-new schema since the expectations that most of us have of jumping off a bridge or a crane don't match with the experience of (successful) bungee jumping. There is often an element of danger in making accommodations to schemas. Activities that require such major adjustment are typically out of the ordinary and may even seem threatening in one way or another. In particular they threaten the status quo.

Interestingly enough, children make major changes to their schemas and construct new ones on a regular basis. Whenever something new comes along, children (and adults) are challenged to fit the experience into what they already know. For adults, this most likely requires an assimilation; for children it often entails accommodation due to their limited experiences. But in either case, the individual has been knocked off of "cognitive balance" and must work his or her way back to feel at ease again. Children often find this intriguing, perhaps challenging, and ultimately rewarding.

So, working one's way back to a condition of cognitive equilibration involves constructing new knowledge by virtue of the processes of either assimilation or accommodation. This is what school is all about, by the way. Educators establish a "constructive disequilibration" in their students that requires the building of new knowledge (from the student's perspective) to be resolved. We call that resolution process *learning*. In any truly educational setting, learning should require the robust application of accommodation-oriented thinking. If that is not the case, we can expect that students in our schools are unchallenged, difficult to "discipline," and failing to achieve at levels that represent appropriate expectations. Is this starting to sound like school as we know it?

In a Piagetian sense, we all process information in this same way, though there can be varying degrees of sophistication to our thinking. That is, your ability to manipulate information (primarily in terms of the use of logic and the ability to work with abstraction) differs from the abilities of children, even though the processes of assimilation and accommodation leading to equilibration are the same in both cases. But what we wish to do now is to consider this idea of schemas in terms of *social institutions*. It might sound like a big jump to go from individual to institutional schemas, but the connection is really quite fundamental.

You can get a sense of the relationship between personal schemas and social schemas with the following exercise. First, you need to find one or two people who have not read this book. With that done, ask each of them to outline the going-out-to-eat schema as we asked you to do. When you examine the outlines, there may be small variations between each (yours included), but there will also very likely be significant overlap among them. That's because within any given culture, the experiences that lead to the construction of schemas are remarkably similar. *Your* particular schema is yours alone because it reflects *your* particular life experiences. However, someone else in your culture, whose schemas are based only on his or her life experiences, has had many experiences that *parallel* your own, even though they don't replicate them exactly. Riding bicycles, falling off bicycles, eating particular foods, observing holidays, *going to school*, learning to drive, and answering to the particular laws of the land all contribute to a significant level of "social sameness" among our life experiences. That your friends' schemas overlap your own should come as no surprise.

Way back in the beginning of the book, when you likely looked up the dictionary definition of culture, you probably found something that referred to the shared beliefs, values, and customs of a people. Perhaps you see now that the true underpinnings of a culture are the shared *schemas* of a people into which their beliefs, values, and customs are woven. Institutions arise out of the desire to perpetuate those schemas we have come to collectively value. We can then see how traditions remain intact, even though changes in the culture can be expected to occur: It is all based on the shared ideas of those who compose the culture. And so, we make that jump from the individual to the institution; institutions are larger representations of schemas that people value and share. Institutions represent schemas that have "grown up."

Changing an institution, by revolution or some other means, is not to be taken lightly. One of the reasons that institutions endure is that they are based upon deeply rooted values. This is important to understand because institutions have a particular talent for defying what is often referred to as "pop culture." That is, the foundation elements upon which the institution is built transcend the ephemeral preferences of differing generations.

The turbulent times of the latter half of the twentieth century in the United States are indicative of this (we take these several decades together so that no group feels that its particular cause is being disenfranchised in our discussion). Changes were indeed made, issues were faced, and many facets of the contemporary society were brought into question. But consider the institutions that were present then in terms of their existence now. Is government significantly different? Are schools substantively different than when you were a youngster? Is our national defense system administered in a clearly different manner when you consider it on a fundamental level? Is marriage still the convention? Are women still typically paid less than their male colleagues? Do ethnic tensions still permeate our society? We ask these questions not to necessarily support the underlying sentiments (how can we still tolerate economic and ethnic discrimination?) but merely to demonstrate that, as we said in chapter 1, institutional change is very much a matter of wrestling with the beast—a beast, by the way, that typically does not want to change.

Therefore, when calling for substantive change in an institution, it is prudent to look inward, as we have already suggested, and ask whether the change we seek is one of abiding quality or one of contemporary cultural preference. It is, after all, somewhat reassuring to know that the values represented by institutions are, on some level, truly noble, virtuous, and laudable artifacts in the story of our culture—not something to be revered through the years but something worth perpetuating *through the ages*.

The Nameless/Faceless Entity

The interplay of personal and social schemas makes it difficult to separate ourselves from the institution, to say that the *institution* must change but we don't have to. In fact, as chapter 2 argued in a cultural context, changing the "thinking" of an institution requires changing *our* thinking.

Given our intimate relationship to social institutions, it seems curious that they are typically thought of as being out of touch with mainstream thinking. Usually, institutions seem to be lacking in that "personal touch" and are oh-so-slow to catch up with the times. Yet, here we've just suggested that the essence of an institution is that it represents the shared ideas of individuals coalesced into an organizational format intended to serve the many; that is, the institution is us! So, there must be another dynamic at play here. There is, and it is characterized by our three recurring themes.

The Recurring Themes

The notions of perpetuation, identity, and survival cannot be minimized in our discussion, for they are the rhyme and reason of any institutional existence. And failure to adequately consider any one of the three negates the value of the other two. For example, an institution that does not pass on (*perpetuate*) the message embodied in its *identity* serves no worthwhile social purpose. Its identity gradually erodes, and its *survival*, as originally intended, is not at all likely. Thus, each represents a critical component in the picture of institutional existence. A mini example of this is a "fad," or the interests of popular culture. Let's examine what this means in the context of each theme.

Perpetuation   A fad plays itself out not by first losing its identity but by first losing its ability to sustain the notion that its message remains valuable. That is, the value remains essentially intact, but as the ability to convince others of the value fades, identity *with* that value message subsequently fades. From a philosophical perspective, we are faced with the idealist proposition that ideas, good or bad, are enduring. Our acceptance of those ideas may come and go, but the idea remains intact. Perpetuation therefore becomes not only a characteristic of institutional existence but also an activity that can take on different demeanors to suit changing times; sometimes institutions make their "voices" heard, and at other times it may be prudent to keep a low profile. The key point, however, is that the inherent value is not what fades first. Rather, first to go is the desire to *perpetuate* the value message.

Do you recall the "pet rock" craze of the 1970s? Here's a fad that offers an example of what we are suggesting. Prior to the mass-marketing of otherwise orphaned rocks, the stones themselves had a particular value. Whether or not that value truly translated into something along the lines of companionship or fulfilling relationships may long be debated. However, the fact remains that before and after the fad, the rocks had some inherent value. The only thing that changed was that, at one point, someone convinced a whole lot of people to purchase these low-maintenance pets, and at another point, people were no longer convinced. The value remained, but the ability to convince people of the worth of perpetuating recognition of that value eroded (so to speak). And that's a characteristic of fads, the fact that there is no deeply rooted value (as is the case with most of our institutions) worth perpetuating. But it was fun at the time.

We have mentioned repeatedly that institutions serve to perpetuate something of collective value within the society. Institutions provide a particular service to the contemporary society and, in so doing, perpetuate the values of the culture. But perpetuation is simply the underlying, perhaps subliminal, task of the institution. That which is to be perpetuated is an entirely different matter.

Identity, Ideology, and Purpose Institutions are nameless, faceless entities. Who *is* education? Who *is* the military, law enforcement, the judicial system, or government? Really, isn't it an amusing notion to think that if you are a taxpayer, you own the aircraft carrier *Enterprise*? What do you suppose would happen if you asked to borrow it for a weekend cruise? No doubt your degree of ownership would be summarily pointed out to you. No one owns the *Enterprise*, though at the same time, we all own it. The translation of individual ideas or values into a collectively held representation of those ideas does take its toll. It blurs the edges of "ownership" and personal identity. And so, it might be suggested that despite the fact that our institutions are made up of shared ideas, once institutionalized, they gradually take on a separate identity.

"Separate," however, may not be the most appropriate word. It would be more to the point to say that institutions take on an ill-defined, perhaps even obscure, identity. We tend to think of institutions as self-perpetuating, forgetting that they are reflections of our own cultural identity. We distance ourselves not only from the operation of the institution but from the spirit as well. As the chasm between individual self and social self widens, the vitality that the institution should represent begins to subside. Neglect plays a part in institutional evolution as people allow their institutions to operate on autopilot. Identity, however, does not disappear. Rather, it evolves into something different, into a generic "institutional" identity.

Is the obscure nature of identity acceptable in a cultural sense? The answer is a matter of perspective. Good works usually enjoy a prominent relationship to someone in particular (or a group of someones). For instance, the Declaration of Independence was conspicuously accompanied by the signatures of those who felt deeply about the imperative for change. Many Americans readily associate the name Neil Armstrong with the first lunar landing that placed a man on the moon, even though he was just one of thousands of people responsible for reaching that goal. But here was a *name*, an identity. There are few just and virtuous causes (if any) that would necessarily suffer if the perpetrators of the cause, or the cause itself, were clearly identified.

On the other hand, less-good, unlawful, or unacceptable works are often characterized by their anonymity, and it becomes the work of other organizations to determine the identity of the responsible parties. In other words, there is a perception of safety (or perhaps of "opportunity") for the individual, or for the institution, when identity is not known, when purpose can be kept in the shadows. We have all had experiences of trying to work our way through the bureaucracy that so often encumbers institutions, whether in terms of educational institutions or the Department of Motor Vehicles, for example.

Finding *definitive* answers is routinely more difficult than finding *contradictory* answers from one level to the next. And yet, all along the way the relative anonymity of the organization, the lack of a clear identity, provides security for each individual we encounter, as well as for the institution as a whole. If you can't find anyone to blame, blame cannot be assigned. As a clearly articulated identity can be expected to lead to allegiance (considering that the institution is reflective of our own values), an unarticulated identity can be expected to lead to disassociation. A sure sign of fading cultural identity is when people no longer feel an affiliation with the institutions of their culture.

Survival   Curiously, the dissociation discussed in the previous section does not lead to institutional demise. In fact, and perhaps not surprisingly, it almost *ensures* institutional survival. As an institution becomes identified more as "an institution" and less in terms of the people either that administrate it or that it serves, it becomes nameless and faceless and takes on a different demeanor. Because the institution serves some social function and is not typically tied to the economic realities of a company or corporation, funding continues to flow. It is rare for such funding to occur at a rate that would allow the institution to flourish, but rather the rate is sufficient to enable *subsistence*. And that is all an institution needs to gradually assume its new identity.

At this point, the institution begins to take on its new identity and internalizes the peculiar institutional characteristic of survival, that is, the force that seeks to protect the institution from threats to its existence. In the case of economic institutions, that force is most typically money. Corporations that have become "institutions" lay off workers by so many thousands at a time that it comes across as actually being nothing more than a business decision—and one that makes sense at that. In the case of "ideological institutions" such as marriage, the perceived threat comes in the fashion of alternative life partnerships. In the case of social or civic institutions, the focus of this work, the threat is change itself. And to combat that force, institutions resist change with all their might.

Institutions resist change because of their leviathan-like nature. Schools have long since passed the point at which they were enterprises consisting of a publicly provided building, a teacher, and a class of students. The closest we come to that scenario (one teacher, several students) in these times is the homeschooling movement. Instead, the modern institution of education involves teachers, administrators on many levels, secretaries, food workers, bus drivers, maintenance crews, pencil- and school-supply vendors, school-supply manufacturers, dairy workers, school psychologists, even university professors and colleges of education that depend upon the high teacher education enrollment to keep the rest of the school fiscally afloat, and on and on. An attempt to change the institution, to redefine it, is a threat to many, many people. And an institution that wishes to survive simply cannot take the chance that such changes will occur.

So, how do institutions survive? In the case of some industries, we see the robust use of planned obsolescence. The computer hardware and software industries have essentially raised obsolescence to a high art. In fact, those industries have for years successfully used the consumer's experiences with their products as their test bed. The automotive industry was pretty much the same until government regulation put an end to much of it for safety reasons. Once folks start filing suit against computer-related industries due to the loss of sensitive data from computer glitches, the same sort of regulation may occur.

In social/civic institutions, however, planned obsolescence is not an option. And for the schools in particular, which are so responsive to their constituencies (or at least to the parents of their constituents), the survival mechanism of choice is reform. The beauty of this approach to perpetuating the institution—and keep in mind that we are referring here to the institution itself rather than the ideology of the institution—is that reforms can come and go. A reform is not really a change but rather an adjustment. Adjustments in one direction can eventually be adjusted back in the other direction, much like your thermostat at home. There is nothing permanent about reform, and in fact, the tertiary level of the institution has made the transience of reform its bread and butter. But whatever means may be used, the bottom line is to keep the institution alive—it's a matter of survival because too many folks stand to lose too much if things change. *Of key importance here, once again, is that the institutional survival of which we speak is a mechanism for the protection of those that the institution supports, not of those that the institution serves.*

Corporations: Baby Institutions

Throughout these pages, we have alluded to the notion that corporations are very much like institutions. We do not want to confuse the issue by acting as if corporations *are* institutions, but they do offer a practical illustration of our argument and will help as we further define the nature of institutions.

Corporations do respond to the same themes we have just discussed: perpetuation; identity, ideology, and purpose; and survival. And in fact, there are companies that, just like the school system, employ so many people that extraordinary efforts to keep them in business are taken from time to time. Some examples would be the guaranteeing of loans on behalf of the Chrysler Corporation in 1979–1980 or the subsidizing of agricultural products, or the support of the airline industry following the terrorist attacks of September 2001.

What is perhaps most interesting about this is that it indicates a movement on the part of the society to treat business entities as if they were institutions. That's dangerous and, if allowed to continue, will play itself out in a most deleterious fashion. For instance, the Chrysler "bailout" of twenty-seven years ago caused a tremendous amount of controversy—and that was over loan guarantees. The automaker did not actually get money from the government. Today's version, as an example, is a direct transfer of funds from the government to the airline industry. The continuing farm subsidies, which pay farmers not to grow crops, is another example.

Summary

So, what we've seen is that institutions, despite the particular defining characteristics of each, possess three idiosyncrasies: perpetuation, identity, and survival. *Perpetuation* represents the tendency to carry on a message that at some point was deemed to be of value for virtually all in the social system. Despite the changes of pop culture, the "baby boom," Generation X, and so forth, the institution strives to continue on.

Identity is the most paradoxical of the three themes. Institutional identity is at once specific and obscure. It is specific to the degree that there is some particular function that the institution is supposed to serve. It is obscure in that the institution is so large, so multifaceted that individual identity with, or within, is lost; that is, the institution becomes an entity in which people work or through which people receive services of some sort. Subsequently, a new "institutional identity" is born.

And finally, there is *survival*. Keep in mind that survival and perpetuation are not at all the same thing. When we speak of an institution's inclination toward perpetuation, we speak of that purpose for which the institution was, well, instituted. But when we speak of survival, we refer to the institution's instinct to protect itself. From what? From change. An institutional existence may not be necessarily exciting, but it can be comfortable.

Does this sound familiar? It should because it goes back to our discussion of schemas and adapting to the environment. You might recall that in terms of cognitive processing, the mechanisms of adaptation were accommodation and assimilation. Where was the "danger" and where was the comfort? Schemas that required only assimilations provided the safety, the security, the comfort zone. That's what institutions want: a little adjustment here, perhaps a change back to the way things were there, but no accommodations please. Institutions, for reasons of survival (maintaining that comfort level) would prefer not to make real changes. In short, doing so threatens their existence.

We've spoken now about institutions within social systems (which implies considerable size, at least in the breadth of the ideas they represent) that possess three generic characteristics. Yet, the point has also been made on several occasions that institutions are defined by an entire set of characteristics. So, let's look at some examples to further develop our understanding of just what we are up against concerning the educational behemoth. Perhaps we can even clarify what is and what isn't an institution.

A LOOK AT SOME WELL-KNOWN INSTITUTIONS

We have been very general in our discussion of institutions thus far, and so, now let's get a little more specific. We will look at several examples of "institutionality" and try to determine just what constitutes an institution. By doing so, we can ultimately look at education and determine what its defining characteristics appear to be. Having done so, perhaps the notion of changing some of those characteristics may not be quite as scary as people think.

Though all of the entities we will discuss answer to the recurring themes of perpetuation, identity, and survival, we are going to have to start being a bit more careful about which organizational structures we refer to as institutions. In popular culture and relaxed language, we tend to think of each of these examples as institutions. But they are not. That is the illuminating light we wish to cast—not so much to expose a structure as being noninstitutional but rather to more clearly understand what an institution is so we can make it more responsive to our needs. So, let's look at three categories: business entities, social/civic structures, and ideological models.

"Institutions" in Business

Do you think of IBM or McDonald's as institutions? Many would quickly say that IBM is because it employs 329,000 people worldwide and has been in existence for as long as any of us can remember. McDonald's, on the other hand, might be thought of as an "emerging" institution because, despite representing hundreds of thousands of jobs, it has been around for only about fifty years. Even so, its corporate size and considerable influence on the fast-food industry would seem to qualify it for institutional standing. We have chosen these two examples because both represent tremendous economic forces (they are among the thirty corporations represented by the Dow Jones Industrial Average), both employ thousands of people, and both are ubiquitous in our daily lives.

IBM

IBM can trace its business existence back well into the nineteenth century. It is a company that has survived the ups and downs of economic cycles, more wars than one wishes to count, and shifting social emphases that literally document the history of twentieth-century America. Change *within* the company has been dramatic as well. IBM is a leader today in a technology that was *nonexistent* when the company was founded. That's a lot of history, a lot of change, for any organization to absorb. Add to that the rather nonbusinesslike practices of focusing on the needs of its employees as pioneered by IBM, and we have a firm that watches out for its own as well as its bottom line.

Here, in this one example, we find corporate longevity, employment for tens of thousands of people, and products and services that are supplied to millions of people around the world. It is a company that packs a tremendous amount of economic wallop, and the repercussions could have far-reaching effects if that bottom line ever bottomed out. Certainly this must be the stuff of which institutions are made.

McDonald's

And then there are companies such as McDonald's. Ray Kroc was fifty-two years old when he first went to meet the McDonald brothers in San Bernardino, California. It seems they were using a lot of the multimixer milkshake mixers that he sold, and he wanted to know what was going on. That was in 1953. Some fifty years later, after "the rest is history" part, had you invested $2,000 in that fledgling "fast-food" business, it would now be worth $7 million! Indeed, at the very least, we are talking about the American dream and the land of opportunity. But are we talking about an institution?

Employing thousands of people, many of whom are experiencing their first paying job, and boasting a national and worldwide presence that is even more recognizable than that of IBM, McDonald's has come to represent more than just a burger. And unlike the development of IBM, McDonald's essentially invented its own industry. Food service was there, and Dick and Maurice McDonald had come up with some innovations of their own, but it was Ray Kroc who saw the potential that no one else had ever considered before. There would, of course, have been *a* McDonald's even without Kroc's appearance on the scene. But there would not have been *thousands* of McDonald's. And though McDonald's was not the first food-service franchise, it was the one that made the difference.

With its thirty thousand outlets around the world, McDonald's is an economic force to be reckoned with. Yet, what would be the effect if the folks at the top in the McDonald's organization decided to just shut things down? Certainly a lot of people would be out of work. And that includes many more than just the direct employees of McDonald's since the effect could be to shut down many businesses that supply the restaurants as well. But once those folks had found new jobs and were working again, what would be the real difference to society if McDonald's was no longer a place to stop along the highway? Would its absence leave a hole in the fabric of society? Very likely not.

Size and longevity may contribute to the notion of institutionality. However, in the case of both IBM and McDonald's, it is also true that they, as with all businesses, are *profit driven*. If the profit is realized, business continues. If no profit is going to be generated, then the business ceases to exist. The typical consequence, beyond the economic inconvenience that a great many people might suffer, is simply that one product or another may no longer be available from that particular supplier. Size and longevity, in a business sense, are direct functions of fiscal profitability. Given that fact, it would be difficult to argue that businesses of *any* size or age qualify as institutions since institutions don't answer to a profit motive but instead *seek to perpetuate something of social value and meaning*. Though funding is often a problem for institutions, their value supercedes economics. Institutions are, in fact, a viable part of our social fabric, whereas businesses are an economic function within a given society.

Remember that we have been trying to establish that the perpetuation aspect of institutional existence refers to an underlying message of value to people as *people* rather than to people merely as consumers. We buy what is available, and changes in corporate existence will affect only that which we find on the shelves. But our existence as social creatures goes far deeper than the profit considerations of corporations. And so, if we can agree that a profit motive is not the driving force behind an institution, then that's good news because it means we may look to something other than money, which is merely a *tool*, a *convention* of society, to solve institutional problems and improve institutional functioning.

Don't get us wrong. We all know that money can go a long way toward solving most any kind of problem, but as a society, we tend to retreat quickly to the idea of "not enough money" as an excuse to *not* solve problems. In contemporary language, it is the equivalent of people using the phrase "I don't know" rather than trying to answer a question. "I don't know" is a phrase that stops thinking just as "there's not enough money" rationalizes the idea of leaving unacceptable situations in their unacceptable state. Rationalizations make things sound "okay," but they do not solve problems.

Civic Institutions

Let's turn now to a couple of examples that can be very much affected by financial circumstances but have never ceased to exist in our history because of failing funds. These examples, government and national defense, represent, on the one hand, very general social desires and, on the other hand, a very specific social enterprise. Are they both institutions? Are either of them institutions?

Government

Government is one of those terms that seems so specific, yet can be so vague. The student council that you may have served on in high school was euphemistically referred to as an exercise in government, the fact being that it was much more an *exercise* than it was *government* (as you may have found out whenever push came to shove with the local school district policy and administration). So, even with our educational experiences in tow, we might need to ask just what constitutes that which we call "government."

What was missing in those high school days was any real decision-making authority. A school's board of education can make decisions for the district it serves. A charitable organization can have a committee that determines how donations will be dispersed. A company can have a governing board that exercises control over business operations. These can appropriately be called governing functions because (with the exception of the student council) each does possess the authority to make decisions. The source of that authority may differ from situation to situation, and the extent of that authority may be narrowly or broadly defined by the particular circumstance, but the bottom line is that a governing agency only exists if it has the authority to make decisions that can be enacted. Yet, if governments and businesses have that authority, and we've established that businesses are *not* institutions, we have a contradiction staring us right in the face. So, there must be more to it.

Let's establish just what we mean in our discussion of government. Perhaps we can stipulate at this point that a government is a body imbued with decision-making authority. However, since our topic is organized public education, we are going to specifically define government in terms of social systems. As such, government represents *a system for determining, administering, and carrying out the needs, desires, and broadly defined expectations of the society it serves.* Businesses, on the other hand, answer to the profit-driven expectations of a narrowly defined constituency. With that in mind, let's continue.

Governments can certainly fit the criteria of size (in terms of employing many people) and longevity that we discussed under the heading of corporations. In fact, it is virtually impossible, much like obtaining an accurate census, to account for *all* of the government workers in our society. It may be possible to find out how many federal-level workers there are and perhaps to get an accurate number of the paid state-level employees. However, by the time we include all of the local-level officials, all of the school board members, and certainly all of the *unpaid* workers on governmental projects (for instance, business leaders as appointed members of state-level educational-reform initiatives and volunteers in social service organizations and schools), the numbers will be changing again with new elections, new issues, and new committees. It would probably be best to agree that government, in the context we've established, definitely has size on its side when considering the characteristics of institutions. And since a government serves its constituents, which in the United States numbers around three hundred million citizens, it would be fair to concede that our particular government serves the needs and interests of many people. So, government is a duly authorized decision-making body that is expansive in size and comprehensive in representation.

Our discussion of IBM included the notion that the corporation had remained in business despite changes in the surrounding social milieu and the technology of the industry. The same can be said fairly of governments. In fact, governments can be painfully slow to change. Ideology is its stock in trade. So, we can conclude that government has longevity, size, and an underlying value or purpose that does impact upon people over time. It's sounding pretty institutional so far.

Of course, there is always another question to ask: Given all we've said about government so far, what constitutes "governmentness"? Isn't it really the case that government is a *model*, perhaps an ideological *structure*, that emerges when the various operations of government are brought together under some grand "control" (for lack of a better term)? Somewhat analogous to the Gestalt perspective of the whole being greater than the sum of its parts, government is what we have when the various departments and agencies of social function are bundled together.

Just like a collection of drawers in a single wooden cabinet (a bureau), government is simply the organizational tool that facilitates the work of the individual "drawers." Centralizing control of those functions gives rise to the *bureaucracy* that we call *government*— for better or worse. There is a negative connotation to the term *bureaucracy* (just as is the case with *institution*), but the first step in changing those connotations is to identify each for what it is. And government, it would seem, is the *bureaucracy* that exercises control over the *institutions* and *regulatory agencies* of a society.

You might wonder why (or, perhaps, if) this is an important distinction to make. We believe it is because it is this distinction that directs the actions necessary to make institutional change. For example, people have a tendency to buy a new car when the engine on their old car fails. Yet, a "car" is more than an engine. In fact, a "car" only exists by virtue of combining a number of discrete components. Now, which makes more sense when there is some difficulty with the car: replacing a component that has failed or replacing the entire unit because of the failure of one component? You probably know what effect profit-driven business and advertising have had on that decision. We see the car as the institution—unchangeable—rather than seeing the part that needs changing. Replacing the part is easier. And institutions are the parts that make up who we are as a society.

If government is the "car" and some institution or agency within it is failing, then it is obvious that the particular component needs attention. What does this mean for our discussion? It means that revolution is neither a scary nor a dirty word if it is directed only at the component in need of attention. We need not destroy the car (as the term *revolution* might imply) to fix the problem. What is the pertinent point? Education is part of a bureaucratic system, and it can be revolutionized so that the entire system works more effectively. Now that's not scary, is it? In fact, wouldn't that be good news? After all, what this tells us is that the beast, though formidable for reasons of institutional survival, may not be as big a beast as we had feared.

The Military

Well then, we are still left with trying to determine just what an institution is so that we can more effectively consider the system of organized education in our country. Since we've brought ourselves to the point of focusing on drawers within the bureau, let's see whether all of those drawers represent institutions or if there are further distinctions to be made. As our example, let's consider national defense, "the military."

Taken together, the army, navy, air force, Marines, coast guard, and their various incarnations of reservists and the National Guard obviously represent a very large force of personnel who provide a service to a broadly defined constituency. So far, we are on the road to an institution. It is also true that while budget cycles can affect everything from hardware to the meals served in dining halls, profit per se is not the driving force behind our combative forces. The possibility of "institutionality" looms on the horizon. Before that image starts to blur, let's quickly add that the mission of the military is founded upon a deeply rooted and widely held value: the preservation of our social system, our nation. Further, while embracing changes in technology— in fact often driving those changes—the military has a narrowly defined purpose and ideology that has remained essentially unchanged throughout its history: the

protection of the aforementioned values against enemies "foreign and domestic."
Can't get much more prescriptive than that—they are to defend and protect the Constitution of the United States against any and all comers. Sounds as though we might
have a winner here! But wait.

When you get right down to it, couldn't we say the same things about another organization widely recognized by its initials? Couldn't we make most all of the same
statements about the Internal Revenue Service (IRS)? True, the IRS does not have
quite the same amount of deadly firepower that the military has, and there likely
aren't many IRS-specific dining halls, but they do utilize progressive technologies to
accomplish a highly specified mission, while employing thousands of people and
serving the "needs" of millions of Americans without regard for ethnicity, creed, or
national origin. While the IRS is not necessarily defending and protecting the Constitution of the United States, its activities are carried out in accord with the provi-
sions of that document. Yet, somehow it just doesn't feel right to say the IRS is an institution in the same way that the military might be an institution. So, what's the
difference?

Here's the difference. Both organizations do in fact serve a legitimate public need.
And both have the various characteristics we've enumerated. However, an agency such
as the IRS performs a *regulatory* function, whereas organizations such as the military
perform a function that people could not reasonably accomplish for themselves. And
that is a characteristic that we must look for to consider some structure as a social institution: It must perform a function that people legitimately need and cannot perform
for themselves. National defense is such a function. The values that underlie national
defense fall within the domain of institutions because specialized attention is needed,
specialized preparation of the providers is required, and the delivery of services must
provide the greatest good for the greatest number. And we have a sneaking suspicion
that education is going to fall into that same category as well.

Ideological Institutions

Our discussion would not be complete without stepping away from the concrete, the
bricks and nails and other hardware, and taking a look at institutions from the perspective of pure ideology. Even though we have delimited our discussion to consider
social institutions, forces exist within those structures that are perpetuated by pure
force of will or belief. Despite changing times and challenges to the dogma of their
messages, they survive despite the lack of mandated funding, the absence of "employees," and the overwhelming and inescapable reliance on faith. Such stamina must involve a lesson worth learning. So, let's consider the topics of "the church" and of marriage as ideologies prevalent in our society.

In taking on these particular topics, it is only fair that we elaborate on our intended
purpose. First, you've probably noticed that we used quotation marks when referring
to "the church." The distinction we want to make is that the church (we'll stop using
the quotation marks now) refers to the organizational structure that delivers an ideological message to its adherents no matter what the denomination.

A consideration of the church is certainly a departure from our focus on institutions
that arise within societies for the express purpose of perpetuating what might best be
described as the secular values of that society, but we want to spend some time con-

sidering "institutionality" in terms of something that is almost purely ideological. Ideology is fundamental to two of our concerns from previous chapters: understanding the American culture and determining the purpose of organized education in that culture. So, our emphasis with the examples of the church and marriage differs somewhat from the derivation of our previous operational definition. In fact, what we are doing now might better be thought of as testing the strands of that emerging definition. With all of that in mind, let's see what can be seen.

The Church

We can acknowledge immediately that though the church may be *prophet driven*, it is not *profit driven* and, so, passes our initial test for scrutiny as an institution. And since we are considering "religion" in a broad sense, as faith-based systems of belief, it can also be acknowledged that size and longevity are on its side. So, too, are the notions of impact over time and the meeting of particular needs (in this case, spiritual needs).

However, the church nonetheless differs from what we've been identifying as institutions in some very poignant ways. Perhaps most important is that religious affiliation is based upon a common faith rather than on the communal acceptance of diversity. That is, the tenets of *a* church (as opposed to *the church*) are not negotiable. Nor should they be. Yet, in an institution it is necessary that a broadly defined constituency be accommodated rather than one that is narrowly defined—and by that we mean a constituency that is bound together by a doctrine that cannot be changed.

We suppose that members of any given church could make the argument that in fact their church *is* an institution that meets the needs of all individuals without exception; the problem is simply that all who are not followers of that particular faith have thus far failed to find the true answer. It is difficult to argue around that.

Nonetheless, this issue is of primary concern for public education. Despite the regular attempts of one group or another to have their religious doctrine become an explicit part of the established curriculum, the social institution of public education (if it is one) must, by our emerging definition, be as inclusive as possible of all and prejudicial toward none. These are two things that religion cannot, or perhaps does not wish to, accomplish.

We might also mention that, as part of its nature, the church is highly resistant to change. In fact, it is so tradition-bound that practitioners are expected to change themselves to better mimic tradition and, thus, exemplify an underlying message. On the other hand, social institutions are expected to change to better match the contemporary constituency, though not at the expense of the underlying message.

In the final analysis, we find that the church qualifies as an institution in terms of the definition we have been building, but only with qualification. That is, *churches* don't qualify because they are too narrowly defined, but *the church* does qualify because it subsumes all denominations and thus is broadly defined. Of more concern for our discussion, however, is the power of an inherent message of value to be perpetuated over time for the good of the many. So, while we may not look to the church as the model for a new institution of education, it may be wise to recognize the value of ensuring that the message the institution delivers and perpetuates is one of tremendous ideological strength. No, the ideology is not the institution, but ideologies are the messages for which institutions are built.

The lesson for our concern with the institution of education is to fashion our ideology well and then build an institution that translates our ideology into a practical expression of who we are. The church is able to do this with volunteered funding and without the reins of legislative control over its followers. Indeed, amazing things can be done when the message is a powerful one.

Marriage

Marriage: no buildings, no organizational structure, no governing body, yet so often it is referred to as an institution. And it does seem to have a number of the characteristics we've been identifying. But is it an institution? We should be getting pretty good at this by now, so let's see how it all breaks down.

Marriage has no organizational structure (keeping in mind that we are talking about "marriage," not *a* marriage such as your own or one between a couple of your friends). Yet, its instigation in our society has some very definite rules. For instance, it is still overwhelmingly considered to be a legal/religious union between one man and one woman. There are many attempts to remove the man/woman aspect so that, at least legally, it is a union between "partners," but the underlying ideology still fights to retain its traditional hold.

Marriage is so paradoxical that it is difficult to discuss. For instance, in religious terms, it represents a sacred bond between two people. Yet, in legal terms, cohabitation for a protracted period of time constitutes common law marriage: no ceremony, no particular agreement of "marriedness," and yet legally as binding as the full-blown, bank-breaking production that your daughter has her heart set on.

Just as curious, though a license is required by most states, the common law marriage is licenseless. And in any event, obtaining the license is no particular trick. Unlike the written and driving tests to get a license for motor vehicles, the most demanding aspect of obtaining a marriage license is paying the nominal fee: no training necessary (other than on-the-job), no testing, not even an eye test every couple of years. In fact, all of this sounds pretty good for driving—a common law driver's license. Do you suppose that would hold up if you were pulled over by a trooper? "No officer, I don't have a traditional license, I'm a common law driver."

Kidding aside, the paradox is real. The ideological basis of marriage is an ancient one. Yet, the practice and support of marriage is left to the two partners. Travel along virtually any street of families, and you will find abundant evidence of marriages—some successful, some failed, some struggling, but all with some semblance of that underlying value that marriage represents. It is certainly not profit-driven (for the most part), and many would argue that its absence would indeed leave a hole in the fabric of our society. But still, marriages in our contemporary culture come and go and may represent little more than the last vestiges of a bygone cultural tradition.

So, is marriage an institution? Certainly not in its ideological form, for we have already determined that ideologies can be the basis for institutions but not institutions in and of themselves. And in practice, we would have to find some sort of service that marriage provides that people could not accomplish for themselves. In the case of marriage, as we have seen, it is left almost entirely to people to manage for themselves, despite the high failure rate and the pressing questions of a changing society. Is it important to defining our American culture? Perhaps. An institution? No.

Summary

And so, let's take a shot at an operational definition of "institution" based on what we have found with these examples. An institution must support, serve, and represent the needs/values of a large and diverse population. (When we speak of institutions in our social context, the numbers involve tens of thousands, millions, or more.) The services provided by this institution must be something that people typically cannot accomplish for themselves, and that is most likely because of the specific expertise required to appropriately provide it. Institutions are based on widely held values that serve a legitimate and enduring public interest that cannot be ignored simply for profit (or lack thereof) considerations. And an institution performs a function whose absence would leave a hole in the fabric of the society at large. It would be evident that some need (and we mean a *need* here, not something that would simply be nice to have) is not being met.

Constructed around these characteristics, institutions in practice adopt the characteristic features of perpetuation, survival, and the establishment of their own identity. These are not characteristics that the designers of institutions (whoever they might be) specifically work into the blueprints. Rather, these are the characteristics that institutional activity fosters in the name and practice of preservation. These characteristics often manifest themselves as institutional anonymity. That is, there is no name, no face to match with the institution. As such, we typically see institutions as being slow to react to changing needs and often as suffering from lack of funding as their anonymity distances people from their identity.

And yet, institutions need not be that way. In fact, the very characteristics that we have cited as representing "institutionality" are characteristics that are dynamic, that could orient the institution toward the future as a provider of human needs. Institutions, imbued with our own vitality, could be cutting-edge organizations that keep pace with society.

We are our institutions. If we find them lacking in respect for human dignity, as has been the case with care for the mentally handicapped, the disenfranchised, and the elderly, it is because we have failed to keep our part of the bargain. If we find fault with the institutions that serve us, we find fault with ourselves. That's not such a bad message really, for it underscores the fact that institutions can be changed. Sometimes that change is in terms of reform if the underlying values of the institution were originally well thought out. And sometimes that change might require revolution if the underlying values were never formally articulated and put in place. If the institution has evolved on its own, revolution may indeed be the remedy.

We have examined this question of what an institution is in a general sense to make our task clearer. Everyday language becomes accepted language, and in the process, meanings become blurred. The dilemma is that when someone approaches a problem such as "an institution," there is so much ambiguity that the issue is perceived as being much greater than it really is. Characteristics identify institutionality and further characteristics identify particular institutions. Changes in those characteristics threaten to change the institution. However, understanding just what we are talking about serves to diminish the "fear factor" in making changes. That an institution is an organization established by and for a society isolates it from the notion of being so big that its problems can't be addressed. Carefully defining what it means to be an institution allows us to look at a particular organization and know what sort of actions it will take to make the changes we desire. For instance, a department or agency can be more easily changed than an institution because the agency is regulatory, while an institution speaks to us and our values. Knowing that change will entail an examination of who we are and what we want, we can then look to the defining characteristics of the particular institution to see where the problem is and what needs to be done about it. In some cases, it may be possible to fix one component or another. Mysterious? No. Mystical or magical? No and no. Beyond human capability? By no means. A big undertaking? Yes.

We now know that there are three sets of qualifiers to be addressed when considering an organizational structure in terms of its being an institution: the characteristics of "institutionality" in the broad sense (size, longevity, message, etc.), characteristics of institutional function in a generic sense (perpetuation, identity, and survival), and the defining characteristics of the particular institution (for example, the political and educational characteristics specific to public schooling).

The characteristics of institutionality suggest that when considering an organization, we should first look to see if the structure itself fulfills the criteria for being an institution: that is, having size and longevity as made possible by an underlying message of social value, serving a legitimate public interest, and providing services to a broadly defined constituency that could not reasonably provide those services for itself. In addition, one must keep in mind that social institutions are practical expressions of the values held by a particular society or culture, and as such, their absence would be conspicuous. The "test of absence" is a key consideration.

If we determine that some structure meets the criteria outlined in the previous paragraph, we can next look for the presence of the three recurring themes that we have identified: perpetuation, identity, and survival. Here, of course, is where things start to get sort of fuzzy. We should be able to establish that there is some message or value statement that the institution seeks to perpetuate, even if it's difficult to articulate. However, it is not uncommon to find that an institution over time drifts from a clear identity into a kind of anonymity. This leads to the third common characteristic of institutional existence: an instinct for survival.

An institution operating at optimum efficiency (stop laughing) would be one that need not have a survival "instinct." Instead, the value of the institution would be evident, as would its personal and collective value structures. It is the "institutional" institution, however, that develops a survival mechanism to protect the many interests *within* the institution, interests that have perhaps come to be more important than those the institution was established to serve. And so, efforts at change are typically unwelcome for they pose a threat to those internal interests, to the jobs that people hold, to the manner in which those jobs are carried out, and to the ancillary services that support the institution's activity. No, it's not pretty, but it's what institutions do to survive after we have turned our backs on them.

And finally, we can look to the very particular characteristics that define the institution we have identified. Now that we have a greater understanding of what it means to be an institution, let us consider the characteristics of public education in the United States.

THE INSTITUTION OF EDUCATION

So, is education an institution? We know that public education does not answer to a profit motive, even though it is left at the mercy of economic circumstances. But let

---

Activity 3.2.
IS EDUCATION AN INSTITUTION?

Before reading further, take a moment to consider education as you know it in terms of the general characteristics of institutions. You need not go into great detail about any of these topics, but try to provide some example of how education passes (or does not pass) the test of "institutionality" as described thus far rather than just giving yes or no answers.

1. Does organized education have a long history?
2. Does education serve a large and diverse constituency?
3. Is it expected to convey a message of social value?
4. Does it serve a legitimate public service that people could not accomplish for themselves to the same degree?
5. Does the providing of an education require a specialized service?
6. If there were no system of public education, would there be a conspicuous absence in the fabric of society?

---

us consider each of the generic characteristics of institutions: longevity, size, broad constituency, message of social value, serving a legitimate public interest, specialized service, and the test of conspicuous absence. Following that, we can consider the recurring themes of institutional existence: perpetuation, identity, and survival. If it all holds together as an institution, we can move to the defining characteristics peculiar to education.

The Generic Characteristics

The characteristic of longevity is definitely on public education's side. In fact, organized education's history in America predates the nation itself. Massachusetts passed the first education law in 1642. Though not particularly establishing "public" education, the law held parents responsible for seeing that their children were educated. It was the Old Deluder Satan Act of 1647 (also in Massachusetts), however, that established organized education at public expense. The signing of the Declaration of Independence was still well over one hundred years away, yet an institution was being born. And since it could be argued that colonial times represented the existence of *a* church rather than *the* church, it could be said that education has a longer history in our country than does any other institution. If we take the Education Act of 1642 as our starting point (and that is conservative, for education was an issue before 1642), then the year 2042 will mark education's *four hundredth anniversary* in what is now the United States. Yes, it would seem to meet the criteria of longevity.

The size of the institution would also seem to be a moot point. At this writing, there are approximately fifty-five million children enrolled in our nation's schools, and they are served by well over five million teachers. If we add in the parents of those children and the ancillary service providers that facilitate the delivery of the educational program, it is obvious that even with a very conservative estimate, nearly half of the population of the United States has a first-hand interest in public education on any given school day. We could extend this further, of course, by including the businesses that depend upon the graduates of public schools to be qualified workers, but with well over one hundred million people directly involved, the size of the institution would seem to be well covered.

It would also seem obvious that organized public education serves a legitimate public interest. At the very least, and perhaps indicative of a blurring of its institutional identity, education provides a day care function. Don't get upset: We said "at the very least." At its very best, education provides an efficient, fair, reliable, and fully sanctioned system for providing children with the basic skills necessary for effective citizenship as it also disseminates and perpetuates (there's that word again) our common culture. Even this notion has a long history, for in the 1800s Horace Mann actively advocated for a publicly funded and equitable system of education, the common school, to accomplish just this. And that was more than 150 years ago! Whether or not it is true that education does these things in this day and age is another story. Yet, the question of providing a service that meets a legitimate public interest is one that we could reasonably answer in the affirmative.

Is there a message of social value that the institution exemplifies? The easy answer is yes. What is that message? That is again an area that becomes exceedingly difficult to articulate. Looking back to colonial times once again, the purpose of education was to teach children "proper conduct." Ostensibly, this was done through strict discipline, obedience, and reading of the Bible. The ultimate goal: salvation. But today is, *to a large extent,* a different story. We qualify that statement because one can find the vestiges of colonial education alive and well throughout our "modern" school system. Nonetheless, there was at one time a clear idea of the message of social value delivered by schooling. We would all like to believe that such a message exists today, even though very few among us, if any, could state that message in a manner that would yield unanimous agreement. We will not suggest that, in this book, such a widely acceptable statement will be made, but we do hope to open the dialogue with an eye toward the future of education in our country.

That education is an institution providing services to a broadly defined constituency is without question. There may be significant concerns about who the curriculum actually serves, but the fact remains that, by law, a free and appropriate education is to be made available to all children of U.S. citizenship up to the age of twenty-one (the age limit of twenty-one applies in particular to students with identifiable learning disabilities or handicaps as detailed in Public Laws 91-142 and 101-476). Our system of public education is therefore open to all. Unlike the circumstance of private schools, public schools do not have the option of simply expelling underachievers or children with incorrigible behavior problems. Nor is the inability to speak the English language grounds for turning children away. And, of course, religious affiliation is similarly not a factor. There likely is no institution in our country that opens its doors as wide as does education.

It would not be difficult to start an argument regarding whether or not public education meets our next criteria in this set of institutional qualifiers, that being the providing of a service that the constituents themselves cannot reasonably provide for themselves. There are, in fact, hundreds of thousands of children in the United States who are homeschooled, and some estimates take that number as high as 1.5 million (Sadker & Sadker, 2000). All states allow homeschooling, provided that minimum curricular requirements are met. And without a doubt, education has long suffered from the widely held perspective that anyone who has gone to school can teach or, in the case of state governments, can effectively legislate school. But is this true?

We need to make a distinction at this point between what is reasonable within our current circumstances and what is most desirable. For instance, private schools, home-schooling, and specialty learning services (commercial tutoring services) make claims for improving student performance that seem difficult to believe given all we know of our public education system. We don't disparage those claims at all. However, we hasten to point out that a parent homeschooling his or her children or a commercial service charging a steep tuition have the luxury of working with children one-on-one or in very small groups. The system of public education cannot, by sheer force of numbers, come close to such a student-teacher ratio. That's why we say it is important to make the distinction between what is and what would be nice. A simple fact in this situation is that a student-teacher ratio of five to one, for example, would require increasing—and paying—the professional workforce by at least 100 percent. That's not feasible. And providing services to accomplish our nation's educational goals must be done under specialized conditions and with personnel educated to meet the needs of many, diverse students. The notion that all children are different is not difficult to accept. The notion that children must be taught according to those differences is not difficult to understand. Providing instruction that at one time accommodates all of those differences does require specialized knowledge and expertise.

The matter of specialized knowledge and expertise leads us directly to the final consideration among the generic characteristics of institutions. We must question whether or not the services of the organization would be conspicuous in their absence. In this case, the answer would be yes. Parents *could* deliver an academic curriculum to their own children; they *could* provide that instruction concomitantly with a message of appropriate social behavior and the value of being a "good" person. But there are other messages that would indeed be lost.

Oftentimes referred to as the "hidden curriculum," schools typically provide a host of experiences and educational messages that are not explicit in the academic curriculum. School is also a socializing process. Through their interaction with many children, each child learns skills related to working with others, disagreeing, finding common ground, accepting differences of all sorts, understanding common culture and tradition, and developing common cultural aspirations for the future. The unsurprisingly biased and ofttimes prejudiced views that children find at home are questioned, balanced, and sometimes ameliorated by the child's interaction with other children and adults at school. A form of tolerance is embodied by the school that parents would have difficulty personifying at home.

Similarly, the "null curriculum" influences a child's educational experience in terms of what is not taught. For example, schools that refuse to teach about the theory of evolution leave their students lacking in an accepted scientific explanation of species-specific biological change and adaptation over time. In this case, students have not made a decision about the viability of the theory but instead are simply ignorant of it.

Without the public school experience, a large measure of cultural cohesion would be lost. Science awareness would almost certainly suffer as parents would pick and choose among the principles of science that they cared to explain or emphasize to their children. Our common language, another area already in deep distress, would disintegrate even further because children would be taught to read, write, and comprehend as their

Table 3.1.   The Broad Aspects of Institutions as Applied to Public Education

Generic Characteristics	
Longevity	Laws have existed since 1642. Public education is the oldest secular institution in the nation.
Size	Fifty million plus teachers, students, staff, parents, ancillary service providers.
Broad constituency	Must accommodate all ethnicities represented by citizenry.
Message of social value	Represents and disseminates sanctioned social values and aspirations.
Serving a legitimate public interest	Essential skills and ideologies are taught that support perpetuation of the society and its values.
Specialized service	Teachers and administrators provide a broad, socially sanctioned curriculum to millions of students based on principles of pedagogy and take responsibility for student welfare during the school day.
Conspicuous absence	Absence of organized public education could be expected to result in a marked decline in communication, calculation, and socialization skills, along with a decline in appreciation of a common culture and social heritage.

parents read, write, and comprehend. In many cases, this might not be so bad, but keep in mind that we are talking about *tens of millions* of cases.

It is obvious that parents cannot be expected to have the range of expertise that professional teachers possess. Yet, the perception continues that if one has completed school (no matter what the degree of success), then one is capable of teaching school. This makes no more sense than to say that if one has ever been sick, that person is qualified to treat sick people, or that one who has lived in a house is qualified to design and build houses. The ramifications of removing organized public education would not only leave a hole in the fabric of our society, but it could be expected to begin the complete unraveling of the society as well. Education, properly administered and presented, is one of the most specialized activities in which a society can engage in its own best interests.

The Recurring Themes of Institutional Existence

Having found that public education meets the broad characteristics of institutions, we can look to our recurring themes for further confirmation. We already know that there is some underlying message of social significance that the institution perpetuates. And we have acknowledged that the message may be a little difficult to uncover. It is also evident that public education has resisted the efforts of parochial *and* secular privatization because, while many students are indeed sent to nonpublic schools, the overwhelming majority of American children participate in public education. Through all of the efforts toward reform, the basic institution remains intact. If that is the case, there must be some message of value lurking within.

Institutional identity is a classic example of all we have discussed throughout this book. Though there was likely a time when the identity of organized education was clearly tied to its mission of providing an equitable educational experience for all, when people are asked about education these days, it is more likely that the first image that comes to mind (and therefore the one with the strongest identity) is a yellow school bus or a red apple. These are cute icons, but they gloss over the lack of a substantive institutional identity.

With regard to survival, reforms are hampered not by a resistance to adopting best pedagogical practice but by resistance to changing power structures (legislatures like to control education, administrators like to control teachers, etc.), resistance to changing economic forces (parents pay taxes, so tuition is out of the question), resistance to changing family-vacation schedules (which would impact the seasonal tourism business), and, ultimately, resistance to changing the status quo.

And so, the survival instinct of an ill-defined institution has taken over. With a clear ideology long since lost, the institution protects itself from being dismantled. A little change here appeases one faction; a little change there appeases another. Eventually, things can get changed back when a new faction comes along, when membership of the school board changes, when new issues capture the attention of the society at large (e.g., the effects on science education following the launching of Sputnik in 1957 or the shift to social issues during the 1960s and 1970s). Education exemplifies the phrase "The more things change, the more they stay the same."

The fundamental problem with education, as we have said previously, is that it is fundamentally an institution. Institutions do not want to change, even if doing so is in their best interests. Do you see how our earlier discussion of the American culture begins to come back to haunt our analysis of public education? Public education is the poster child of institutional evolution: It perpetuates *something*, its identity is *as an institution* rather than as reflecting the mission the institution serves, and it fights tooth and nail to survive in order to protect the interests of those working *within* the institution more so than to protect the needs of those the institution was intended to serve. That's where we are with public education, and a look at its own defining characteristics will bear that out.

Table 3.2. The Recurring Institutional Themes as Applied to Public Education

The Recurring Institutional Themes	
Perpetuation	Public education has repeatedly survived efforts to replace it with parochial and secular privatization. There is undeniably an inherent message that the institution seeks to perpetuate, though the message has become vague, distorted, and difficult to articulate, and agreement for it on a broad scale seems to be problematic.
Identity	Education is a classic example of institutional evolution. School has an identity, but it is tied more to yellow school buses than to academic excellence or a clearly defined institutionwide mission. Thus, it has evolved from its educational identity into a nebulous institutional identity that is accepted but little understood.
Survival	Education's resistance to substantive reform is a clear indicator of its inclination toward institutional survival rather than ideological integrity. That is, the institution survives intact to preserve the interests of those supported by the institution more so than to meet the needs of those served by the institution.

Defining Characteristics of the Institution of Education

When considering change, the generic characteristics of institutional existence give us a sense of the enormity of the task. They also provide guidance to those who would establish a new institution. These are not discussions to be entered into lightly, for they impact many people and will continue to do so for many years. The recurring themes of institutional evolution provide insight into how an institution will hold on to the notion of perpetuating *something,* even when its identity is subject to change and struggling to survive, having lost sight of its original purpose. These themes remind us of what happens when we forget that our institutions should be dynamic manifestations of our own values.

All of the characteristics discussed are those that we might expect to encounter if and when we come to wrestle with the institutional beast. However, each institution is defined by its own set of *defining characteristics.* Contained within such a list are the artifacts of the original institution, as well as the current realities, the characteristics that are threatened by the notion of change. And so, the survival instinct takes over to avert, ameliorate, and occasionally adapt to change rather than face redefinition. But substantive redirection is rarely the case when working with institutions.

What are the defining characteristics of the institution of education? Compiling an exhaustive list would be, well, exhausting. But creating a list of a hundred or more items that define what goes on with and at "school" is not so difficult. Keep in mind that we are not identifying "problems" with school but rather characteristics. For instance, the amount of "paperwork" involved is a complaint in most any enterprise that has extensive record keeping, and that represents a problem rather than a defining characteristic. That students are assessed and evaluated on a regular basis (referring here to classroom assessments as opposed to standardized districtwide assessments) is a distinguishing characteristic. How often are you assessed on the job? How often does someone come along and put a grade, or a smiley face (or sad face), or gold star on the work you have just completed? This is what happens regularly to children, and it is one of the more traumatic changes from the carefree world of the child to the accountability world of school. Whereas at one time mom and dad said that everything their child did was wonderful, suddenly some third party (the teacher) is making very real judgments about that child's work, and he begins to notice that not everybody in the class is receiving the same grade. That is a defining characteristic of an educational setting.

We have listed some of the defining characteristics of public education in three categories. Table 3.3 lists items, such as the grading situation just discussed, as *instructional* characteristics. Table 3.4 offers characteristics that deal with the *administration* of public education, and table 3.5 lists descriptors that could be broadly classified as *political* issues. You may also want to jot down a few of the items we haven't included here—and there are many. A revolutionizing of the institution will require that we identify and resolve more items than these, but this should provide a start for understanding some of those things that we tend to overlook from day to day.

Instructional Characteristics

In this category list, we refer to the grouping, instructing, and assessing of students. As you consider additional items for this category, it might be good to think in terms of anything that directly impacts upon the student. These certainly would include the

Table 3.3. Defining Characteristics of Public Education: Instructional

Instructional Characteristics

1. Classes have one teacher with one, two, or three or more dozen students in one large room.
2. Classes are held on a 180-day/year schedule with an extended summer break.
3. Students are assessed and graded on a regular (daily) basis.
4. Some sort of writing surface (typically, a chalkboard even in new schools) is affixed to the front wall.
5. Each student has a desk to which the teacher has access. The teacher has a larger desk, which represents sovereign territory.
6. There are report cards! And interims, and updates, and notes.
7. Classes are conducted with a distinctly nondemocratic authority structure.
8. In virtually all schools, some form of tracking and/or ability-grouping takes place.
9. The teaching force is predominantly female and predominantly white.
10. Children are typically grouped into grade levels by ages rather than cognitive ability.
11. Some 50 percent of children are not on grade level but are kept in "age-appropriate" grade levels.
12. Though students can drop out of school, it is essentially impossible to "flunk out" of public school.
13. Elementary schools have one teacher per class for all academic subject areas.
14. From middle school on, teachers "specialize," though not necessarily in the field for which they are certified. The schools' needs drive assignments.
15. English language is the dominant language but not the official language.
16. Teachers are expected to supplement consumable supplies and materials because that's how they are.
17. School brings the world to the students rather than taking students to the world.
18. School is responsible for the dissemination of our common culture.
19. Teachers are nurturing by nature.
20. Daily accomplishments are ill defined. Just ask a child, "What did you learn today?"

teacher and his or her education and credentials, the curriculum materials that children use, the instructional techniques and strategies that the school advocates, the grouping of children, the source of supplies, and, to a degree, the appearance of the classroom (not the entire building—that's administrative) and the atmosphere that it establishes. You should be able to see that the items listed here, and that you list, as reflective of school today are often unsettlingly similar to school when you were there, no matter how long it has been since you were in elementary school or high school.

Administrative Characteristics

As you consider the characteristics of school, you will likely find that many items apparently overlap categories. We have attempted to avoid repetition in the tables presented here but want to emphasize the importance of understanding the multidimensionality of many characteristics. For instance, the typical 180-day school year with an extended summer break has a direct impact on *instruction* and student learning. The curriculum must be organized and lessons structured to present that curriculum within the allotted time. However, it is also an *administrative* characteristic in that teacher contracts and subsequent salaries are based on nine months rather than twelve months. An obvious repercussion of this is when the discussion of year-round school comes up.

Table 3.4.　Defining Characteristics of Public Education: Administrative

Administrative Characteristics

1. Schools are run with a distinctly nondemocratic authority structure.
2. The "business model" characterizes school operations.
3. District/state student transportation system. Yellow school buses!
4. Teachers have no opportunities for advancement without leaving the classroom.
5. Testing of students is used extensively for district planning and evaluation.
6. Accountability is a relatively new buzzword whose meaning is still poorly articulated, yet it is driving student standardized assessment, as well as school and teacher evaluations.
7. A weak philosophical orientation. Schools often post their "philosophy," but the institution avoids doing so, perhaps to avoid disenfranchising one group or another.
8. Teachers are expected to fulfill the roles of educator, guidance counselor, behavior manager, clerical workers, community (parent) liaison, etc.
9. The principal sets the tone for the entire school, and that tone is at the principal's discretion.
10. The school board rules the principal vis-à-vis the superintendent.
11. Policy making is considered as being beyond the ability of classroom teachers.
12. Typically a K–12 structure, though there is increasing prevalence of pre-K programs.
13. Students graduate at age eighteen.
14. Despite the test results, there is an overwhelming academic emphasis and very little explicit emphasis on social skills in the curriculum.
15. Despite the requirements for certification and postgraduate work, teachers work for lower salaries than those in occupations with similar educational requirements.
16. "Portables" (temporary classrooms) are preferable to future-oriented planning.
17. Teachers are expected to participate in regular professional-development activities.
18. Extensive use of substitute teachers. Though schools have existed for centuries, the use of substitute teachers is still almost synonymous with "free time."
19. Discipline and obedience are still central themes (there's that perpetuation again), and some states still condone the use of corporal punishment to ensure that obedience.
20. Schools can make do with the funding. Rarely do schools shut down (though it happens).

If days are actually added to the school year (rather than just reallocating those 180 days to include the summer), then the matter of salaries comes back into play, and we all know that schools are always searching for funds to keep going on the present schedule. That, of course, becomes a *political* issue because more money for salaries (it's not really higher salaries, just longer contracts) means more appropriations from the state, and that means higher taxes assessed somewhere or another. Really, it's not difficult to see why people become disillusioned with, and eventually disassociated from, institutions: The issues can boggle the mind. But in the final analysis, they are just that, issues. And the more clearly delineated the issues (as we have tried to do with this chapter), the easier it will be to find viable resolutions.

Political Characteristics

Chances are good that the U.S. Air Force never contacted you for your opinion about building the B-1 bomber. It's not likely that the army consulted with you before constructing some facility for its personnel. And we'd be willing to bet that you haven't been to a bake sale any time in the recent past to help the navy finance a new ship. Yet, these are all functions that have an impact upon you. They are funded with your tax dollars, and they afford you a level of protection that you could not otherwise manage on your own. But you probably didn't have much input anyway. Correct?

On the other hand, if the school district needs a new building, there will be a bond referendum in which you can cast a vote that will determine whether or not that building becomes a reality. You can, if only by being the squeaky wheel, have an impact on what foods are served in the cafeteria, which teachers will teach your children, and which textbooks will be adopted by the state and district. Certainly, it is possible for you to be involved on various levels with political movements local, state, or federal, but your most immediate and perhaps influential political role is with regard to our public schools. We say this knowing that both good and bad news accompany the message. For instance, the public education system in the United States does afford you the opportunity to be a player in the determination of how and what children are taught. The bad news is that there's a reason why the armed forces probably didn't contact you about the issues discussed previously, and the same reason can (and often should) apply to education: credentials.

Parents typically don't like to hear this. We will admit right now that if the air force had asked either of us about the B-1 bomber, we would have been so lacking in the required aerospace expertise that we would have had little to contribute to the discussion. The same would be true if the local fire department called asking for recommendations regarding the fighting of fires. Even political candidates must show that they have some qualifications for the offices they seek; just saying "I'd like to win this election" is usually not enough.

In education, however, there is an *assumption* that anyone who has children or has attended school (whether he or she finished or not) has the credentials to make

Table 3.5. Defining Characteristics of Public Education: Political

Political Characteristics

1. Education is funded primarily through state and local taxes. Federal funding is available for special programs.
2. Policy making and legislation is top down.
3. Legislators and other elected/appointed officials make the assumption that they have the credentials to teach/administer/legislate education.
4. Community-centered schools.
5. Education must be responsive to many constituencies.
6. Parental involvement in school is ill defined and inconsistent.
7. The "equality" of educational experience is largely economics driven.
8. School curriculums are often and easily changed.
9. Separation of church and state is still an issue for public education.
10. An overwhelming assumption exists that anyone can teach.
11. Children are entitled to a free and appropriate education.
12. Textbook design and content are driven by the demands of the major markets (states).
13. Schools support a wide range of ancillary materials and service providers (the extended institution).
14. Schools (the facilities) are the property of the community/state.
15. The desired outcomes of education are poorly stated (this differs from a listing of standards).
16. Education can be legislated without major influence from educators.
17. Schools are the mechanism for solving social problems.
18. Education is the job of the school (unless the parent disagrees with the education).
19. Standards, benchmarks, frameworks, etc. States attempt to establish a laundry list of standards, assuming that they collectively will yield the appropriately educated individual.
20. Extracurricular athletics are just as important as academics.

decisions that can impact upon the lives and learning of hundreds, thousands, and perhaps even millions of children. The acceptance of this assumption has made education an inherently political animal. Please notice that no one has said that parents (and others) cannot acquire credentials for meaningful decision making with regard to the public schools—and there are many ways of gaining such expertise—but the simple facts at the moment are (1) no credentials are required, and (2) that's considered okay. So, as we look at some of the political characteristics that define education, it will become evident that they cover a lot of territory. And when we speak of revolutionizing education, it is the political aspect of the institution that will be *most* resistant to substantive change.

Summary

Words can illuminate our thinking. Language can be our ally, and it can be our enemy. Discourse and dialogue can inform our perspectives and guide our resolution of problems. But meanings and messages can just as easily become obscured by the faulty assumption that all in the conversation are speaking the same "language." The common acceptance of the misuse of words can make that which is understandable incomprehensible.

Having derived and applied a set of criteria for separating institutions from other organizational structures has shown that public education is indeed a manifestation of our social identity. The *broad characteristics* of institutions are present, and that means we are considering something that is not motivated by financial profit or reflective of passing fads. The *recurring themes* demonstrate that education is going the way of institutional evolution as its message is less and less clear, its identity increasingly clouded, and its survival instinct well honed to stave off all attempts at substantive change. Its *defining characteristics* speak to the political nature of organized education, despite the fact that the largest single population within the school building each day is distinctly nonpolitical. The students pay no taxes and cast no votes for legislators or for school board members. They neither hire nor fire faculty and administration; they have no say in the development or presentation of curricula. This sort of paradox should sound familiar after our earlier attempts to understand the American culture. Adding our listing of defining characteristics to the other criteria should also serve to make the entire enterprise more understandable. And from that understanding, we can begin to effect the changes that would make this particular institution once again reflective of who we are, who we want to be, and what we dream of for our children. There are more characteristics to consider, of course; it is not so difficult to find them. The confusion is a matter of trying to "fix" things without taking the time to first define the entire nature of the problem. So, before we move on to questions of the reform model, of the wants and needs of the practitioners within education, and to speculation about the schools of the future, we invite you to take some time to list a few of the characteristics we have not yet considered. Ask others for their perspectives as well. There is absolutely no danger in compiling a long list.

Activity 3.3.
EDUCATION'S DEFINING CHARACTERISTICS

It's your turn now. Use the table below to list what you would consider to be the defining characteristics of the institution of education.

Defining Characteristics of Public Education

FINAL THOUGHTS

Institutions have gotten a bad name in our society. Most folks don't think of "an institutional approach" as being a good thing. Rather, the tendency to distance ourselves from the organizations created to serve our own best interests is at the heart of what we might call "institutional decline." But it need not be that way.

Our institutions express who we are and what is of importance to us. They are the physical representations of ideologies and collective philosophy. It would be useful for each member of a society to spend some period of service with a social institution, such as the prison, mental-health, and elder-care systems, the armed forces, and certainly education. Preparation for such service could be part of students' educational experience. In this way, the vitality and freshness that should be characteristic of our institutions might be rekindled and sustained.

Of course, the key to such an initiative is a clear understanding of what constitutes an institution. To that end, this chapter has focused on delineating the characteristics of institutions in general and public education specifically. The many facets of the issue can be regarded as pieces of the overall puzzle. And since institutions are established by people for people, the puzzle is not one without a solution. Our task as authors and yours as our readers is to make the puzzle manageable, to take what is often perceived as mysterious and "someone else's concern" and make it understandable and worthwhile. Then decisions can be made to keep things as they are, change them, or perhaps—just perhaps—revolutionize them. As education in our country approaches that four hundredth anniversary, it is not unreasonable to think that while the ideology may remain the same, a more exemplary institution may need to be constructed.

4

The Reform Model in Education

> If there is a lesson to be learned from the river of ink that was spilled in the education disputes of the twentieth century, it is that anything in education that is labeled a "movement" should be avoided like the plague.

> —Diane Ravitch

Reform in education is an ongoing activity to the extent that if you attended a public school in the United States, you did so during a period of educational reform. During the past several decades alone, we have seen the emergence or reincarnations of "the new math," phonics, whole language, the alphabet programs of science (ESS, S-APA, SCIS), Success for All, Back to Basics, progressivism, behaviorism, humanism, the great books, vocational education, the subliminal message of "traditionalism," and on and on. Carolyn Orange (2002) lists 125 different programs that she and her colleagues reviewed as representative of contemporary education. And these 125 are the ones they *selected* to review; the list was too long to take on all of them.

The topic of reforms, interventions, and innovations could easily occupy several books (and does) taking many different perspectives. However, in this chapter, we do not want to provide an extensive discourse on reform in American education through the ages. Nor do we want to promulgate the false dichotomy of *traditionalism* versus *progressivism* that is so prevalent in the education literature. But there are several salient points for you to know not only as a conscientious education consumer but as an agent for change as well. Actually, that last sentence exemplifies one of the points we would like to make: We do not wish for you to become a *reform* agent but a *change* agent.

CHANGE AND REFORM

In virtually all things, from academics to Zen, from business to biology, from weather to work, the common denominator is *change*. People grow up and, in some cases, out. Businesses adapt successfully to fluctuating market conditions or say adios. Times *do* change. But have you ever noticed that when it comes to education, the call is not for change but for reform?

The Difference between the Two

The difference between change and reform is that change can be fortuitous, serendipitous, purely accidental, caused by force of nature and, sometimes, by force of will. It can seem good, or it can seem bad, can be a consequence of our actions or a goal toward which our actions are directed. People don't always embrace change, but it is something that we can live with and, in fact, something to which we occasionally look forward. And, as Heraclitus taught, the one thing we can count on is change.

Yet, we need to recognize that reform is always instigated out of dissatisfaction. Rarely, if ever, do folks sit around and think of ways to reform things that are going really well and paying handsome dividends. It's not too often that people will say, "Hey, this is working so well, why don't we do it all differently?" Rather, reform is something done because people don't like what is happening. And it is difficult to find any period in the history of U.S. education when someone did not have some complaint about "school." In the 1800s, the problem was that schooling was not extended to enough children, and there was a failure to communicate a common culture. In the restless 1900s, the concern was that school was neither relevant nor effective in meeting the needs of an industrialized society, and people could not agree upon the common culture to disseminate. Dissatisfaction has historically been the impetus for change, and reform has been the mechanism of choice. But that leads to another question.

Where Were You When Dick and Jane Ambushed Phonics?

If reform is something undertaken with purpose in mind, then why have the results been disappointing? People have long had access to the workings of education, and

---

Activity 4.1.
REFORMS YOU HAVE KNOWN

Before going further in the discussion of reform efforts, it might be good to get a feel for how the topic is seen by folks in education. For this activity, consider contacting the schools you have attended or perhaps working with a local school. Make an appointment to speak with a teacher or the principal and ask the following questions:

1. What are the most effective reform efforts he or she has seen in the school in the past five years? Examples might include site-based management, outcome-based education, single-gender classes, coed physical education, reading programs, and inquiry-based science.
2. Which of those reforms does the teacher or principal expect to see still in place five years from now? If the expectation is that the initiative will not be there in five years, what reasons make him or her think so?
3. What makes some reforms succeed and others fail?

many influences have been brought to bear on what happens in school. And this has taken place over the course of *hundreds* of years. So, if dissatisfaction still exists despite all sorts of reform efforts, and in fact current dissatisfaction is voiced over the *reforms themselves*, one can legitimately ask a number of poignant questions. Who made these apparently ill-informed decisions? Where was everybody when education became secular rather than a matter of religious indoctrination? Where were the parents when the common school shifted parental responsibility from *educating* their children to seeing that their children *received* an education? Where were the legions of educators when the "progressivists" accomplished their coup d'état over the "traditionalists" in the early twentieth century? Who stood in the schoolhouse doorway when the innovators and interventionists came along and challenged the entrenched curriculum? How can it be that "Dick and Jane" are icons of American education *and* the poster children of what many consider to be all that is wrong with reading education (that is, the replacement of phonics with the "look-say" method, a precursor to "whole language")? Where were the accomplished teachers, at any point in our history, who backed up their work by demonstrating that all children *were* learning under their tutelage? And where was business throughout all of this?

You can get a sense for where these people may have been by attending a meeting of your local school's board of education. You need not be a parent to attend these meetings; after all, they are supported by your tax dollars to serve the needs of your children and your community. We must caution you however. Don't go to the meeting expecting the above questions to be answered. Rather, go to the meeting so that you can see why these are (still) viable questions to ask.

What you will typically find at a meeting of the board of education is a sparse crowd that remains relatively silent (unless there is some "hot potato" item on the agenda, such as the teaching of evolution—*still* an issue more than seventy-five years after the Scopes trial of 1925). Chances are good that there will be a few teachers, some building-level administrators (particularly those who hope to be recognized for advancement), local reporters, and perhaps a small number of concerned parents and citizens. Check with the district office before going to the meeting just to find out how many children are enrolled in the school district. If they are willing to tell you how many families that number represents, so much the better. While at the meeting, count up the number of folks in attendance and do a quick computation of what percentage of the families in your district are represented. If you do this, particularly for several sessions, we expect that you will find a number that represents an abysmally low percentage. Yet, these are open, announced meetings and are being conducted by people who have been voted into service on the school board by the public at large. This is not secret stuff; nor is it by invitation only. So, again we ask, where were (are) the parents, the concerned citizens, the "dichotomists" who believe that all that was good and noble was thrown over by a group of wild-eyed radicals known as the progressivists, or the essentialists, or the fundamentalists, or the perennialists, or whichever group was (is) in fashion at the time?

When education was "commandeered" a hundred or so years ago in what is often overgeneralized as the "progressivist" movement, it was not in the dark of night or with the kicking and screaming of angry parents. No, a new line of thinking was ushered in because a hundred years ago, as was similarly the case two hundred years ago and as was the case during your own school experiences, there was dissatisfaction about what the school was accomplishing and where the country was headed.

It is easy enough to recognize that at the turn of the twentieth century, a young and prosperous America began to take on the same aristocratic demeanor as the folks from whom they'd fled. And this contributed to the climate for reform. The tidal wave of immigrants inundated the land with people who spoke limited, if any, English and were not considered to be on par with the rest of "us"; the thinking was that something needed to be done about this. As we noted in chapter 1, there was significant anti-immigration legislation enacted to stem that tide. In fact, there were a whole lot of children, immigrant and otherwise, who were quite simply destined for factory work in the new industrial age, and their studying Greek, Latin, and mathematics just seemed like a waste of everybody's time.

The Industrial "Revolution" itself was a major contributor to the relative success of efforts in the first two decades of the twentieth century to break from the traditional academics-based curriculum (though many would argue that there has never been any success from the progressivist movement). Particularly in the burgeoning urban areas, the need was for workers, not scholars. And since business was prosperous at the time, it made sense to provide workers to man those machines. Though a reading of the educational literature gives one the impression that leading scholars of the time, such as John Dewey (whose philosophy of pragmatism was convoluted into what came to be known as "progressivism"), G. Stanley Hall, Edward Thorndike, and Lewis Terman, among others, instigated and accomplished the wholesale revamping of education *for reasons of social value*, the fact remains that they worked in an environment that was willing to accept such change. Certainly there were dissenters—loud and vocal—but the milieu, and in particular the business and economic milieu, favored the changes that child-centered education offered to the machinery of industry. Not surprisingly, the forces behind educational "research" and debate at the time included the names Carnegie and Rockefeller.

What happened in the twentieth century was that "reform" became entrenched in education as the "reform model." That is, reform itself became institutionalized in the very manner that we discussed when considering the nature of institutions. The people who showed up for and influenced school board meetings and district administrative personnel at conventions and conferences made reforming the school into a business. As parents and other citizens acquiesced and let the institution "run itself," the institution turned into something else. "Reform" became an obscure term that could mean virtually anything from "back to basics" to the new frontier. The model provided sponsorship opportunities for business with no particular regard for outcomes and a bottomless well of "research" opportunities for higher education, again without any particular need to dwell on the outcomes—if this didn't work, they could always try something else.

In the early twentieth century, the credentials of the professors leading the charge were, along with the degree to which the charge matched the needs of business, sufficient to convince many people that educational progress was in good hands. Whether the hands were good or not, we would rather not argue. But the fact that more hands should have been involved in fashioning a new educational order is without question. But even here, we are talking about a relative handful of people, and these folks were academicians, businesspeople, and politicians. Reform is rarely initiated in response to a ground swell of dissatisfaction. More often, reforms are instigated by folks who have a vested interest in education from one of three perspectives: higher education (involving not only teacher education but other academic pursuits, such as research and development); business (both the demands of the business community and the business of supplying schools); and politics. Yet, the school board meeting exercise we recommended will demonstrate that *all* of the blame cannot be placed on these three groups. In fact, if nothing else, these three groups are the vocal groups.

It is not our intent to argue in this book that parents and the community at large should run the school system. On the other hand, it is our intent to indicate that the schools should be run with the *informed* cooperation among all *four* groups sharing a common vision of what the schools should accomplish. As you will see, the suggestions we provide for evaluating reform efforts include asking pointed questions of each of the constituencies with regard to the expertise they bring to the discussion. You can count on the other three groups to show up for the meeting having done their homework. The question now is whether you will be there as well.

Summary: The Responsibility of Accessibility

The questions that needed answers in the past are the same questions that we have been asking you in this book. Since they were left unanswered in years gone by, is it any wonder that the same issues are unresolved today? Issues such as whether nonnative speakers should be taught to read and write in English *before* doing other coursework (in English) are still unresolved. Should schools use a bilingual approach to education? Or do "those children" need to have an academic education at all? Do *any* non-college-bound children need academics? Should everybody have a liberal arts background? Is education indoctrination, mind expansion, or pure propaganda? These questions were, and still are, at the heart of what constitutes the American culture and where that culture wants to go.

These can be very disturbing questions, can't they? As Americans, we like to see ourselves as tolerant and accepting of people. Without question, to a great degree we are. Yet, our history with Native Americans, enslaved Americans, and the early-twentieth-century immigrants is not pretty. And though the Industrial Revolution is something that most speak of as a remarkable human achievement, it was carried out on the backs of many poorly paid and constantly endangered workers who simply tried to scratch out an existence.

These examples certainly do not represent all of what is "American," but neither does a representation that leaves out these examples provide a complete appraisal. We have mentioned earlier in this work that perhaps we are reluctant to truly consider who we are because it is very possible that we will not like the picture that emerges. The key point, however, is that without allowing the picture to emerge, we are unable to determine what changes to make. This is nowhere more important than in determining the direction of the schools. The best news among all of this is that our own founding documents, revised as they have been by the amendments, are visionary enough to celebrate humanity without discriminating against gender, ethnicity, or spiritual belief. We simply need to know who we are and where we want to go. Unfortunately for the progressivists and the traditionalists before them, the function of school in our society has never been clearly defined. And that lack of definition, along with all of the other factors at work at the time (any time), has resulted in what Ravitch (2000) refers to as one hundred years of failure in educational reform.

If those fundamental questions had ever been answered, then through the years education would likely have *changed* to keep up with progress in technology, global awareness, science, politics, economics, and so forth. But in the absence of those answers, education has always been subject to reform, a dance that we do around the burning issues to make it look as though we are actually confronting and resolving them. Continued efforts at reform will only perpetuate continued dissatisfaction because reformists never see the need to answer those fundamental questions. Instead, let's become agents of change who do the reflection needed to institute something worthy of our time, efforts, and attentions as a nation. From that point on, change can be what education undergoes to *continue* its mission rather than what it goes through to find one.

We all have an appropriate part to play in determining the goals and objectives of formal schooling. But people need to take part in an *informed* capacity rather than leaving it to the "academics," the business leaders, and the politicians. We all need to be at the meeting if education is going to continue to function with considerable local control. And though the thrust of this book is toward revolutionizing our concept of what school should do and how it can be done, a practical starting point is for us to become better educational "consumers." Let's not confine ourselves to the reform model as we become change agents, but for now, let's take a look at (1) the reform model, and (2) reform and intervention efforts (so that we can start to see the curriculum in its component parts). In chapter 5, we will discuss a method for evaluating reforms and interventions that are being used in, or considered for, your local school.

THE REFORM MODEL

In the early twentieth century, educational leaders often claimed that theirs was a *scientific approach* to social progress through the schools. But the emphasis on schools as the solution to social problems lost sight of the fact that the "science" of education (a young, viable, and legitimate intellectual concern) was in the *pedagogy of learning* rather than in schools as the instrument of social progress. Neither was the science of atomic energy, for example, dependent upon the development of an atomic bomb. The science was in nuclear physics and its potential to generate phenomenal energy. Social change might result from learning, but for educators, the science is in how people learn and how to facilitate that process for millions of children.

Even so, a reading of the history of education in our country leaves one with the idea that educational reform was the hot topic across the country from 1900 through to the late 1930s. The idea is given that heated and intellectually stimulating debate was provided every Saturday evening so that the townsfolk could consider the latest commentary of Bode, Bagley, Bigham et al. The impression is made that children across the country were throwing their old textbooks out of the classroom windows and settling into discussion circles to consider what worthy home membership means. But such was not the case. These were essentially discussions among academicians, educational administrators, business leaders, and politicians, and school today is largely the same as school was hundreds of years ago, though with two major exceptions: Reform has become a part of the institution of education (a big and powerful academic, economic, and political part), and somewhere along the way, the American culture was lost. Let's consider three aspects of the reform model: higher education, business, and politics.

As you read through these discussions, keep in mind that our context is education in its institutional sense and the forces that impact on that institution. Our perspective on higher education, business, and politics is also one of an institutional nature rather than a focus on the performance of *individuals* within those domains. A complaint against programmed instruction in the 1940s, 1950s, and 1960s was that its emphasis on discrete bits of information made it difficult for the learner to conceptualize the whole. That's what we are trying to avoid. Let's try to see this larger picture so that we may then understand how its parts interact. One rarely sends an afflicted organ to the physician and asks that it be cured. Rather, the physician begins a pathological investigation of the entire person and works toward isolating the specific ailment. So, don't be offended as you read if you are in higher education, business, or politics (that covers quite a bit of territory, doesn't it?), for we are discussing the *domain*, not the individual. With all of that said, let's consider the forces at work as Culture X goes to school.

The Reform Model Finds a Home in Higher Education

Scholars had long been curriculum consultants and disseminators of knowledge, but as primary and secondary education became social institutions, the new academic discipline of *pedagogy* (the study of the teaching of children) emerged within colleges and universities. It is not surprising, then, that schools of education have evolved into principal players (no pun intended) in the conduct of school today. Professors are involved professionally in everything from the academic content of instruction and the pedagogical "science" of teaching, to the preparation of teachers and administrators, to the writing of textbooks. Though steadfastly maintaining their autonomy from the K–12 organization, departments and schools of education have nonetheless become ingrained as components of the overall institution.

What is curious is that despite this close relationship an atmosphere of animosity often exists (at least in the larger institutional sense) between "the schools and the scholars." There are those who argue that higher education's "ivory tower" perspective does not facilitate the work of classroom educators. It is a tenuous relationship fraught with the perils of unrealized potential. McEwan (1998), who blames essentially all educational woes on the progressivist movement of the twentieth century, complains that professors "are protecting their own self-interests: tenure, opportunities to publish, and the golden-carrots of government-funded research" (68). To her credit, McEwan does not place *all* of the blame for failing schools on higher education, but she does suggest that the tertiary influence is just as harmful as it is helpful. To a degree, she is correct, though it is also the case that professors complain that despite all of their efforts to impart new instructional techniques, novice teachers tend to adopt the same traditional methods as their supervisors and induction-year mentors.

It is true that professors seek tenure (and protect it as well, though we're not exactly sure of what McEwan means by that) and that government-funded research is one of the avenues for publication. Tenure does foster an atmosphere conducive to the free exchange of ideas, a condition that is essential if one is to question the status quo. And government funding of research does facilitate investigation in academics and pedagogy that otherwise would not be possible. In fact, the "publish-or-perish" pressure can even be said to force the development of new ideas and new understanding, as well as to encourage a high quality of writing and clarity in communication. So, these are not necessarily bad things. The problem arises because the reform model that has evolved operates in the absence of what Senge (1990) refers to as a "shared vision." The various constituencies are not necessarily at cross-purposes but simply have never come together to define a *common* purpose.

The result of all of this is a system that trades on reform. Professors and their graduate students do research and develop programs based upon their research because that's what higher education folks do. Some of that work manifests itself as new programs to be tried in the schools, while other research serves to illuminate a bit more of the path along the way to new insights and new instructional techniques. Government agencies fund research and facilitate work that otherwise could not be done but are at the same time hesitant to continue funding the *same* research. Funding sources want to see new and different ideas developed. So, it is not at all surprising to find a lack of continuity, and it is easy to see the emergence of the reform model. With no real definition of what the schools are supposed to accomplish (academic education? character education? democratic education? individualized education?), there is no need to focus all of these efforts, and dollars, on a common goal. Thus, all research is viable, all reform efforts are legitimate (if the current climate accepts the premise of the reform), and despite the fact that nothing really changes, it always *looks* like something is happening. And that perception is enough to satisfy the current generation of reformers. The reform model keeps everybody happy.

Higher education can be expected to perpetuate this system because the model keeps people busy in academic pursuits and keeps funding coming in without the requirement of proving that any given program actually works. As we've mentioned, in the world of research, failed programs contribute to the accumulated body of knowledge just as successful programs do. And after all, the nature of the relationship between higher education and K–12 is such that the one does not have control over the other: The schools don't direct the research that universities undertake, and the universities cannot control all of the factors at play in the schools (e.g., readiness to learn, parental involvement, socioeconomic factors). It's almost as if the failure of reform efforts is built into the system. That, of course, is what we've been suggesting all along. It's much like investing in the stock market: The investor is unable to control what happens within a company but is responsible for making the buy and sell decisions. The broker, however, is paid a commission whether the investor makes or loses money. In our situation, the institution remains intact and essentially unchanged whether the reform effort succeeds or fails. And everyone seems to accept that as making sense.

But does it *have* to be that way? In subsequent chapters, we will look at higher education's involvement in a revolutionized school system. There will be more work to do than higher education could possibly handle even if there were a common goal—not to mention that the "gatekeepers of knowledge" should take a leadership position in synthesizing that goal. As it stands now, however, the reform model of minor changes here and there that do not substantively affect the institution *keeps higher education in business*. Attempts to change this condition are likely to be met by a strong survival-based reaction from the institution.

Business and Education

It is worth asking why higher education failed, and continues to fail, to take a guiding role in building a foundation and infrastructure for effective public education. Perhaps those in academe were swept up in the momentum of reform movements and lost sight of the need for long-term thinking, though we know that the reform model does not take a long-term perspective. Perhaps those professors and academic administrators were intoxicated by the elixir of putting their ideas into practice in a consequence-free environment, for as we've indicated, failed efforts (no, no, no, let's say "nonoptimal approaches") also contribute to the body of knowledge—a legitimate academic outcome. Or perhaps those in higher education were simply suffering from a scholastic naïveté that blinded them to what was really happening. Who knows? But if we stand far enough back from the college campus, we can see that there were other forces that had much to do with the path that higher education followed.

Those external forces can be categorized in a generic sense by the terms *business* and *politics*. Given its prominence in a capitalist economy, business has never failed to make its interests known or to miss an opportunity to direct the course of events. With regard to primary and secondary education, business quietly influences change without taking responsibility for what happens. In the same manner as the parent who knows that *speaking to* the board of education can be more effective than *serving on* the board, business merely *influences* local and state education decisions; they don't *make* the decisions. Thus, responsibility for what happens in the American schools cannot be handed over to the business leaders. Now, our intent here is not to indict business. However, it is important to realize not only that business impacts education within the current model but also that it could impact education in a much more effective manner within a new model. So, let's look just a bit closer.

We place this brief discussion of the role of business in education between the discussions of higher education and politics because that is precisely where business works. Whether it represents a buffer zone that holds the hands of politics and higher education and keeps them on "the right track" or it acts as a catalyst that forces action in what might be considered a covert or "behind-the-scenes" manner is a topic for spirited debate. For our purposes, let's just stipulate that business is entrenched in what is right *and* wrong with the institution of education as it influences it in three ways: tax funding, involvement, and demands.

Tax Funding

Perhaps most apparent in the consideration of business and education is that business can significantly affect a school district by virtue of the tax base that it provides. A community with no business presence (that is, something of the corporate variety that employs many people) tends to suffer in terms of total funding available. The school will receive the base funding supplied by the state but will not receive any significant supplements from local tax revenue. This effect trickles down to the salaries that can be paid for teachers and other personnel, the sophistication of instructional equipment that can be purchased, and the ability to keep a school supplied. One cannot fault business, per se, for this situation, and it is only fair to acknowledge that businesses paying tax dollars to a school system are entitled to have a say in what goes on, like every other taxpayer does, through a vote, a presentation to the school board, or the opportunity to serve on school committees. But be prepared to hear more than that from the business community. You may also want to listen closely in the coming years, for the movement toward *school choice* will surely engender a response from businesses as their tax dollars are stretched further and further to accommodate students coming into the district from "underperforming" schools. The question is what that response will be.

Involvement

Involvement in the educational enterprise, that is, apart from taxes, is another significant business activity. We refer here to sponsorship, grant funding, and scholarships. Let's begin with sponsorship. When attending an athletic event at a local school, you have likely noticed that the scoreboard has been "donated" by business concerns. Logos representing the gamut from shoes to soft drinks are prominently displayed. On the one hand, it can be argued that without such "sponsorship" (it's really advertising space rather than sponsorship), those scoreboards would not be there at all. But that's only in terms of the current model. If business were truly *supporting* the school rather than simply using it as an advertising venue, there would be no need to include the corporate crest on the board. And so, for as important a concern as public education, it may be worth questioning the motives of those funding sources and watching to see who blinks first. Will parents and schools refuse the money if it represents selling advertising space, or will business decide that philanthropy is not in their best interests? Chris Whittle's Channel One, which brings video advertising to millions of students at the beginning of each school day, would suggest that the schools have so far blinked first. This speaks volumes about our culture.

Involvement also takes the form of the grant funding that we've previously mentioned. Many large corporations do in fact contribute millions of dollars to education in the form of research grants to colleges and universities. To their credit, these foundations support a wide range of studies, though each, legitimately enough, may impose various restrictions and requirements. It is worth mentioning that not a lot of fanfare is made with regard to these grants. Though such funding is of great importance in the academic world, companies rarely seem to bring a lot of attention to their grant-funding activities with regard to the general public. Unfortunately, it also comes as no surprise that the range of projects that get funded, given the millions upon millions of dollars made available, lack a common focus. This is not to imply that all researchers should be studying the same thing, but one would expect that given all of the money spent on educational research and development through corporate grant funding alone, greater strides in pedagogy would have been made by now. Yet, Horace Mann's call in the mid-nineteenth century for the need to disseminate a common culture is repeated in this work in the twenty-first century, and John Dewey's emphasis on solving real problems as part of education, suggested in the early years of the twentieth century, still rings true. Could it be that the reform model serves the interests of business in the same manner that it serves the interests of higher education? Is it at all possible that in a climate that seems to cry out for innovation, there is a whisper saying, "Just don't change"? It takes no stretch of the imagination if you understand the nature of the reform model.

Demands

Then there are the demands of business. And those demands are significant. That businesses see the schools as the source of their future labor force is good. That business sees the purpose of school *as preparing people for work* is a philosophically troubling matter. It is even more disturbing that the reform model has turned schools into the training programs for business. The return that business wants for its "philanthropic" dollars is a workforce competent, capable, and *trained*. The reform model not only provides this training but expects schools to shift gears with the changing demands of the work environment.

Of particular interest in terms of the entire notion of school as a training ground for workers is that organized education originally took children *away* from job training and apprenticeships. This offers a good example of the notion that with regard to reform, the more things change, the more they stay the same. Consider that the paradigm shift that introduced "practical studies" (work skills) to organized education goes back as far as the introduction of English grammar schools in the 1700s to counterbalance the academic orientation of the Latin grammar schools. Throughout the 1800s, debate continued over whether vocational training had a place in the public schools. Eventually, Baltimore opened the first public manual-training high school in 1884. Since that time, vocational education has soared. A contemporary high school is likely to have an expansive vocational-education program, wing, or building providing job training in everything from woodshop to fast-food restaurant work. This model can be extended to other aspects of publicly funded training for private enterprise. A prime example would be university athletic programs that essentially serve as the well-paid farm teams for the professional sports entertainment industry. The model is far more pervasive than is evident to the casual observer. That's the covert aspect we mentioned earlier.

All of this suits the business world just fine. Today, one will not hear a demand that schools provide liberally educated young men and women able to read, write, do mathematical calculations, and understand their own culture in the context of the world so that businesses can then train them to do the work they need done. Instead, you will hear business demand that vocational education shift its focus to a greater degree onto computer-technology training. In years gone by, the emphasis was on manual and clerical skills. In the years to come, we will likely see a shift to biotechnology and, perhaps, eventually to something such as laser-based teleportation devices that facilitate global or galactic business enterprise.

What is lost along the way? The American culture. Lost along the way is Aristotle's contention that our purpose as *human beings* is to think and, through that thinking, to understand our world. In its place, we find the idea that our purpose is to facilitate business. A clearly focused purpose in education, a purpose emphasizing the human capacity to think and understand, is anathema to this agenda. The reform model that precludes the "need" for synthesizing such a purpose protects established interests.

Business is not all bad, of course. But as we discussed in chapter 3, when people allow institutional forces to operate in absentia, it is to be expected that the influences that remain will take greater control. We would argue that this has happened in the case of public education. For example, you have no doubt heard the notion that if schools would just operate according to accepted business practices, all of public education's problems would be solved. We find this interesting, for schools already operate under a business model. Through much of the 1900s, that situation was often extended to what has been called a "factory" model of education. You will still hear people refer to it, even though in the early 1950s the tide had begun to turn against that approach as postwar America sought relief from the frantic pace of the previous decade. Still, a typical school today is operated by virtue of a system of workers, mid-management personnel, and executive administrative personnel. Students are the "products," and teaching is the tool that forms those products. Salaries, facilities, and privileges all relate directly to the level on which one is working. Management commands the highest salaries and the "perks" of administration. And teachers—despite the requirements of college degrees (and continuing graduate work), licensure credentials (based on coursework, experience, and testing), and ongoing evaluations (by peers, school officials, and state-level administrators)—are at the low end of the scale in terms of power, prestige, and salary. What's more, at this point, a teacher's only option for advancement in the system is to leave the classroom for administrative work. The schools already have more of the business model than is healthy for anyone.

We make that statement because school is not, *and never will be*, a business. It is a unique social institution with unique characteristics. There is no bankruptcy protection for children when the economy changes or "accepted business practices" fail. There is no provision for shutting down to restructure when corporate leaders make mistakes that could put the company out of business. And education is not an interest to be cultivated in good economic times and ignored when the economy does poorly. No, education does not fit the business model. Given the stock market events of the early years of the twenty-first century, it is a wonder why anyone would turn to a businessperson for advice on how to run education.

Remember, we determined that education is not a profit-driven enterprise. It cannot pick and choose who will be taught. It doesn't even control its own funding sources. Leadership has a part to play. Vision is important to the enterprise. Compassion, competency, commitment, and cultural literacy are key characteristics that educators must possess. Business does not understand that particular combination of attributes or that the bottom line in education is completed with blood, sweat, and tears, as well as ink. Business *does* have a role to play in the functioning of the institution, but not the role it has become accustomed to playing.

Politics and the Assumption of Expertise

Business is about profit, but politicians control the purse strings when it comes to education. The bad news in this regard is that there never seems to be enough money. The good news is that *money is not necessarily education's biggest problem*. That statement may seem counterintuitive, and you can be sure that it was not well received when mentioned in response to the district office's request for ways to improve morale back when one of your authors was teaching middle school. In fact, when word of the comment worked its way back to the school building, the assistant principal made a point of announcing it, out of context of course, in a gathering of faculty members. But the comment was relevant then, and it is relevant today as well. This is not to say that education has all the money it needs and is certainly not meant to encourage legislators to cut education budgets even further; we simply suggest that throwing more money at a seriously flawed institution will not necessarily solve its problems.

Consider that across the country during the 1995–1996 school year, the combined spending of all states for education was nearly *$400 billion* (NCES, 2000). Education is typically the most expensive line item in a state budget. A small state such as South Carolina will have an education budget in excess of $3.5 billion a year for primary and secondary education. A state such as California commits upwards of $30 billion. Include public higher education in such figures, and expenditures in these two states are closer to $5 billion and $43 billion a year, respectively.

In 2003, the federal government's on-budget funds for education topped *$124 billion* (NCES, 2004), which comes in about fourth after defense, welfare, and interest paid on the national debt (now *that's* a wake-up call!). The national average for expenditures per student per year based on these figures is almost $8,000. A teacher with a second grade class of twenty-five students is staring at approximately $200,000 worth of revenue. Though this is a simplification, we all must be aware that there *is* money going to education. The question is, *where* is it going and *why*? That is why a casual comment in a middle school hallway caused such a stir among the school's administrators more than twenty years ago. We are talking about a lot of money. But who is controlling it?

It would make sense with all of the money going to education that the decisions about how the money is to be spent would be the responsibility of educators. But politics is a chimerical entity. It is a term that vaguely describes the nebulous give-and-take of the legislative process. It is a notion that outwardly purports to be all things to all people when, in fact, the best it can possibly deliver is the greatest good for the greatest number of people. It is the "flavor" of a process carried out by people who endeavor to resolve a mind-boggling array of issues, despite not having any real credentials for working with the matters they must address (that is, at least not any credentials that are required *before* taking office; there is no licensing involved, no competency testing, no required coursework). It would not be uncommon for a legislator to encounter issues regarding grain subsidies, environmental-impact debates, nuclear fuel and/or weapons concerns, the ethical ramifications of cloning, and . . . whether or not to approve funds for all-day kindergarten. The scope of the task, let alone the details, can be overwhelming.

The ideological umbrella of "politics" manages to make such a system of policy development and decision making acceptable, even though no other social concern would ever operate in such a manner. The medical community does not come to elementary school teachers for advice on how to provide health services. Boeing does not ask a wheat farmer for decisions with regard to the design of new aircraft. The wheat farmer does not ask Boeing for agricultural advice. Has the fire department come to you lately and asked for a decision as to which equipment would be best to purchase for the station house? Of course not, because these decisions require expertise that only experts are legitimately expected to have. In politics, however, particularly with regard to education, there is an *assumption* of expertise.

You may already have noticed that the ambiguity that accompanies politics (and our emphasis here is on "politics" more than on the legislative responsibilities of elected officials), combined with the legislative and economic power that politicians wield, is a perfect fit for the reform model we have been discussing. As is the case with education and reform, the meaning of "politics" is ill defined. The Thirtieth Annual Phi Delta Kappa/Gallup Poll of the Public's Attitudes toward the Public Schools (Rose & Gallup, 1998) asked respondents which of the two major political parties was more concerned about improving public education. The results were 38 percent for the Democrats and 28 percent for the Republicans. Neither party received more than 40 percent of the vote for an issue that dominates virtually every campaign from local school board elections up to that for the president of the United States. This has to indicate that what people say and what people do are not the same. To avoid this stigma, many candidates campaign today with the message that they are not "politicians." Perhaps they aren't, and were this the case in one or two political terms, it could more easily be tolerated. But a lack of clarity and follow-through have characterized American politics for generations. That sounds a lot like the reform model in education: providing the perception of change without any real change occurring. It does indeed satisfy constituents for the time being.

There are other characteristics of the political world that make it work well with the reform model. Given the range of issues with which politicians are involved, it is virtually impossible for them to devote time toward understanding what Jerome Bruner (1960) would refer to as the "structure" of education (or of any specific subject, but we'll stick to education for now). Certainly, these men and women can come to grips with the surface issues swirling around some school topic, but it would be patently unreasonable to expect that they could, *or should*, have a conceptual grasp of the deeper structure of education (which includes its mission, objectives, pedagogy, techniques, facilities, ancillary responsibilities, credentialing, funding needs, support services, cultural impact [or lack thereof], etc.). The political perspective of education is typically a superficial perspective simply due to the nature of politics.

A natural consequence of a superficial approach to any issue is that there will also be a lack of ideological vision related to the ultimate purpose of education. Though we would argue that determining the vision for education would be among the first steps toward revolutionizing the institution, our concern in this chapter is with understanding the reform model as it exists. From that perspective, we would suggest that it is necessary for participants to understand the structure of the institution so that they can then fashion a mission statement, new or adjusted.

We might expect that political leaders would turn for advice specifically to those who do have an understanding of the structure of education. But that's not how the model works. You have likely heard someone in politics include the phrase "when I was in school" when talking about what to do with education. Many people say this, but when it's mentioned by someone in politics, there is particular reason to be concerned. That's because "when I was in school" is being offered as some credential for teaching or administering school when in fact it is only representative of what it was like to be a student. It makes no more sense than to walk down to the local hospital and offer your advice about how the facility should function: "Well, when *I* was sick. . . ." It would be difficult for a candidate or elected official to similarly say, "When *I* was designing laser-guided smart bombs . . ." followed up at the next meeting with, "When *I* was running the blast furnace. . . ." But they've all been to school, and so it seems legitimate for politicians to campaign with a message of what they will do for education. Perhaps you've entertained this notion as well?

If it is the nature of a political perspective to lack depth when policy makers assume expertise based upon their political positions, then it follows that there will be a concomitant lack of vision in the decisions they make and the policies put forward. Goals 2000: The Educate America Act, which we discussed in chapter 1, provides an excellent example. As you will recall, each of the eight goals were phrased in classically political tones (i.e., goals that will be all things to all people). For instance, the first goal was that all children in America would start school ready to learn. How can "readiness to learn" possibly be legislated? And if programs derived from Goals 2000 begin with students who are not ready to learn (that would be the presumption, correct?) to get them ready, how does that differ from where we are? If they start with younger children, they have simply extended the responsibility of education to prekindergarten and perhaps pre-prekindergarten children. What we saw with Goals 2000 was the reform model in action from the political perspective. The goals sounded great, but they obviously lacked a deep understanding of the structure of education. The vision was nice, but it was wishful thinking. And when it came right down to it (in 1994), who was going to remember any of this by the year 2000 anyway? That's the reform model from the political perspective: the perception that things are changing, an accepted failure to clearly articulate what will happen and when, and a complete, though sanctioned, failure to take a perspective that lasts beyond a political term or two.

Summary

We would suggest that the nature of politics is such that the power to make and enact decisions breeds an assumption of expertise on the part of the decision maker. With particular regard to education, an experience common to virtually all members of the society, the result is that decisions are made by people with a minimal understanding of the structure of education, little thought toward an articulated purpose of the institution, and even less consideration for the long-term effects of those decisions.

Politics and the assumption of expertise do not provide the fuel for the reform model; that comes from business. As the key economic force in our society and the management model that pervades government and education, business has always provided the impetus and momentum for whatever has occurred in education. It is a subtle and powerful influence. But it fuels the reform model for *business* interests rather than *social* interests. It cannot accept all of the blame for this because the responsibility for defining what organized education should be and what it should accomplish fell to another constituency—and it failed to get the job done.

Nor is politics the incubator of the reform model. That role falls to higher education and those components of it that impact upon the educational enterprise. From their positions as disseminators of knowledge to their work as synthesizers of new knowledge, professors and other faculty members should have long ago taken the lead in conceptualizing a system of public education that would have paralleled other great innovations pioneered in the United States. Instead, higher education has embraced a model that is a revolving door of research opportunities that never requires tallying up the wins and losses. It is particularly distressing that a national cadre of highly educated people dedicated to learning have abdicated their intellectual responsibility in favor of what often amounts to little more than academic busywork. Aristotle would be hard pressed to find evidence of the fulfillment of human purpose in the majority of tertiary and postbaccalaureate studies, and Plato would shake his head and wonder if anybody is concerned with a truth that endures beyond the next semester.

So, neither the fuel nor the incubator is politics. Where do politicians fit into the context of the reform model that has stalemated educational progress? They are the players, and the campaign trail, the state house, and the halls of government are their stages. Politicians come and go, each promising substantive change for education. If all of them lived up to the rhetoric, we would have to ask how much change any one institution can stand. But that's really not a problem, for school today is essentially what it was when you were there, when your parents were there, when their parents were there, and so on. Teachers still scratch chalk across blackboards even in brand-new buildings. All of the elements of the reform model fit perfectly with the characteristics of politics, and so, each generation is entertained by the current board member, the incumbent at the state level, the challenger, the old administration, or the new "reform" administration that is taking office. Yet, as was the case with business, politics should not shoulder all of the blame. There was another constituency that had a responsibility in all of this and failed to show up for the meeting.

You may have noticed that we did not include *parents* as one of the domains under consideration. It can certainly be argued that parents find a comfortable fit with the reform model because most, passionate as they may be about their involvement with the schools, are only committed to educational reform while their children are in school. And it would be fairly safe to say that many parents are concerned with *their* children in school rather than with *all* children in school across the state and nation. It is also true that many parents are guilty of the same assumption of expertise by virtue of having attended school as we found in politics. The lack of a long-term vision for education as an institution perpetuating our culture, *the culture which represents our children's heritage,* along with a superficial understanding of education's structure, contributes to an atmosphere conducive to the failure of reforms and interventions. The reform model fits. But we differentiate between parents and the other three domains because higher education, business, and politics are all *conventions* of society with a vested interest in the practice and product of education. Parenting and social affiliation is, at its base, a biological function. The other three exist only by virtue of the unique cognitive abilities of human kind, and they have a responsibility to more effectively serve the society that created them. So, parents are off the hook in that regard.

However, parents are not blameless. In chapter 1, we discussed education as a political exercise for the people. There has been ample opportunity for parents to form a collaborative relationship with the schools that not only facilitates their work but also could structure the institution of education itself. Parents have historically been afforded access to the rhyme and reason of schooling, but they have consistently remained, as a majority of the stakeholders in the enterprise, at arms length. The tendency is to complain about what bothers them. For example, in the extensive "reforms" of education in Texas during the 1980s, a major complaint from parents was with the "no pass, no play" rule that tied their children's academic performance to extracurricular-activity eligibility. For this teacher, the memory is still vivid of a parent adamantly stating that the school was not going to tell her son he couldn't play football just because wasn't passing his classes. Yet, parents are willing to turn as much parental responsibility over to the school as possible. The schools are specifically charged with protecting the safety and health of students while in attendance, a condition referred to as "in loco parentis," or in the place of a parent. Even organizations such as the Parent Teacher Organization and Parent Teacher Association (PTA) have failed to live up to their potential. McEwan (1998) does not spare them from her disdain for professional organizations when she writes, "In many local districts, the PTA is merely a giant group of cheerleaders and fundraisers for the administration" (71). Parent involvement in the success of organized education is a key to our social and cultural future, and that is what this entire book is about. But that involvement, as is the case with business, higher education, and politics, is not the same involvement to which they have become accustomed.

There is a place for parents in the new institution, an important—and even critical—place, but parents cannot wait for someone else to lead them there. They need to come to the meeting ready to learn, ready to participate, and ready to go. The next two sections of this chapter are intended to facilitate that readiness. We will discuss examples of reforms so that you are familiar with some of the efforts that have found their way to the schools. We will then provide you with the tools to become an informed consumer, advocate, and change agent in this most important of all social endeavors. Will you be at the table?

Activity 4.2.
TALKING WITH THE DECISION MAKERS

This activity will help you broaden your perspective of education beyond children and teachers in the school. Identify one individual for each of the five categories to interview about education: (1) a person in higher education (a professor or dean would be a good choice, and he or she does not have to be in the college or department of education), (2) a classroom teacher, (3) someone from the business community, (4) a politician on the local, state, or federal level (don't be afraid to write a letter to your state senators and congressmen), and (5) a parent. Ask each of these people the following questions:

1. What do you expect from the schools? What should the schools accomplish?
2. If you could change one thing about education, what would it be?
3. How many of today's issues in education are related to money?

Consider their responses:

1. What common themes, if any, did you find?
2. How do the opinions differ?
3. What are the implications for the work of a classroom teacher?

A LOOK AT SOME REFORMS AND INTERVENTIONS

Hundreds, if not thousands, of educational-reform or improvement programs are in the schools across the country today. A school that has closed down for the summer will still have administrators, teachers, professors, graduate students, parents, and business leaders sorting through the results of last year's programs and/or preparing for what will be done next year. There are grants being written, and the logistics of implementation are being laid out. All that has been discussed up to this point in the chapter should indicate to you that "reform" can sometimes appear to be as big an undertaking as the whole of the educational institution.

Any attempt to outline the various programs with an impact upon the nation's schools would have to be highly selective. And it would be virtually impossible to discuss the "top ten" reform efforts because any program is a function of the particular needs of the particular school. Perhaps the reading curriculum in your local school is simply fantastic, but science is in need of attention. For another school, the situation could be the reverse. Therefore, what we want to do is offer some distinctions between reform efforts and provide an example of each. When you start to visit schools and talk with educators, board members, and perhaps politicians in your community, you will be able to start organizing what you hear about to better understand just what is going on. We see all of this as a warm-up for the section to follow, which will discuss the evaluation of reforms in detail.

Throughout this entire discussion of education, we have attempted to maneuver around clumsy terminology. There are only so many synonyms for words such as "school" or "reform," among others. So, we have tried to be as clear as possible about our meaning for each term. As we turn our attention to specific programs, we now want to become more precise about the context in which we use the word "reform." In its generic sense, reform can refer to all of those activities that serve to do things differently than is traditionally the case. Of course, the problem we run into is that who knows what "traditional" means in a truly comprehensive sense? And so, having differentiated between change and reform earlier in this chapter, we now want to break down reform to be more specific. We've actually used the new term quite a bit in this chapter, but have not taken the time to define it.

The terms we want to use are *reform* and *intervention*. This distinction provides an immediate indication of the intended scope of an effort that might be under consideration at your local school. A *reform* is a program that seeks to replace some aspect of the current educational operation. It could be a matter of philosophy, administrative style, curriculum, instruction, or conceptualization. What has been done up until the point of the reform effort will be eliminated, and something new will take its place. For instance, if we refer back to our earlier example of reading instruction, we have seen that the look-say method (Dick and Jane) replaced the phonics approach in many schools. Schools did not provide phonics to some children and look-say to others; instead, they reformed their reading-instruction program by replacing one approach with the other.

An *intervention* is some effort that supplements normal procedure, either by providing remediation or enrichment or by extending or reducing responsibility or authority. Interventions typically respond to some specific need and often do not have the intended longevity of a reform. For example, programs that pull specified children out of the regular classroom for remedial reading instruction would exemplify an intervention. The regular reading program has not been replaced, and the child's remediation can be discontinued if she improves her reading ability. The same would be true of enrichment programs. A child is provided enhanced educational opportunities but is not deprived of what the school is responsible for providing. And, by the same token, if that child "no longer qualifies" for the enrichment program, she can return to the regular program, which is still in force.

You can see that reforms and interventions have different characters. We also want to point out that given the vast range of efforts and explorations in education, there will be many times when it is difficult to decide which of these categories best applies. That is not a particular problem for us at this point. For now, we want to find ways to make what is going on in education more understandable. The distinction between reforms and interventions is a first question to ask when seeking clarification about the need, claims, and extent of a program that a school is considering.

Reforms and interventions can be further subdivided according to the institutional component to which they pertain. There could be many other ways of categorizing these efforts, but we have chosen to think in terms of curricular, administrative and/or conceptual, and instructional programs. Curricular programs are concerned with *what* will be taught in school. Instructional programs are involved with *how* subjects will be taught. And our administrative/conceptual category, admittedly a very broad, catchall group, is concerned with *why* something is going to be done.

Reforms

Perhaps you have read in the paper that the test scores in your district were very low, and so, a recommendation has been made to change to a new reading-instruction program. In this situation, the message is that the *curriculum* is in need of reform. If the newscast mentions that the school is going to adopt an "open-concept" approach to teaching, then you know that one *instructional* approach is going to be replaced by another. Each of these would represent big changes and are not to be entered into without significant research and deliberation. Here are some more examples.

Curricular Reform

You may have heard that your state has adopted curriculum benchmarks, frameworks, or standards for each of the subject areas taught in the school. Each of these represents curriculum reform because they involve determining what students will learn. These particular efforts revolve around establishing standards—the minimum learning expectations for all children. Benchmarks spell out the hierarchy of knowledge and skills for which students are responsible at each grade level. See "State Departments of Education" in the compendium for websites that will provide the standards for your (or any other) state.

Instructional Reform

Programs in this category seek to find better ways of teaching information, particularly in view of the diverse nature of students. An example would be the *whole-language* approach to reading instruction. Some might argue that this represents a curriculum issue rather than an instructional issue. We have placed it in this category because, in terms of what is happening to the student, it is a matter of how she eventually gets to the point of reading (phonics, for example, being another approach). Thus, we consider it here as an instructional reform.

In our earlier discussion of educational history, it was mentioned that the look-say method of reading instruction replaced the phonics approach in many public schools. Whole language is an approach to reading that extends the look-say method: Rather than breaking reading down into component skills and discrete sounds (phonemes), which are then reassembled to make up words, language is left intact—whole—and learned in a context of authentic literacy events. Proponents argue that people learn language in this way and, so, should learn to read this way as well. Opponents argue that this leads both to guessing at the meaning of words and problems with spelling.

Administrative/Conceptual Reform

Perhaps the most pressing reform issue, once people get past the phonics versus whole-language debate (which really shouldn't be as dichotomous as it is often portrayed), is likely that of multiculturalism. We have argued passionately through the early chapters of this book, and will do so in later chapters, that cultural confusion is at the very heart of the problems in our society. Though we understand and embrace the fact that ours is a culture made up of many cultural influences, we adamantly maintain that our focus as a society must be on how those influences combine to yield one, cohesive, American culture. In the meantime, you will find that virtually all subjects can now be taught from a "multicultural" perspective (e.g., Robertta Barba's *Science in the Multicultural Classroom: A Guide to Teaching and Learning*, 1995).

What is most ironic about efforts toward multicultural education is that the most likely casualty will be the American culture. Proponents suggest that multicultural education provides children with a respect for, and appreciation of, the world's cultural diversity, though one could certainly ask at what age children are prepared to understand and appreciate cultural differences and global-community membership. At this point in time, multiculturalism as a reform movement is, perhaps, well intentioned, though ill defined and lacking in cohesive goals, and has "absolutely nothing to do with learning to read, write, do math, or understand history and science" (McEwan, 1998, 163). This brings us back to the question of what the schools are supposed to accomplish. Do you see how important these questions have become?

Interventions

The examples we have discussed so far were classified as reforms because they sought to replace one perspective, approach, or curriculum with another. Interventions, on the other hand, seek to supplement, without replacing, a program. Though an intervention can be intended as a short-term remedy for a specific problem (e.g., supplementing a child's regular mathematics instruction), it can also be a program added to the curriculum with a long-term perspective. Enrichment programs under the heading "Gifted and Talented" would be an example. In such a situation, the regular school program remains intact, but special opportunities are made available to students who qualify for the experiences. Thus, interventions typically supplement rather than supplant.

Curricular Intervention

The multicultural movement that was discussed previously fell under the heading "Administrative/Conceptual Reform" because it seeks to change the "tone," so to speak, of the entire curriculum. *Character education,* on the other hand, represents an intervention designed as supplementation with experiences not overtly addressed in the explicit curriculum. The intent here, for example, is not toward "character education–based science."

The debate over character education can be traced back at least a hundred years. In the tumultuous 1920s and 1930s, John Dewey was a strong advocate for character education. His suggestions contradicted the educational research of the day, which indicated that character education did not significantly affect children's behavior. In the years since, that perspective has been brought into question.

A major problem facing character-education efforts today is the difficulty of defining just what sort of character should be inculcated. Thomas Lickona (2000) suggests a program directed toward core ethical values. There is disagreement among the various constituencies as to which character traits should constitute such values, and there is an ongoing, fervent debate as to whether or not the school should be responsible for teaching them. Is all of this sounding painfully familiar? It is not at all plausible to argue *against* character education, and many would argue that it is impossible to provide a value-free educational system. Personal interaction necessarily involves the communication of value statements. What are our common core values?

Instructional Intervention

An example of instructional intervention is Reading Recovery. Developed in New Zealand, this program was introduced to the United States in 1974 through the National Reading Recovery Center at Ohio State University. It is a pullout program providing one-on-one reading-remediation instruction with a whole-language orientation to the bottom 10 to 20 percent of first graders.

Reviews of the program (Northwest Regional Educational Laboratory, 1998; McEwan, 1998; Orange, 2002) acknowledge both the effectiveness of the program and its cost. The program is labor intensive and requires a contractual agreement with the parents of children enrolled to provide support for the activities. Thus, some are inclined to concede that it makes sense that an extensive one-on-one program should show significant results, but the costs involved can be staggering. Orange and McEwan go on to mention that questions have been raised about the reporting of the results, which brings the numbers into question. Neither author discounts that the program can be successful, but both indicate that there could be a credibility issue. And finally, though neither the program developers or those who implement it are at fault, one must wonder if there is not another question to be addressed if significant numbers of *first graders* are candidates for a "recovery" program.

Administrative/Conceptual Intervention

An intervention that has become quite popular in recent years is that of "mentoring." It is a program that can be directed toward various groups. We include it under the heading "Administrative/Conceptual Intervention" because one of those groups could be beginning teachers (thus, the program would have an administrative orientation), or it could be directed toward students (in which case, the orientation would be along the conceptual lines of socioemotional development as opposed to academic instruction).

Sweeney (1990) has identified five forms of mentorship with regard to teachers in their induction year: orientation, collaboration, sharing, joint problem solving, and encouragement. A mentor may assist a beginning teacher through the stages that Wong and Wong (2005) identify: fantasy, survival, mastery, and impact. In any case, mentoring programs are designed to intervene at this crucial time for the express purpose of improving the transition to the classroom so that the student's educational opportunity is not adversely affected by the teacher's instructional inexperience.

Mentoring programs established for the students offer a relationship that differs from that between a student and teacher. There is less formality to the mentorship than that which exists in the traditional instructional setting. For this reason, mentorship programs can be an effective utilization of parental/community involvement. Typical impediments to sound mentoring programs are the failure of schools to provide adequate training for the volunteers and that ever-present nemesis in education, the failure to clearly articulate the goals and objectives of the program. This can be particularly problematic with the use of volunteers because "mentoring" becomes synonymous with "buddy." That is not what a mentoring program is about. A mentor is a person with some particular knowledge, wisdom, or expertise that needs to be imparted to the student in a guiding, facilitating manner. Students learn from mentors by finding their own way to internalize the value of the mentor's experience and example.

This is a sophisticated endeavor. It is not a crime if your school is actually going to implement some sort of "buddy" program, but if that is the case, do not be fooled into thinking that it is all about mentorship. Look carefully and critically, but openly, at the claims of all reforms and interventions.

Summary

We apologize for all of the jargon that shows up in our discussions. However, this represents the terminology of education, and that terminology does in fact facilitate communication between the various constituencies involved. McEwan refers to it as "educationese," and we are sure that there are many other much more colorful references out there. But none of this is secret. None of it is intended to keep people from understanding what folks are talking about. It is simply the responsibility of those who want to be involved in the conversation to learn the lingo, so to speak. So, be neither overwhelmed nor intimidated by the foreign language of education. Instead, become conversant in that language, and you will be amazed by the new worlds it opens up. Learning is not confined to a school building, even if you are learning about education.

FINAL THOUGHTS

It is deeply ironic that one hundred years of reform in the United States have done little more than maintain the educational status quo. But it is not surprising that long-ignored questions of cultural identity have come back to haunt us. Higher education, the so-called "gatekeeper of knowledge," has incubated the reform model through academic busywork and a revolving-door research machine. Businesses have demanded good workers without requiring well-rounded thinkers. Politicians, assumed to be experts because of their elected office, have been charged with making fiscal decisions without great understanding of the structure, the purpose, or the long-term effects of their allocations. Besides, politicians are only as good as their term limits.

No one of these three groups is solely responsible for thwarting substantive educational change in this country. But the American people can no longer leave it to the academics, the business leaders, and the politicians to know all the answers or even to ask all the questions. As parents, you have the ability to wield considerable authority, particularly when you've done your homework and speak with reason and diplomacy. This chapter has discussed reform and intervention so you can better understand the practices as well as the terminology. It is now time for you to pick up the tools of assessment and evaluation, to further your growth as informed educational consumers who have a right to know what's going on at school.

II

REFORMING REFORM

5

What Makes a Reform Effort Worthwhile?

> If we hope to implement change in schools that desperately need it, we first need to understand what we must do differently, and why a new approach will work when so many other innovations have failed or been forgotten.
>
> —Anne Wescott Dodd

As you can see from our discussion thus far, reforms and interventions are everywhere. There are scores of "unofficial" interventions as well, those that may have been established at a local school between teachers, community members, and parents. And though it is often the case that these efforts are supported by the building principal—perhaps even put in place by the principal—the likelihood of such efforts having a sound research base, a proven record of success, a plan for accurately assessing educational impact, or the involvement of credentialed individuals is very low. These efforts are high on good intentions and may even produce some positive results, but they are not sound elements of pedagogy. Yet, other people's children are involved. Hospitals rarely allow volunteers to perform surgical procedures. The armed forces rarely (hopefully never) allow untrained, nonmilitary personnel to operate their aircraft, ships, or guns. And even the volunteer fire department requires that their volunteers be rigorously trained. Why should education be any different? As we'll see, when you examine these programs with the guidelines we provide here, they should not likely be condoned.

Yet, there is a place for these activities somewhere in the new schools of the twenty-first century, perhaps as a system of paraeducators or expanded advisory boards. And in the present, your review of a program can identify weaknesses that need to be addressed or important elements that have been omitted, essentially strengthening good intentions by helping to provide a sound foundation. The result is that everybody wins: The school has helped to develop a stronger program, the volunteer has gained a deeper understanding of pedagogy and has a more effective program to offer, and the children will receive a valuable instructional experience. Keep these thoughts in mind as we construct an instrument for assessing and then evaluating the reforms and interventions that are in your local schools. Even one of your authors, who formerly developed such a program, has subsequently scrutinized it by this method.

Activities 5.1 to 5.5

As you read through this chapter you will find forms for each of the five components of the reform evaluation process. Some forms will require that you speak with particular individuals, while others can be completed with research that you do independently. We suggest that you contact a local school or your state department of education and identify a reform initiative that is under consideration. You may be able to get information by attending a meeting of the local school board.

Having identified a topic, follow the guidelines presented in this chapter and use the forms provided to do your own evaluation of the proposed reform or intervention. Be warned, however, that the institution is always suspicious of folks asking questions! You can assure the powers that be that you are simply completing an exercise and are not out to get them (you aren't, are you?).

THE REVIEW INSTRUMENT

The review instrument that we offer here has four major assessment components and an evaluation component:

1. The Need for the Program
2. The Nature of the Program
3. Implementation
4. Assessment
5. Evaluation

We admit that this is not intended as a simple-to-use five-minute checklist of the do's and don'ts of educational reform. You may be using this format for considering a program that will cost your district millions of dollars over some number of years or for a program that the teacher of your first grader would like to offer; it needs to be something as comprehensive as possible, yet practical in the context of providing *informed collaboration*. As you read through these pages and use the format several times, you will find that it is a straightforward series of questions that build toward making sound decisions. You need not earn a PhD or read all of the literature related to the particular program—that was the job of the program developers. You merely need to ask the questions that will provide a clearer picture of what is being done. No doubt you will spend more time reading this description of the forms than working with them.

Though you could take any one of the first four categories and work with it in isolation, you will find that there is a progression built into this approach. The questions become increasingly sophisticated or detailed as you move through the assessment. If you find that the answers to the very first category of questions are unacceptable, there is little need to collect the rest of the data. So, if the principal cannot give you a sound reason for *considering* the intervention (something like "for the good of the children" should fall into your category of *unacceptable answers*), then it is a legitimate conclusion that the intervention itself is not sound.

It is likely that if you were to go to a dealership to purchase a new car, you would ask the sales representative a series of "pointed" questions. You might ask about the horsepower of the engine, the warranty on the car, the towing capacity, and, of course, what other colors are available. You are not being confrontational; you simply want the information that will help you decide whether this is the right car for you. The same is true of assessing school programs (we'll use the term *program* to mean reforms and interventions). If the automobile salesman answered your questions with "It's got plenty of horsepower, I think the warranty is pretty good, I bet it could tow some stuff, and (as Henry Ford would say) you can have any color you want as long as it's black," you probably wouldn't buy that car—at least not from that dealer. Similarly, if the answers you get from the appropriate school or legislative personnel are inappropriate responses, then you should do what you can to see that the school does not pursue that program—at least not until satisfactory answers can be provided. Doing so isn't confrontation, just common sense.

Category 1: The Need for the Program

As you look at the Program Evaluation Form for Category 1, you'll notice that it provides a space for you to write in the name of the program (each of the forms provides this space so that you can keep things in order), followed by a space for identifying the contact person. It may take you a bit of work to find the most appropriate name to list in this space. For instance, if you hear from your children about the "new program" they will have in class, begin by contacting the teacher. She may have the information you need. On the other hand, she may indicate that this is a schoolwide program and that the principal is the one to contact. Find the person who can actually answer your questions. For the sake of future reference, you may want to indicate on your form whether that person is on the state level (e.g., a local representative or state department of education official), someone in the district office (e.g., a curriculum coordinator, assistant superintendent, or superintendent), a building-level administrator (e.g., assistant principal or principal), a classroom teacher, or someone else (e.g., someone in the organization responsible for the program, a college or university professor who is conducting the program, a consultant at a research-and-development center, or someone from a local organization such as the PTA. Keep their contact information handy by writing it in the space provided.

Why Is This Program under Consideration?

Before inquiring about the nature of the program, it is reasonable for you to ask why the program is being considered at all. In the absence of a reasonable response, there is no need to spend time considering it. If there is a clear need for this program, then indicators should point to any changes, additions, or deletions to the established curriculum. Or, if the program is one of professional development for the teachers, either in terms of credentialing, assessment, or continuing education, there should similarly be identifiable reasons for conducting it. It is no secret that school district funds are almost always lacking, so it is worthwhile to ascertain whether the proposed activity is a worthy use of available local, state, or federal money. There are many people (including the authors of this book) who would argue that simply throwing more money at the schools will not solve the problems they face. There's more to it than that, and one of those things is the *appropriate* use of the funds available.

Suppose a university basketball coach decides to put her team through two-a-day workouts in mid-season. During this time, there are regularly scheduled games, classes

Activity 5.1.
THE NEED FOR THE PROGRAM

Program Assessment Form	*Category 1: The Need for the Program*

Name of the program:

Contact person:

___ state ___ district ___ building administrator ___ teacher ___ consultant ___ other

1. Why is this program under consideration? Considerations: What has indicated the need for this program? Test scores? Teacher observations? State mandates?	
2. What evidence is available to support the need for this program? Considerations: Standardized tests? Teacher-made tests? Anecdotal records? Incident reports?	
3. What purpose will the program serve? Considerations: What can we expect will be different as a result of the program? How significant a difference can be expected?	
4. Are there any other programs like this available? Considerations: Is there a particular reason that this is the only program being considered? If so, how was the decision made to consider this one?	

to attend, homework assignments to be completed, and papers to write. If she were asked to justify this action and simply answered, "Because it will make them better people," then one would have grounds for further questioning of the decision. Why? Because to add additional practice sessions to the day, something else must be taken away from the schedule. We won't enter into a discussion of what that might be, but the simple fact is that to do one thing, something else has to go—and that involves making a value judgment.

However, it is more likely that the coach will indicate something such as the fact that the players have lost five of their last six games, all of which they were winning, because they "ran out of steam" in the second half. Obviously, better conditioning could play a big part in changing this situation. In that case, particular observations (and results) have indicated the need for a change. So, too, with the schools. There is only so much time in the day, only so much teaching staff available, and only so much money that can be spent; therefore, doing things differently requires that someone be able to indicate that there is a *need* for the change. That's all there is to question 1: What indicates that we need this program?

It could be that the principal will tell you that the program is being implemented as a response to a state-level mandate. Principals are allowed to say this, for even though they are at the top of the chain of command within the school, they are nonetheless responsive to directives sent down from the district. However, don't accept this as the final answer. If the principal (assuming that is who you are speaking with) is unable to explain the state mandate, then you are not speaking with the most appropriate individual. Politely ask who would be able to explain the need for the program and begin your research anew with that individual. The good news, of course, is that you've only gotten to question 1 thus far, so you haven't wasted any time but in fact have established relevant school contact and have conveyed the message that at least one person would like to have some real answers about what is going on. There should be no animosity as a result of your inquiry. If it were the case that your child would be dropped from the school because of your questions, at least one of your authors would never have gotten through the public school system.

There is another point that you should keep in mind throughout the process of working with these guidelines. That is, as you work with Categories 1 to 4 you are doing an *assessment*. You are collecting information that you may use at a later time to conduct an *evaluation*. The difference between the two is that an assessment simply compiles information about something (hopefully in the most appropriate manner and in the most appropriate form), whereas evaluation, as the name implies, places some *value* on that information. Thus, all evaluations involve assessments, but not all assessments are evaluations. This is important because as you speak with your contact person(s), it is not necessary to argue points with them or to express opinions (positive or negative) about the responses you receive. For the time being, collect the information. Category 5 will address evaluating the assessment data you have compiled.

What Evidence Is Available to Support the Need for the Program?

Question 2 asks for the evidence to support what was said in question 1. *Evidence* and *documentation* are not foreign terms to school personnel, and they come in many forms; it's just that some forms are more appropriate than others.

With regard to student performance, appropriate evidence may be provided by standardized test scores. Do not be intimidated by jargon-rich responses that speak of percentiles, z-scores, and standard deviations. In any case, they're just numbers intended to quantify some aspect of achievement, aptitude, or potential. If you are presented with such data, ask for explanations of the meaning of those numbers *and* an explanation of the population upon which those numbers are based. Standardized tests are only as good as the norm group used to set the standards. Be sure that the norm group for the test matches the characteristics of your school district.

Teacher-made tests are good indicators of student performance if the program under consideration is intended to provide services to one or a small group of students. Those tests, however, should be available for review, and their design should be something that can be explained plainly and logically. It is not typical that a teacher is "out to get" some child, but it is also not uncommon that children are tested in inappropriate ways. The classic example is that of a nonnative speaker of English being tested and evaluated in English. If the test is of English-language skills, that's one thing. But if it is something such as a science test, and the student has failed because he can't read the questions, not because he doesn't know the science, then the problem is with the test and not with the student.

Teacher observations also represent a good source of information. If this is the situation, those observations should be documented. The date, time, and circumstances surrounding the observations represent data that should not be dismissed out of hand. The use of anecdotal records is not inappropriate, but as Stiggins (2001) indicates, relying on nothing more than one's memory of an event is rarely, if ever, a sound foundation for evaluating a situation.

What Purpose Will the Program Serve?

If you get as far as question 3, then things are actually going pretty well. It doesn't mean that you have a great program on your hands, but it does mean that the chances of collecting worthwhile data about the program are increasing.

At this point, we want to know what will be different as a result of this program. If this is a reading program, will students be better readers? Better at comprehension, at word recognition, at sounding out unfamiliar words? If this is a math program, will the students be better at calculations, at word problems, at problem framing? There are many dimensions to virtually any undertaking in the school curriculum, and your contact person should be able to tell you just what impact the program will have. There should also be some indication of the degree of significance of that impact. Will students improve an entire grade level (watch out if this is the claim)? Will they be able to speak a foreign language fluently? Will they lower their cholesterol to a number below the national average? An educational program under consideration should also be able to indicate what the difference will be by making a change to this new, or at least different, method.

Are Any Other Programs Like This Available?

The final question of Category 1 asks what should be an obvious question: Is this the only product on the market? People do comparison shopping on a regular basis and with reference to a host of criteria. The education market is very big, and competition is fierce. There are many products out there. So, if the program you are considering comes in several varieties, it would be worthwhile to know why this particular model is being considered.

It is also very often the case that the program *is* the only one of its kind available. Perhaps the deliberations involve a grant-funded project with a university or a classroom-level program that will utilize the talents of local parents or community members. If that is the situation, fine, you simply need to know this up front because the information will direct you (or your contact person) to the appropriate sources to find out about credentials, backgrounds, and the pedagogical basis for the proposals being made. There is no crime in expecting those who work with children to demonstrate that they know what they are doing and can be held accountable for that instructional time. Ultimately, the school bears this responsibility and benefits from clear answers to these questions.

Category 2: The Nature of the Program

As we have already mentioned, reading about Category 1 is more overwhelming than putting it into practice. As you review the questions, it will all make sense. Yet, as we've also mentioned, our intent is that you become an informed consumer and change agent. The time you spend with this will prepare you to speak intelligently with any level of the educational institution and not be intimidated or put off.

Category 1 provides the opportunity to jot down notes while in conversation with your contact person. For Category 2, most of the information is recorded in a checklist format. In all cases, you can seek elaboration on any point, but the basic information can be obtained in a short-answer format. Our emphasis here is on what the program is all about. Category 3 will address implementation (including personnel, training, time, and cost). For now, let's try to get a picture of how and why the program has been devised.

To begin with, find out who is responsible for the development of the program. This may be collaboration between school personnel and faculty from a college or university or, perhaps, with local businesspeople or parents. It could be the case that the program is a "sophisticated" product marketed by some educational enterprise. It is possible that the program was developed "in house" at the state, district, or school level. You need not identify each professor and graduate student, but find out who the lead individual is behind the program under consideration. This information alone will give you a good idea of how well the program has been thought out.

Program Characteristics

There are four basic program characteristics that should be clearly identified. Begin by determining whether the program is intended as a reform, an intervention, or something else. Essentially, a reform will make the claim of changing the way things are done on a fairly broad scale. Interventions, you will recall, tend to leave daily operations intact but exert an effect on some small, problematic segment of what is happening. The importance of the distinction is in the scope of the efforts. Reforms can be expected to be expensive and expansive, to require changes in pedagogical philosophies, and almost always to necessitate training of personnel. Interventions of an instructional nature, on the other hand, can often be put in place with little additional

---

Activity 5.2.
THE NATURE OF THE PROGRAM

Program Assessment Form   *Category 2: The Nature of the Program*

Name of the program:

---

1. Program developed by:

---

2. Program characteristics:

   a. ___ reform ___ intervention ___ other

   b. ___ curricular ___ instructional ___ enrichment ___ administrative ___ credentials

   c. ___ student/small group ___ class ___ grade level ___ school ___ district

   d. ___ temporary change ___ long-term change ___ incident specific

---

3. Program development:

   a. There is a documented research basis.   ___ Yes ___ No

   b. The program has been tested in other schools.   ___ Yes ___ No

   c. Field-testing was in schools similar to this one.   ___ Yes ___ No

   d. Program results are available for review.   ___ Yes ___ No

---

4. There is evidence that the results of the program are:

   a. Valid   (assessments were measuring actual program outcomes) ___ Yes ___ No

   b. Reliable (the program yields consistent results)   ___ Yes ___ No

---

5. The developer(s) make the following claims about the program and its effectiveness:

---

6. References (other schools that have adopted and continued this program):

---

funding and with little bureaucratic attention. It is true that sometimes it is not an individual child that needs remediation but rather an entire school or district. In this situation, a state department of education or other state agency may "intervene" for the purposes of remediating the district's problems. This may seem like more than a small segment of the operation, but from the perspective of the state agency, a single school district represents one part of the overall system.

The "Other" category can cover a lot of territory but still provide important information in assembling a picture of the program. A good example would be a site council established at the school to bring teachers, parents, higher education faculty, and businesspeople into the decision-making process. It is not really a reform since it is not replacing district policy. When push comes to shove, or simply if a new superintendent is elected, the site council approach could easily be overridden by the perspectives held in upper administration. Nor is the program an intervention since the typical administrative operating procedure has, indeed, been replaced rather than just supplemented. Hence, it is an "other," and that designation often tells us that the program is likely "experimental" and that it probably does not have an *instructional* orientation.

The next three items within this section serve as tools of further clarification. What is the specific target of the program: curriculum change, instructional change, administrative change, enrichment, or something to do with credentialing (for administrators, teachers, or staff)? Substitute teachers, teacher's aides, parent volunteers, and student teachers (along with their college or university supervisors) are expected to have some sort of credentials.

For a program that claims to impact upon the curriculum (either in terms of the "standard" curriculum or the provision of remedial services) or to provide enrichment activities (which can include academic or extracurricular activities), it should be noted how broad the impact will be. While some programs may address the entire district, others are provided for just one child at a time. Determine whether the program you are assessing is targeted toward individuals, a classroom, an entire grade level, a school, or the entire district.

Finally, ask that it be made clear whether the effort is intended as a long-term or temporary change or whether it is addressing a specific incident. If the response is that the change is permanent, you will want to be certain that careful deliberation is provided for something that is supposed to remain in place for a long time. If the change is temporary, you will want to ascertain that all of the necessary support will be provided so that the program can be implemented successfully.

Program Development

Before we get to the actual claims made by the program developers (item 4), there is still more background to consider. If the responses you have been receiving thus far make sense, and the responses to this next series of questions are satisfactory, *then* it will be time to let the developer(s) tell you about the wonderful things their program will accomplish. If you find that the contact person insists on talking about the merits of the program first, let that be a red flag warning you that all might not be right with the proposal. No amount of fast-talking or slick marketing should substitute for the information you are gathering.

A research basis was one of the four dimensions that the Northwest Regional Educational Laboratory (NWREL) required in considering reform models. In fact, it was the first of the four dimensions. For programs that are offered through a college or university or one that is a published program, there should certainly be a research base that supports the claims of the program. Do not assume that the foundation is there just because it has higher education folks involved or because the program comes in a nice box with three-color graphics on the front. Step 1 is to ask whether such a basis exists. If the answer is yes, flip your assessment form over, ask for details, and take notes. If the answer is no, proceed with open-minded caution.

Item 2 asks whether the program has been tested in other schools. The fourth dimension of the NWREL screening of programs asked for evidence of replicability, that is, that the program can be used in other schools. We are not emphasizing that dimension here because you are concerned with what is happening at your local school. However, two points need to be kept in mind. First, a program that has had success somewhere else has a greater chance of being successful in your school. It is not necessarily so (for many reasons), but it is likely that many of the initial problems have been worked out already. At this point, it is a question of "fit" more than a question of viability. If the program has been tested in other schools, the follow-up question is whether or not those schools are similar to your school (item 3b). A program that enjoyed great success in a well-to-do suburb is not necessarily a good match for an underfunded urban setting. Again, as we continually hasten to add, this is not to say that it can't be adapted, simply that people need to be aware of these conditions *before* charging forward believing that success in all applications is guaranteed.

The second point, referring back to item 3a, is that all programs have to be done *somewhere* for the first time. So, if the answer to this item is no, that does not automatically work against it. In particular, local programs involving community members are going to be specific to a particular school. Exportability of the program is not an issue, and field-testing is something that will be carried out on site. In such a situation, the program needs to be clearly recognized as experimental, indicators of positive *and* negative results have to be identified before beginning, and the progress should be closely monitored and documented.

Finally, if the program has been piloted or implemented elsewhere, ask whether or not the results are available for review. And if the answer is yes, ask to see them. This could be a difficult situation. If you feel that you are being kept at a distance, watch the calendar for the next school board meeting. Check with the district office to find out how to be placed on the agenda, or ask whether the meeting will include time for questions from those in attendance. You need not prepare for battle; simply stand up in the meeting and say that such and such a program is being considered but that you have not been allowed to review the results from previous implementations of it. Indicate that you are concerned that the school may be spending money on something that doesn't match its needs. Start the ball rolling. In a situation like this it is probable that you will either (1) be given access to that information, or (2) begin to understand why we are calling to revolutionize the institution of education.

Evidence of Program Results

If you are reviewing a published program rather than something locally developed, and evidence of prior results is available, there are two important issues to explore: validity and reliability. In assessment terms, validity refers to whether a testing instrument measures what it is supposed to gauge. For instance, when a teacher deducts points on a science test for grammatical errors, the validity of the test suffers (unless the teacher has specifically indicated that this would be a test of science and grammar, in which case grades should show up for that student in both of these categories). Reliability refers to whether or not the assessment yields consistent results. A test that students always ace is reliable. A test that students always fail is also reliable. And a test that some students ace, a higher percentage get average grades on, and a few don't do so well on is reliable as long as the results are consistent. Of course, in test design, those patterns tell the designer something, and adjustments are made accordingly.

In the context of our program-review process, validity refers to whether or not the program does what it is supposed to do. If you look at the way the results are measured, or your contact person explains them to you, they need to be an obvious match for the situation for you to check this one with a yes. If things are otherwise, maintain a healthy skepticism and ask a few other folks about the matter. It is possible that you will be the one getting educated in these discussions, so remain cooperative rather than combative.

Reliability is easier to address as more sites use the program, but if yours is the first to use it, look to the evidence provided and ask for clarification of anything difficult to understand. You'll only have to seek help a few times before you are the one explaining it to others.

The Claims

Now is the time to find out the specific claims of the program as you are ready to do so from a more informed perspective. You already have determined whether it has a solid foundation and a record of success (or is untried), as well as precisely what the targets are in terms of program characteristics. All of this casts a very different light on what you will be told the program can accomplish.

Space has been provided on your "Program Assessment Form" for writing in the claims. If more space is needed, use the back of the page. However, as you take notes about the claims, keep in mind that no program can be all things to all people. If the list seems endless, then pay close attention to the nature of the claims. For instance, goals and objectives are often considered to be synonymous when, in fact, they are not. The goal of a particular program may be to increase the reading comprehension of fourth graders by one grade level. Objectives might include ascertaining the reading level of each child who participates and designing appropriate experiences to allow that child to gain one year's reading improvement. Under these conditions, it is possible that at the end of the program, no child will be reading on a fourth-grade level, and yet, the program could be a tremendous success. How? If all of the fourth graders were reading on a second-grade level to begin with (not at all a far-fetched possibility), then one year's improvement could still have them one year behind. Whether this is a good thing or a bad thing is another question. However, knowing this up front is a good thing. As you listen to the claims, try to separate the goals from the objectives and ask for clarification whenever the two seem to be getting confused, particularly whenever goals seem to be giving way to desires.

References

Finally, if the program has been used elsewhere, ask for references. If it has never been implemented before, ask for the credentials of those who will be designing the program and interacting with the children. Neither is an insulting request. Student teachers must submit fingerprints for an FBI background check before they are allowed into the classroom. In the future, they may have to do this before being allowed into a classroom as a freshman or sophomore doing clinical internship work. Knowing who will be working with the children and their qualifications is a legitimate area of concern. And knowing what other people have to say about a program that was offered in their school (particularly the opinions of those who actually implemented it) can go a long way toward bringing the program into sharper focus.

Category 3: Implementation

The tale of reform efforts in this country is punctuated with good programs poorly implemented. And so, we now must ask how this program will become a reality in the schools. Who will actually do the work of implementing it? Is it really feasible to ask teachers to do yet another task? Are there funds for hiring specialized personnel? Chief among the flaws of implementation is inadequate preparation of those who will deliver the program. Personal experience shows that this was a problem thirty and forty years ago and remains one in contemporary practice. That's why we recommend asking about the training of those who will conduct the program as well as about the costs involved.

Who Will Do the Work?

Good ideas are wonderful things, but they need people to implement them. Folks in higher education or in politics tend to be prolific with ideas for how the schools should work. Parents frequently recommend what schools should do. But despite the twentieth-century impetus to use the schools to solve all of society's problems, the facts still remain: Even with more than six million teachers, administrators, and staff in our country, they are already worked to the limit. We won't argue that all the work for which they are responsible represents the best use of their time, but the limitations of time and resources make it important to consider additional workloads very carefully.

For this reason, item 1 of Category 3 specifically asks who will be doing the work. This could be a rather complex answer, and it may be necessary for you to jot down a number of notes as your contact person answers the questions. For instance, it may be that the work will be done by community volunteers but that students' availability will be coordinated by the teacher. The teacher, then, must account for a different class size for her own instruction and make sure that participating students don't lose ground in other academic areas. If administrators will be responsible for implementation, that can avoid the loss of instructional time but still indicates that special scheduling will be necessary if the program involves students or teachers. It would be great if the folks who represent the program are going to implement it, but this, of course, is going to involve additional funds (see item 4, below).

What Materials Will Be Needed?

It is reasonable to ask whether additional books or other printed materials will be needed for the program. How about additional computer hardware, software, or other "technologies"? What about specialty work areas, special materials, or consumables? Consumables are supplies that get used up during a lesson or activity and must be replaced for the next time around. For instance, using batteries in a science class will require that those batteries get replaced at some point. Working with paints in some sort of creative-thinking program would also require consumables. We're sure that this

Activity 5.3.
IMPLEMENTATION

Program Assessment Form	*Category 3: Implementation*
Name of the program:	
1. Who will do the work? Considerations: Will teachers implement this program? Aides or volunteers? Consultants or program representatives? Administrators?	
2. What materials will be needed? Considerations: Are books or other printed materials required? Computer hardware and/or software? Special space considerations (e.g., science labs)? Consumables (i.e., things that get used and must be replaced)?	
3. What training will be required? Considerations: Will teachers need training? Who will train them? When will this take place? How long will it take? Do volunteers or aides need training and/or orientation?	
4. What costs are involved? Considerations: Will new personnel be required? Consultants? Program costs such as license fees, tuition, registration? Are there costs for equipment and/or consumables?	

probably sounds obvious to you, but if you chat with a teacher or two, you will find that many a great program languishes in storage closets and bins because after the first time through, there was no budget for replacing used materials.

What Training Will Be Required?

Will it be necessary to conduct training sessions for those who will eventually deliver the program to the participants? You can probably recall, as we do, some point(s) in your own educational experience when a brave new program was put in place. The materials were there, renovations to the classroom area were complete, and all was ready to go. The only problem was that no one ever got around to teaching the teachers how to do this new, neat thing. Perhaps it was the new math of the mid-1960s or the shift to "open classrooms" in the mid-1970s. Or it could have been any one of a hundred different reforms. Time and planning are needed to prepare people to do something different from what they've done before. This is an aspect of implementation that needs to be just as well conceived and arranged as any other element.

This also extends to nonprofessional personnel. If community members are recruited, they must be made aware of the many restrictions under which the school operates. What can and cannot be said to a child is not an issue of meager importance. Whether or not it is permissible to put a hand on a child's shoulder can be part of school policy today. The way people dress to come work with children is an important concern. Ask your contact person whether these people will receive indoctrination, professional oversight, and, as we will mention in Category 4, any evaluation.

What Costs Are Involved?

It is not necessary to access detailed budgets at this stage of your evaluation. Actually, if the program involves salaries of particular individuals, it may be virtually impossible for you to review such a thing. However, you *can* get an idea for the project's scope. And if you have completed Categories 1 and 2 on your way to this point, you will have a much better perspective from which to consider the dollar amounts that you hear. If the principal tells you that this program will cost the district $100,000, you should have a good idea of whether that seems reasonable. If a teacher tells you that the program she is going to run won't cost anything, you probably have a pretty good idea of how reasonable that is as well.

As ever, we are not trying to launch you on a career as an investigative journalist or get you branded as the local educational gadfly. But there are two things that should be kept in mind: One is that whenever you hear about money being spent on one program or another, some of those dollars are your dollars, and you are entitled to know whether they are being well spent. A second point is that by virtue of the involvement you have had through this inquiry, you can share in the "ownership" of this project and should be prepared to offer your assistance in any manner that is suitable. This sort of inquiry is but one aspect of being a change agent, that is, helping to determine whether this is the right change to make. The other aspect is helping with the change.

Category 4: Assessment

Category 4 represents the final information-gathering form of your program assessment exercise. Category 5, "Evaluation," will combine the results of the first four forms to arrive at your conclusion about the program. For now, the topic is the assessment component of the *program*. For example, we previously offered a scenario about purchasing a car to illustrate the fact that people gather information to make a variety of decisions. Well, in the case of the new car, once the decision has been made to buy a particular model, there comes a time when the buyer tries to determine whether the right decision was made. That's what we are talking about here. Suppose the program is adopted and implemented; at some point, a decision will be made as to whether or not it accomplished its goals. The making of that decision should not be haphazard or left to the eventual surfacing of complaints. There should be a plan in place for assessing the program from the very beginning. This is not strange or unusual practice in most any industry—with the possible exception of education, which is somewhat ironic considering that teachers regularly assess their individual students, and administrators regularly assess the academic progress of entire schools and districts. As you are well aware, those assessment efforts are currently tied more to "accountability" efforts than to educational decision making. We won't argue the relative merits of these activities but will indicate that "assessment" is nothing new to education. And any good reform effort or intervention will have a sound assessment piece laid out in advance.

The form that we suggest here has four components: who, when, how, and for what purpose. As was the case with Category 2, the questions that you ask about assessment can typically be answered in a short format. You need not uncover the fine details of assessment-instrument construction or weigh the relative merits of an ANOVA or a VANCOVA statistical treatment of the data. Some programs will not require such number crunching. You are entitled to the reasonable expectation that the folks presenting the program have done their "homework" in putting the program together. You don't need to learn how to design a program to assess it any more than you need to understand how to design an automatic transmission to assess how well it works in your car. However, you do have a responsibility as a "consumer" to be well prepared in this activity. We don't want you favoring, or speaking against, a program with the argument of "just because."

The Who of Assessment

There are two aspects of assessing the results of a program from the "who" perspective. First, you need to determine who will *be* assessed. If the particular program has an instructional orientation, it needs to be known whether students will be assessed individually, as a group, as a school, or as an entire district. This answer will be addressed again in item 4 when you ask about what is to be done with the assessment results. For instance, will the results be used to give students a grade and/or credit? Will the numbers be reported in a manner that identifies individual students or stratifications of students (such as by grade level or perhaps between sections of math, English, or science classes)?

But there is another dimension to this question of who will be assessed. That is, are the students the *only* ones being assessed? If the teachers are being asked to teach something new or something in a new way, then they should be assessed as well. This is not necessarily a matter of determining whether they did a competent job but rather whether the training component of the program (from Category 3) was adequate.

If the program is being presented by someone without educational credentials (for example, local volunteers), there must be some sort of assessment that at the very least

---

Activity 5.4.
ASSESSMENT

Program Assessment Form   *Category 4: Assessment*

Name of the program:

---

1. The Who of Assessment:

   Those assessed:

   a. ___ students ___ teachers ___ admin. ___ volunteers/aides ___ consultants

   b. ___ individual ___ class ___ grade level ___ school ___ district ___ special group

   Those assessing:

   c. ___ teachers ___ administrative personnel ___ volunteers/aides
      ___ consultant/program representative

---

2. The When of Assessment:

   Assessment of participants:

   a. ___ no testing ___ pretest ___ ongoing formative assessment(s) ___ posttest

   Assessment of presenters:

   b. ___ no testing ___ prior to presenting program ___ following completion
      of program

---

3. The How of Assessment:

   Instruments prepared by:

   a. ___ teacher/presenter ___ district ___ published tests ___ program materials

   Format:

   b. ___ selected response ___ essay ___ performance ___ personal communication

   Scoring:

   c. ___ criterion referenced ___ norm referenced ___ rubric ___ subjective

   d. ___ teacher ___ trained rater ___ consultant/program representative ___ other

4. What Is to Be Done as a Result:

   Participants:

   a. ___ criteria for successful completion is established ___ no criteria established
      thus far

   b. ___ grade ___ credit ___ certification ___ other recognition

   Program:

   c. ___ one-time presentation ___ reviewed ___ revised ___ expanded
      ___ continued/discontinued ___ adopted as part of permanent curriculum

provides that individual with constructive feedback about the presentation and effectiveness of the program. Professional consultants or representatives of packaged programs (if they are responsible for either training or program presentation) are also subject to assessment. There are many ways to accomplish these goals, and we will discuss some of them when we get to item 3.

You may be wondering about the program itself. The questions you asked in Category 1 specifically addressed issues that involve the assessment of the program. Those responses, along with item 4 of this category, will combine to give you a picture of the efficacy of the program.

The second major aspect of the "who" question is who will *do* the assessing? Assessment is a responsibility, not an afterthought or something that will be done in the last five minutes of class—if there's time. It is an important task that must be assigned at the outset and for which the person taking on the responsibility must be prepared. That's one of the reasons why, as a follow-up question to item 1c, you should ask whether the assessment instruments or, at the very least, the assessment plans have already been prepared. More about this can be discussed in item 3, but if the answer here is no, don't hold out high hopes for what you will find out as you continue with this line of questioning.

The When of Assessment

This may seem like an obvious matter to you; after all, assessments are done after the program is finished. On the one hand, that is true. On the other hand, an assessment properly conducted begins *before* any of the participants are exposed to the "program" itself. For example, if the intent is to provide a reading intervention, the teacher (or whoever is presenting the program) should begin with some sort of pretest to establish exactly where a child is in terms of reading ability. This is not one of those "testing children to death" situations. Rather, this assessment component, referred to as a "formative assessment," can be accomplished in many ways that may not even strike the student as a testing situation at all. But it is a critical activity in terms of both instructional planning and determining the final results of the program.

If you are told that students will be assigned to such and such a program based upon their scores on such and such a test or on grades received in class, someone is making the same assumption as saying that a child in the fifth grade must be reading on a fifth-grade level because he's in the fifth grade. Check out these numbers with the school's principal, and you will likely find that relatively few children are actually on a reading level that matches their grade. You might also be suspicious in this case of how children can be assigned to a "new and different" program based on old and questionable data.

It should become obvious why it is important to know who will be taking on the assessment responsibility—and that said person is aware that she is taking on the responsibility. There's no use going any further in asking about the nature of the assessment plans if it turns out that nobody's already thought about the questions you've raised. We hope you will find plans in place to assess the program both in terms of student gains and presentation (which can help substantiate that the program was responsible for those gains) and to conduct pre- and posttesting, along with formative assessments along the way. Actual dates for the planned assessments would be ideal, but an explanation of at what points during the program the various assessments will be carried out would suffice. None of these activities should put a crimp in anyone's style, and if the claim is made that they will, then take a very long, serious look at the program—there may be other areas that have not been thought out very well.

The How of Assessment

There are three aspects to the "how" of assessment that we believe you should consider when investigating a program: How (or by whom) are the assessment instruments prepared, what format (or method) will be used for carrying out the assessment, and how will the scoring be accomplished? These are all straightforward assessment components, and all should be easily explained. If there is any difficulty with regard to accounting for them, then that is cause for concern about the integrity (not the intentions) of the program.

There are at least four sources for the assessment instruments that might be used with the particular program. One would be tests designed by the classroom teacher. If this will be the case, you should ask about the teacher's qualifications for designing effective assessments. That the teacher has "been here forever" is not an acceptable response. Why? Because the design of assessments is often given little emphasis in teacher-education programs. By and large, teachers use the assessment materials that are provided with the textbook series that schools adopt. There are good and bad points that accompany this situation. A good point is that often (but not necessarily) the materials that come "with the book" are very specifically keyed to what is presented there. From that perspective, one could expect that the tests will definitely match up with the content. However, the designers of those tests have never met your child or the students using it: They don't know their cognitive abilities, their readiness for the particular topic, their attendance patterns, or exactly what transpired in the class from an instructional perspective. All of these are things that the classroom teacher *should* know but that tend to be deferred to the publishers. So, if the teacher (which also includes aides or volunteers) is going to design the assessments, it would be a good idea to ask to see either the tests that will be used or, at the very least, samples of tests that the presenter has designed in the past.

Depending upon the nature of the program under consideration, it could be that the district will design and/or provide the assessment materials. The most likely scenario in this case is that the assessor is assessing personnel. For instance, the principal in each school within the district could be evaluating faculty members according to a district-designed system. Such evaluations vary widely around the country and can include formative and summative components, along with a mix of assessment formats. This could also be a likely approach to a program that is being conducted by community members such as businesspeople or parents. There probably will not be a formal evaluation procedure in place, but for the sake of *all* involved, there should be some plan in mind at the outset.

Of course, published tests, more typically known as "standardized tests," are frequently used for a variety of assessment purposes. We have briefly touched on this topic already and made the point that a standardized test is useful only to the point that the norm group (the folks who set the standards) matches with the people to be assessed in the program you are reviewing. If school district personnel have determined that a published test is going to be used, they should be able to tell you about the norm group. If, indeed, that group sounds like your population, then the next step is to consider the assessment instrument itself. You almost certainly will not be allowed to review the test (test security is a legitimate concern), but you can ask questions such as those in item 3b so that you will know what sort of format will be used.

The fourth possibility is one we have already discussed: program materials. This could be a matter of such things as assessments included with a textbook series, questions included in an instructor's manual, or the testing materials that a consultant will use as part of an in-service presentation. However, program materials are typically a bit more formal than the teacher-made materials we have discussed. The difference is that if the district is buying into a packaged program, the assessment materials should all be prepared and ready to review at the same time as the instructional materials. The question then becomes whether or not those materials represent an appropriate (and acceptable) means of assessing the results of the program. By this we mean that if the program is, just for example, a course for teaching swimming, then an assessment consisting entirely of multiple choice questions answered with pencil and paper is not the most appropriate approach. At some point, it will be necessary to see the student swim (a performance test). At this point, the question is simply whether or not assessment considerations have been made. Let's switch perspectives now and consider what some of those testing methods might be.

Item 3b refers to the method that will be used to assess the program results. Whether or not it is the best or most appropriate choice may be open for discussion, but has the method been identified? Chances are good that if the response to item 3a was anything other than "teacher-made," this information will be easily available. If the teacher or presenter will be designing the test, it's possible that this question has not yet been decided. It's good for you to be investigating because these issues should be resolved!

Selected-response formats are all of those that provide an answer to the test taker: multiple-choice, true-or-false, matching, fill-in-the-blank, and even short-answer formats are characteristic of this approach. Typically, selected response provides a highly structured approach that is easily and quickly scored. It's at its best when asking for little bits of information but is woefully lacking when testing for comprehension, attitudes, and skills.

Essay tests, as you will recall, are time intensive to complete and score and are famous (infamous) for allowing people to write everything they know in the hopes that something in there might actually be the correct answer. Essay questions that are well designed delineate the information being sought and simultaneously provide the opportunity to express attitudes, opinions, and demonstrate understanding. If the program, however, is supposed to result in products (making, building, or designing something) or skills (acquiring the ability to do something), then essays are not the most appropriate way to go.

Performance assessments are what you should expect whenever the participant will be required to produce something or demonstrate a skill. In our aforementioned swimming example, a performance assessment will show if the student has learned to swim. Students in choral, band, art, or athletics programs are all assessed regularly in a similar manner. But so, too, are those who must design a lesson plan, demonstrate how to teach a topic, give a speech, or write a poem. There are many, many opportunities to employ performance assessments, though the preoccupation with multiple-choice tests that dominated the twentieth century has, to a tremendous degree, replaced the pressure of "performing" with that of "recalling."

Personal communication is yet another method, and this one involves a talk between the assessor and the assessed. There should, of course, be a list of questions to be presented, but the real strength of a personal-communication assessment is in allowing the assessor to pursue avenues that had not been anticipated or to seek clarification and deeper understanding relative to the conversation. This assessment technique is especially valuable when the concern is with opinions, attitudes, and an acceptance of diverse perspectives.

Items 3c and 3d are concerned with how the scores are referenced and who does the actual scoring. With regard to referencing, it should be known as the project begins whether participants will be compared to a standard for mastery (criterion referenced), to the performance of others (norm referenced), to a rubric (a predetermined evaluation scale), or to the subjective determination of a scorer. You've often seen that last approach used in athletic competitions (such as figure skating or diving), beauty pageants, talent contests, and even political elections. Needless to say, if a "panel of experts" (whether that panel is one expert, several, or, in the case of voters, millions) is going to have assessment authority, it should also have sufficient expertise for those being tested to accept its judgments.

Following up with the point about subjective evaluations, it is important to know who will assume the responsibility for scoring the assessments. This is not the same as conducting the assessment. For instance, when a child takes the annual achievement-test battery at school, it is conducted, typically, by classroom teachers. The scoring, however, is entirely in the hands of the testing agency. Here we want to know who will do the scoring. If someone is going to assist the teacher, then that person needs training so that a consistent standard of judgments is maintained. If it is the program consultant or some "other" individual (which could also refer to a machine that scans bubble-type answer sheets), then we want to know that as well.

What Is to Be Done as a Result?

The final area of concern with regard to assessment is what will be done with all this assessment data once it is collected. Assessments well conducted provide information with which to make better-informed decisions. So, here it is worthwhile to find out what the plans are for that assessment information as regards the participants and the program.

Have the criteria for successful completion of this program already been established? If the answer to that question is no, then all of the assessment data that has been collected is of little value. Even more to the point, this tells you that the program proponents do not have a good idea of what all of this effort will accomplish. We can think of many situations in which doing something just to see how it turns out might be a fun and adventuresome sort of thing to do, but on operating tables, during final approaches to landing, and in classrooms, there is an implied responsibility to have a better grasp of the consequences of one's actions.

Also of concern for the participants is how the results will be used. Will they receive a grade? Course credit? Certification? These are all serious matters and should demonstrate the seriousness of the assessment. Perhaps the results will be used for recognition, such as "master teacher," or "student of the year," or valedictorian, or some other such distinction.

And what of the program? If this is to be a one-time presentation, then the assessment information is useful, of course, in determining the relative success or failure of what's been done. However, if there is a longer-term emphasis on this project, it would be helpful to know whether the assessment information will be specifically used for making decisions about the program. What are the options? Will it be reviewed? Revised? Will the information be made available to folks like you? As we've said, assessments provide information for making decisions. The intent of item 4 is to ascertain what sort of decisions are going to be made.

Category 5: Evaluation

At this point, you have more information about the program than most parents ever have about their children's entire school experience. We hope that you also have a healthy respect for all that educational programs entail, for the efforts of those folks who are at the school each day, for the constraints under which they operate, and for the need for careful evaluation. We also hope that you have earned the respect of the people you've discussed these questions with as being a conscientious and concerned supporter of education. But now it is time to look over your four pages and determine what conclusions can be drawn.

Category 1

In the space provided for Category 1, write in a summary statement of the four points you investigated about the need for this program. Now, don't feel that you are confined to the space on the evaluation form. Just as we have avoided reducing all of the information you have accumulated into a number or score, we similarly do not want you to feel that your opinions and conclusions must fit into a little rectangular space on the page. We do encourage you to look carefully at the four items (why consider the program, what evidence supports the need, what purpose will it serve, and are there other versions) and try to synthesize a statement or two that captures the essence of what you have found. Maybe there is an obvious need for the program based upon districtwide achievement testing, but other programs could be considered. Then say so. If you find yourself presenting this case to the principal, school board, or PTA, then you can elaborate with information taken from your Category 1 page. But for now, try to put together as clear a statement as possible *based upon the evidence you have acquired*. That is, if all of the information you have indicates that this program is unnecessary, but you really like the glossy brochure that the consultants provided, you need to show that the evidence does not support a need for this program. If you ultimately decide to support the program anyway, that's your business. But in this evaluation, you should stay with the facts as they've been presented. This page is your big-picture summary. Focus that picture accurately, and then make your best decision.

Category 2

This may be a little bit easier than summarizing Category 1 because the items were basically discrete bits of information. You should be able to look at item 2, for instance, and say something such as, "This program is an intervention intended as an enrichment activity that will be conducted with students in the fifth grade. It is a temporary program that can be continued based on the assessment results." Items 4 and 5 can easily be summarized in a statement that will give a clear indication of the program's foundation.

Activity 5.5.
EVALUATION

Program Assessment Form	*Category 5: Evaluation*

Name of the program:

Category 1:

Category 2:

Category 3:

Category 4:

Recommendation:

Pay particular attention to the claims made in item 5. You might want to write them on your evaluation page, but first consider whether they really seem viable. Do they try to be all things to all people? Chances are slim that anything so broadly defined can be accomplished. If that is the case, you need not reject the program; just ask that the developers address the issue.

You might ask for that same sort of clarification if the claims are vague. Schools, for better or worse, have long been academic laboratories. In the first half of the twentieth century, notable examples like John Dewey's lab school at the University of Chicago and the Lincoln School of Teacher's College at Columbia University were open experiments in the relationship between education and society. As the reform model took hold, public schools soon became the test beds of what higher education developed. Today, *collaboration* between colleges and universities with education programs and local education agencies, that is, the schools, are typically required when seeking grant funding.

The fact is that research and investigation (experimentation is really not the appropriate term) will continue with our current institution of education. However, it is not necessary that any idea that comes down the pike should have ready access to schools and children. There does need to be a gatekeeper. Rest assured that if you begin to take on this role, there will be tremendous resistance to your efforts. Yet, it will not hurt any program to be able to satisfactorily answer to the assessment suggestions that we have provided here.

Category 3

Your summary of Category 3 will take a form much like that of Category 1. Item 1 is simply a statement of who will do the work. The only confounding aspect to this might be in the interrelationships of various constituencies involved. Nonetheless, it should be obvious who will bear the brunt of the effort.

You may want to try stating a summary of items 2 and 3 together and then providing a final statement of how item 4, the cost, factors into the equation. Of particular concern here, however, is whether items 1 to 3 are adequately represented in the program plans. If you feel the developers have addressed each of them sufficiently, that's the real issue. If only one or two have been accounted for, that's the telling statement to be made. You can then ask the decision makers if they are aware that these concerns have not been fully resolved.

Category 4

You may find that people are taken aback by the amount of information you have compiled regarding assessment. We mentioned earlier in this chapter that assessment is an area that receives less emphasis than it should in teacher-education programs, and you will find that a careful job of completing the Category 4 page will put you on the brink of being the resident expert on the subject. So, take some deliberate time to consider all that you have on the assessment page and write out a careful summary statement. If you keep to the items that you asked about, no one will be able to dispute your statement. It may be true that you were given inaccurate data, but that also serves a purpose by bringing information out into the open.

A key aspect of your Category 4 information is that you have tried to identify all who will be assessed, including the program itself. It is very easy for the contact person to say, "Oh, yes, the children will be assessed quite formally at the conclusion of the program." Well, that's great, but what about the program itself and the people who presented it? Only with information about all of these components is it possible to determine if the program has succeeded and was responsible for any change, as well as to isolate any bugs (to use a technical term) in the system. The real purpose of assessments is to direct appropriate change. The fascination with the assigning of grades is another matter entirely.

Recommendation

You have done a lot of work to get to this final item. What, then, is your recommendation? We have provided just a small space so that you will be gently pushed into committing, one way or the other. Do you support this initiative or not? We feel confident that the other items on the Category 5 page will provide the support for your recommendation if someone should be wise enough to ask that you elaborate.

We have asked so much of you up to this point that there is one last concern that we left off of the form. That is, based upon your recommendation, what *suggestions* would you make? You may wish to reflect on this particular question. To one degree, it is not your responsibility to design the program for these folks, but to another degree, you are now the one with the clearer picture and the information in front of you. *You* are the informed consumer.

Summary

Reading about these assessment guidelines is likely more tedious than actually working with them. But the bottom line is that with just these five assessment pages, appropriately utilized, you have a tool that parents are rarely given. And if teachers were to apply these criteria to new programs, then many doomed efforts could well be avoided. If program developers knew that they would have to answer to a constituency greater than just one or two district administrators, then programs would be better prepared for inclusion in the school day. And if the folks in higher education knew that each time a professor wanted to try out a new idea or a graduate student wanted a forum for her dissertation study they would have to satisfy folks like you asking legitimate questions, then "reform" efforts in education might become more focused. Just to avoid alienating all of higher education, a field in which some of us work, let us hasten to add that in subsequent chapters we will discuss the fact that a revolutionized educational institution very much needs what higher education has to offer. Higher education, however, will have to be willing to join in that revolutionary process.

FINAL THOUGHTS

You've probably noticed that we made a shift in emphasis over the course of this chapter. Though the activities mentioned earlier in the book asked for your own beliefs, as well as the opinions of others, this chapter has encouraged you to pursue information in a more "official" manner. Our intention was to expand the notion of an informed consumer from one who knows *about* something to one who also knows *how to find out about* something and make effective decisions. It is important that you understand that the perception people have of you may well change from this point forward. That's not necessarily a bad thing, but you should be aware.

How will perceptions change? First and foremost, an institution, any institution, that finds itself being questioned also finds itself threatened. You need not lead a march down Main Street or write vitriolic letters to the editor to be perceived as a danger to the status quo. You simply need to start asking questions. And if you appear to ask informed questions and have some understanding to back them up, then that's even more cause for concern. Since you and the school system essentially have the same "goals" in mind, it may be a bit difficult to find yourself held in suspicion by the institutional eye. But don't let that bother you. Unlike much of what has happened in reform over the years, your questions are designed to bring things out into the open so that we all understand the whys and wherefores of what will be done in school.

It is also important, however, that you keep the fundamental problem in mind. That is, even with a more informed perspective on the reforms and interventions that take place in your local school, reforms are no more than minor adjustments that the institution will tolerate for the time being. Don't be lulled into thinking that a well-researched and well-implemented intervention will turn the schools around. In her epilogue to *The Quick Reference Guide to Educational Innovations*, Orange (2002) relates the story of an innovations graveyard in the district where she worked:

> Schools from around the city sent materials [here] from their abandoned programs: whole kits; used but mostly unused products; lots of manipulatives, workbooks, and books. Everything was delivered to the doorstep of the facility. I was told that on one delivery day, the products were left at the front door in the breezeway and most of the delivery was destroyed by rain. Brand-new, beautiful materials were literally thrown into rooms that were already stacked to the ceiling. The materials lay there untouched for over a year, dead in the sense that children were not using them. They had been sent to the graveyard of abandoned programs to rest in peace. Appalled at such blatant waste, I questioned the reasoning behind it. Why would schools that claim to have little money waste it on programs that they apparently did not want to keep? Perhaps the glamour of a program wears off as soon as a new program appears on the scene. Perhaps schools have a genuine lack of knowledge about the programs or practices appropriate for their educational setting. Unfortunately, they adopt a trial-and-error approach—and the error inevitably generates a lot of waste. (120)

There are flaws in the defining characteristics of the educational institution that necessitate revolutionizing the institution itself. Even if you wrestle with the beast, the beast still remains. But your efforts toward more worthwhile reforms and interventions now will be a practical exercise in seeing school in a whole new way. As we have said all along, reforms come and go, but children still show up for class everyday.

As you become a change agent, do not be confined by the reform model, watch for signs of institutional resistance, and start talking to the men and women who have dedicated their lives to education. You might find that many of them share your desire to make public education work for each child. Mortimer Adler (1982) said, "There are no unteachable children. There are only schools and teachers and parents who fail to teach them" (8). Chapter 6 will specifically ask that you investigate how the administration, teachers, and support staff see their responsibilities and what sorts of assistance they would like from those "outside" (parents, businesspeople, and politicians). Your work as a change agent with efforts currently in progress, along with building a collaborative—rather than combative—relationship with the schools, will point toward how best to make education in the United States the very best in the world.

6

A New Educational Institution

The powers not delegated to the United States by the Constitution, nor prohibited by it to the states, are reserved to the states respectively, or to the people.

—Constitution of the United States of America, Bill of Rights, Tenth Amendment

There are few political documents that challenge the poetic diplomacy of our own Declaration of Independence or the pervasive social perspective of the Constitution of the United States and its subsequent Bill of Rights. We have alluded previously to a consideration of whether some of the language in the Constitution is visionary or exclusive, but nonetheless it is a document that has begged to be tested and has managed to "talk with crowds and keep [its] virtue and walk with kings nor lose the common touch," as Rudyard Kipling might say. Still, it is curious that with the obvious vision for the future that went into the drafting, writing, and adopting of those documents, there is no mention of a system for the education of the young in a fledgling nation. Education is a responsibility of each state by virtue of that single sentence in the amendment quoted above: Anything not covered goes to the states. And despite the twenty-seven amendments that have made their way to ratification, there have been none to say that we will embrace education as a nation. None. Why do you suppose that is the case?

By this point in your reading, you should be able to come up with some possible answers to that question. There are, in fact, many obvious reasons why the institution would resist a national orientation toward education. And, of course, a myriad of less obvious reasons exists as well. For example, a look at our history as a nation would indicate that efforts seeming to attack the sovereignty of the individual states can be expected to be met with resistance. Others would argue that, apart from questions of sovereignty, there are concerns that the diversion of funds from *state* taxes to *federal* taxes would gobble up the purchasing power of those dollars before they ever got to the school system. These thoughts, among the many others that could be bandied about, are legitimate concerns. They are not, however, *necessarily* limiting concerns. That is, they should be issues considered and accommodated as part of the educational revolution rather than as reasons not to revolutionize in the first place.

CONTROL OF THE SYSTEM

Ultimately, the "control" of public schools must be at the local level, for that is where schooling occurs. Students are not shuffled around the state or exported to school districts in other states like so many businesspeople being assigned to corporate operations around the country. Public schooling is, and always will be, an extension of the home-based process of human development (there can, of course, be many incarnations of what constitutes "home," but in all situations, there is some nonacademic entity that fosters child development).

The foregoing does not mean, however, that public education should necessarily or exclusively rest solely with the state. There are arguments for and against state control of education, just as there are arguments for and against national control. As we begin this discussion from the state-level perspective, keep in mind that the design of a *new* institution should not be fettered by preconceived notions about the locus of control.

The State

Please notice right away that we have labeled this section as *the* state, not *your* state. Our society is one that likes to compare and rank anything and everything, and "education" from state to state is certainly not immune to that exercise. There are numerous factors that could wind up as a fifty-item list with one state at the top and another at the bottom, and we will have to bring some of them into this discussion, but by and large, the differences from state to state reflect regional heritage, focus, and priorities, all of which might be considered in the context of curricular issues, economics, the physical facilities required, and a very strong civic undercurrent. However, we want to couch our discussion in terms of any state being the controlling force in the education of children because the *institutional* nature of state control is virtually the same from Alabama to Wyoming. And *that* is the nature we particularly want to address.

In the State's Favor

A strong argument for expecting states to take responsibility for education within their own boundary lines can come from a basic foundation of civics. Even in our highly mobile society, we tend to educate children "as our own," that is, with the expectation that they will grow up and become prosperous and contributing citizens in that same state. That's reasonable enough, of course, and difficult to argue against. States can legitimately be expected to emphasize the lifestyles, values, and economic needs (for instance, the skills and capabilities needed for the workforce) unique to the particular state. So, it makes sense that students in a particular state should spend more time studying the history of that state than the history of other states. And again, it is reasonable to expect that the curriculum, explicit and implicit, will reflect the values and mannerisms that the particular state embraces.

One of your authors experienced those regional differences firsthand as a high school student. The move was from the greater New York City area to a suburb of Houston, Texas, in the early 1970s. The expected, if not required, use of "sir" and "ma'am," though nice-enough courtesies, was something foreign to a young man from the Northeast. Similarly, moving from an area that encompassed many religious denominations to an area that was predominantly of one devout orientation offered changes in curricular emphasis that otherwise one would have thought were consistent throughout the nation (e.g., the teaching, or nonteaching, of evolution).

These experiences do not reflect aberrations of human value and virtue; nor do they represent a corrupting of the youth in some manner detrimental to the strength of the nation. They simply reflect the diversity that is at the heart of our American culture. Though many teachers would likely say that they try to educate their students to be successful members of society *wherever* they live, and that now includes the perspective of the "global community," most legislators would just as likely say that the responsibility of the state is to educate the children with an eye toward their becoming the community members and *community leaders* of that state as well. The idea, therefore, that it is most appropriate for states to assume the responsibility for public education as a means toward preserving the cultural values of, and civic pride in, that state is a reasonable one indeed. In essence, state control preserves the notion of *statehood*.

The states can also make a cogent case for controlling the public schools on the grounds of the "ground," so to speak. Schools take up real estate, and real estate is what states are made of. Therefore, given the amount of space that needs to be provided for schools, it would make sense that the individual states control the schools within their borders. How much space is involved? Well, we don't have figures on the actual acreage involved at this point, but we can get some idea of the magnitude involved by extrapolating from some numbers that are available.

Figures have not been compiled to account for the value of the land that public schools occupy throughout our country, but figures are available for the value of land held by degree-granting institutions. As of 1995–1996, the value of land and buildings (this excludes equipment owned by the institutions) was in excess of *$161 billion*. The land alone was valued at more than $11 billion (NCES, 2000). Of course, colleges and universities tend to take up more space than does your local elementary school, so for comparison purposes, consider that as of 1999 there were 4,070 degree-granting institutions in the United States, and at that same time, there were *91,062* public elementary and secondary schools. If you have ninety-one thousand of just about anything large enough to hold at least two people (for instance, a student and a teacher), it's going to require a significant amount of area.

The space argument is a good one in favor of state control of education. Were the federal government to control public education, it would require states to relinquish control of sizable tracts of land throughout the state. Add in the property already occupied by federal buildings, national parks, and military installations, and the whole issue of sovereignty could be expected to arise with full force. "Where will this incursion end?" states may be expected to ask. Even in the case of military installations, which can occupy quite a bit of real estate, they tend to occupy large areas that, once established, maintain restricted status to one degree or another. Schools, on the other hand, represent smaller parcels of land that exist deep within communities throughout the state. From a land-acquisition and -control perspective, the advantage goes to the states if we are compelled to adopt an "either/or" mindset.

We have already alluded to the issue of curriculum, but it would seem to be worth further consideration. In a generic curriculum sense, what is taught throughout the country is driven to a great extent by the standards and requirements set by just a handful of states. Due to the nature of publishing, the content of most public school textbooks is determined by California, Texas, and New York. These states represent such huge markets for curriculum materials that it is prudent, in a business sense, to be certain that the standards required of these three states are addressed in their publications. No company wants to write off a state that has the potential for purchasing tens of thousands of their books. Nonetheless, geography virtually demands some degree of a regionalized curriculum.

The United States is unique in that its reach is from the tropics to the arctic. It is bordered by three major bodies of water, each of which represents a very different sort of influence upon patterns of trade, aquaculture, and shoreline residency (particularly in view of the weather patterns that emerge). It is also bordered on the north and south by sovereign nations with distinctively different cultural foundations. Each impacts our nation as a whole in general and the states along their borders in particular with their cultural influences. And between the East Coast and the West Coast, we have pastures, plains, deserts, mountains, the Great Lakes, and rivers that dictate the quality of life along their banks. It makes logical sense that each state is an "expert" in the resources of that state and that a study of those landmarks, industries, and other resources should be part and parcel of the education of children. Those concerns are, in the final analysis, what defines the state, and identity is at the heart of any educational experience: who we are in relation to our immediate world, who we are as a state, who we are as a nation, who we are in the world, and—in a philosophic and/or religious vein—who we are in the universe. There is not enough time in the day to provide every child with a complete and rigorous grounding in the identity of every region and state in our nation, and so it is more likely that each state will pursue its own emphasis within its own borders.

States also pay the greatest share of the cost of education. So, they are responsible for raising and allocating large amounts of funds for the various programs in the schools. Increasingly, they are being challenged in court to ensure educational equity as well, an issue that has characterized virtually the entire history of education in our country. In a recent major example, the Kentucky Supreme Court ruled in 1989 that the education system of that state was ineffective and unconstitutional. It directed the governor and legislature to develop a proposal for a new state system. In 1990, the legislation was enacted into law as the Kentucky Education Reform Act. More cases are working their way through the court system.

In 1997–1998, one-third of all expenditures of state and local governments were for education. Thus, $450 billion of $1.3 trillion went to the public schools. Elementary and secondary schools received $318 billion, while colleges and universities received $112 billion. As you can tell, the greatest share of the education budget for public schools comes from state coffers. However, the proportion of the budget that comes from a state varies considerably, with some states providing almost all of the nonfederal funding, while other states rely on individual school districts to fund their schools.

It would seem from the previous paragraphs that the states are indeed the most appropriate entity for assuming the responsibilities of public education. However, it is possible that there are one or two reasons (or maybe a few more than that) why state control makes the whole process more difficult. Let's consider some of those possibilities as well.

Limitations of the State

It's only fair to admit that there are some powerful arguments emphasizing the limitations that states face in providing a uniformly outstanding educational experience in the twenty-first century. At the very least, it is obvious that the "states" in United States referred to a much smaller number when the Constitution was drafted. So, when we think in terms of the nation that we have *become*, it is not difficult to understand that while the challenges of public education have remained the same on some levels, they have been greatly extended on others.

For example, if you have school-age children, you have probably noticed that parents these days are responsible for sending their children to school with a host of items that appear on lists of supplies that many schools distribute. Items such as paper, pencils, markers, crayons, and so forth are referred to as "consumables." Schools, like most institutional entities, use large quantities of consumables but very much dislike having to purchase them. In essence, once purchased, they represent a debit against the financial accounts of the institution, and that value is lost. Equipment, on the other hand, requires expenditures but remains an asset that continues to contribute to the institution's fiscal strength. Thus, a principal will be more willing to authorize the purchase of a telescope (equipment) that will be used over and over again than art supplies (consumables) that will be used up once and be gone.

Where does this show up? It actually shows up in several ways that directly impact upon classroom instruction. Many schools purchase various "instructional kits." These could be kits for the teaching of math or science, for instance, and at first purchase represent equipment. The kits, however, contain consumables that must be replenished after several uses. As we've mentioned, budgets rarely account for the ongoing restocking of the consumables, and so, after being expended, not only are there no more materials available, but the cost of the kits is no longer justifiable. You can check this for yourself with a visit to a local school. Don't ask the principal, but instead ask a teacher whether she has any such materials. It is not uncommon that all of those boxes either become pedestals for stacking other materials or are shipped off to some curriculum graveyard, the contents of which will astound you—if only in terms of dollars wasted.

That the schools now expect parents to provide the consumables for students to use during the school year exemplifies the budget crunch that education faces. It also demonstrates that the states are more than happy to pass on these expenses to the parents. If it is not already happening, we can certainly expect that the trend will broaden to the point that parents must purchase the textbooks that their students use and/or supply the computer hardware and software that schools elect to use instead of hardcopy textbooks. We can agree that parents should be responsible for expenses associated with extracurricular activities and participation in occasional nonrequired activities (e.g., field trips to an event or a site that requires an admission charge), but books, pens, pencils, paper, and the like are the necessary materials for conducting classes in organized educational settings. Such materials should be provided. Would a company office require their employees to provide paper for the copying machine? Would a legislator be expected to pay for the consumables needed by his or her office? Not likely.

This matter of parents providing the materials so that teachers can teach is not brought up as an indictment of the schools. Rather, it is an indictment of the states' ability or willingness to properly fund the education of its citizens. As mentioned previously, parents have seemingly accepted the present burden. It will be interesting to see what happens when schools do, in fact, find that they must pass on the costs of textbooks to the parents. We hasten to add at this point that anything that is the fault, or due to the delinquency, of the state actually illustrates the arguments that we have put forward in previous sections of this book: The citizenry of the state, of the country, has failed to identify who we are as a people, where we want to go, and what we want of the schools so that we can move in that direction. In the context of our current topic, however, it exemplifies why the states (who *are* responsible for the education of their citizens) may not be the best stewards of the educational enterprise.

So, it may also be the case that while the states' responsibility for funding education favors the notion of their then having control over education, it could also be the case that the funding of education at the hands of the state represents a rather obvious limiting factor when we look at the national picture. Likewise, the amount expended by local and state agencies varies considerably. For instance, in 1997–1998, some states (Indiana, Iowa, Michigan, Texas, Utah, and Wisconsin) allocated approximately 40 percent of their funds to education. The District of Columbia allocated about 17 percent, and Hawaii and Alaska slightly less than 25 percent. Three states (Connecticut, New Jersey, and New York) and the District of Columbia spent more than $10,000 per student in average daily attendance in 2000–2001. At the other end of the spectrum, Utah spent less than $5,000 per student in average daily attendance (NCES, 2003). It is important to remember that with increased public focus on education, the numbers (although not necessarily the ranks) may change.

In any case, there are gross financial disparities between some schools and others. It is easy to recognize, for instance, that a state that leaves education financing to its local education agencies will see significant differences in the amounts of money provided to the "rich" districts (those with a strong tax base because of industry, technology, tourism, etc.) and "poor" districts (those in predominantly inner-city or rural areas). Thus, the case can be made for a state's funding all of its schools, at least at a basic level. In fact, the U.S. Supreme Court has ruled that the absence of significant state funding across the board may unconstitutionally deprive students of equal educational opportunities. A relevant case is *San Antonio v. Rodriguez*, which has resulted in a number of lawsuits in which the courts have required that the financial resources of the state be distributed more equitably among its school districts (Henkoff, 1991).

From a broader perspective, the same concept applies across the country. Some states, for instance, are far wealthier than others; thus, the students in some states have far greater access to financial support than do their cohorts in other states.

Of course, this argument also applies at the microlevel, the individual school district. Within any school system, there are schools with many affluent parents, involved business partners, and active parent volunteers eager to engage in fund-raising activities. Just a few miles away, there are schools with little or no family involvement in school activities and no discernible tax base. The case can just as easily be made that these latter schools are unable to provide equal educational opportunities. While our purpose here is not to debate the relative merits of various funding formulas, you may still wish to raise some issues related to this topic and consider them from time to time. You will find that there are no easy answers.

The Nation

Perhaps ironically—or, more likely, paradoxically—the same civic argument that we made as favoring state control of education can be made for national control, or at least for a national emphasis in education. That is, we are a *nation*, and it is a legitimate expectation that an education in this nation should be characterized by those things that bind us together as such. Particularly in the context of "global communities," international commerce, and international competition, Americans are seen by the rest of the world as members of a nation rather than as individuals from one state or another within the nation. And so, perhaps to a greater extent than ever before, our local, regional, and state isolationism may need to give way to a greater emphasis on our national culture and identity. And this would not be without precedent.

In chapter 3, we briefly mentioned the 1957 launch of the Soviet satellite Sputnik, which was part of the impetus toward reform in science and math education in the United States. Actually, the launch of Sputnik was the final straw. The U.S. military, which does testing of enlistees, had already noticed during World War II and the Korean conflict that young American men were woefully lacking in mathematic skills and science literacy. The streaking of Sputnik across the sky served as the exclamation point. The federal government became a major player in funding academic-reform initiatives and, subsequently, hosts of programs in education as part of the 1958 National Defense Education Act. The federal government did not take over public education by any means, but it did become a dominant influence by virtue of the strings attached to the funds made available to the states. Nonetheless, it was in the name of national interests, specifically *national defense*, that this precedent was set.

The frenzy with federally funded curriculum-reform initiatives has long since subsided. But now, a number of federal departments contribute funds, products, or services to the public schools. These include the U.S. Departments of Education, Health and Human Services, Agriculture, Labor, Defense, and Energy. In fiscal year 2001, it is estimated that the federal government spent $92.8 billion on education. A total of $36.8 billion (approximately 40 percent of that total) came from the Department of Education. Another $19.5 billion came from Health and Human Services, and $11 billion from Agriculture.

Of the $92.8 billion total, $48.7 billion was allocated for elementary and secondary education institutions, $15.3 billion for postsecondary institutions (e.g., colleges, universities, technical institutes, community colleges), $22.8 billion for research (mainly at educational institutions), and $6 billion for other programs. Many entitlement programs and programs that provide special services to children (for instance, by virtue of the Individuals with Disabilities Education Act) are funded by the federal government. So, from an economic perspective, it can easily be argued that the federal government already has a very significant involvement in public education, even though it remains the responsibility of the individual states. In fact, expenditures from the federal budget for education ranks fourth after defense, interest on the national debt, and welfare.

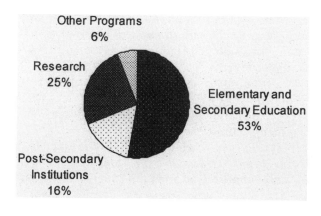

Figure 6.1. Distribution of Federal Expenditures for Education

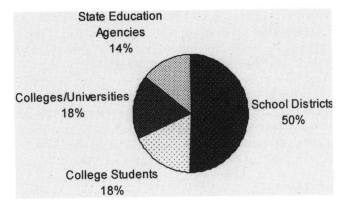

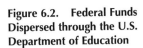

Figure 6.2. Federal Funds Dispersed through the U.S. Department of Education

Of the $36.8 billion distributed by the Department of Education, $17.6 billion (about one-half) went to school districts, $6.2 billion to college students, $6.1 billion to institutions of higher learning, $4.9 billion to state education agencies, and small amounts to subsidize student loans.

As you can tell, we're talking about a lot of money. After being adjusted for inflation, the amount of federal funding for education increased 56 percent from 1985 to 2001 (NCES, 2001). In 1993–1994, 33 percent of public school students (30 percent of elementary students, 22 percent of secondary students) received free or discounted lunch (NCES, 2001). If you were not one of those students, did you get anything free in your lunch? Could you buy the same lunch in town for the price you paid at school? Of course not. The federal government subsidizes school lunches for *everyone* by providing surplus farm products to the lunchroom program. That's a $9.5 billion contribution by the Department of Agriculture identified above.

Approximately 13 percent of elementary and secondary education students received Title I services in 1993–1994 (NCES, 2001). These services (about $8.5 billion worth) were provided by the Department of Education to students with low levels of achievement (according to standardized tests) in schools with high concentrations of families with low incomes.

The second largest amount of money from the Department of Education ($5.8 billion) was allocated for special education services. In 1999–2000, those funds helped to serve over six million people between birth and the age of twenty-one. (Notice that this figure includes people before the age of school entry and after their departure.)

A third source of funds was $3.3 billion for school-improvement efforts. If your school was engaged in such an effort, you might have been aware of it. However, it is altogether possible that you really were not aware that faculty were being (re)trained or that special programs were being implemented.

Another $1.7 billion was provided for vocational and adult education. Some of your classmates, for example, may have dropped out of school and later obtained a General Equivalency Degree, or GED, instead of a high school diploma. Some of those people attend college and do very well when their circumstances are altered.

The Department of Health and Human Services provides $6.2 billion for the Head Start program, one of the most popular education endeavors of the federal government.

The Department of Labor administers a number of training programs involving education. These programs, funded for $4.2 billion in fiscal year 2001, include training under the School-to-Work Opportunities Act. This act is intended to help bridge the gap between education and the workplace and has strong support among business-people, who have long complained about the lack of preparedness of many of the new members of their workforces. Smaller amounts are expended for a myriad of other federal programs. They range in scope from Indian education, to bilingual education, to the construction of educational facilities, to the Junior Reserve Officers' Training Corps.

With the funding of programs comes the set of regulations under which they operate. Politicians are spending your money, and they want assurances that the expenditures yield results. So, there are regulations and still more regulations. If schools want the money (and they actually can decline it, as private schools often do), they must accept stewardship of the money, develop plans for using it in a way the law intended it to be used, and then document expenditures and uses of the funds and the resulting benefits.

Curriculum: the question of what is to be taught in schools. Of the three topics we are discussing in the context of controlling the institution of education (civic perspectives, funding, and curriculum), curriculum may be the most divisive. Economics, of course, is not so much divisive as it is another exercise in control.

At this point, you know that the fundamental issue in education is its institutional basis and that as an institution of our society, it is confounded by a failure to articulate our civic identity. That failure leads to the economic-control issues that have resulted in the spending of billions of dollars (begrudgingly, perhaps) on education, yet with the establishment of an infrastructure of widely varying quality from school to school, district to district, and state to state. The infrastructure problems manifest themselves in terms of facilities, some of which are far beyond the needs of a public school while others are outright health hazards in which no child should be expected to remain throughout the day. All of this, however, confounds the development of a meaningful curriculum. Interestingly enough, it is in examination of the problems in curriculum that we can see our other problems. Unfortunately, we keep missing the message.

Does It Matter?

Yes, locus of control matters. It matters in terms of equity in funding, the building and maintenance of appropriate facilities, and the perpetuation of our cultural values,

---

Activity 6.1.
WHO'S IN CONTROL?

The debate over whether there should be national or state control of public education has gone on for a long time. There are many who adamantly oppose allowing the federal government to take control of education because it would turn education into an even greater bureaucracy with an even more homogenized curriculum. Others argue that "public" in public education refers to our national identity.

What is your position?

1. Should the locus of control for a new institution of education rest with the federal government, state government, or some other arrangement?
2. What would be the tax consequences of shifting control of public education to the federal government?
3. Ask three of your friends or colleagues to respond to questions 1 and 2. What sort of patterns in thinking do you find?

beliefs, and identity. And the curriculum, as a reflection of our national character, is the key. It is the topic around which we must come together to face our issues, it is the flag around which a nation can then rally, and it is then the blueprint by which our culture can prosper. So, in the next section, as we look at the revolutionizing of the institution, and considering the collaborative role that state and federal influences might play (as opposed to taking an either/or perspective), we will *begin* with the curriculum.

A NEW COLLABORATIVE FOR A NEW INSTITUTION

The sovereignty of the states and the broad diversity of the nation preclude the possibility of a national curriculum being developed in isolation by either of the two entities. What's more, a curriculum written by either a state or the federal government is one that necessarily foists compromise (at best) on the other. For example, a curriculum from the federal government is almost certain to slight one state or another simply because there is not enough time in the day to provide a thorough treatment of the history and contributions of every state. A state-based curriculum would similarly be expected to emphasize that state's culture to the neglect of the perspectives of other states. Curriculum development, therefore, must be a collaborative effort not only between each state and the federal government but between the *states* as well.

To accomplish this, we will need a new organizational structure with a shared vision. It would make sense, after all, to begin the building of a new institution with a new approach to design, and our suggestion would be the Education Congress of the States (ECS). We see this as an opportunity for the states, the nation, and the instructional materials industry as well.

The Education Congress of the States: Foundation for a New Institution

The Education Congress of the States will be the guiding body for public education in the United States with primary responsibilities for the development and dissemination of the common curriculum (see the 622 Curriculum below) and policy matters in that regard, the sponsorship and dissemination of educational research, and data analysis and reporting based upon standardized examinations of student achievement; it will also serve as a forum for educational debate and development. Established by virtue of a constitutional amendment, the ECS should be housed in a permanent facility, most likely located in the nation's capitol, and will meet *as a full congress* annually through its first four years of existence and biennially thereafter. Telecommunications and electronic technology make it unnecessary to invoke the expense of meetings of the full congress on a yearly basis.

The daily work of the ECS will be accomplished by full-time staff recruited from outstanding educators across the country who will serve three-year, nonrenewable terms. Ideally, these will be teachers who would then return to teaching in their home districts or collaboratives (note: collaboratives are discussed later in this chapter). Our suggestion would also be to impose term limits on the delegates. The reason is simple: Delegates to the ECS should serve as education professionals and not as "politicians." When delegates begin to be concerned about whether they can be reelected or reappointed, the emphasis tends to shift, as we know of institutional entities, to self-preservation.

The national conferences will be funded by the federal government (travel, lodging, conference expenses) through the U.S. Department of Education, which shall be charged with this responsibility. Permanent staff and compensation for officers elected from within the congress will be supported by the federal government. Compensation of delegates to the congress will be the responsibility of the states.

Composition of the Congress

The Education Congress of the States shall be composed of a minimum of five delegates from each state, U.S. district, possession, or territory. The participation of these five delegates in the work of the ECS when the congress is in session will be sponsored by the federal government. All states may provide additional delegates to the ECS, though support must be provided by the state.

With regard to the five official delegates to the ECS, each must hold current and valid teaching credentials in the state they represent. Because the establishment of the ECS would precede possible changes in the administrative structure of schools, individuals holding a valid education-administration credential, but who do not have teaching responsibilities at the time of their service, may be named as delegates. However, at least three of the official delegates of the state must hold a teaching credential and have, during the term of representation, classroom teaching assignments (though, at the discretion of the state, these responsibilities could be reduced to no less than a half-day teaching load).

All districts/collaboratives within a state will identify an educator to serve as the liaison between the school and the ECS delegation. These individuals could also represent constituencies beyond the public school. Each state could choose to support the participation of these representatives at the meetings of the ECS, though their participation would be as nonvoting delegates.

State departments of education would, under the current system, be the logical choice for providing the mechanism to identify delegates and for facilitating their work. However, the ECS delegation *would not* represent an arm of the state department of education or be seen as the voice of the department in affairs of the congress. Clearly, if a state department were to direct the delegates, we would have nothing more than the institution attempting to preserve itself. We do not make this point as an indictment of state departments of education but simply as a reminder that our intent is to abandon the myth of reform. It would be to a state's credit if the activities of the department were in concert with the activities of the congress; after all, the goal is to put a system of excellence in place. Even more impressive would be to see state departments of education looking to the ECS delegation for guidance.

In all voting matters, each of the five official delegates will be entitled to one vote. Delegates will be expected to vote as educational professionals and, so, will not be required to vote as a state. This is a crucial point because the intent of the ECS is to find a collaborative voice that represents the interests of the states and the nation in an environment dedicated to building a shared vision rather than perpetuating special interests.

Constitutional Amendments

Revolutionizing our public education system, unlike the reform approach that has prevailed for so long, will require substantial commitments from many of the stakeholders involved. In the case of educational reform, there has never been any real consequence, other than perhaps a financial one, for beginning, continuing, or terminating an initiative. That aspect of "reform" is what has made it so well suited to an institution: Reforms come and go and the institution remains largely unchanged. Actually changing the institution, however, will require abandoning the myth of reform. And so, having the weight of a constitutional amendment behind it is a primary distinction between a reform and a revolution.

One of the major indicators of whether or not our society takes this matter on as a legitimate national obligation will be through the passage of, or failure to pass, a constitutional amendment (or amendments) specifically addressing education. Let us hasten to add that a constitutional amendment does not mean that responsibility for education is shifted to the federal government. In fact, our suggestion is simply to make explicit the shared responsibility of the states and the federal government. As you know, the Constitution presently makes the implicit statement that education is the responsibility of the individual states.

You may have noticed that in the previous paragraph, we alluded to the possibility of more than one amendment. Admittedly, it is difficult enough to propose, pass, and ratify one amendment, let alone making multiple additions. And that is as it should be. The Constitution is not something that should be easily changed. It is a testament to its strength that after more than two hundred years, there are only twenty-seven amendments.

However, we would argue that there are at least two issues that are so pervasive and so fundamental that they are worthy of amendment status. One, establishing the Education Congress of the States and delineating the shared responsibility for education between the states and the federal government, is arguably the easier of the two since it is essentially a clarification of the Tenth Amendment. The other, establishing an official language for the United States, is likely the more controversial of the two.

Establishing the Education Congress of the States and Acknowledging the Shared Responsibility for Education   The Education Congress of the States and its specific charge should come into being by virtue of a constitutional amendment if a *rebuilding* of our educational system is the aim. Such an amendment would indicate the following:

1. A system for the education of children and young adults in the United States at public expense is seen as integral to the social prosperity of a free and democratic people.
2. Such a system is the shared responsibility of the federal government and the individual states.
3. The Education Congress of the States is established as a collaborative entity among the states for the development, dissemination, administration, and review of educational policy, practice, and curriculum in the United States.
4. The Congress of the United States shall pass no law that imposes policy, ideology, or sanction on the activities of the ECS so long as the ECS remains a duly constituted body representing the majority opinion of its state delegate constituencies.

The activities of the ECS, as mentioned previously, shall include:

1. service as the guiding body for public education in the United States with primary responsibilities for development and dissemination of the common curriculum
2. consideration of policy matters in the development of such a curriculum

3. sponsorship and dissemination of educational research, as well as data analysis and reporting based upon standardized examinations of student achievement
4. service as a forum for educational debate and development

The Education Congress of the States would not supplant the U.S. Department of Education or assume the roles currently performed by that agency. The U.S. Department of Education would, however, work collaboratively with the ECS rather than in the "us and them" arrangement that we presently see between the federal agency and state governments. In fact, the intention of this organizational structure is to make the work of the U.S. Department of Education and the public school system far more effective, efficient, and economical. The Education Congress of the States would have the particular charge of defining and maintaining a shared vision of excellence for education in this country.

An Official Language   Either as a stand-alone amendment or as a compromise embedded in the Education Congress of the States amendment, we believe the time has come for the United States to identify its official language. It has been suggested much earlier in this work that our society has a multiethnic nature and that, as a people, we are willing to assimilate those ethnicities into a single culture. Language, however, is the means by which those in a society communicate with one another.

It is possible to label foods and products and to put up aisle markers and menus in local businesses using multiple languages. But even here, there is a limit to how many languages can be represented. More importantly, it is prohibitive for the infrastructure of a society—street signs and highway markers, official forms and documents, monetary systems—to be routinely represented in multiple languages. At the very least, the argument about using such signage demonstrates the fact that, at some point, it would have to be determined how great a critical mass, in terms of the population using a given language, is required before a language will be added to the list. If, ultimately, we are willing to establish a minimum population figure for including additional languages in education and commerce, would that not beg the question as to why we did not simply adopt a common language for the nation?

Activity 6.2.
AN OFFICIAL LANGUAGE FOR THE UNITED STATES

As you can imagine, as time goes by, it becomes increasingly difficult for the United States to adopt an official language.

1. What is your position on the notion of adopting an official language? List five reasons in favor of doing so, and then try listing five reasons why it would not be a good idea.
2. Take the time to write a polite letter to your state legislators and to your federal congressmen and senators. Ask each of them for their reasons in support of, or opposition to, establishing an official language for the United States.
3. If you favor the idea of a constitutional amendment, research the process for putting such an effort in motion. What is required to accomplish proposing and passing an amendment?

The issue of a common language is elemental for any society. It is, indeed, among the defining characteristics of the social system. Yet, whether Americans, even now in the twenty-first century, are prepared to commit to an official language remains to be seen. It would seem, however, that nothing short of a constitutional amendment would give such action legitimacy.

There is another possibility, though it still would include an amendment. That would be to include the identification of an official language as part of the constitutional amendment establishing the Education Congress of the States. In essence, such an amendment would at least mandate the language of public education in the United States. Such a compromise would enable the process of education to proceed as a nationalizing exercise and clear the way for programs that seek to teach that language to children for whom it would be a second language, yet would not be seen as an effort to "outlaw" or subordinate other languages.

In any event, whatever the American culture is ultimately determined to be, its existence will depend upon the ability of people within that culture to communicate with each other.

The First Meeting of the Education Congress of the States

It will be necessary that the ECS discuss four topics in particular at its first meeting: election of a governing board from among the delegates; bylaws for the governance of the congress; the design, implementation, and assessment of a common curriculum (see the 622 Curriculum below) model; and the American culture. It is not anticipated that all of these issues will be resolved in the first meeting of the congress, but rather that the discussions will be initiated and decisions made about how to pursue the topics to conclusion.

Because it is our purpose here to suggest rather than to prescribe, we will not attempt to detail what organizational structure the ECS might embrace or to outline the bylaws that might be adopted. These are matters to be addressed by the individuals who serve as delegates. However, the recurring questions about the American culture and a framework for curriculum have been consistent themes throughout this book and, so, are topics that should be addressed in the context of the Education Congress of the States.

The American Culture Discussion   If defining the American culture simply required bringing a couple of hundred people together for a two- or three-day conference, then it is possible that the task would have been accomplished long ago. To this point in your reading, you may have come to terms with your own definition of the American culture, but if you've tried it out on more than just a few close friends, you've probably found that there are many different perspectives. So, we do not suggest here that the Education Congress of the States could convene one time and get the matter hammered out.

They could, however, come to the understanding that a clearly articulated statement of the American culture will be the cornerstone, if not the foundation, of a curriculum designed to serve the needs and interests of a nation. With that in mind, it will be the responsibility of the congress to determine how best to address this task. Remember, the statement that the congress ultimately adopts will be a public statement. There is not likely to be unanimous agreement throughout the country on this (maybe someday, but certainly not to begin with), but the perspective that the congress identifies will have to be something that represents well who we are and who we aspire to become as a people. Though the delegates to the congress will be in regular communication with each other throughout the year, it is the magnitude of this project, along with discussions of curriculum design, that will require annual meetings through the first four years of the Education Congress of the States. You should be a participant in that process.

Curriculum Design, Implementation, and Assessment It is our suggestion that a meaningful curriculum cannot be designed without a clear understanding of who we are as a people. However, the congress could immediately begin, from at least two perspectives, an analysis of the curricula that exist. The first perspective would be to consider curricular frameworks and the intent of a curriculum. This discussion is apart from the actual content to be taught in schools. Rather, it is a discussion of how to structure what is to be taught and what purposes various structures might serve. Below, we describe one possibility: the 622 Curriculum Model. There are, however, multiple approaches that can be considered, such as the explicit curriculum (the subjects actually taught), the implicit curriculum (the additional messages of school, such as cooperation, competition, character/citizenship), the null curriculum (those things that are intentionally left out of a curriculum), and even the extracurriculum. It is our intent that the 622 Curriculum Model will eliminate the need for, or at least the presence of, an implicit and a null curriculum by building in the possibilities for alternative perspectives on subjects and by making plain what the curriculum is intended to accomplish. Neither of those conditions is clearly addressed in contemporary curricula.

The second perspective is to analyze what is (or isn't) being taught in contemporary curricula around the country. From this analysis, a clear picture would likely emerge that addresses what we refer to as the "common curriculum" in the 622 Model. It is also likely that regional emphases and topics worthy of broader consideration would emerge.

Obviously, these two perspectives could be investigated at the same time by different task groups within the congress. It would be at that first meeting, however, that the initial goals and objectives of such investigations were determined.

As a final comment with regard to the Education Congress of the States, let us emphasize that we do not see this as a deliberative body, an "all-knowing" body. That is, the expectation would be that the delegates to the congress have the specific charge of seeking out information and opinions from all stakeholders in the educational enterprise, and that could include children and young adults in school as well. But certainly, parents, legislators, taxpayers who are not parents, and the interests of business and commerce must be represented in the work of the congress. It is for that purpose that the congress will be established: that its members may be investigators, deliberators, decision makers, and initiators of action.

The 622 Curriculum Model

The 622 Curriculum that we propose, if only as a point of departure, provides the ECS with a structure that can address national cohesiveness while recognizing regional and state perspectives. Though it may be a tough pill to swallow, we would suggest that the greatest portion of the curriculum (60 percent) be allocated toward a national, or "common," curriculum because, in our increasingly global economy, our collective identity is in terms of the United States and not in terms of a single state within the nation. The 622 structure, however, allocates 40 percent of the curriculum to regional

(20 percent) and state (20 percent) concerns, and since much of the common curriculum is found throughout the nation already, to a significant degree the 622 format may
be allocating even more time to regional and state perspectives.

Structure: A Curriculum for the Culture

In the 622 Model, curriculum is considered in three contexts: the common curriculum, which reflects a national orientation; the regional curriculum, which could, for
example, represent larger territories within the nation, such as the Northeast, South-
west, West Coast (the noncontiguous states and territories may either be considered in
a single category or subdivided as appropriate); and the state curriculum, which may
specifically address the history, heritage, and economy of individual states. Taken together, the intent of the 622 Curriculum structure attempts to find agreement about
that which all citizens of the United States should know and be capable of doing, while
providing states and regions opportunities to expand the curriculum—and perhaps
even dissent on some points in an academically defensible manner.

The Common Curriculum   It is not our intent to write out the curriculum in any one
of the three components of the 622 structure. That is the work that must be done by
the ECS in cooperation with the people they represent. We can, however, provide an
outline of what such a curriculum might look like (in particular, see chapter 8).

The common curriculum portion of the 622 structure would emphasize those studies
that all children in the United States should complete. Among these would be the reading, writing, and speaking of standard English (or whatever language or version of language the Educational Congress of the States shall identify as the language of the United
States), as well as mathematics, science, U.S. and world geography, other languages,
world and national history, American government, and the pragmatics of citizenship.

At this time, the United States has not designated an official language. As mentioned
in the previous section of this chapter, "The Education Congress of the States: Foundation for a New Institution," a constitutional amendment that accomplishes this
(whatever language may be chosen) is a critical first step in a detailed and long-lasting
approach to curriculum design. There can be no lack of consensus on this point: A nation needs a language. In the absence of such a decision, curriculum design is destined
to continue as little more than a game. For too long, we have taken the easy way around
this issue by simply refusing to address the matter.

As a nation, we have demonstrated a distinct lack of vision, something that the
founders of this nation seemed to have in abundance. Social scientists will argue that
the failure of a people to share a common language is a key ingredient for civil war. We
do not make these comments as an attack on programs for nonnative speakers of English, though adopting an official language may well lead to a new approach for providing a higher quality of education to students across the board. This will be a tough
sell, but it will also be an early and significant indicator of our ability as a nation to
revolutionize education.

The Regional Curriculum   Determining what constitutes "regional" could be determined within or across states. The states of the Northeast, for example, may wish to collaborate with regard to issues that would impact the region, whereas states such as
Alaska, California, and Texas may want to identify regions within their state. In any event,
the regional aspect of the curriculum is intended to afford a narrower focus than that provided in the common curriculum but a broader focus than specific state interests.

Programs for nonnative speakers of English would likely be considered as part of the regional curriculum, as could programs for the teaching of additional languages. With the adoption of an official language, schools could provide programs that teach the official language to nonnative speakers for at least 20 percent of the school day (and up to 40 percent if the state portion of the curriculum were used as well). Students who are native speakers of the official language could spend this 20 percent of the day in programs for learning additional languages. In either case, the emphasis could be on becoming conversant in the language rather than trying to accomplish all things at once, as has been the attempt of bilingual education programs. There is not as much an issue with "falling behind" because electronic technologies make the grade-level approach obsolete. Scheduling of students across "achievement levels" by subject should be easy to accomplish.

The State Curriculum   The state portions of the 622 Model offer flexibility for attending to topics and issues of more selective importance. Though the common curriculum will be derived from the standards recommended by learned societies, the states, and districts within states, there are those who may take issue with some of the topics. The teaching of evolution is an obvious example. Evolution as a scientific explanation for the development and extinction of species is among the standards of the National Science Teachers Association, which are derived from the work of the National Research Council under the advisement of the American Association for the Advancement of Science. However, feelings run deep about the teaching of evolution in a number of states around the country. The portion of the 622 Curriculum apportioned to the state can be used, if it is so desired, to teach alternative explanations to the theory of evolution.

Topics of particular interest for a given state, job orientation to the major industries of that state, or even visionary approaches for preparing students for a global community could be addressed as part of the state's portion of the curriculum. Programs in the fine and performing arts could easily find a home here in the state portion of the curriculum.

Testing and Accountability

Students would be held accountable for all topics included in the common curriculum, but we emphasize that the common curriculum represents what people should know (which does not necessarily mean "believe") in a national and global society. States may just as legitimately expect students to be able to intelligently demonstrate knowledge of alternative perspectives on topics, such as in our evolution example, and to require such demonstration as part of their graduation requirements. In fact, as we express in several sections of this work, students (and schools) should be held accountable as part of graduation requirements for *everything* that is contained in the curriculum. Anything included in the curriculum, but considered "expendable" with regard to testing, should be eliminated. Now don't get upset! This doesn't mean that everything has to be tested—that would be impractical—but everything that represents a planned educational experience is subject to testing. If this criterion cannot be met, then the presence of the activity should be questioned. However, if the schools are responsible for teaching character traits and cooperative attitudes (often thought of as the implicit curriculum), then some assessment of results of these activities must be accomplished.

Activity 6.3.
THE MODEL IN GENERAL

Suppose a new institution of education were to adopt a 622 Curriculum Model (you can substitute a different model if you like). In general, what would be the essential topics that you would allot to each of the curriculum divisions?

Common Curriculum: What do you believe all students in American schools should learn and/or study?

Regional Curriculum: How would you divide the United States (or even individual states) in terms of regions? If you'd like, just consider your own "region" for now. What topics or issues do you see as important for students in your region to study?

State Curriculum: The final 20 percent of the curriculum is dedicated to state issues. What issues or topics do you believe are important for students in your state to study?

Standardized testing programs would monitor the progress of the student population to identify strengths and weaknesses by nation, region, and state. Data regarding trends on these three levels would be communicated to the states. Responsibility would be assumed at the state level for evaluating performance at the district and school level. Districts/schools failing to achieve could transition into a common curriculum improvement phase that bracketed the underperforming grade levels so that students who were failing to meet the standards would receive additional instruction, and the students would be better prepared coming into the problematic course levels. If the new institution were to adopt the 622 Curriculum Model we have discussed previously, it would be possible to target specific levels in need of attention rather than labeling entire grade levels. The additional time necessary for academic improvement programs would be derived first from the regional emphasis portion of the 622 Model and then, as necessary, from the state portion. If both the regional and state portions were based on the use of electronic instructional materials, the transition to a common curriculum emphasis would be of limited difficulty. Similarly, as student achievement in the common curriculum improved, transitioning back to regional and state emphasis would be readily accomplished.

The 622 Curriculum is a starting point. We don't claim that there is anything magical about this apportionment of the curriculum but simply that the *common curriculum*, which represents the curriculum that will be presented to all students in U.S. public schools, should constitute the greatest portion of the overall course of study. Allotting 20 percent to regional study provides the opportunity for addressing large-scale characteristics of geographical regions. And, perhaps most importantly, the 20 percent of the curriculum left to the discretion of the states can allow for either in-depth study of topics or values characteristic of the state or an opportunity to provide alternative views to topics included in the common curriculum, or both.

FINAL THOUGHTS

There is one more notion that needs to be raised in this chapter. Just as you would not try to do repairs to your car while traveling down the highway at seventy miles per hour, it is not reasonable to expect that the schools could be revolutionized all at once and for everybody at the same time. It simply won't work: Consider the litany of failed reform attempts as your evidence of this fact.

The substantive, systemic revolutionizing of public education will require the sacrifice of a generation. We'll give you just a moment to get over that. Okay, just as we indicated early in this book that "revolution" is not necessarily as nasty a word as one might at first think, the same could be said of "sacrifice." We do not suggest an entire generation of students will be tossed aside and given a patently inferior education, but it is the case that we, as a society, will have to decide where the revolution will begin— some students will be on one side of that starting point and others will be on the far side. This will be discussed in greater detail in chapter 8, but now is the time to start thinking about it.

Two issues will have to be addressed in the development of the new institution. The first will be the manner in which the new institution will come to replace the old. The second will be how to persevere through the lengthy process of change. We have never said that this would be an easy process, let alone an easy sell.

It is evident that there is a problem with public education in the United States. "Pretty good" should not be our standard of excellence. That it *can* be changed is evident. The question is really one of whether it will change because we see that it must be so or because we allow the system to collapse (from internal or external forces) and then have no choice but to rebuild. As we look at the world today, we have to wonder whether we would ultimately give up a voice in the rebuilding as well if we were to await a collapse. So, to bring this chapter to a close, we leave you with the words of Rabbi Hillel: If not you, who? If not now, when?

7

Logistics of the New Institution

Excellent schools are transparent in their operation and intellectual in their purpose, which makes them legitimate in the eyes of their constituencies.

—John Merrow

So, let's begin thinking in terms of a new institution. What changes could be made that would redefine what we know of as "school"? You may recall that in chapter 3 we discussed a number of characteristics, dividing them into the categories of institutional, administrative, and political. For this discussion, we have broadened the categories just a bit. In chapter 8, we will take a closer look at curriculum in particular.

Some of these ideas may strike you as very "doable," while others may seem just a trifle outlandish (wait a minute, can there be such a thing as a "trifle" outlandish?). In any event, take these thoughts as starting points and pursue them to whatever ends you can conceive of as the institution is fashioned into something new and effective.

Each of the categories that we discuss in this chapter could be developed as chapters themselves. We have tried to be brief, but, nonetheless, with seven topics this chapter is a lengthy one. To make it a bit more manageable, we have divided the chapter into two parts. In Part I, "People and the Institution," we address the roles that people play within the institution: national and local perspectives, organizational concerns, professional considerations, and parental responsibility. In Part II, "Issues and Decisions for the New Institution," we will discuss issues that relate to decisions that must be made about school: financial considerations, electronic technologies, and physical facilities.

PART I: PEOPLE AND THE INSTITUTION

NATIONAL AND LOCAL PERSPECTIVES

As we have discussed at length, it would seem that the new institution must accomplish the very difficult task of providing an education for the nation while maintaining a local perspective. In practice, this will require some strong commitments from politicians, parents, and educators, among others, but ideologically it is not really a stretch. In a very real sense, it is obvious.

There are at least two ways to approach the situation. One would be for the federal government, representing the national interests, to assume responsibility for public education and to essentially dictate to the local level just how things will be done. We see this happening already as the various federally funded entitlement programs and, of course, the No Child Left Behind Act threaten the states and local districts with the possibility of losing federal dollars if they don't toe the line. There can be few arguments in favor of such an approach (there are many excuses for it, but few arguments on its behalf).

The other approach is for the local level to adopt a measure of national perspective as part and parcel of what it means to be American. This, of course, again returns us to the necessity of identifying who we are as a culture and where we want to go, but we would argue that it is because people have tried so hard to *avoid* this exercise that we find ourselves in this predicament to begin with! A common curriculum exists to one degree or another already. In fact, an examination of that curriculum may be a useful first step in the broader task of defining the culture.

ORGANIZATIONAL CONCERNS

The business model of top-down administration has been used in public education since early in the nineteenth century. Based on Frederick Taylor's work in *scientific management*, it has become a part of the institution. Unfortunately, this approach has made the institution top-heavy with administrators and administrative salaries and kept teachers—who are required to hold college degrees and state credentials and to take part in continued professional education—to a level not quite as elevated as "mid-management."

But education is not a business. It does not operate with the intent of earning financial profits for its stockholders. And any attempt to refer to children and young adults as so many "products" is offensive to most people. Nor does education enjoy the recourse that a business entity might avail itself of in times of need. Schools cannot just shut down for a while to retool. They cannot do a bit of market research and simply change the curriculum from one month to the next in response. Schools can order textbooks, provide bus transportation, or expand their facilities only after lengthy approval processes at the local, district, and state levels. Schools do not have the option of telling a parent that his or her child is unable to learn or that the child is too disruptive to keep in class (without extended expulsion hearings). No, schools are enterprises, but they are not businesses. Any effort to substantively change the institution will have to address this particular point.

Building-Level Administration

We would like to suggest, first and foremost, that the business model of educational administration be eliminated. There is no justification for believing that the highest-paid individuals in an institution dedicated to teaching should be people who do not teach. And we certainly do not advocate the notion that the CEO of a school district (that is, the "chief educational officer") should be *anyone* other than a fully credentialed, *practicing* professional educator (that is, one with ongoing classroom teaching responsibilities).

The concept of top-down management in which legions of highly educated individuals are herded about by principals, assistant superintendents, and superintendents is completely out of place. There is no task done by an educational administrator that could not be performed as well by a properly prepared teacher doing an administrative rotation. And if our society is compelled for some reason to retain the antiquated and uninspired administrative structure that education now endures, then at the very least the power structure should be reversed so as to empower the educators and make all administrative positions into tasks that first and foremost support the activities of the educators.

We would maintain, however, that with the possible exception of tasks that are professions in and of themselves, such as accounting, all administrative positions within a public school should be held by teachers. All teachers hired to ongoing, nonprobationary contracts would at some time serve an administrative rotation in which that person's teaching load was reduced by approximately two-thirds. Teaching responsibilities would not be eliminated. We believe it is critical for those who perform administrative duty to be regular participants in the classroom experience.

The elimination of "principal" positions would immediately free up considerable amounts of money for use within each school building. Teachers on administrative rotation would be paid a stipend for the increased responsibility that is assumed in an administrative capacity. They would also "work into" their administrative duties. For example, let's assume that administrative rotation is a three-year term. For each teacher in the rotation, the first year would be completed with the assistance of a mentor. During the second year, that teacher would assume full administrative responsibility for the school. In the third year, that teacher would mentor another teacher, beginning the first year of the rotation. In this way, the second-year teacher would always have an administrative partner who had been mentored by an individual who was just leaving the position. It might look something like this:

Year 1: Bob (first-year assistant)/Lesley (third-year mentor)—Chris (second-year lead teacher)

Year 2: Mary (first-year assistant)/Chris (third-year mentor)—Bob (second-year lead teacher)

Year 3: Emily (first-year assistant)/Bob (third-year mentor)—Mary (second-year lead teacher)

In this manner, each individual is involved with administrative matters of the school for a three-year period but, more than that, is mentored by a previous "principal" and serves as the mentor for an incoming principal. In this way, administrative continuity is maintained. Add into the equation the idea that principals will be charged with seeing that school policy is properly administered rather than establishing school policy, and you can see that the school will be well directed by individuals who keenly understand what is happening in terms of teaching and learning. Not a matter of charts or statistics. Not a matter of the child said this, the parent said this, the teacher said this. Instead, those doing the teaching—who have not been removed from that milieu—will be guiding the work of *colleagues* rather than *subordinates*. Indeed, when one speaks of teacher empowerment, this is what should come to mind.

Paraprofessionals

Schools have long relied upon community volunteers and "teacher's aides" to make the work of the classroom teacher more manageable. There can be no faulting the dedication of such individuals, for as volunteers their remuneration is entirely in terms of self-satisfaction for having made a contribution. For teacher aides, dedication to the cause must also be a high priority, for the salary, if there is one, is typically very low.

The unfortunate result, however, is that something that may have been done at one time to alleviate a particular problem has now become a standard practice in schools throughout the nation. The qualifications for serving as a volunteer or as an aide are little more than an enthusiastic nature and perhaps a high school diploma. Again, we do not fault these folks in the slightest degree, and there certainly have been exemplary volunteer programs in many schools. However, we do fault an institution that has willingly accepted the efforts of such individuals rather than accepting the responsibility for funding more teachers to meet the workload (research indicates that class sizes below fifteen students show significant gains in achievement) or providing a paraprofessional level of credentialed teacher assistants.

An individual who has completed a rigorous, two-year associate's degree as an education paraprofessional would be a valuable resource in a professionally operated system of public education. Such an individual could be assigned specific duties either within a particular grade level, perhaps working in concert with all of the teachers on that level, or could be assigned to a "series" of teachers. In this case, the paraprofessional might work with a group of teachers, each representing a different grade level. Thus, the paraprofessional might work with some of the same children as they progressed from one grade to the next. This would provide children with special needs a consistency of instruction that is not possible across grade levels. The paraprofessional would also be able to lend true professional assistance to the classroom teacher because she would be able to advise teachers at each new level with regard to learning preferences, developmental abilities, and learning rates, for example, of the children with which she worked. The two educators would then be able to more appropriately tailor special learning opportunities for the children in question.

Even though it would be expected that paraprofessionals would be paid less than certified classroom teachers, funding is not out of the question. At the very least, a cadre of appropriately educated teaching assistants would save money in terms of avoiding duplication of services and providing a higher quality of service without the need for experienced-based ("on-the-job") training. Further, if the new institution were to embrace an education-based model rather than a business-based model of administration, many positions could be filled with the money saved on administrative salaries. For example, if we figure that there are approximately 4.5 million public school teachers staffing the approximately ninety thousand public schools in our country, that averages out to about fifty teachers per school. Speculating that a well-prepared teaching assistant could be assigned to five teachers, which works out to ten paraprofessionals per school, it would not be unreasonable that the shift in administrative salaries could cover the salaries of at least three to five of those individuals.

A full-fledged paraprofessional program could open the opportunity for nine hundred thousand new credentialed education-oriented jobs in the nation. The work done by paraprofessionals could also be credited as an experiential education component of a program leading to certification as a professional educator (a teacher, that is, though in our new institution, *teacher* would be too antiquated a term to refer to the responsibilities that professional educators accept). This could also reap benefits for teacher-education programs because students coming to them for initial certification would do so with a solid foundation in education (from the associate's degree work) and viable experiences working with children (as opposed to the less structured, "as needed" involvement of volunteers and aides). Programs of teacher education could therefore become more rigorous as well, emphasizing an understanding of how children (and adults) learn rather than the mechanics of teaching, pursuing opportunities for individuals to become empowered as decision makers and educational administrators (in the context of the new institution) rather than staff members herded about by a principal, and most importantly of all, infusing innovation and facilitating inquiry and creativity into the development of children rather than finding ways to make it until Friday, or until testing is over, or until summer.

PROFESSIONAL CONSIDERATIONS

There are a number of issues that will need to be considered as we reconceptualize what it means to be a professional teacher in our country. Two of the prominent issues will be establishing teaching as a profession and teacher empowerment.

Is Teaching a Profession?

This may seem like an obvious question to you, but when considering just what constitutes a profession, it becomes apparent that there are questions about the status of teaching as being a true profession. What does it mean for something to be considered a profession? Typically, professions require specialized study and extensive training, and that is true of teacher education as well. Professions are also typically seen as occupations that require some sort of government credentialing process because they provide some sort of essential social service. That, too, is consistent with teaching. But driving a car requires specialized study, training, and governmental licensing, and yet, we would not say that it constitutes a profession.

The American Association of Colleges for Teacher Education (1976, 6–12) identified twelve characteristics of professions. Teaching matches up with most of them (the items we have already discussed being among the twelve), but there are five areas in particular where the notion of teaching being a profession comes into question:

1. The members of a profession are involved in the decision making in the service of the client.
2. The profession is organized into one or more professional associations that are granted autonomy in control of the actual work of the profession and the conditions that surround it.
3. The profession has agreed-upon performance standards for admission to the profession and continuance within it.
4. There is a high level of trust and confidence in the profession and in individual practitioners based on the profession's demonstrated capacity to provide service markedly beyond that which would otherwise be available.

5. There is relative freedom from direct on-the-job supervision and direct public evaluation of the individual practitioner: the professional accepts responsibility in the name of his or her profession and is accountable through his or her profession to the society.

Let's consider each of these items in turn. In our current institution, teachers are involved in decision making in a cursory manner. State legislators, officials in state departments of education, local school boards, district personnel, and the building principal all have priority over teachers when it comes to what, when, and how school is to be taught—and then there are parents whose influence can overturn decisions that teachers make within the classroom. Yet, individuals who complete a traditional program in teacher education are well educated and hold at least a baccalaureate degree in *addition to* licensing by their state's certification agency. The only way for a teacher to become a significant member of the decision-making or policy-making process is to leave teaching for administration or politics.

There are many teacher and/or administrative professional organizations in education. The largest of the generalized organizations (as opposed to subject-specific organizations) are the National Education Association, founded in 1857, and the American Federation of Teachers, a teacher's union established in 1916. Neither of these entities, however, is granted autonomy in control of the actual work of the profession and the conditions that surround it. Both organizations represent their memberships, advocate for education, and provide ongoing educational opportunities for teachers, but they do not exercise any authority over the institution of education. Similarly, the many state-level professional organizations represent their memberships and are advocates for education and educators, but their influence is advisory rather than their having the authority to make policy for education in a state.

We have recently been in a social cycle that is delirious over standards and accountability in education. Establishing curriculum standards, as you have found throughout this book, has been a difficult process simply because, as a nation, we do not know what we want the schools to accomplish. The immediate rush for specificity (standards) has pushed teaching toward an exercise in *training* rather than education. If you watch carefully over the next few years, you may notice a repeat of what education went through approximately fifty years ago in the same regard. In the late 1940s and 1950s, schools had become very much focused on the transfer of discrete bits of information from the teacher to the student. This emphasis on rote memorization, along with the burgeoning psychology of behaviorism and "teaching machines," eventually was swept aside in a movement against the factorylike approach to education that children were experiencing. In response to the launch of the Soviet satellite Sputnik in 1957, unprecedented funding went toward the improvement of math and science education in American schools. Trying to establish standards and holding students, teachers, and schools accountable for achievement have been at the core of the educational agenda ever since.

With particular regard to the work of teachers, the National Council for Accreditation of Teacher Education establishes standards for teacher-education programs; the Interstate New Teacher Assessment and Support Consortium has established expectations for beginning teachers; and the National Board for Professional Teaching Standards provides the opportunity for voluntary advanced certification of in-service teachers (this is an advanced certification, not a degree). Each organization has its own standards, principals, or propositions, but they have yet to be coalesced into a single set of expectations for the teaching profession.

One of the problems that educators face is that many people believe that because they have "gone to school," they know how to teach school. Few people would say that because they have flown on a plane, they are qualified to fly the plane. And few would say that because they have been ill at some time, they are qualified to be a physician. But many folks take a different perspective when it comes to teaching, especially if the person happens to be a parent. Yet, it is not uncommon for a principal to tell you that the way he or she works with students in a school is not necessarily reflective of how he or she behaves as a parent. And that is because teaching, working with other people's children, requires more than just a parental perspective. However, until educators can show a demonstrated capacity to provide service markedly beyond that which would otherwise be available, the impression that "anyone can teach" will thrive. The actions of legislatures and departments of education that allow alternative paths to teacher certification (a heavily funded initiative trying to gain ground today would require payment of a fee and passing a written test) perpetuate this perspective.

Despite the credentials that they hold, teachers represent the lowest rung of the professional ladder in a school. Interestingly, in many schools you will find that the teachers refer to the principal as Mr. or Ms. So-and-so rather than by first name. The work and conduct of teachers is monitored and directed on a daily basis. Certainly, when you consider that what goes on in school reaches the ears of parents in some version of the reality of the matter, you can understand that teachers are evaluated by supervisors and the public routinely. And it is these people, not a peer review board, to whom teachers must answer when a problem or issue arises.

Teacher Empowerment

If the institution of education is to change for the better, empowering teachers as professionals working in a professional capacity will be essential. It is incongruous to think that states license and certify individuals to be teachers but then turn to businesspeople and layman to tell them how to run the schools. On the other hand, we do not suggest that this is some sort of "magic wand" approach whereby teachers will suddenly be (1) empowered, and (2) worthy of such empowerment. There is work to be done on either side of this issue.

Because we are talking about approximately four million teachers, all of whom would be public employees (we are confining ourselves to public education), it is not reasonable to suggest that education could have an organization similar to the American Medical Association or the American Bar Association. Because this cadre does, typically, represent state employees, an organization of educators, perhaps an American Education Association (AEA), could legitimately be expected to exist in cooperation with some governmental agency. Obviously, our recommendation would be that the AEA operate as an arm of the Education Congress of the States (ECS), which would exist as an interstate coalition in collaboration with the federal government. It would, in essence, represent the profession of education.

The AEA, in concert with the Education Congress of the States, would take upon itself the task of establishing standards for teacher education and a code of ethics for teacher conduct, and it would be the review body for consideration of charges of misconduct or failure to perform appropriately. That is, the AEA would have the

---

Activity 7.1.
OPINIONS ABOUT TEACHER EMPOWERMENT

What do you think?

1. Should teachers become the primary players in the design of curriculum and the administrative aspects of school?
2. Should state governments shift their focus from the input of businesspeople in school affairs to a substantially greater input from classroom teachers?
3. Would the empowering of teachers with regard to broader responsibilities (and, of course, commensurate pay) as professional educators have any influence on the institution of education?

Ask these questions of parents, teachers, school administrators, and legislators (if possible). Are there any common threads among their responses? Does one group in particular favor or oppose the idea? What does that tell you?

---

responsibility of establishing the guidelines for admission to professional education and continuance within that role. The AEA and ECS would also be the organizations responsible for seeing that educators, with more than a token voice or vote, are included at all policy-making levels.

The other side of this recommendation is that professional educators must demonstrate the "capacity to provide service markedly beyond that which would otherwise be available." Sadly, it must be admitted that teachers (taken here in the generic sense) have acquiesced to the business model in education that has left them with little authority beyond the classroom door. Professional educators, empowered educators, will have the responsibility of demonstrating to the public that their knowledge and expertise are to be highly regarded. Perhaps it would be best to say it this way: We advocate that teachers be given the opportunity to become empowered as professionals.

Providing such an opportunity, as a new institution is conceptualized, would represent a "good faith" effort on the part of the community. What educators did with that opportunity would go a long way toward determining how much of the responsibility for our current state of education should be placed at the door of one's local school. We suspect, however, that teachers will seize the opportunity, that they will favor rigor in teacher education rather than "fast-track" programs, that they will not be tolerant of teachers who are not competent to teach, and that they shall be willing and able to demonstrate that theirs is a proud and noble profession that benefits society in a manner no other institution can match.

PARENTAL RESPONSIBILITY

Parents can be the most impassioned of influences with regard to education. Particularly on the local level, parents can, and do, have a profound effect on what is taught in the school. Admittedly, their perspective tends to be narrow in that their primary concern is with their own children in school at the given time. Nonetheless, every parent of a school-aged child has a vested interest in what happens between the morning bell and the dismissal bell. In terms of numbers, aside from the students, parents represent the largest constituency with a direct interest in the school, and studies show that their involvement has a positive effect on learning (Darling & Westberg, 2004).

In our current system, parents can have an impact on the school by formal or informal means. By "formal," we are referring to participation as school board members or in parent organizations such as parent-teacher associations (PTAs). As school board members, which usually are locally elected positions, parents can have direct influence on the decision making in a district.

School boards, however, are made up of a limited number of members. Organizations such as the PTA provide the opportunity for greater numbers of parents to speak with a unified voice. Parent-teacher organizations usually serve as support groups for schools by raising funds or contributing time and labor for school projects. However, at those times when volatile issues sweep through a community, the opinions of a parents' organization are something to which school boards need to be attuned.

Similar to the possibility of serving as an elected member of the school board, parents are often invited to serve as members of site-based councils in schools that have such a management structure or on a "board of directors" for a charter school. As is the case with service on a school board, the numbers of parents serving in such formal positions is very limited.

Parents can also have an impact on curriculum through informal means, and many prefer to do so. Some parents feel that they can speak to the board more frankly from the podium than if they were confined by the "politics" of being an elected board member. Short of slander or libel, individuals in the community are free to raise topics and press issues that they deem important without worrying about offending voters. If people agree with them, fine. If people disagree, well, that's also acceptable. Elected officials who wish to remain as elected officials must have more guarded opinions and must express them more carefully.

Though parents can make their opinions known in discussion with other parents, in conversation with their child's teacher, through dialogue with the principal, or with the district superintendent, addressing the board of education represents an appeal to the top level of the local education agency, often with an emphasis directed toward curriculum matters. Sheurer and Parkay (1992) have noted that in a survey of Florida schools, it was reported that in a one-year period, one-half of the complaints received by districts were about the curriculum. These complaints included the undermining of family values, overemphasizing globalism, underemphasizing patriotism, teaching taboo subjects such as satanism and sex, and the increasing use of profanity and obscenity. The underrepresentation of minorities in history textbooks has long been an issue that parents bring to their local school boards. We increasingly see attempts to ban various books from school libraries—and this runs the gamut from children's fairy tales and Harry Potter to the perennial complaints over *Catcher in the Rye*. Thus, the influence of parents cannot, and should not, be discounted. But it must also be considered as the double-edged sword that it represents.

Aside from these formal and informal influences, perhaps the greatest direct involvement of parents is through what might be called "unofficial" capacities. These parents, ostensibly volunteers, chaperone students, participate in or offer special programs, work in the classroom as teacher's aides, and otherwise contribute in ways that facilitate the work of the classroom teacher. This represents a tremendous resource for the school not only in terms of a workforce but, more importantly, in terms of emphasizing the "public" in public schools. All in all, as was mentioned in chapter 1, parents have unprecedented access to the institution of education—as decision makers, policy makers, and participants—as contrasted with any other institution in our society.

The Reform Model Dilutes the Efficacy of Parental Involvement

It should come as no surprise to you that parents find a comfortable fit with the reform model, for all of the examples that have been mentioned represent transitory involvement. That is, for all the efforts expended there is no long-term impact on the operation of schools. Understandably, most parents are only committed to educational reform while their children are in school. And it would also be fairly safe to say that during that time, most parents are concerned with *their* child in school rather than with *all* children in school across the state and nation. And so, programs or changes that can accommodate the constituency du jour can come and go without significantly altering the institution. The reform model does, as we have seen, manage to keep all constituencies occupied in such a way as to make them think that substantive changes are occurring.

The interesting result, after looking over the history of education in our country, is that very little has changed. A clear example is the current trend toward single-gender schools. It took hundreds of years to win equal educational opportunities for females and to overcome the segregationist doctrine of "separate but equal." Yet, early in the twenty-first century, we find a movement toward separate but equal and toward various forms of segregation (e.g., ethnically, cognitively, and by gender). And the impetus for both of these approaches comes very much from parental influence. Is this the fault of the school? Is this because educators cannot decide how children learn? No, it is because we continue to fail to make decisions that carry any vision for the future. It is so much easier to let the institution run us. The reform model within the workings of an institution is just such a comfortable fit. Parent involvement, however, should have greater efficacy than the reform model affords.

We come back again to the question of what the schools are supposed to accomplish. In the context of parents, the purpose of schools depends on the people to whom you speak. Some parents consider schools as a baby-sitting service that also provides free or inexpensive meals. You will recognize these parents when they are concerned about what to do with days during which children are dismissed early or are not expected to attend (as during teacher work days). Other parents expect the school to assume total responsibility for the academic, physical, emotional, and social development of their children.

There has been ample opportunity for parents to form a collaborative relationship with the schools. Though parents have historically been afforded access to the rhyme and reason of schooling, they have consistently remained at arm's length (there are always individuals who become very much involved with their child's education, but we refer here to parents in a generic sense representing the tens of millions who do not become involved). The tendency is to focus on what bothers them about the functioning of schools. Yet, at the same time, they are willing to turn as much parental responsibility over to the school as possible. For instance, one study shows that high school parents tend to be as disconnected from the school as their sons and daughters are (Newman, 1997–1998). Another study indicates that 50 percent of all parents have no rules about what television programs their children can watch (Hymowitz, 2001). Today, the schools are specifically charged with protecting the safety and health of students while in attendance, a condition referred to as "in loco parentis," or in place of a parent.

Even parent-involvement organizations such as the Parent Teacher Organization and Parent Teacher Association have failed to live up to their potential. As we have mentioned, McEwan (1998) writes, "In many local districts, the PTA is merely a giant group of cheerleaders and fundraisers for the administration" (71). Parent involvement in the success of organized education is a key to our social and cultural future. But at the same time, the reform model only supports the short-range, "while-my-child-is-in-school" perspective typical of so many parents.

Still other parents see school as another item on an elaborate "to do" list for their children. In his classic work *The Hurried Child*, Elkind (1981) expresses considerable concern about parents who push their children into a veritable merry-go-round of activities: sports, dancing, music, baton lessons, cheerleading, and so on. In school, these hurried children are pushed to excel. Thus, they may have tutors (not because of remediation needs but to accelerate progress with good grades, high school honors, and college scholarships as the goal), and they may have parents who "do their assignments" for them, for instance, science projects, term papers, and homework.

There are also parents who see themselves as part of a team dedicated to producing the best possible results and who see the schools as the enablers of their children's futures. So, different parents have different expectations of the school. The result is that no one really knows just what school should accomplish. That condition makes it difficult to effectively utilize the resources that parents offer.

We would suggest that as one looks at the institution of education today, it becomes obvious that (1) parents as a constituency have failed to take advantage of the opportunity to directly involve themselves with a vital institution of our society, (2) the institution has failed to embrace and effectively utilize the tremendous resource that parent involvement represents, and (3) the haphazard approach to collaboration on the part of both entities (organized education and parents) is largely to blame for the mediocrity that we not only see in education today but that we try to convince ourselves is "not so bad."

Meaningful Parental Involvement

In a new institution of education, it will be necessary to find meaningful and legitimate ways of utilizing parents as a resource. We add, however, that parental involvement in the new institution should, if the institution is still going to be in the hands of the community, be seen as a parental *responsibility*. And we recommend that local control of schools does remain in the hands of the community. After all, one of the distinguishing characteristics of a public education system will continue to be the significant amount of time that children spend under the guidance and influence of adults other than their parents. (We do not deny the possibility that, one day, schooling will be home based and electronically delivered, but that will require revolutions in more than just the institution of education, and so, we will confine ourselves to just one institution at a time.)

Activity 7.2.
PARENT INVOLVEMENT WITH THE SCHOOLS

This section of *A School by Every Other Name* suggests that parental involvement across the board should be raised to the level of an acknowledged responsibility. That is, parents would have responsibilities for *involvement* in the education of children in addition to the current responsibility of having children *attend* school.

Assume that you are the teacher/administrator at a neighborhood school. What would be your minimum expectations for parental involvement with the schools? What would be your upper limit for the involvement of parents?

Write a brief "letter to the parents" that explains your perspective on their involvement at your school. If possible, allow a teacher and a current administrator to review your plan.

Involvement in a new educational institution could be thought of as having four dimensions for parents: at home, at the school, in the school, and finally, parents *and* the school. We see an expectation for all parents to be involved in at least one of these four dimensions, though participation in several areas would be strongly encouraged. We will discuss some possibilities for each of these dimensions but want you to notice that throughout all four, the key difference between the old institution and the new is that parental involvement is seen as an organized, formalized responsibility.

Parents at Home

The most basic form of parental involvement with a child's education is that of support provided at home. As classroom teachers can attest, parental support of the school or the needs of the school (signing forms, checking for homework, supporting a teacher's authority in the classroom) is something that is provided in some households and not in others. The difficulty that very quickly arises is that students wind up being held responsible for parental lapses or, in disciplinary matters, empowered by the parents' disinterest. It is true that teachers hear something like "my mother forgot to sign it," when in fact the student forgot to get a form signed, but sometimes the student is telling the truth: The parent forgot to sign the form or simply refuses to sign forms. And so, what is the school to do? Is the child held responsible?

The easy part of this particular discussion is to say that parents need to be formally introduced to the expectations that schools have for involvement with a child's education. A program of orientation, one that takes more than an hour on a weekday afternoon, could be developed in principle by the Education Congress of the States and then fine-tuned by the local education agency for any given community. It would not be stretching the limits of decorum to expect that any parent enrolling a child in a public school be required to complete such an orientation program for each level of schooling that a child enters. (You might recall that we have suggested that grade levels be abolished, but that does not mean that the broader grouping of students, e.g., elementary, middle, and high school, need be eliminated since these groups serve a socializing function.)

An orientation for parents could provide not only information about parenting and child development (as appropriate for the level in which the child is enrolling) but also explain how to support and facilitate the work of the school with regard to the individual child and how to work with the school when issues arise with which a parent may have a question or disagreement. These orientations could also include an overview of school law so that parents could understand the rights of their children, as well as the restrictions under which the school is required to operate. Such a program might be convened at the beginning of the school year and also have two or three follow-up meetings over the course of the year.

As we have said, that's the easy part. And likely, for a large percentage of parents, such a program would be very workable. It might even be the case that attendance at education orientation programs is seen in the same civic-duty light as jury duty. That is, employers are obliged to release workers to attend. The difficult part is with the parents, who, as nonsalaried employees, may be released to attend but also forfeit a day's wages that they can ill afford to lose. Or the difficulty could be with compelling parents to attend when they are more concerned with where the family will sleep that evening or, even more sadly, when they are simply not interested in the life of the child.

Well over two thousand years ago, the philosopher Plato indicated that parents were not necessarily the best-qualified people to raise children in the state. His plan in the *Republic* took children away from parents and put them in the hands of those people designated and trained by the state to raise children. While such an approach is not an option for us, it is worth noting that the basic problem that Plato identified has not changed: Parents (and once again, this is in the generic sense and not meant to offend the many caring and outstanding parents that there are in the world) have not been educated about *being parents*. The biological instinct is enough for conception, gestation, and birth, but it is not "wired" into the growth of an individual in a broad-based social system. There should be some expectation for parents to learn to be parents and to be parents to their children in school. And that expectation should be a formalized aspect of what schools do.

We see discussing a child's schoolwork, homework assignments, and activities as a responsibility of parenting. Asking for assistance from the classroom teacher when a parent feels that he or she does not clearly understand a topic sufficiently to help a child should be part of the organized and formalized way that parents and teachers interact. Electronic technologies can easily facilitate this sort of cooperation, but there must also be convenient mechanisms for families that do not have access to computer-based systems.

Parents at the School

Across the country, there are beautiful schools with bright lighting, clean floors, and well-landscaped grounds. Indeed, many students are fortunate to attend school in inviting and exemplary facilities. We would hope that parents of children in such schools might see a civic responsibility to keeping those schools in pristine condition.

Unfortunately, there are also thousands of schools around the country that are antiquated and in disrepair. The grounds around the school may be depressingly desolate as well. More often than not, the claim is that the district is unable to afford the upkeep, let alone the outright renovation, of these buildings beyond a minimally adequate level. Having visited many such buildings, we question how any community can tolerate allowing their children to spend hours a day, everyday, in such conditions. We are also aware that the conditions themselves send a message to students each day.

The inequities of educational funding (note: this is not necessarily a matter of the amount of money spent on education in the United States but rather a matter of the distribution of funding) may well be at the heart of many of these circumstances. We would encourage states to actively recruit business and industry to economically depressed regions to stimulate both the economic *and* educational growth of ill-funded communities. Unfortunately, the political perspective is typically to say that because of the economic depression and poor quality of schools, businesses will not locate in such areas. We would suggest that stimulating economic development be an integral part of the new institution of education and that states work collaboratively with their educational entities to routinely include this perspective when recruiting and promoting business development.

In the meantime, we believe that no school should be a disgrace to a community. Schools should, in fact, be the centerpiece of any community. We suggest that there are no failing schools, rather there are communities (local, state, and national) that have failed their schools. We have already indicated that entities above the local level should address the inequities of funding, but we also wish to recommend that the parents in a local community be organized to improve the schools that their children attend.

Though public education should not be seen as a charitable cause, a "Habitat for Education" perspective may be very appropriate in situations that have dire need. Teams of parents under the guidance of professionals in various trades could accomplish a wide range of tasks at the school. At the very least, classrooms and other student areas could be freshly painted. We hasten to add that this is not a plan for having parents take over custodial services in a school. Keeping a building clean and environmentally safe for students is a basic responsibility of the school. However, there are many upkeep and renovation tasks that could be accomplished by parents rather than simply being left to deteriorate. Let us add that the recommendation is that parents be organized to provide the workforce, not the materials. Again, the school and the state should not be allowed to dodge their responsibilities.

It would not be unreasonable to expect, particularly with regard to middle and high schools, that students be involved as well. If parents and students take part in establishing and maintaining a worthy learning environment, then they will also begin to share in the ownership of their efforts, take pride in the facility, and tend to exercise greater care on a day-to-day basis.

Parents in the School

Though we roundly advocate putting the responsibility for instruction in the hands of credentialed educators, it is also true that individuals who see the school from a perspective outside the classroom can offer ideas and support for instructional experiences. Though a "fresh set of eyes" likely does not include as strong a foundation in child growth and development, special needs, school law, pedagogy, and state-based standards as the professional educator possesses, this different perspective can provide the opportunity to see innovative ways of addressing the needs of students and, so, should be cultivated as a resource.

Some parents bring skills in conceptualizing programs, others are good organizers, and still others are anxious to work with children. Some parents, of course, bring all three talents to the table. Their ideas and willingness to do the work (note: we are specifically talking about parents who are offering to participate, not those who simply want to tell the system that there's a better way that they could be doing things) can have many positive influences on student achievement.

There is a caveat, however. Because all programs are part of the curriculum and because every minute of every school day is funded at taxpayer expense as instructional time, program ideas or proposals brought to the school by a parent or group of parents should be evaluated using the same evaluation criteria we detailed in chapter 5. Proposals for an individual school should be brought first to the principal. Proposals for a coalition would go first to the superintendent (or someone in a similar position) of that coalition. In any event, the proposal should be reflective of (1) the need for the program, (2) the nature of the program as it meets the identified standards and learning objectives of the school/coalition, (3) how the program will be implemented, and (4) how the students *and the program* will be assessed. Obviously, the most expedient approach would be that proposals be formatted in a manner that addresses each of the questions in Categories 1 to 4 as discussed in chapter 5. This process does not have to be made into something that, in and of itself, discourages the offering of ideas, but it is a legitimate expectation that the process be formalized. After-school programs conducted in a parent's home may not need as much rigor, but anything conducted during the school day in a publicly supported organization should be held to a considerably higher standard.

What must be lost is the haphazard or patchwork approach to parental involvement that presently characterizes the schools. For instance, even a brief discussion of school law would require a lengthy chapter in this book, yet school volunteers have little exposure to the legislation that directs how people will work with other people's children. The meaningful involvement of parents in the education of children is critical, but the reform model that has driven it has allowed worthwhile programs to prosper only in small pockets and for relatively brief periods of time; even worse, it has allowed poorly conceptualized and implemented programs to waste valuable instructional time.

Parents and the School

Previously in this section of the chapter, parental involvement as school board members, in parent-teacher organizations, or on site councils was referred to as "formal" interactions with the schools. Since a common theme for each of the four venues now under consideration (at home, at the school, in the school, and with the school) is that the relationships be formalized, we need a new descriptor for this section. When we speak of parents and the school, we refer to opportunities for parents to work as decision makers and policy makers in the work of schools. The examples we have given represent such a level of involvement.

The primary difference between working with the schools in each of the previous three venues as compared to this last one is that the activities at this level move an individual away from the "for my child while my child is in school" perspective. That parents have policy-making positions at the local level (e.g., on the school board, site council, or board of directors) is an important and distinguishing characteristic of the institution of education and that collaboration should exist. There are, however, at least two concerns that the new institution should address: credentialing and breadth of authority.

Credentialing of Parents as Policy Makers   Parental involvement at the policy level
of education today is consistent with the requirements for parenthood; there are essentially no requirements. For a parent to serve on a school board at the local or state
level or to serve on an advisory board appointed by the governor, the only qualification is that one get elected or appointed. And very often, individuals appointed by a
governor, for example, are more likely to have a business background than a professional education background. Can you imagine a multinational corporation forming
a board of directors and the only qualification required is that the individual may have
used the corporation's product at some time? Yet, *in education it is possible to be elected
to a policy-level position with no background at all in education.*

The Education Congress of the States, should it ever be established, could take the
lead in developing what might loosely be referred to as a credentialing process for
parents (or nonparents) who wish to serve at the policy level of any school entity,
whether at the local level or a broader one. As it stands now, a comprehensive "Introduction to Education" textbook, as is found in teacher-education programs, could
serve as the basis for such credentialing. Some of the topics routinely included in in-
troductory textbooks are

- pedagogy
- curriculum
- assessment
- history of education
- ethics and law
- social issues affecting education
- student diversity
- teacher credentialing
- classroom management
- philosophy and education
- governance and funding
- education organization

If they were assessed on these topics, even on just the highlights rather than the
specifics, we suspect that few parents running for a school board position would post
an exemplary grade. Likely, they would say that it wasn't necessary for them to know
these topics to conduct the business of the school board. We would counter, however,
that if they are not able to demonstrate competence in these areas, then they are, at
best, poorly qualified to make policy decisions about education. The credentialing of
candidates for policy-level positions does not have to be tantamount to earning a license (though a good argument could be made for it), but the sort of foundation
building described here should be seen as a legitimate expectation of the community
before an individual is eligible to run for or accept a position with such responsibility.

Breadth of Authority   How much authority should a local, regional, or state
school board (or other such entity) hold? Having come this far in *A School by Every
Other Name*, you should know that this is a function of decisions that we make as a
nation about what we want the schools to accomplish. For the purposes of our discussion, let's assume that a new institution adopts a professional organizational
structure such as the Education Congress of the States, and that the ECS adopts

something similar to the 622 Curriculum Model for organizing the educational experiences for public school students.

In all cases, it would fall to the ECS, as a national education collaborative, to act as the mediator between the short-term wishes of parents and the long-term needs of the school and society. That is, the ECS would have the responsibility for determining that changes in the provision of educational opportunities at the local, regional, or state level remained in concert with the goals of the nation for the education of its children. It is important to remember that the ECS would be specifically intended to represent the interests of the nation while protecting the sovereignty of the states. It would act not as an arm of the federal government but as a collaborative organization of the states.

However, and this is a big "however," under the 622 Curriculum Model, local communities have complete control over 20 percent of the curriculum provided to their students, and the regional/state level has another 20 percent. If the school board wants to be certain that the children under its jurisdiction are exposed to a particular educational experience or an alternative viewpoint, it has the authority to make that happen.

Local boards should also retain the authority for conducting the day-to-day business of the school. Personnel matters for noncertified positions would be the domain of the local board. Personnel matters involving the hiring and firing of teachers would be handled at the local level under the guidelines established by the Education Congress of the States, which may well require a peer review process. Remember, as discussed in a previous section, "Professional Considerations," the new institution would require a professional organization for teachers that established standards, guidelines, a code of ethics, and professional expectations held by educators for educators. The end result would be that local boards might have more stringent guidelines to follow, particularly in the dismissal of a teacher, but rules of professional conduct for teachers would have first been more formally articulated.

*   *   *

Much like the discussion of adopting an official language, expecting parents to assume a formal role in education may be a difficult sell. However, it is our contention that a contributing factor to the problems in public education is that nothing but a biological capacity is required to be a parent. Many locales require a license to go fishing, but assuming the responsibility for a human life, for its welfare and cognitive/emotional/social development, has no condition placed upon it. Our after-the-fact approach to parenthood preparation is something that should be addressed in the new institution. One of the ways it could be addressed is through the expectation of parental involvement and the providing of services to make that possible.

Perhaps most crucial of all with regard to this outline for parent involvement is that the new institution of education be worthy of the trust and confidence of parents. Asking parents to take on the responsibilities outlined here, which many may interpret as being directed by the institution, can only be amenable if parents can sense that they are indeed valued participants in the educational process and that the enterprise is succeeding. Public education is too important a function for our society to allow it to fail, and its success can only be realized when it takes on the character of a truly collaborative effort between educational professionals and the constituencies that they serve.

PART II: ISSUES AND DECISIONS FOR THE NEW INSTITUTION

FINANCIAL CONSIDERATIONS

The funding of education is always where the true colors are shown. Editorials, letters to the editor, guest commentaries, political sound bites, and the parade of experts that we hear from in what has become the "newstainment" industry on television will talk about the variety of schools that we need. We often hear of how schools need to differentiate so that the various learning styles of students can best be accommodated. We are told that competition needs to be infused into the system at the level of the classroom teacher and at the level of schools within a district so that parents have a clear option for where to send their children. It all sounds so obviously simple—a no-brainer, so to speak.

Well, that is until someone asks whether the individual offering these ideas is willing to accept the price tag that comes with it. There can be little doubt that if we were to double or triple the funding that goes to education, there may well be a myriad of changes that could be made. We would suggest, however, that such changes would not make the differences in education that we seek. There comes a point at which options become burdensome in themselves and cause us to lose sight of the fact that *options* are not the substance of the enterprise. We offer the notion of Occam's razor: *All things being equal, the simplest answer is probably correct.* Dressing matters up with so many options dilutes the basic, fundamental aspects of education.

In the context of our discussion, the simplest answer is found in Robert Maynard Hutchins's suggestion that "the best education for the best is the best education for all." That is, rather than establishing a buffet of educational options from which we pick and choose among various components, we need to determine what the best education is *for all* and then provide a system that delivers it.

Does this approach dodge the "competition" argument that is so prevalent today and is supposed to bring down the cost of education? Certainly not, for those who espouse the notion of competition as a panacea have a fatal flaw in their reasoning. We do not oppose competition, but it's the context that is problematic. We can look at other public institutions for examples. For instance, with regard to our national defense, we do not establish several versions of the air force in the hopes that the best one will put the second-best out of business. People do not have the option of choosing *which* air force will defend them.

And what of business, from which the competition model ostensibly arises? "Business" is not an institution. Within the economic domain of business activities there are megacorporations, such as General Motors or IBM, but they compete with other companies of their own genre, not with themselves.

The argument can be made, nonetheless, that schools *do* compete, even today. The public schools compete with the private schools. Private schools in fact compete for a very small percentage of students, and the public school must take responsibility for those who cannot avail themselves of a private school education for one reason or another. Even so, if it is argued that the competition is only for the "best" students or for the wealthy students, it is because public schools *are not allowed* to compete openly. Are we willing to make this a fair competition? If so, rather than continuing with the misguided perspective of eliminating "failing schools," we must allow the public schools to turn away underperforming students or those who present ongoing discipline problems. That would be fair, wouldn't it?

Even more problematic to the vague suggestions that competition among schools will be financially expedient is this question: If competition is clearly the answer to failing schools, why haven't entrepreneurs set up private schools for low-performing students? Why don't we see private alternative schools in virtually every district around the country? We can suggest a reason: Those private schools can only "guarantee" success if they operate under parameters unavailable to the public schools, such as extremely small class sizes (if not one-on-one instruction). Neither vouchers nor tax credits would be sufficient for private enterprises to make a profit.

We suggest that the question of funding schools in a manner that reflects academic excellence is confounded by the popular notion that the blame in education falls squarely on the shoulders of schools and teachers. With an eye toward revolutionizing schools, we again make the statement that *in fact there are no failing schools, rather there are communities (local, state, and national) that have failed their schools.* This one statement has broad implications for both the structure and funding of schools. With that statement comes a contemporary sacrilege in the educational debate: Though funding is often a critical component of the problem, money is not necessarily *the* problem with our approach to educating the children of this nation. As detailed previously in chapter 6, incredible amounts of money go toward education. It is the business model, however, top-heavy with administrative salaries and expenses, that is a chief problem in the funding of our schools. There are many other ineffective and wasteful uses of funds. Our recommendation is, as it has been throughout this book, that we make fundamental decisions about the education we want for the children of our society and that we find the most expedient means of providing that education. That approach will require that stakeholders within and without the school once again assume critical responsibilities that have quietly been passed on to the schools.

ELECTRONIC TECHNOLOGIES

Get ready for another modern-day sacrilege: We do not consider computer technology to be the savior of education. There is a place, a significant place, for educational tools that use electronic technology. But the notion that civilization has been waiting five thousand years for computers to come along makes no sense at all. Think of it, computers were conceptualized and designed in the absence of computers, right? The foundation of modern aviation and space travel depended more on slide rules than on computers. Language acquisition and scientific inquiry have never been dependent upon electronic technologies. This is not said to minimize the impact that computers may well have on education but to point out that we are currently in a period of infatuation with computer and electronic technologies, and the novelty of it may be clouding our judgment about its most appropriate use (Oppenheimer, 2004). We would like to suggest that apart from the mesmerizing games (and the computer's obvious potential for offering remedial-education opportunities), there may be some more substantive applications for electronic technologies that could indeed change the way we have been looking at "school" for centuries.

One clear potential for the use of electronic technologies in education is to enable the strengthening of neighborhood schools without the necessity of duplicating ancillary services. That is, computer technologies can facilitate a wide range of administrative tasks, such as:

- scheduling
- attendance
- academic-progress monitoring
- testing programs
- inventory
- energy-resource monitoring
- faculty credentialing
- transportation
- food services

Education Coalitions

The establishment of "megadistricts," with their accompanying cost-effectiveness, becomes a viable administrative structure with electronic technologies. In essence, what emerges is a centralized administrative structure (which many see as a necessity from an economic perspective) without the assumption that *instruction* must be centralized as well. Rather, electronic technologies would allow neighborhood schools to take advantage of all the things that small size offers while answering to a centralized administration. The savings in administrative salaries alone, as duplicated administrative positions are eliminated, would offer more resources to the instructional end of the enterprise. Perhaps if we think in terms of *education coalitions* (which implies a broader collaboration) rather than the traditional school district (which implies an autonomous entity), the picture may start to come into focus.

In a standards-based environment, the coalition structure makes even more sense. The academic expectations of the schools are already established as a function of the state and, so, are in place for each school within the coalition. But this structure would allow individual schools to take advantage of the 622 Curriculum format that we discussed previously. That is, within the governance structure of the coalition and of the neighborhood school, there could be room for curricular enrichment programs that could come from a wide range of possibilities that suit the local constituency.

All of this is not to say that computer technology would be absent from the classroom. Rather, we are simply making the point that such technologies hold *immediate* potential in terms of the task that computers already do very, very well: data management. *And that, after all, is all that computers do.* It is important that we keep in mind that computers do not solve problems. They do not make value judgments. They manage and manipulate information in a value-free environment. It is only through the human interpretation of data, through the human determination to examine and manipulate particular data and to select particular courses of action based upon that data, that value is added into the equation. *Valuing is a function of humanity.* Therefore, as an instructional tool, we want to see computer technologies assume a seamless integration into the process of instruction, but we do not want to perpetuate the notion that computers can or should do anything but supplement the interpersonal dynamic of students and teachers.

Recognizing the Obsolescence of Grade Levels

With all that is known today about how people learn (e.g., differences in rates of learning, learning-style preferences, the impact of personal interest and thus motivation to learn, and cultural differences in learning styles), there is really only one argument in favor of using the traditional "grade-level" approach to school, and it's a poor one: It's traditional. Interestingly enough, the one-room schoolhouse of 150 plus years ago is closer to the model that education should embrace than is the model we have today in which children are grouped essentially by age. However, it must be added that we are not talking about a room in which all students are doing the same work, but, instead, we refer to a room in which students could be working on appropriate levels of learning but all in the same room—a very big distinction.

If you consider the age-level grouping of students for more than just a few minutes, you will realize that such an approach has no pedagogical value whatsoever. It does have value as a means of categorizing and scheduling students, and it could even be argued that it has value in terms of the socializing process that occurs at school. This latter point has considerable credence. In the 1980s and 1990s, schools tested the idea of what we might call "in-between" grade levels when students who were unable to progress beyond the eighth grade were isolated in a sort of academic purgatory. Parents did not want fifteen- and sixteen-year-old students mixed in with their twelve-, thirteen-, and fourteen-year-old children, but the older students were not academically capable of moving on to high school.

Many a student of education, as well as those who have studied cognitive development and/or the principles of operant conditioning as applied to education, have heard the phrase "stages, not ages." The meaning is that students should receive instruction based upon their cognitive stage (their current ability level) rather than being grouped based on their ages. Embracing this notion wholeheartedly allows one to recognize that it goes even further. That is, as any parent knows, a child who may be struggling in math may simultaneously be thriving in language arts. In such a case, it makes no sense to keep a child who "fails" math on the same grade level for all subjects due to this one area of weakness.

The argument against the grade-level approach is strengthened when considering the *gain scores* perspective toward school achievement. Gain scores open up the discussion to an entirely different line of thinking in terms of how student achievement should be measured. As opposed to simply meeting or not meeting a predetermined standard, gain scores measure student *progress*. That is, a system based on gain scores will determine precisely where a child stands, academically speaking, prior to instruction and then measure the progress made after instruction is complete.

Let's use reading as an example for this discussion. It is not at all uncommon that by third grade many students are reading below grade level. So, let's assume one child enters third grade reading on a 2.2 level (that is, second grade, second month according to an achievement test). Another child in the same class begins the year on a 3.4 level. At the end of the year, our first child is reading at a 2.9 level, while the second child in our example is reading at a 3.5 level. Our first child has gained seven months in terms of reading ability but nonetheless has failed to reach a third-grade level. Our second child has gained only one month over the course of an entire school year, yet *is* on the third-grade level. How should each of these students be graded? Notice that we are not asking about effort in this example. One student has gained seven times as much as the

Activity 7.3.
GRADE LEVELS AND GAIN SCORES

We admit that this activity might be just a bit sneaky. The idea would be to chat with a local school principal, a district-level assistant superintendent for curriculum, and a district superintendent. It's sneaky in that we don't want you to ask anyone to justify the grade-level structure of schools; we just want to find out why they favor it. So, while the underlying question is whether a gain score–based structure would be more pedagogically sound, just ask for a brief explanation of why schools are organized along age-based grade levels.

What patterns, if any, can you find in the responses? Do the responses suitably justify a grade-level structure? What do you suppose the response would have been if you had asked about switching to a gain score system. (Note: some may say that gain scores are another name for "mastery learning." They are not. Gain scores are a measure of learning over time. Mastery learning seeks to provide sufficient time to "master" a topic). If you have a good enough relationship with the people you have asked about the current structure, go ahead and ask about gain scores as well. Don't be surprised if the answer is, "It would be a scheduling nightmare!" We know that computers are made for such nightmares.

other. Do we consider that failure? Admittedly, there is a catch to this example. Schools are currently structured to grade students on the meeting of objectives rather than on how much they have gained during the year. So, our question to you is really one of broader educational policy: Is our current structure the most appropriate perspective for the assessment of *learning*, and how does that structure vary from school to school?

Electronic technologies are tailor-made for freeing the schools of the grade-level tradition. Monitoring of student progress or achievement, if you must, can easily be accomplished with computer technologies, and students can then be assigned within any school to the most appropriate *academic level* for any given content area. And, of course, rather than obliterating the movement toward educational objectives, the placement of students by academic level for each content area makes the reaching of objectives all the more plausible. Benjamin Bloom (1976) pointed out decades ago that the problem with mastery learning approaches has been the assumption that given the same amount and quality of instruction, all students will learn at the same rate. Such is not the case, and using computer technologies to efficiently place students wherever they may need to be along the continuum of instruction will transform schools from grade-level-based facilities to centers for learning.

Instructional Innovations

What might *teaching* be like in the years ahead? After literally hundreds of years, organized education is presented in much the same way that it always has been. And that seems curious. A new school being built today will have roughly the same layout as the schools you may have attended as a youngster. The expectation continues to be of one teacher with a large group of students, and even some of the educational tools will be the same.

For example, a new school will likely have a chalkboard in each classroom. Chalk? For how many years do you suppose teachers have been using chalk? The educational innovation in that area is represented by whiteboards and dry-erase markers in many schools. Yet, markers are much more expensive than chalk, and in a budget crunch, replacing those markers becomes problematic. What other innovations (other than dry-erase markers) can you identify that have truly changed instruction? Let's take some time to consider possibilities for change in the way an education is delivered.

Instructional Delivery Systems

When we consider instructional delivery systems for the future of education, there is no escaping the impact of computers and electronics. However, it is a good idea to keep in mind that even when the power goes off for one reason or another, school must be able to continue. It already sounds as though we are singing the praises of chalk, doesn't it? You have likely had an experience at a store or in dealing with a company over the phone when the salesperson or customer service representative was unable to take care of you because "the system" was down. The fact that the system is down has no effect on your immediate need or situation, yet it has become an excuse for shutting down all sorts of business operations. Education, however, does not enjoy the luxury of just shutting things down and sending everybody home. So, the real challenge is to create ideas within ideas, that is, ideas that have backup systems built in.

The Electronic Wall   What if we were to replace the chalkboards (or dry-erase boards) in your school of the future with electronic walls? Two classrooms, for instance, could be arranged with a narrow electronics service hallway between them. The wall of each room that backs up to either side of the hallway will be the electronic wall for that room, which will also be the front of the classroom, much the same as a typical classroom has a chalkboard on the front wall. In this scenario, however, virtually the entire wall will be a display area. The display comes to within two feet of the floor so that even in the earliest grades, the students should be able to write on the surface. Vertically, the display area goes to the ceiling, and horizontally, it stretches from one end of the wall to the other. This is not one of those "smart boards" that you may have heard of but rather an entire electronic wall.

Such a wall could have many uses. In one upper corner, or wherever the teacher wished it to display, could be the clock. Using a wireless keyboard, the teacher could bring up clocks with the time displayed for several countries around the world as well. Somewhere else on the wall, the day's academic objectives would be displayed. Another area could provide class rules and, in the event of emergency, instructions for exiting the building. As sophisticated as our wall would be, it could even be programmed so that as students entered the room, they would place their thumbs on a scanner that took attendance for the main office and also popped up a picture of each student at his or her desk as part of a "seating chart" display. As the display would highlight empty desks, the teacher would be able to see at a glance whether or not all of the students were in class and ready to begin.

The most important use of the wall, of course, would be for instructional purposes. The wall would connect directly to the teacher's computer, probably an easily carried "task slate" (that has a school-like sound to it, doesn't it?) that could include a touch-sensitive keypad or could be written upon. Whatever the teacher wrote on the pad or whatever program was called up through the computer could be displayed on the front wall as well as on individual student consoles. As the teacher moved about the room and found a student with a particularly good solution to a problem, that student's work could be displayed on the front board.

The wall could also display individual or group responses to questions. Students would enter in their responses to the problems the teacher presented. The results could be displayed numerically or graphically on the front board, allowing all to see how the class had responded. Video programs from disks (Disks? What will replace disks in the future?) or television could also be displayed on our electronic wall.

To make the wall even more useful, the surface would be such that the teacher or the students could come up and write on the board just as if it were a dry-erase or chalk board. Perhaps a stylus or just a finger could be used to write across the board. Whatever was written on the board could be saved, revised, and/or deleted, just as with any other computer-generated information. And when the electronic wall was shut down or when the power went off for one reason or another, the wall would have a white appearance and dry-erase markers could be used on the outer surface. If we could think of a way to make that surface chalk-user friendly, we'd really have it made! You probably know that all of the technology for a wall such as this is readily available today. What would it take to make it a reality?

Experiential Education

Experiential education is an approach that seeks to find ways to make what is taught as part of school as realistic as possible. This is not a new notion, and in fact, the idea of experience-based education can be traced at least to the beginning of the twentieth century. Both the pragmatist philosophy and the progressivist movement advocated such an educational structure. A philosophical approach to education in use today, *constructivism*, is based on providing students with experiences upon which to build— from which to learn. The difficulty that we face is how to make such an approach integral to classroom instruction.

Before determining which experiences from the real world can be applied to instruction in the world of school, it will have to be decided what education in the future is supposed to accomplish. Does that sound familiar? Why do we learn algebra? Is it to do algebraic manipulations? To an extent, that's true. But what of calculus or the dissections students do in biology classes? What must be asked at this point is, what are the experiences students will face in the real world? Secondly, it should also be asked how best to prepare them for those experiences. Certainly, providing experiences rather than abstractions is the best way to go; after all, "experience," "expertise," and "expert" all seem to have some common thread, don't they?

The Internet

At first, the Internet was a research tool that served to exchange information from mainframe computer to mainframe computer. It provided the foundation for the *information age*. Now, the World Wide Web has become largely a marketing tool. And while it is true that there is much information to be found via the Net, it is also true that the ease with which information can be posted has led to a lot of information of dubious quality. This is not meant to disparage the Web but rather to make three educationally important points: (1) the Internet is just as much a part of everyday life for vast numbers of people as is television, (2) information from the Web must be accepted with the same guarded skepticism as that which is provided through other media sources (just because something is posted on the Web doesn't mean it must be true), and (3) it is changing. It would not be unreasonable to expect the Internet to change at least as drastically in the next twenty years as it has over the past twenty years, and probably at a much more rapid pace. What we might see is a "splitting" of the Web. That is, the highly commercial aspect will continue its own development, while research and educational functions, for example, may develop in their own directions.

As you begin to think about the possibilities for education, our suggestion is that you focus on the idea that education fosters the development of an individual's abilities and also develops the skills for putting those abilities to use in solving problems. In essence, our recommendation is that you reconceptualize the Internet so that the next generation moves from the information age to *the age of problem solving*. The question becomes one of determining in what ways an electronic network of information sharing can contribute to that mission?

Local Issues   Among the most interesting by-products of the Internet has been its global nature. The phrase itself, "the World Wide Web," conjures up the notion of people from distant countries being in communication with one another. Yet, we already see that the shorter "www" or "w³" is serving to let people take the global aspect of the Net for granted. In other words, the Internet is more "computer" than it is "global." That's unfortunate, for rather than breaking down the distance between people, it has opened up a new territory, "cyberspace," that fosters high-tech anonymity.

One way of getting around this issue, particularly with younger students, could be to put the Internet to work on local issues. Children face enough of a challenge understanding the concept of a local community without trying to conceptualize a global version. So, we would do well to identify problem-solving scenarios that could be developed addressing either particular subject areas or integrating subject areas that would put students to work on locally relevant concerns. What are the current characteristics of the Internet that would facilitate such activities? What necessary characteristics does the Internet lack at this time that would contribute to meaningful problem solving for students in K–12? How might a curriculum strand for elementary school children be designed using a local issue? Perhaps this approach could be extended so that the middle school curriculum could contain a strand (or theme) that addressed a state-level issue. High school students could focus on national issues or global issues.

We hasten to add that we don't want to abandon the global capabilities that the Internet of today or tomorrow offers. Rather, we want children to build their appreciation of community, of society, through several levels, much as Bruner (1960) advocated with his spiral curriculum approach, which increased in sophistication as students learned more and more.

The Global Community   An extension of what we have been saying could be the establishment of a Global Creative Problem Solving Consortium as part of the curriculum. A project such as this would allow schools in the United States to form problem-solving partnerships with schools in other countries. Students could be involved in multiple subject areas, with multiple cultural perspectives, and with genuine problems to solve. Ebert and Ebert (1998) refer to one such model as Topic Integration for Macro-Learning Experiences, or TIME. In this particular model, students work in collaboration with their partner schools to consider the problem from three perspectives: (1) the cause of the problem, (2) the effect the problem has on people, and (3) the possible effect of the problem on the future. From that foundation, the students work to find a solution that would be acceptable from all cultural perspectives involved.

Instructional Materials

Books have been in use for a long time, and books have changed the world. But one has to wonder whether the preeminence of the printed page has passed. A visit to a public school will reveal that students, particularly in the younger grades, carry virtually all of their books in book bags. There are those who are seriously concerned about the physical development problems that may be looming as students walk about leaning far forward to counterbalance the weight of the book bag. In addition to the question of health and safety, there are at least two more dimensions of this issue that should be considered as we conceptualize the school of the future: print media versus electronic media, and textbooks (print or electronic) in general.

Electronic Books   Electronic books (e-books) likely have a place in the school of the future, though there are viable arguments for and against the use of such technology. Not surprisingly, we may find that many of the arguments on either side are not based on pedagogical concerns but instead are business concerns. Does this mean that the future of education is destined to be constrained by the same influences that impact upon it today? That could be the case, but remember that "education" does not have a mind of its own; it is an institution guided by the minds of people. Here are some points to consider as you begin to think about the pros and cons of e-books for school.

Points in Favor of Electronic Books

1. All of the books that students now carry could be reduced to a single memory stick that is played on a lightweight and portable monitor. No more overloaded book bags.
2. Use of memory sticks means no moving parts. Thus, electronic books would have minimal power-supply needs. In fact, it is possible that they could utilize "windup" power technologies, such as that used in radios.
3. Font size can be changed at will by the user. No straining one's eyes to read the text.
4. An electronic book may occasionally be damaged, but textbooks must be routinely replaced due to wear and tear.
5. It is easier to search an electronic text than a paper text.
6. Highlighting or bookmarking text does not damage the page (for the next user).
7. Memory sticks (or whatever technology you envision) can be easily reprogrammed and updated. An entire textbook series could be updated rather quickly.
8. It is possible that the costs of equipment could parallel the costs of stocking and restocking sets of books for each student and each subject area.
9. Electronic book publishers could key all state academic standards to the materials that they publish. As standards changed, updating would be relatively easy. (Ebert & Culyer, 2008)

That list is enough to get us started. What other benefits can you identify for switching from paper media to electronic media for student textbooks?

Points Opposing the Use of Electronic Books

1. An electronic book is only as good as the power available to run it.
2. Equipment is too valuable to entrust to students.
3. Textbook publishers are set up for print. (Actually, many publishers of print material already make their listings available electronically.)
4. An electronic book can only display one page at a time. It would be difficult to switch back and forth between pages or to view pages from different "books" at the same time.
5. Paper producers would suffer drastic losses in business.
6. Equipment is more susceptible to damage than is a traditional book.
7. An increasing reliance on the storage of information in electronic form imperils the archiving of cultural history. That is, a simple electronic virus can do a lot of damage.
8. Students would have to find something else to throw at each other. (Is that a pro or a con?) (Ebert & Culyer, 2008)

Though this may seem like a simple sort of question to you, perhaps even a "non-question," it is concerned with how we will handle the written word, both in presentation and degree, in the years to come. What sort of changes should there be? Is it possible that publishers of electronic textbooks will see that their profits are in the "intellectual property" of the written word and, so, will make the equipment available to schools at little or no charge? After all, only those who have the machinery to run the books will be inclined to buy the books. Therefore, the textbook industry might go out of its way to see that there's an electronic book on every desk the first day of school.

Textbooks So far, we've discussed the way in which textbooks might be presented, but the entire question of *content* remains to be considered as well. Much of the content in textbooks is influenced by the several largest textbook-buying states. It is an influence that is purely a matter of economics. It is possible that the whole electronic book idea will change all of that. It may well be possible that a department will be formed within each state's education agency that will be responsible for the content of textbooks for that state. Publishers will make their materials available to those committees, and the committee members will then pick and choose what they want to appear in the electronic versions for their state. This, of course, is not a technology that is years away. As you read these words, electronic publishing can easily accomplish such a task.

This scenario is one that may indeed have ramifications that could empower education on the one hand and sow the seeds of civil conflict on the other. As you are well aware, at this point states can choose the topics they want to include in the curriculum and which ones they wish to exclude. As education remains a matter of state's rights and technology allows more customization of teaching materials, education across the nation could become more dissimilar than similar. Under our current system, such differentiation is held in check by the encumbrances of print media. Remove those encumbrances, however, and the situation could change dramatically. A framework such as the 622 Curriculum Model described in chapter 6 may make the development of electronically delivered materials not only viable but practical as well.

PHYSICAL FACILITIES

Design of School Facilities

Across the United States, you will find examples of buildings that seem to be the very representation of school as an institution. These old buildings typically involve a lot of masonry work, wooden floors, tall windows, and an overall "massive" sort of demeanor. Such buildings are often multilevel, and access to upper or lower floors, perhaps even to the front doors, is by staircase. Buildings of this type were not inexpensive, and so it is no surprise that they have been occupied in various states of repair for decades on end. Today, it is not uncommon to find one or more "modern" buildings attached to the older structure by a hallway or breezeway or, at the very least, a village of "portables" (temporary buildings housing one or two classrooms) mushrooming around it. In 1999, 39 percent of all public schools were using "temporary" buildings (NCES, 2004). For schools of six hundred students or more (that's approximately twenty-eight thousand schools), one-half use temporary buildings. But take a look at the cornerstone of that original building, and you will find dates that go back to the early twentieth century.

Buildings such as these tend to become icons in and of themselves. These are the buildings we think of when imagining the footsteps of the great people who once roamed the hallways of public schools. As venerable examples of the institution of education, it is rare that these buildings are demolished to make way for newer ones. This does not suggest, however, that the buildings are necessarily maintained in a manner that preserves their glory. As of 1999, a full 50 percent of the approximately seventy-eight thousand public schools in our country had one or more building features rated as less than adequate (NCES, 2004).

The National Defense Education Act of the late 1950s brought a sharp national focus to education as a response to several disturbing world trends and events. Along with the development of new curricula, there was a building boom of American schools. In fact, some might argue that the real reform in education was in terms of construction techniques.

Rather than the large, labor-intensive structures that we know of from the pre-1950s, new buildings were often some variation or another of a general plan: cinder block walls, metal-framed window units, welded steel roof trusses, and flat roofing systems. Schools had less height and more sprawl. With legislation affecting equal access and special services, new construction often adopted the "one-floor" design that eliminated, or at least minimized, the need for staircases or elevator systems for physically challenged students.

We can nonetheless identify at least a few common threads between the old school buildings and the new. First, whether single-story or multistory, schools take up a lot of space. Another commonality is that the space that schools and their surrounding properties occupy is typically open area. The truly urban inner-city school may be an exception, but even in such a case, the facility occupies an open area to one degree or another. Third, the basic design of a school continues to emphasize the movement of people, a lot of people, and often at the same time. Thus, schools are typically an arrangement of classrooms along a large hallway. And finally, schools never seem to be big enough. A brand-new school that opens as you read this book may well have a contingent of portable buildings mushrooming in its backyard within a year.

New Possibilities

It would not be feasible to simply eliminate all the schools we have and start over, so let's try to think in terms of what we can do with the old schools, along with coming up with ideas that could be incorporated into the design of new schools. Try to keep in mind that having new ideas is not sufficient to make these things happen. The real challenge of developing a shared national vision for education remains. It is the shared vision that will sustain the impetus for innovation in education.

Considering that schools take up so much space, one idea that can apply to old as well as new is that schools generate at least a portion of their own power. School rooftops, out in the open sun, are obvious candidates for arrays of solar collectors. By using passive collectors for heating water and photovoltaic collectors for generating electricity, schools could generate not only their own power but possibly generate excess power that could be sold back to the utility company. Wind-generated energy is also a possibility. So, rather than utilities being a major drain on the school budget, generating power may actually become a source of revenue. An increased cost in the building of the school may result in a school that is less costly to operate.

Schools typically have large, heat-absorbing parking lots on their grounds. Perhaps during construction of such lots, a type of flexible tubing could be embedded in the pavement. Water running through the tubing could then be heated throughout the day. The water could either go to use for the hot-water needs of the school or could be delivered at a higher temperature to the school's power-generating facility, thus requiring less energy to heat for use in generating electricity. Perhaps there is an engineering entrepreneur who could develop such a system and patent it (it could certainly have applications beyond schools), with the stipulation that the technology must be made available to schools at no cost.

Students represent another major source of energy. As we have mentioned, the traditional trend in school design moves students from room to room. This means that in many schools, there are literally thousands of students walking through the hallways at peak times throughout the day. Imagine a floor system that made use of the energy that a floor (and those expensive athletic shoes) usually absorbs as people walk across it. Perhaps a thin water-filled channel could be sandwiched between two layers of waterproof material. With each step on the top layer, water would be forced through the channel until it eventually passed through a turbine that generated electricity. Multiply the action of one person walking across the floor by the hundreds or thousands of students that walk through the hallway each day, and the possibility exists for schools to capture "student power."

As with the parking lot heat-transfer project, such a technology might easily be adapted to other high-traffic areas, such as airports or stadiums. Perhaps the designer of such a system could insist that the manufacturer provide "power floors" free of charge to public schools in exchange for the right to market it for nonschool use.

Design of School Buildings

The sheer size of schools and their various buildings has come to be of concern for a number of reasons. While there are many factors that influence the design of schools, most of those factors are not *pedagogical* concerns. Instead, they often involve questions such as the moving of students, controlling who gets into the building, how quickly large numbers of students can be moved through or out of the building, and the concerns of equal access for all students. Yet, it is also true that school "sprawl" results in the necessity of moving students greater distances, even within the building. What if instead of conceptualizing school buildings as classrooms emanating from a central hallway, we thought in terms of hallways that surround classrooms? Certainly such an arrangement would make it easier to provide the electronic capabilities for clusters of classrooms that we discussed previously (not to mention electricity and plumbing) because such utilities could be more centralized.

While considering the size of the building, one ongoing debate to consider is that of class size and, subsequently, the size of classrooms. Research has shown that class size has a long-term correlation to academic achievement ("Benefits of Small Classes Found to Last Years," 1999) and that benefits are retained even after students return to regular-size classes (Finn, 2002). Because of this, many schools—and even entire states—have mandated that class sizes be reduced. But there are at least two factors that have diluted the success of such initiatives: Class size must be reduced to about fifteen students ("Small Class Sizes Produce Long-Term Benefits," 1999) to realize increases in achievement (thus far, class-size-reduction efforts have only brought class limits to around twenty to twenty-two students), and current classrooms *and classrooms in newly designed schools* are sized with the idea of accommodating several dozen students. In the latter case, it is a matter of "if you build it, they will come." That is, as long as schools provide space for larger numbers of students per class, eventually larger numbers will be placed there. So, how daring an initiative would it be if a school were designed specifically for smaller class sizes? How might this work out in terms of the overall school design? Could it be the case that breaking this conceptual block is what is necessary to pave the way for more innovation in education?

Expandability is another aspect of school design that holds great potential for the creative thinkers concerned with education. Schools are typically designed for a finite number of students, even though they just as typically have changing enrollments. We have already mentioned that this often leads to the use of temporary buildings even as

---

Activity 7.4.
THE SMALLER CLASSROOM

Take a moment to think over what schools might look like with smaller classrooms. If we keep the idea of developing virtual districts but neighborhood schools, the whole notion becomes even more workable.

The outside dimensions of the school would likely remain about the same because the building still has to accommodate the same number of students. But draw an outline for a school (be creative; use any shape you'd like) and then subdivide the building for the essential rooms, such as the office, a media center, and the like, but then divide the rest of the building using rooms sized for no more than a dozen students at a time.

After drawing your master floor plan, draw a more detailed plan for just one of the rooms. Will you still use desks for twelve students, or will you use a single large table? How would you set up a room to create a more conducive environment for learning? Would a language classroom look different from a math classroom? Would such classes be held in different rooms? Break out of the classroom "box" idea with this activity!

the concrete continues to cure in the new building. What really confounds the problem is that enrollments can rise *and* fall. It would not be practical for communities to build structures that far exceed present needs based only on speculation about the future, and it would be just as inefficient to build large schools that eventually have need for only 50 percent of the space available. However, suppose expansion and contraction were part of school design. Meeting the future demands of enrollment would not have to occur in such a haphazard manner.

This could be the beginning of an entire industry arising around the design and manufacture of "modular schools." We are not suggesting portable buildings, which are often lacking in structural integrity (for long-term use), appropriate heating, cooling, plumbing, and, not least of all, aesthetics. (Though it's easy to ignore the aesthetic aspect, keep in mind that children spend their entire day at school, and the condition of the building and classrooms, whether portables or permanent structures, teaches an implicit message about the value placed on schools and the people in them.)

If schools were designed as modular units, a district or community could purchase a set of modules for their particular needs. There could be administrative modules, instructional modules, special needs modules, *energy modules*, and so on. These units could be manufactured in such a way that would allow schools to seamlessly add new modules as the need arose. Even more innovatively, it could be the case that as needs changed, modules could be removed and replaced with different modules that served different purposes. Old modules could be refurbished, updated, and reused in other settings. Modules that were no longer needed by the school could be moved and put to use for other community activities, such as community centers, youth centers, or senior centers. Now *that* would be a switch in our contemporary approach to education: schools giving hand-me-downs to the community rather than the other way around!

What types of modules should be developed for our new schools, and how should they be equipped? What should be included in a "classroom module" or in a "physical education module," or a "media center" module? And more importantly, *how could the module concept be employed so that schools never become the antiquated buildings that are found throughout our country?* With this idea, we are looking at a system that keeps schools on the cutting edge and allows others to benefit as well. Designing expansion and change into a building system does not eliminate the "art" from architecture; it challenges it!

Necessary Facilities

All of these ideas lead to a discussion of necessary facilities. If you were about to put pen to paper for the purpose of designing a new school, what does that school really need to have? Try not to begin with the "big box" model for schools with which we are all so familiar. Instead, consider some of the things that go on at school and work from there. Perhaps the old design will prove to be the best—but let's see.

What constitutes a necessity? For example, the library has given way to the more contemporary "media center." Does a media center really need to occupy as much space as once was claimed by a library? Is a band hall that is separate from an auditorium necessary? Does parking, at a new school, have to be outside of the building? Perhaps parking garages could be built into the basements of new buildings. And is it necessary to provide parking for students? Perhaps parking spaces could be provided as recognition of academic excellence or for social/civic contributions rather than providing hundreds of spaces that could be better used for other purposes.

It may well be the case that when you examine the necessities of schools, you will find that there is duplication and, in many situations, extravagance. This is not to say that education does not deserve the best that can be provided, but many schools have less than the best as it is. Some schools have fine facilities but no money left to replenish consumables (paper, supplies, etc.), and still others use storerooms and closet space to accommodate academic activities. Think outside the school as you know it. How can new schools benefit from a new perspective?

Flow

No matter what we do with the school of the future, it will likely require the movement of large numbers of people from one place to another. Even if we see a return to greater use of neighborhood schools by virtue of the education coalitions mentioned in this chapter, movement of students is a fact of school life. This might involve not only getting students to and from school but getting them from one place within the building (or its surrounding facilities) to another. Even if electronic technology eventually makes school an "at home" activity, there will still be a need for coordinating the activities of many people. We refer to all of this as the "flow" of the school.

As we see schools today, elementary students tend to be assigned to one classroom and one teacher and to stay there throughout the day. Middle school and high school students have a homeroom but move throughout the building to many different classes and many different teachers. Is this the best model?

While teaching at a university in China for a semester, one of your authors had the opportunity to observe a different model. When students arrived at the university in their first year, they were assigned to a particular classroom. This became "their" room for the duration of the collegiate experience. *Each student had a key to the room, and together they were responsible for keeping the room clean and orderly.* Professors would come to that room throughout the day to teach the different subjects. The classroom became the meeting place for the students after classes. Students would come there to study and to talk, and occasionally they would have a class party. The model was that students, of whom there were many, stayed in one place while professors, of whom there were few, moved from room to room.

Could a variation of this same model be used in American middle schools and high schools? Keep in mind that it is already the model we use for the elementary schools. Rather than putting several hundred students in motion every hour or so, a model such as this would do away with much of the lost time between classes, the delays in starting classes when students arrive late, and the lost time at the end of a class as students prepare to depart before the period ends.

What affect would such a change have on the design of new schools? Would hallways need to be as big? If hallways were not as big, could that space (as square footage in the overall building) be utilized differently or perhaps eliminated, thus decreasing the cost of the building? It may be that the additional square footage would make building more classrooms of smaller size a viable possibility. Perhaps, as we have mentioned before, the hallways could surround a pod of classrooms rather than dividing the rooms. This arrangement might be better suited to providing several different specialties, such as a general classroom that opens into a science room, that opens into an arts room, all without the need to leave the central area.

Time spent moving about is lost instructional time. According to Burns (1984), at the elementary level there are thirty-one major transitions occupying 15 percent of the instructional time available for the day. That's nearly an hour a day, and elementary students don't move from room to room for each subject!

Use of School Facilities

There was a time when schools were thought of as the "heart" of a community. That's not difficult to understand since it was the place where the children were sent to learn. School was a socializing experience funded in large part by the local community. Contemporary schools, unfortunately, have a more distanced relationship to the community. They are provided to accomplish a particular (though still ill-defined) purpose, they are funded by a community that is often concerned with the high rate of taxes and fees that its members must pay, and it is not uncommon that the only time people (other than students and school personnel) show up to the school is for various extracurricular activities.

This issue of the school's relationship as a community facility certainly has at least two sides: (1) schools are established and funded for the purpose of educating students, but (2) the school is a public building that sits idle in the evenings, on the weekends, and for several months each year. In view of this, it would be worth our time to consider how the schools could be more fully utilized.

Year-round School

Probably any child who has attended school has cringed at the thought of having to go to school all year long. The debate regarding keeping schools open on a year-round basis is decades old. Arguments range from better utilization of the facilities to increased retention of prior learning. After all, a three-month hiatus from what one has just learned hardly contributes to improved achievement. (Actually, if we really wanted to know what students had learned in a given year, the time to test them would be on the first day back after the summer break.) Arguments opposed to keeping schools open tend to emphasize parents' summer vacation plans, as well as the increased costs of keeping the facility up and running for three additional months, especially at a time when schools around the country are forced to close early because funding has run out. Considering that literally hundreds of millions of dollars worth of real estate remains idle for a quarter of every year, it is easy to understand that this is an area in need of attention.

Year-round-school proposals do not typically involve extending the 180 day "school year" model. Rather, days spent in school are simply distributed differently. For example, students may have a week-long vacation after each six weeks of school with a four-week break after the third and sixth six-week periods. The 45–15 and 60–15 days on/days off models are the most common. It would also be possible to stagger the starting date of different grade levels. For any of these options, the number of days does not change, just the distribution of them.

Though each of these plans has legitimate pedagogical purposes, they all wreak havoc with working parents who depend on school to provide day care for their children. However, it is also true that a school system using the six-week plan mentioned above also provides the opportunity for entrepreneurs to develop day care programs that specifically work with the school's schedule; after all, that's what they do now.

The first question with regard to better utilization of school facilities is really just one of innovative scheduling possibilities. As you redefine what school is, watch for opportunities for new businesses to arise. Schools have lost much of their efficacy because they have been forced to assume the roles that could be provided by ancillary businesses (see "Ancillary Businesses" below). If the current arguments over forcing schools to compete with each other were augmented to include having entrepreneurs and ancillary businesses compete for the opportunity to provide the noninstructional services that schools require, *then* a new wave of innovation and competition could be expected to appear on the horizon.

Community Activities

There probably are not many school principals who would like to hear this, but the truth is the truth: Public schools are public facilities. There could be some debate as to whether they are owned by the community, the county (parish), or the state; nonetheless, they are bought, built, and operated with tax dollars. Public schools are often used as polling places during election time, but it is not unreasonable to suggest that they be used for civic purposes to a much greater degree.

We certainly understand that there are probably few teachers or principals who welcome the idea of the community at large traipsing through the building when school is not in session (for example, in the evenings, on the weekends, or during vacation periods). We share their concern. Yet, a community that takes responsibility for its activities at the school also sets an example for the students who attend that school. It also allows for the possibility of taking more pride by virtue of "ownership" in the school itself. In a previous section of this chapter, "Meaningful Parental Involvement," we encouraged parents to become directly involved in the upkeep of school facilities. This alone would make community use of the property less destructive because people would appreciate the effort that it takes to maintain the educational environment.

If we follow this train of thought further, there are at least two categories of community use to be considered: nonprofit and revenue producing. Nonprofit activities are those that might be allowed for such things as community government (town meetings), civic-organization meetings, or summer (vacation) programs for the children in the community.

Revenue-producing events, on the other hand, could involve using the school auditorium for concerts or lecture series for which an admission price is collected. Continuing education programs could use the facility in the evenings, and a portion of the participants' tuition could go toward renting the space. Opening a newly designed physical fitness center might also be an opportunity for producing revenue. Individuals who use the exercise equipment during the evenings could reasonably be expected to pay a "membership fee" or "community-use fee" of some sort because they are, after all, using equipment that must be maintained and/or replaced. Private businesses could lease the space during off hours and provide fitness classes of various types to community members. In this way, funds for the continued maintenance of the facility would be provided without taxing the school's academic budget.

Of course, possibilities such as these are not ones to be entertained lightly. It is a sad fact of our society that there are those who might abuse the access that is being granted. There might also be organizations that the community, for noble or less than noble reasons, does not want to grant access. Would the community have a right to allow some activities and not others? Keep in mind that the underlying issue that we are addressing is how the school facilities in their generic and specialized senses can be better utilized.

Ancillary Businesses

Even with all of the responsibilities that modern schools have assumed, they still involve many ancillary businesses. Throughout this book, we have been discussing education as an isolated entity. However, long gone are the days when school was just a building in town where children met with a teacher. "School" today also includes transportation services, food services, supplies, medical attention, and diagnostic testing by professionals in a wide range of physical and psychological disciplines, to name just a few of the nonteaching aspects of school. To a degree, this is the result of the school's being seen as more than just an institution of education. To a considerable extent, it has become a holistic child-care institution. From the perspective of social reconstructivists, the school is seen as the mechanism for solving society's problems. Thus, schools provide breakfast to children who receive none at home. They provide lunch. They provide after-school programs for children who have nowhere to go until their parents can leave work for the day.

What we want to add to the discussion is the notion of ancillary businesses and the schools of the future. Our question is this: What services should the school provide, and what services should be provided to the school by businesses? For example, should schools and school districts also be in the transportation business? Is this something that could be better provided by a private school bus service of some sort? Obviously, in large cities the public transportation system is used for moving students to and from schools. Is there a possibility for entrepreneurship in suburban and rural communities? As another example, is food service something that schools should provide with district personnel, or should this be contracted out as well?

We would suggest that schools just might be better off if they could focus on education alone, so to speak, rather than also being responsible for repairing buses, providing before- and after-school programs for monitoring children in loco parentis before and after school hours, or assuming the task of feeding hundreds of children. We would also suggest that a shift in perspective that encouraged ancillary businesses to take on many noneducational tasks would stimulate the growth of new business, as well as provide healthy competition for the best product at the best price. What effect could this have if we saw a shift that allowed schools to emphasize schooling rather than an overall package of child welfare? Could we legitimately expect parents to take a greater responsibility? If free and reduced-price lunch programs, breakfast programs, and so forth are what the community wants, they can remain as state and federally subsidized programs. The *providing* of the service, however, could be done by an ancillary independent business.

FINAL THOUGHTS

These last sections have not been intended as an exhaustive look at what needs to change and how to go about it. Rather, these have been starting points. Perhaps even more importantly, the intent is to demonstrate that in revolutionizing the institution, there are no sacred cows. There are no preexisting conditions that cannot be called into question, with the exception of one: The adults in our society, not the children, bear the responsibility for providing an educational experience characterized by excellence, and we cannot ask children to wait around for a few years while we get our act together.

Throughout this book, we have attempted to provoke your thinking about the American culture and the purpose and organization of schools, and we have *not* tried to *prescribe* what should be done with regard to public education. In this chapter and the one that preceded it, we have been trying to identify broad mechanisms for change and major categories of "schoolness" that those mechanisms might address. In the next chapter, we will look more closely at curriculum. But as you can see from recommendations such as the Education Congress of the States or the American Education Association, conceptualizing a new institution is something that must involve many players who find a common vision rather than just looking at a plan described by several individuals. It is for this reason that activities have been included throughout each chapter. If you have been completing (or at least considering) the activities, you are already becoming one of the players.

8

Education in the New Institution

Feedback from employers who hire public school graduates has not been generally positive. Employers find graduates weak or inadequate. Many graduates cannot read, write, or calculate. In other words, performance standards of schools are too low.

—Irving Buchen

It can easily be argued that performance standards are too low in our schools. However, it is not simply a matter of having higher standards. We must first have a curriculum that reflects a shared vision of what an education in the United States should accomplish.

There are many factors influencing curriculum in the modern school, and it may be impossible to determine which has the greatest effect on what ultimately reaches the student. It's possible that the folks who had the most significant impact on the American educational curriculum in the last five decades were a group of Soviet scientists working away on a basketball-sized satellite back in the 1950s. It was the launch of Sputnik (the first man-made satellite) that initiated the spending of unprecedented amounts of federal money for the revision of school curricula in math and science so that we might catch up with, and surpass, the technological achievements of the Russians. In fact, it was the National Defense Education Act of 1958 that appropriated nearly $1 billion primarily for math and science curriculum-reform efforts. Since that time, the funding emphasis has switched from one area to another in accord with the prevailing social climate. Much of the furor that once existed has subsided, but the use of *federal* taxpayer dollars to support educational research and development continues despite the fact that education is each *state's* responsibility.

CONSIDERING THE CURRICULUM

Our look at curriculum is intended to help you see the depth and breadth of this fundamental aspect of organized education. The issues that arise when discussing curriculum can be divisive in communities, states, and the nation. Questions of school prayer,

171

uniforms, the suitability of certain books in the library, and even scientific perspectives cannot be resolved within the pages of this chapter, but it is hoped that you will gain a better appreciation of what curriculum is as we consider what students should be exposed to as part of school.

UNDERSTANDING "CURRICULUM"

There is considerable discussion these days about policies such as requiring public school children to wear uniforms to school or prohibiting the wearing of clothing that displays "culturally offensive" messages. Would you consider the policy decisions about these issues to be part of the curriculum? Did the high school *you* attended have a dress code? Would you consider that as part of the curriculum? What about the food served in the cafeteria? Many schools today are removing soda machines and no longer offer sugary beverages for sale because they are not considered to have nutritional value. And what of the offering of "ethnic" foods in the school cafeteria? Is this part of the curriculum? Would the teaching, or not teaching, of evolution as a topic in science classes or the removal of books considered to represent "new age" philosophy from the library bookshelves? In your opinion, do any of these issues enter into determining what constitutes curriculum—the message of the school?

Defining "Curriculum"

Arising in medieval Europe was the *trivium*, an educational curriculum based upon the study of grammar, rhetoric, and logic. The later *quadrivium* (referring to four subjects rather than three, as represented by the trivium) emphasized the study of arithmetic, geometry, music, and astronomy.

This perspective on curriculum should sound familiar. The emphasis on single subjects (such as those identified in the trivium and quadrivium) continues even today. Very likely during your own school days, you moved from classroom to classroom, particularly throughout your secondary education, studying a different subject with each teacher. Yet, there was much more to your education. Perhaps you participated in athletics, or the band, or clubs, or student government, or made the choice *not* to participate in any extracurricular activities. All of these (including the option not to participate) constitute what we might call the contemporary curriculum.

Curriculum is indeed much more than the idea of specific subjects as represented by the trivium or the quadrivium. It requires extensive planning and organizing that incorporates built-in flexibility. It must have a clear purpose but not have a structure that fails to allow for the fact that all classrooms are composed of *individual* children. It can be characterized not only by what it *does* include but also by what it intentionally *excludes*.

Some say that the curriculum consists of all the *planned experiences* that the school offers as part of its educational responsibility. Others would suggest that the curriculum includes not only the planned but the *unplanned experiences* as well. For example, incidents of violence that have occurred at a number of schools across the nation are by no means a planned component of the curriculum. However, the manner in which these situations are addressed before, during, and after the actual event does send a very definite message about how people in our culture interact and how the laws of our nation are applied. We will also mention here that events of great joy and accomplishment are also powerfully charged as lifelong experiences. Given that schools are expected to take a particular perspective on all events that take place within their jurisdiction, we could say that the curriculum *does* include unplanned experiences as well.

There is also a perspective that suggests that curriculum involves "organized" experiences rather than planned experiences because any event must flow of its own accord, the outcome not being certain beforehand. Competitions, for example, whether academic or athletic, can be organized, but the outcomes will depend on a myriad of factors that cannot be planned. All of this brings us to the notion of emphasizing *outcomes* versus *experiences*. The focus now would be on what the schools are supposed to accomplish with the students rather than simply on what the student *might* be exposed to as part of school. The curriculum, therefore, would be that program by which the school meets its educational goals.

This shift to the notion of *outcomes* is in keeping with the contemporary trend toward *accountability* in the public schools, that is, the perspective that there are indeed specific things that the schools are supposed to accomplish with children. District personnel, school administrators, and teachers are to be held accountable for ensuring that those objectives are met.

What this leaves us with is an enormous task that cannot be overestimated. Hirsch (1988) has written, "During recent decades Americans have hesitated to make a decision about the specific knowledge that children need to learn in school" (19), and "There is a pressing need for clarity about our educational priorities" (25). In this book, we have discussed a number of mechanisms for addressing this need, but none of them can be effective until the decision is made to bring an end to the hesitation that Hirsch mentions.

So, if in a challenging situation you should happen to be asked what "curriculum" means, what should you say? Though much of the message of school is strikingly similar throughout the country, there are differences from state to state—and even between regions within a state. Curricula are always intended to serve a particular constituency, and you likely know the constituency where you live better than we do. From a broader perspective, however, we suggest that you think of the curriculum as *the means and materials with which students will interact for the purpose of achieving identified educational outcomes.* "Materials" refers to the identified subjects and topics to be presented to the students and to the various media formats in which those topics are presented (for example, books, videos, computer software, etc.). By "means," we refer to the strategies teachers use to foster interest, expand perspectives, and encourage learning. Modeling, investigating, and even drill-and-practice are among the methods a teacher might consider for stimulating inquiry, creative and critical thinking, and attitudes of persistence and respect. Taken together, the materials and means represent the curriculum.

The definition we have suggested is necessarily flexible but is also specific on a couple of points. One is that there must be *clearly identified desired outcomes.* This is not to say that all students are expected to reach the same mark in the same amount of time but simply that everybody should know what the mark is, whether it's a particular level of achievement in mathematics or the ability to function as a contributing member of the community. Clearly articulated purposes, goals, and objectives underlie sound curriculum design, instruction, and assessment. As Anderson and Krathwohl (2001) have noted, the more specific the learning experience, the better defined the objectives should be.

A key aspect of the definition we have suggested is that the curriculum is only that part of the plan that *directly affects* students. Anything in the plan that does not reach the students constitutes an educational wish, not a curriculum. Rutherford and Ahlgren (1990) argue in *Science for All Americans* that "the present curricula in science and mathematics are overstuffed and undernourished" (viii). That is, there is too much information and not enough depth. This is the result of years of tinkering with curricula that may have originally represented sound educational objectives. Nearly half a century ago Bruner (1960) wrote, "Many curricula are originally planned with a guiding idea much like the one set forth here. But as curricula are actually executed, as they grow and change, they often lose their original form and suffer a relapse into a certain shapelessness" (54). Any chapter that is not addressed in class and for whose content the students are not held responsible is not part of the curriculum, even if it was part of someone's "plan."

The Purpose of Curriculum

From colonial times with lessons in reading and Bible study, to the secular emphasis on grammar, rhetoric, and logic, to the efforts to make education more "relevant" in the real world, curriculum has responded to social issues, concerns, and priorities (notice that it has *responded* rather than being proactive). Surveys conducted by the Committee for Economic Development and the College Board indicate that employers look for three traits in school graduates: an ability to learn, literacy, and a positive attitude toward work (Committee for Economic Development, 1985).

Authors such as Theodore Sizer (1985) and Mortimer Adler (1982, 1983) have been considerably more specific in their expectations, however, advocating an emphasis on intellectual development. Perhaps the most prescriptive of all has been the call for a focus on cultural literacy, that is, those things that "every American needs to know" (Hirsch, 1988). Whether that reduces education once again to the memorization of facts and figures is worthy of discussion. However, the spirit of the message, a viable one, is that we owe it to ourselves and to our children to be able to articulate our expectations for their education.

Yet another perspective involves placing an emphasis on "character education." The Center for Advancement of Ethics and Character, an organization that sees the school curriculum as lacking in moral authority and ethical language to the point of being sterile and meaningless, looks for a "return" of American values to the school curriculum. It is easy enough to imagine how "sticky" this issue could be. For instance, an English teacher may want her students to read Henry David Thoreau's work *On Civil Disobedience*, yet obedience to the laws of the land is an ethical trait that citizens are supposed to possess.

When the debate includes the question of *time*, a paradoxical question that could stump thinkers for decades becomes apparent. That is, should schools prepare their students for the known present or the unknown future? Without doubt, education as we have known it has been based on the past and directed toward contemporary and practical applications. It is true that high school seniors, college bound or not, will likely be putting their skills to work within days or weeks of graduation. In those cases, a reasonable argument can be made that education should focus on the time in which they live, with today's world, today's needs, and today's expectations of public school graduates. Yet, we also need to consider the youngster on his way to his first day of kindergarten. That child is beginning an educational adventure that will occupy thirteen years or more. It is reasonable to assume that in that length of time, the needs of the community, nation, and world may be very different than they are today. Will there be new ways of communicating, of doing business, of building buildings, and of repairing automobiles? Likely, the answers to these few questions will be yes. The challenge, then, is in designing a curriculum for a future that as yet is unknown.

The curriculum provides opportunities, and the teacher does his or her best to guide the students through those opportunities in a manner that helps to accomplish a desired goal. But a school cannot predetermine all of the educational experiences that a student will have (and often not the most influential experiences). Instead, the school provides the opportunities that could result in experiences of value to the student. Whatever the parameters are or may one day be, the curriculum must prepare the student to thrive within the society as it is, and that includes developing *the capacity for positive change and growth*. That's quite a responsibility: educating people in the present, based on the past, to be prepared for the future.

There Is More Than Just One Curriculum

To this point, we have spoken of curriculum as if it were just one entity. As we look more closely at the structure of curriculum, we find that there are essentially four curricula at work in most educational settings. These four are the explicit, implicit, null, and extra-, or co-, curriculum. Though you are probably familiar with the notions of explicit curriculum and extracurricular activities, the real *intrigue* of curriculum debate and design comes into play with the implicit and null curricula.

The Explicit Curriculum

"Explicit" means "obvious" or "apparent," and that's just what the explicit curriculum is all about. This aspect of the school curriculum is concerned with the subjects that will be taught, the identified "mission" of the school, and the knowledge and skills that the school expects successful students to acquire. These are, in a sense, the published elements of school. If you speak with an administrator at a school and ask about the curriculum, it is this publicly announced (and publicly sanctioned) explanation of the message of school that will be explained to you.

You will hear of the explicit curriculum discussed in terms of time on task, contact hours, or Carnegie units (high school credit courses). It can be detailed in terms of specific, observable, and measurable learning objectives. When students complete the annual district- or state-adopted achievement tests, two dimensions of the educational process are being measured: the school's success in effectively teaching the explicit curriculum and the students' success in learning it.

The Implicit Curriculum

The explicit curriculum does not account for all of the messages presented in school. Sometimes referred to as the "hidden curriculum," the implicit curriculum refers to the lessons that arise from the culture of the school and the behaviors, attitudes, and expectations that characterize that culture. Lessons in good citizenship may comprise part of the explicit curriculum. A particular ethos that promotes multiethnic acceptance and cooperation may also characterize a particular school. This is not to suggest that parents, teachers, and administrators sat around a table and said, "Hey, let's promote acceptance of diverse ethnic values in the context of the American experience." As nice as that might be, it tends to fall into the category of the explicit curriculum. Rather, what we might see is that, by virtue of a high multiethnic enrollment, a particular school may have a "culture" of multiethnic cooperation. Another school, "isolated" in that its enrollment is primarily of one ethnic group, would develop a different sort of culture.

Schools are unique social systems. Even individual schools within a district that share a common *explicit* curriculum can differ greatly with regard to the *implicit* curriculum. You can readily observe this in a district with two high schools. Each school will seek to develop its own identity, and interscholastic athletic competition is one of the prime vehicles through which this is accomplished. The two schools have the same explicit curriculum, but they distinguish themselves based on their implicit curricula. This is not an altogether bad situation, but, to a great degree, the implicit curriculum is subjected to less scrutiny than is the explicit curriculum. It is important to consider the implicit messages that are being transmitted and to consider whether they are messages that should be perpetuated.

There are many aspects to the implicit curriculum, and, interestingly enough, it is the students who pick up on these messages. If you should have the opportunity to visit a school, notice how the classrooms and common areas are decorated. These decorations will demonstrate what the implicit curriculum of the school values. Watch the children to see how they interact with each other within the class and throughout the building. Is there an emphasis on how students are to walk through the halls? Does the school display student work throughout the building? Is there an unwritten but obvious rule that children are to be seen and not heard, or do you hear the voices of children enthusiastically and actively engaged in learning? These are just a few of the many examples that contribute to a very particular message sent to students about expectations, demands, and codes of conduct.

If you speak with some elementary school students, you can investigate the implicit curriculum further. Ask what is required to get good grades or the approval of the teacher. Your expectation may be something about studying for two hours every night or completing homework correctly, but don't be surprised when they tell you things like "sitting up straight," or "being quiet in class," or "being on time." The implicit curriculum, difficult as it is to identify and articulate, is something that students understand very quickly. Bruner (1960) speaks of the need to address intuitive understanding of a subject in order to learn increasingly sophisticated aspects of that subject. Well, here is a very practical example of intuitive understanding. When young children explain the expectations for a student in school, it will likely be the implicit curriculum that they discuss.

The Null Curriculum

Eisner's (1994) concept of the null curriculum is equally compelling as investigating the implicit curriculum. In this instance, we refer to "the options students are not afforded, the perspectives they may never know about, much less be able to use, the concepts and skills that are not a part of their intellectual repertoire" (106–107). The decision to *exclude* particular topics or subjects from a curriculum affects the curriculum by their very omission. The teaching of evolution provides an example. For more than seventy-five years, this topic has been an issue of debate. The decision by individual states or school districts within states not to include this topic within its explicit curriculum places it in the category of the *null curriculum*. You will note that the 622 Curriculum Model discussed in chapter 6 attempts to provide schools with the opportunity to move null curriculum topics into the realm of the explicit curriculum, making them open, observable, and subject to intellectual discourse.

There are other aspects of the null curriculum that are important for curriculum designers to consider as they design the educational programs of the new century. Artistic activity, creative endeavor, imagination, inventiveness, innovation, and the solving of ill-structured problems (the most prevalent of real-life problems) receive little emphasis in the traditional explicit curriculum and are often the first to go when budgets are being trimmed. This provides somewhat of a cultural contradiction when you consider that ours is a country that, to a great degree, has succeeded based upon a spirit of innovation and risk taking, yet these tendencies are not fostered within the curriculum to the same degree as conformity, procedure, and discipline. As Eisner (1994) states, "We teach what we teach largely out of habit, and in the process neglect areas of study that could prove to be exceedingly useful to students" (103). While the future of education is wide-open given the electronic access to information, it is equally restrained by the firewalling of electronic access in the name of the null curriculum. Another paradox? Yes, another.

Extracurricular Programs

The final aspect of curriculum that we will discuss is that of the extracurriculum, or *cocurriculum*. This curriculum represents all of those school-sponsored programs that are intended to supplement the academic aspect of the school experience. Athletics, music, drama, student government, clubs, and student organizations all fall under the heading of "extracurricular activities." Unlike with the explicit curriculum, student participation in these activities is purely voluntary and contributes neither to grades nor credits earned toward promotion from one grade to the next or to graduation. And also unlike the content of the explicit curriculum, which is ostensibly required of all students, extracurricular activities are open to all, but participation often depends on skill level.

By the early years of the 1990s, more than 80 percent of all high school seniors participated in extracurricular activities. In particular, students from smaller schools and those with stronger academic backgrounds tended to participate. Holland and Andre (1987) suggest that the value of extracurricular activities extends beyond school. Their findings indicate the following:

1. Extracurricular activities enhance student self-esteem.
2. Athletics, in particular, improves race relations.
3. Participating students tend to have higher SAT scores and grades.
4. Involvement is related to high career aspirations. (437–66)

Not everybody agrees, however, and there are opponents to the extracurricular activities we see offered in schools today. Brown (1988) suggests that the effects of participation in extracurricular activities are "probably positive" but are modest at best. Even more to the point, students who could most benefit from involvement tend to shy away from such programs.

It is also important to face the "dream" aspect of extracurricular activities, particularly in terms of athletics. It is often said that sports are what keep many youngsters in school. Aspirations for professional careers are the stuff of which rags-to-riches movies are made. Yet, of the more than five million students competing in varsity sports, only one out of fifty will play for a college team. And of those, only one out of one hundred male athletes will play for a professional sports team. It is not surprising that critics of the extracurriculum, such as Gifford and Dean (1990), question the academic value of programs that do little to prepare students for achievement tests, exit exams, and college entrance exams.

This brief look at extracurricular activities is not intended to suggest that they should simply be banished from the schools. However, with the considerable amount of money that goes into some programs and the dearth of funds made available to others (in particular, academically oriented programs), now would be the time to question whether the "traditional" extracurricular structure is working to achieve best purposes. As we work to reconceptualize the institution of education, it would be worthwhile to make the attempt to design an organizational system that (1) integrates the extra programs into the academic program, (2) allows the academic program to become more engaging, (3) opens extracurricular programs to a wider range of participants, and (4) does not allow the abdication of parental responsibility by providing extended "child care" and prefabricated social and intellectual stimulation.

PRIMARY AND SECONDARY EDUCATION

With an understanding of what "curriculum" is, we can move to a consideration of what the curriculum might contain. As a new curriculum is designed, we need to take a hard look at a contemporary curriculum that "is overstuffed and undernourished," does not interest students, tries to be too many things to too many people, and willingly offers extracurricular activities as an incentive to sit through an otherwise boring use of a child's time. Perhaps the greatest shame of education is that children typically begin kindergarten or first grade wide-eyed and enthusiastic, yet by the end of the eighth grade, their eyes glaze over at the thought of school. This does not mean that school should take on the character of an amusement park or a video game; instead, it demonstrates that we are failing to capitalize on the innate intellectual curiosity that children bring to school.

New Goals

It will always be the case that the four curricula discussed previously will exist in the schools. If the task were as simple as saying, for instance, that the null curriculum would be eliminated (eliminate something that isn't there?), education might have changed for the better years ago. But it is a fact of human interaction that all communities will have in mind those ideas to which they do not want their children exposed, and all schools will develop an implicit curriculum based upon the culture that arises as a function of the unique individuals who compose the faculty, administration, and student body. The challenge is in finding ways to make the explicit curriculum more comprehensive without its becoming frivolous and in making the entire curriculum relevant for all students. A curriculum framework such as the 622

Activity 8.1.
SCHOOL DAYS

As preparation for considering a new curriculum, spend some time thinking about the curriculum you experienced while attending school. It doesn't matter whether you attended public, private, or even homeschooling—each of the four curricula were represented to one degree or another. Do not worry about putting together a detailed list of topics, just try to summarize what you recall as being the emphasis or message of each type of curriculum we have discussed.

Remembering the School Curriculum	
The Explicit Curriculum— These were the actual subjects studied. There were probably textbooks and printed materials that were used in class.	
The Implicit Curriculum— These were the more subtle messages that you picked up on in school. These things didn't show up on the standardized tests. It could include things such as conformity, following rules, being polite, or even political views.	
The Null Curriculum— You likely didn't think much about this while in school. What topics or issues can you identify that seemed to have been "missing" from your education. This could involve political views, alternative lifestyles, particular books, or particular scientific perspectives.	
The Extracurriculum— Did your school have an extensive or limited extracurriculum? Did it emphasize some things more so than others? Why did you, or did you not, participate? What lessons do you think were learned in this curriculum?	

model and an emphasis on gain scores rather than grade levels would help to better articulate the curriculum while also emphasizing individual achievement. Electronic technologies make this a very workable situation.

The National Council for Accreditation of Teacher Education, which is a leader in the accreditation of teacher-education programs, evaluates colleges of education with regard to the knowledge, skills, and dispositions (attitudes) that students acquire. The same three categories may be useful in the conceptualization of the public school curriculum.

Activity 8.2.
ANOTHER LOOK AT THE CURRICULUM

Take another look at the table you completed in Activity 8.1. As you examine the items you have listed, what changes would you make? Are there subjects/messages in any of the four curricula that you feel must remain? Are there others that you feel could be eliminated? Are there subjects/messages that need to be added? And perhaps most importantly, what would you move from the implicit, null, or extracurricula to the explicit curriculum? Make your changes on the table below.

Revising the School Curriculum	
The Explicit Curriculum— These are the subjects/ messages that must appear and that contribute to graduation.	
The Implicit Curriculum— These are messages that students should learn, but need not be held accountable for in terms of grades or graduation.	
The Null Curriculum— These are the topics, issues, or messages that students should not be exposed to as part of formal schooling.	
The Extracurriculum— These are the activities that students should be able to choose whether or not to engage in. They would not have any bearing on graduation.	

Cognitive Skills

Through the course of their formal education, we could expect students to acquire cognitive skills such as mathematical calculation, scientific inquiry, and language use, but we should also emphasize the use of these skills for the solving of problems. It is often said that we are now living in the information age. Our suggestion is that rather than emphasizing the amount of information that is available to us, we should emphasize the utilization of that information for solving problems. In other words, let's make this *the age of problem solving.*

Problem-Solving Skills   The idea of organizing a curriculum that engages students in solving problems using the skills they learn in class is by no means new. The progressive education movement sprang from John Dewey's pragmatic philosophy nearly a century ago. The movement, however, never realized its potential for the very reason we have been discussing throughout this book: a failure to clearly articulate a set of goals and objectives under a single and comprehensive philosophy. The Education Congress of the States may be the vehicle that the progressive education movement lacked so many decades ago.

Language usage (whether native or additional), mathematics, scientific inquiry, and problem solving all represent skills that students should acquire in school. Though we have listed these subject areas in order of their typical prioritization in schools, the first three are actually the tools that are used in accomplishing the fourth. That is, problem solving is the natural activity of the brain whether or not language, number systems, or skills in scientific inquiry are extant. However, each of the three makes the solving of problems easier. We could, therefore, consider all of education in the context of problem solving (which could also include distinctions between *creative* problem solving and *critical* problem solving, depending upon the problem being addressed) and each of the other three areas as skill systems that facilitate the process. If the curriculum were designed around age and the developmentally appropriate experiences of childhood, then the process would reflect Dewey's suggestion that genuine thinking begins with a problematic situation. How do you suppose that outcomes of education may change if children, from a very early age, were taught "how" rather than being told "what."

Scientific Inquiry   Science, as an investigation of the world around us, provides an excellent context not only for developing the skills of scientific inquiry but also for developing language programs (with regard to the content of what students read on their way to becoming readers). Of course, all materials must be written in developmentally appropriate forms, but that is simply a matter of how nature is described in language systems; it is not a function of nature itself. For instance, children can learn about clouds and their relationship to the weather of the day without first having to memorize the technical names of each cloud formation, understand the water cycle, and become keenly aware of the interplay between high- and low-pressure systems. In a spiraling curriculum, however, the time for those higher-level lessons will come.

Mathematics   A particular benefit of this grouping of subjects as skill systems could allow mathematics to be taught not only as a means for calculation but also in terms of its beauty as a system for finding order amid apparent chaos and for describing patterns and relationships. And by the way, we see the ability to do mathematical calculation as a skill worth learning—we are speaking of problem solving (a mental function) rather than solution finding (which can be done with calculators and other electronic technologies). The understanding of concepts, something that we would argue has been lost in contemporary education, would be at the heart of the educational enterprise. Scientific inquiry, mathematics, and language would be the tools for building that understanding.

In 1989, the National Council of Teachers of Mathematics (NCTM) released curriculum and assessment standards that enjoyed wide acceptance by teachers around the country. As opposed to more traditional drill-and-practice, the standards emphasized reasoning, problem solving, communication, technology, and the practical applications of mathematical concepts. The newer Standards 2000 emphasize five mathematical content standards and five mathematical processes for the acquisition and use of mathematical knowledge. The standards recommended by NCTM have been adopted in over forty states.

The Content Standards	*The Process Standards*
1. Number and Operations	1. Problem Solving
2. Algebra	2. Reasoning and Proof
3. Geometry	3. Communication
4. Measurement	4. Connections
5. Data Analysis and Probability	5. Representation

Language   In any contemporary social system, a system of spoken and written language is a necessary skill system for communication. The spoken portion of language acquisition is a function of one's immediate environment. Few, if any, children show up for school without the ability to understand their basic, spoken *native* language. Unfortunately, that verbal ability can often be confounded by regional or cultural influences that must be unlearned (a very difficult task) for standard language use to be achieved. For instance, when one of your authors was teaching for a semester in China, he traveled briefly to Beijing. While visiting a local school, he was asked whether he had learned any Chinese. After reciting the few words he knew, his hosts responded, "Ahh, Shanghai dialect." The influence of the region in which language is acquired can have an impact on the teaching of a standard version of that language.

Our current educational system suffers from a number of problems, the influences of culture and dialect among them. In our age of word processing and text messaging, language conventions (particularly in terms of reading and writing) suffer mightily. As long as the message gets across, spelling, punctuation, and syntax are all of secondary consequence. Making the situation worse is the fact that, as we have discussed previously, an official language has never been adopted in our country. School systems, publicly funded though they may be, can have a difficult time arguing against the use of regional preferences, let alone dialect. And to make matters worse, what we now have is an educational approach to the teaching of reading and writing that, while not ensuring failure, makes it very difficult to catch up once one falls behind—and many students fall behind very early on in their educational experience.

Perhaps most disappointing with regard to the learning of languages is that childhood is the prime time for developing fluency not only in one's native language but in others as well. For that reason, we would suggest that the early instructional experiences emphasize an official national language *and* additional languages as well. All children should be learning at least two languages in the early levels. Though the clear focus is first and foremost on learning the standard official language, introduction to additional languages should begin on the first day of the child's educational career.

We have already argued against the grade-level approach to structuring the school system and in favor of a gain score approach. A new curriculum approach might well incorporate a number of subject areas (perhaps arranged as we have suggested here, with a problem-solving context surrounding a scientific-inquiry theme) but would restructure a student's school experience in concert with his or her reading and writing proficiency. That is to say that a student who excels in reading and writing will broaden his or her curriculum as time goes on, while a child who does not achieve proficiency may narrow the curriculum to focus more on reading and writing until substantive progress is made. Once that achievement is realized, broadening the curriculum once again will be of little difficulty because the increasing sophistication of any curriculum comes with an increased emphasis on reading and writing ability. As it stands now, the child who falls behind in first grade and *is required to work with second-grade materials* (across all subject areas) in the next year simply falls further and further behind.

Knowledge

Apart from the teaching of specific skill systems, schools are also the disseminators of knowledge, the traditions and expectations of the nation that supports the school system, and cultural values, beliefs, and customs. Ostensibly, the academic standards that states adopt are reflective of the elements that appear in the explicit curriculum, and those standards are derived from the recommendations of learned societies in each of the subject areas. In addition, various authors have provided prescriptions for what students should study (e.g., Robert Maynard Hutchins and Mortimer Adler's compilation of *Great Books of the Western World* or Hirsch's more contemporary series, of what every student should know [organized by grade level]), and research groups have developed curriculum programs in various subject areas. Even so, there remains an ambiguity as to what should be the "standard curriculum" in terms of the knowledge that students should acquire in school (this is apart from the skill systems we have already discussed).

A curriculum framework such as the 622 Model may make this matter less vague as 60 percent of the curriculum could be devoted to a nationally consistent curriculum, while states still have the prerogative of teaching alternative perspectives in one of the other 20 percent divisions. Nonetheless, a determination of what students should learn "about" in school will be dictated by some philosophical perspective. As you know by now, it is our suggestion that the better articulated the perspective, the better articulated will be the curriculum. So, let's briefly consider four of the prevalent perspectives of philosophy in education that have driven curriculum design over the years.

Philosophical Perspectives That Guide Curriculum Design Four of the prominent philosophies in education are perennialism, essentialism, social reconstructivism, and progressivism. Each brings a perspective that informs the sort of content to which students will be exposed. As you read through each of the four, you will likely find similarities to your own experiences as a student.

Perennialism Perennialism maintains that there are ideas and truths that are, well, perennial. The perennialist perspective asserts that such ideas have transcended time and remain as vital today as they ever were. These themes are found in the great literature of the ages and provide insight into the universe and the place of humanity within it. Education, from the perennialist perspective, should represent an organized effort to make these ideas accessible to students and to guide their consideration and understanding of those ideas.

Perennialism is considered to be a *culturally conservative* perspective because it is based on classic works and reveres the foundation laid by tradition. Universal truth is unaffected by pop culture or the circumstances of a given time. For curriculum designers, there is stability and constancy in the perennialist approach. If you can accept the notion that the more things change, the more they stay the same, then the perennialist perspective is one that you may well embrace.

As an educational philosophy, perennialism poses some substantive challenges for American public schools. With only two hundred plus years of history, ours is a heritage still in process. Despite our Western roots, our national complexion is very diverse. For a perennialist perspective to survive in the twenty-first century and beyond, it may well be necessary to examine the truths of civilizations and societies that have not been "traditionally" included in the American portrait.

Even so, perennialism offers guidelines for the conduct of schools, as well as for the students within those schools. Two of the leading proponents of the perennialist approach in the latter half of the twentieth century were Robert Maynard Hutchins and Mortimer Adler. Adler's *Paideia Proposal: An Educational Manifesto* (1982), which pays homage to Horace Mann (equal education for all children), John Dewey (education should promote reflective thinking and skills that will improve a student's life), and Robert Hutchins (education should draw out the "common humanity" of those being educated), is a fascinating treatment of how a perennialist approach could be implemented in the public schools.

You will find that subject matter is at the heart of education for the perennialist. Schools must focus squarely on the skills of reading, writing, speaking, and listening, particularly in the early grades so that students will ultimately be able to study the great works of literature, history, and philosophy in the later grades. Drill-and-practice will prepare students for the intellectual challenges that await them. A perennialist curriculum would severely curtail the use of textbooks and lectures as students would be engaged in seminars and debate. Vocational training would be eliminated. From the perennialist view, the school is responsible for the cultivation of mental discipline that affords the ability to assume a lifelong quest for the truth. Job training, they would argue, is the responsibility of an employer.

Essentialism   At one time or another, you have probably heard someone say that what education needs is to get back to the basics. If so, what you were hearing was a call for an *essentialist* curriculum. This perspective suggests there are core skills and knowledge that all students should acquire, skills that are essential for sustaining our social order. As we saw with perennialism, essentialism seeks to preserve a society's cultural heritage.

Essentialism, however, emphasizes the training of the mind by virtue of a subject-centered curriculum. It is a philosophy that came into being during the first half of the twentieth century when leading educators vigorously debated the purpose and the future of organized education. Essentialism's most vocal proponent at the time, William C. Bagley, firmly believed that the purpose of school was not to change society but rather to preserve it. School should provide the skills with which a student could study the culture and understand its traditions. In that regard, essentialism is similar to perennialism as a culturally conservative philosophy of education.

In contrast, the perennialist goal of understanding truths and universal principles takes a back seat to the essentialist goal of preserving the culture. The focus is clearly on academic skills. Rather than leading to seminar and dialogue, an essentialist education emphasizes lecture, memorization, practice, and assessment. The early years of schooling should be devoted to the learning of skills in reading and computation, and in the later years, those skills will be put to work in studying the people and events that have fashioned our culture, our traditions, and the institutions that have arisen within our society. Vocational training, again, is not condoned by this perspective; nor are social promotion and course offerings that fail to advance the rigorous, culture-bound curriculum.

Despite the fact that essentialism was a contender in the educational debates of the early twentieth century, it is by no means just a footnote in educational history. Throughout the past century, and even now in the twenty-first century, the back-to-basics call has been repeated in very strong voices. The landmark 1983 report *A Nation at Risk* warned of the watering-down of the American public school curriculum. It recommended a core curriculum for high school students that included English, mathematics, science, social studies, and computer science.

The movement toward essentialism did not end with *A Nation at Risk*. In 1988, Hirsch published *Cultural Literacy*, in which he acknowledges the lament of essentialists from fifty years earlier: Schools are failing to provide instruction in the common culture that binds a nation together, there are skills and knowledge that all students should acquire, and the continued failure to provide a rigorous and culture-based education will be detrimental to the nation itself. "There is a pressing need," Hirsch (1988) writes, "for clarity about our educational purposes" (25). The message that the essentialist curriculum is a curriculum for all students in a democratic society has been argued persuasively for nearly one hundred years in our nation. As Hirsch (1988) suggests,

> Although nationalism may be regrettable in some of its world-wide political effects, a mastery of national culture is essential to mastery of the standard language in every modern nation. This point is important for educational policy, because educators often stress the virtues of multicultural education. Such study is indeed valuable in itself, it inculcates tolerance and provides a perspective on our own traditions and values. But however laudable it is, it should not be the primary focus of national education. It should not be allowed to supplant or interfere with our school's primary responsibility to ensure our children's mastery of American literate culture. The acculturative responsibility of the schools is primary and fundamental. (18)

An effective essentialist curriculum requires that teachers be subject-area specialists. This contrasts with the liberally educated teachers called for in the perennialist tradition, though it is very much in keeping with the No Child Left Behind Act of 2002 that mandates highly qualified and credentialed teachers in each subject area. The contemporary emphasis that we see on achievement testing is central to an essentialist approach. Similarly, the move toward "accountability" of students, teachers, and schools falls within the "academic rigor" advocated by an essentialist philosophy.

Progressivism The 1800s represented the United States' first "full century" as a nation. During that time, the visionary tenets of democracy laid out in the late 1700s were tested in many ways, not the least of which was the divisive state-against-state struggle of the Civil War. The nation withstood these internal tests, accepted throngs of immigrants, made a dramatic shift to becoming an industrialized society, and entered the 1900s with an innovative vigor. That this same momentum might trickle down to the public schools is of no particular surprise.

From the perspective of the cultural conservatives, the culture "had arrived," and school was the experience that would teach that culture to a new generation. The progressivists, however, felt that the time was ripe for change, and in their philosophy, the focus would be on the positive changes that individuals with a particular educational background could provide. Change was based on "doing" more so than on "knowing" and on solving problems more so than on passing on the culture as it existed. This would mean a shift from the subject-centered perspective of the traditional curriculum to a child-centered approach.

The progressivists followed the teachings of John Dewey and adopted the perspective that people learn best from experiences that are meaningful in their lives. Talk of disciplining the mind to pursue universal truths was replaced with talk of the relevance of life experience. There was a high regard for the individual as progressivists embraced the pragmatist ideas of a scientific method in the development of thinking and the solving of problems, scientific or otherwise. Combining this with the acceptance of change made the progressivist philosophy in education an obvious fit for a changing, developing country with high aspirations. In 1938, Boyd Bode, a leading progressive proponent and watchdog in the fight to maintain philosophic integrity within the movement, wrote, "The emphasis of progressive education on the individual, on the sinfulness of imposition, and on the necessity of securing free play for intelligence, is a reflection of the growing demand, outside of school, for recognition of the common man" (11).

In theory, in a progressive curriculum one would never hear a student ask why she had to learn one thing or another because the value of the learning would be self-evident. As Carlton Washburne (1926), superintendent of the Winnetka schools in Illinois, wrote, "Childhood is a beautiful section of life, and children should be given a chance for free, full living. . . . We believe in colorfulness, coziness, homines in our classrooms; in an opportunity for spontaneity. We want children to want to come to school" (349). Ideally, all this was good. Practically, however, any innovation has to answer for the results, and that seemed to be a problem for the progressivist movement, particularly in light of the inconsistencies that were developing within the movement.

Interestingly, the progressive movement mirrored much of the enthusiasm and innovation that the youthful American culture seemed to embody and, yet, found itself in the same sort of identity crisis that we have discussed throughout this book with regard to the culture at large. The progressivists were never successful in fashioning a statement of philosophy that spoke for the entire movement, though they did agree on aspects of the traditional school that they disliked, such as a textbook-based curriculum, teachers as disseminators of information rather than facilitators of thinking, and the school's relative "distance" from what happens in the real world. They even agreed on some of the things they favored, such as the child-centered curriculum, the teacher as a facilitator, and stimulating interest through the use of direct experience. But unanimity for carrying out that philosophy was conspicuously lacking. In the late 1940s and 1950s, the combined discovery of exceedingly low literacy rates among young men entering military service and the Soviet launch of Sputnik served as notice that changes needed to be made. The 1989 report *Science for*

All Americans suggested that the school curriculum had become "overstuffed and undernourished" (viii), indicating that education had lost the very academic rigor for which the perennialists and essentialists had argued.

Social Reconstructionism   Social reconstructionism is a perspective that specifically sees the schools as the agency for solving the problems of society. The schools will provide the future leaders for the community, state, and nation and, therefore, must present a curriculum that prepares students to meet the very real challenges that lie ahead. With this said, you might get the impression that the social reconstructionists take a *proactive* approach to education, that is, looking toward educating a generation of problem solvers. The more accurate statement, however, is that proponents of social reconstructionism are *reacting* to the significant social problems that exist today (and "today" could have been seventy-five years ago, or it could be as you read this in the twenty-first century) and threaten to unravel our culture and social system.

As a reaction to inequities within a socioeconomic system, social reconstructionism is not really a philosophy but would appear to be more of an antidote to social problems that use the schools as part of the prescription. It is a perspective that does seek to preserve cultural heritage but, at the same time, recognizes that ours is a culture constantly in transition. Unlike the perennialists and essentialists, who wish to "solidify" a particular cultural identity, social reconstructionists instead search for ways to make the emerging culture more equitable for all.

The problem, from a social reconstructionist perspective, was that schools were building a caste system that favored the wealthy and subjugated the poor. The opportunities that were supposed to be afforded to all were being systematically denied to many. They argued that schools fostered the knowledge and skills that empower the most privileged and very much established class distinctions. Such socioeconomic distinctions can be true of private schools almost by definition, and they can legitimately choose to cater to a particular clientele and their desires. Yet, even within the public schools today we find specialty schools (schools for science and math, schools for the arts, etc.), magnet schools, and, increasingly, charter schools that may or may not be required to meet state-imposed quotas for ethnic representation. The social reconstructionist perspective would oppose all of this.

In a social reconstructionist approach to education, classroom teachers would have an affective emphasis (focusing on attitudes and feelings) and would engage students in questions of moral dilemmas as a means to understanding the implications of one's actions. This sounds somewhat like the ideas that were offered by the progressivists. It is important, however, to remember that the reconstructionists maintain an agenda of *social reform* rather than simply fostering problem-solving ability.

*   *   *

Where does all of this leave us with regard to a new institution of education? We would suggest that the educational enterprise aims toward developing the well-educated child. What constitutes "well-educated" is, of course, the million-dollar question, but it certainly does not refer to minimal competency. And as we consider the philosophies discussed, it would seem that elements of each, rather than an emphasis on any one, would serve our purposes best. Though the schools should not be used to solve the problems of society, they should be the mechanism through which society develops problem solvers. Though preparation for work in the society

---

**Activity 8.3.
A BRIEF LOOK AT EASTERN PHILOSOPHY**

We have discussed four of the educational philosophies that have characterized education in the United States primarily over the past 100 to 150 years. However, Eastern philosophy, which has not had as great an influence on education in the United States as has Western philosophy, can be expected to be seen in the schools as the Asian/Middle Eastern populations increase. This activity is suggested so that you can consider a perspective that you may not have had the opportunity to consider before.

Select one (or more) of the schools of thought listed below, and use the Internet to find information to help you answer the questions that follow.

Buddhism	Hinduism	Confucianism
Zen Buddhism	Islam	Taoism

1. How does the school of thought you have chosen differ from Western thought as you know it?
2. How is it the same?
3. How could an Eastern philosophical influence become part of the culture of school as we know it? Would it be part of the entire culture? Would it be something recognized only during a selected month of the school year?
4. Which of the Western philosophies most closely parallels the Eastern philosophy you have selected?

---

is an obvious responsibility of a formal system of education, vocational training is the job of employers (the school's responsibility is to provide employers with individuals with the skills and abilities to learn a job). Though the traditions and customs of a culture should be disseminated by the schools, history should be presented as an accurate chronicle of events and their significance to a society rather than as a romanticized version of a favored perspective.

Obviously, the content knowledge of a new institution will require a significant rewriting of many of the instructional materials that are used in the schools today. Even more to the point, it will require that the society at large be willing to tolerate more objectivity of perspective, which can then be the source of informed discussion at the higher levels of the curriculum, and to rely less on the "George Washington and the cherry tree" mythology that pervades early education in particular and confounds later education as students unlearn the fables they learned as children.

What might we call a philosophy that honors the transcendent messages of fine literature, that recognizes essential skills and elements of knowledge that children in our nation should possess, that sees the need to make learning, from the earliest grades, relevant to the life of the student and meaningful for the future, and that appreciates the fact that schools prepare people to solve social problems and issues? The name is not particularly important, of course, but for the sake of having some sort of reference for the well-educated child, let's call it "eruditionism" (from the Latin, *eruditio*, pertaining to learning).

Scientific Awareness, Cultural Awareness, and Knowledge of the Wider World   As education has been the responsibility of each individual state, curriculum has lacked a national cohesiveness, even though it has developed a significant national "sameness." The tension between forces advocating state control on the one hand and a national orientation on the other has resulted in a fragmented, though purposeful, approach to curriculum designs. The sovereignty of the states, a key element of our political foundation, remains intact at the same time that there exists a degree of educational consistency from sea to shining sea. Still, some wonder whether this has been the most expedient process for the development of a high-quality system of formal education.

The development of national educational standards that guide curriculum development has emerged from national organizations such as

- National Council of Teachers of Mathematics
- American Association for the Advancement of Science
- The National Science Teachers Association
- National Council for the Social Studies
- National Center for History in the Schools
- American Council on the Teaching of Foreign Languages
- National Council of Teachers of English
- National Association for Sport and Physical Education

In many cases, these organizations represent the professional organizations for educators in that discipline. In all cases, the standards offered are voluntary. States may wish to adopt all or some of the standards of any given discipline. They may amend the standards to emphasize or de-emphasize a particular topic or strand. However, the hallmark of these efforts at developing standards is that they represent a nonpolitical approach to identifying the important concepts and knowledge of a particular discipline. This is by no means to say that the standards have not introduced new controversy but simply to acknowledge that practitioners in the given subject area have been responsible for deriving the standards. There are those who believe that the development of these guidelines represents just one more step toward the eventual establishment of nationally imposed standards. That remains a matter for speculation. Others (e.g., King-Sears, 2001) maintain that standards clarify the curriculum and provide a guide for selecting instructional content.

The academic disciplines are taught on many levels and by virtue of many course offerings. There are, however, eight major categories of academics that serve as the basis of the contemporary curriculum: math, language arts (including reading, writing, grammar, literature), science (increasingly including technology and the social impact of science), social studies (including history, geography, political science, economics, sociology, psychology, and anthropology), foreign language, the arts, physical education (including physical, mental and emotional health, sexuality, nutrition, substance abuse, and prevention and control of disease), and vocational education (including career awareness, job training, and school-to-work education). We have already indicated that language arts, additional languages, and mathematics would be taught under the heading of "cognitive skills." The remaining subject areas are those that we would consider under the heading of "knowledge." (Note: Physical education is somewhat of a difficult fit. The current approach to physical education [PE] may seem to be better considered as a form of skill training. The recommendation here, however, is that these skills should be reconceptualized as knowledge and applied knowledge.)

We would suggest that with regard to content knowledge, the well-educated child should have a solid foundation in scientific awareness, cultural awareness, and knowledge of the wider world. Note that we speak here of "awareness" rather than the popular "literacy." The reason for this is because true literacy in any subject area is a tall order, let alone literacy in six or seven subject areas (for instance, math, science, government, history, geography, and art). We would look for literacy in language (whatever the official language might be) because, in this one area, literacy is a legitimate expectation of all students in the absence of cognitive dysfunction. In addition to its being difficult to obtain such a level (do you recall when "computer literacy" was the wave in education, something that has since been replaced with the mere ability to operate a computer much as someone might have operated a typewriter in years past?), it would be even more difficult to design a curriculum that qualified an individual as literate in each area. For example, an astronomer with a vast knowledge of planetary motion, galactic structure, and black holes may know little, if anything, of marine science. Would we consider this person to be scientifically illiterate? Of course not.

It is not necessary that all people have extensive knowledge of all subjects, or even of any one. That's what college and graduate school are for. However, we should be able to identify those things in several domains of which all students should be sufficiently aware to be conversant in the subject. We would also recommend that in all subject areas, we keep with the recommendation of *Science for All Americans* and seek depth over breadth. That is, let's choose those things about which students should know—not trying to be everything to all people—and investigate those topics in depth. It has been said that if one were to select any object and study it in all of its aspects, the journey would ultimately lead to the origins of the universe itself, with a healthy dose of theology in there as well. We need not go to that extent, but it illustrates the potential power of a depth-oriented educational process over a superficial study of more topics than are reasonable to entertain. If we think in terms of scientific awareness, cultural awareness, and knowledge of the wider world, we should be able to design a curriculum that would be representative of an eruditionist philosophy; the well-educated student would be a child of our nation and a citizen of the world.

Scientific Awareness   Scientific awareness would include studies of physical science (physics and chemistry), life science (biology and ecology), and earth/space science (astronomy, meteorology, oceanography, and geology), but it would do so in the context of the additional content areas in science recommended by the National Research Council (1996): science as inquiry, the history and nature of science, science and technology, science in personal and social perspectives, and unifying concepts and processes.

The current science standards developed through a somewhat circuitous route. The science curriculum (and math as well) garnered significant public attention in the late 1950s. The ensuing development efforts concentrated on the development of science curricula rather than on the development of standards for the teaching of science. The National Science Education Standards, released in 1996, were developed by the National Research Council of the National Academy of Sciences. Their work followed the preparatory work done by the American Association for the Advancement of Science. Also involved was the National Science Teachers Association's Scope, Sequence, and

Coordination Project. The National Science Education Standards emphasize learning through investigation and inquiry rather than presenting science as an isolated compendium of facts and figures to be memorized.

Cultural Awareness   Cultural awareness is similar to what has become "social studies" in the modern curricula. Social studies is not a discipline in itself but rather a collection of disciplines. Different grade levels, particularly in terms of bulk divisions of the K–12 experience (elementary, middle, high school), have emphasized different disciplines within the social studies. For example, the lower elementary grades have focused on family and community. Upper elementary and middle school curricula transition into history, geography, and civics. U.S. history, government, and more narrowly focused courses in world history, sociology, economics, and so forth can be found at the high school level.

Current issues in the social studies revolve around the relative inclusion or exclusion of minorities and non-Western cultural perspectives in the curriculum. Given our brief national heritage and burgeoning ethnic diversity, one can expect that debates on these issues will begin to yield a less Eurocentric presentation of social studies topics as curriculum materials develop over the next decade. In 1994, the National Council for the Social Studies released these ten strands for national standards.

Expectations of Excellence: Curriculum Standards for Social Studies

1. Culture and cultural diversity
2. Human beings' views of themselves over time
3. People, places, and environments
4. Individual development and identity
5. Interactions among individuals, groups, and institutions
6. How structures of power, authority, and governance are changed
7. The production, distribution, and consumption of goods and services
8. Relationships among science, technology, and society
9. Global interdependence
10. Citizenship in a democratic society

Though they are not within the domain of social studies, we would recommend that the arts be placed in the domain of cultural awareness, though there can be obvious overlap with the third domain, knowledge of the wider world. The four comprehensive arts are dance, theater, music, and the visual arts. Within the context of these four areas, programs in the arts seek to develop an ability to create art, an understanding of art in its cultural context, and an aesthetic appreciation of the various art forms. We see this as where the emphasis should be: art in a cultural context.

Most prevalent of the programs in the arts is music, likely because it serves as a group activity. That is, the band or choir in a school can accommodate a large number of students under the direction of one teacher. Even so, in times of budgetary cutbacks or another round of "back to basics" in the curriculum, programs in the arts are often first to suffer. A clear example was during the movement for curricular reform in science and math during the early 1960s. As the social climate changed in the 1970s, programs in the arts began to reemerge. That momentum has continued to the point that in the "magnet school" environment that we now see, schools, particularly in larger metropolitan areas, are likely to have a school dedicated to an emphasis on the fine arts.

In the new institution, the study of art as we have described would be an integral component of the curriculum. However, just as magnet and charter schools represent a desire to find a more worthwhile and engaging curriculum, we would hope that the new institution would make those efforts unnecessary. Further, programs such as band, orchestra, and chorus, which are only made available to a few students relatively speaking, should fall into the realm of extracurricular activities unless graduation is somehow made contingent upon the successful completion of such programs. This would be a difficult pill to swallow, but a reconceptualization of the arts in school is a necessary exercise.

We include physical education in the knowledge category of the curriculum because it should provide students with knowledge of the functions and needs of the human body *and* knowledge of how to achieve and maintain physical fitness (i.e., applied knowledge). However, over the years, fairly or not, physical education has been the target of two complaints: It is not particularly physical, and it is not education. Due to the metamorphosis of PE from calisthenics to its emphasis on competitive sports, programs in physical education were destined to attract the students with athletic ability and to discourage students who did not possess skills that were up to the challenge.

During the 1970s and 1980s, a change began to occur in physical education programs. Not the least of these was Title IX in 1972, which required that physical education classes be coeducational. Much gender segregation even within coed classes persists today. However, the scope of physical education has expanded to encourage the use of lifelong sports to maintain physical fitness and more rigorously address issues of health, disease prevention, human growth and development, and combating substance abuse. Yet, you will notice in the statement of the National Association for Sport and Physical Education that neither individual nor team competition is mentioned at all when describing the *physically educated student*; rather, such a student

1. demonstrates competency in many movement forms and proficiency in a few movement forms
2. applies movement concepts and principles to the learning and development of motor skills
3. exhibits a physically active lifestyle
4. achieves and maintains a health-enhancing level of physical fitness
5. demonstrates responsible personal and social behavior in physical activity settings
6. demonstrates understanding and respect for differences among people in physical activity settings
7. understands that physical activity provides opportunities for enjoyment, challenge, self-expression, and social interaction

The purpose of physical education is to teach an awareness of the needs of the human body, how to maintain its musculature and other systems to provide for a healthy life, and how to "fuel" the body. Notice that playing dodgeball or walking around a playing field is not among the purposes of PE. In fact, sports and exercise in general—be it the teaching or the playing of them—represent physical *activity*, not physical *education*.

Yet, physical education is clearly as important as any other education in terms of the "whole student." As a society we take our physical condition for granted at the same time that we spend literally billions of dollars a year on health care. It is estimated that 61 percent of the adult population in the United States are overweight or obese (*National Health and Nutrition Examination Survey*, 1999). Over 10 percent of preschoolers are overweight (Vail, 2004). Moreover, 15 percent of American students from age six to eleven may be severely overweight (Buchanan, 2005), which is defined as having a body mass index exceeding 95 percent of their peers (Tanner, 2003). Approximately 16 percent of students from age twelve to nineteen are overweight; twenty-five years ago, the figure was 5 percent (Buchanan, 2005). The American Dietetic Association (Amschler, 2002) contends that 11 percent of American children are "clinically overweight," and another 14 percent are at risk of becoming overweight. The Centers for Disease Control uses the 25 percent figure for children who are, or are at risk of becoming, obese. That's a message that should have direct impact on the presentation of physical education in our schools. Children are not too young to learn about the care and feeding of their bodies, and they are not too young to learn habits of fitness and conditioning that could indeed last a lifetime. These habits have a major impact because overweight children are more likely to develop high blood pressure, asthma (Vail, 2004), and diabetes (Amschler, 2002; Vail, 2004). Because of the widespread nature of this health issue, federal law requires school districts to establish wellness policies including "goals for nutrition, physical education, and other school-based activities" (Buchanan, 2005).

What are the implications for physical education in our school of the future? For one thing, it means that we need to rethink just what PE is all about. This exercise can easily be carried over to other subject areas, but a consideration of PE provides a good starting point for practice in switching perspectives. Here is a brief list of suggestions for you to consider. For each, consider the possible implications. Add more items to the list as you think of them. In all cases, however, open up your thinking rather than being bound by "what you've always known."

1. The focus of PE is understanding the needs of the human body.
2. PE should provide students with guidance in fulfilling the needs of the body to maintain optimal health.
3. Sports can be used sparingly as a technique for exercising the body. Competitive sports, however, should only be used as extracurricular activities.
4. The topics of teamwork, competition, and striving to achieve a goal can be objectives of a physical education program. If so, they should be explicit objectives. Better yet, they should be explicit objectives of the overall curriculum for the school. Exercises to foster these traits should be evident across all subject areas.
5. Age-appropriate exercise equipment and the teaching of exercises that require no equipment should characterize all physical education programs.
6. High school (and perhaps middle school) physical education facilities should (1) tend toward physical fitness machines rather than sports equipment, (2) be of a quality that is higher than one would expect of "home" exercise equipment, and (3) be made available to the community.
7. Physical education programs should be held accountable for identifying fitness models and routines for each child. This is so important that it may be reasonable to require some sort of physical fitness individualized educational plan for each student. This plan could be started in kindergarten and expanded, revised, and improved as children grow up.

By the way, as of 2005, only five states had comprehensive standards for physical and motor development (Scott-Little, Kagan, & Frelow, 2005). Again, our look at PE is not intended as an attack. As we mentioned previously, PE as a subject area offers a good start in reconceptualizing what school is all about.

Knowledge of the Wider World   The category "Knowledge of the Wider World" is perhaps the most exciting new development that curriculum design faces. With a tighter common curriculum in cognitive skills and in the scientific and cultural awareness portions of the knowledge component of the curriculum, this category offers the potential for students to study other cultures in terms of art, politics, economics, religion, and customs and beliefs without trying to act as though the American culture is representative of all of them. We can have a curriculum that celebrates the multiethnic composition of our own culture and then allows our children to consider how we are the same as, as well as how we differ from, other cultures around the world.

An effective curriculum in this category would neither chip away at our own national culture nor water down the study of other cultures. Rather, students—and this is something that has been a long time in coming—might even be able to understand how cultures have influenced each other over millennia (for example, many of the words that you read in this book are of Greek or Latin origin, and many "innovations" that we enjoy today are of ancient Chinese or Egyptian origin).

Perhaps most impressive of all is that an education with a strong common curriculum would provide students with an identity against which to consider the wider world. It is not a matter of one people or culture being better or worse than another, but it is a simple fact of our existence that people want to "know who they are" and to embrace an identity of their own. It may very well be the case that, at some point in the future, we will find that we are not alone in the universe. If so, in an instant we will all become fellow earthlings, and that will be the identity that we take in our perspective toward new worlds. In the meantime, we hope that curriculum designers, educators, and members of all disciplines (that is, across the sciences and the humanities) might see that development of a curriculum around the theme of knowledge of the wider world offers the opportunity to understand our human existence to a greater degree than has ever been offered before.

Dispositions

Dispositions, or attitudes, are a by-product of all human experiences. No matter what the particular situation—paying for groceries in a supermarket or sitting through a semester-long class on educational assessment—people come away with some perspective that includes the "mechanics" of what has transpired, as well as a value judgment of some sort regarding the situation. The combination of the two, the mechanics and the value statement, are what we refer to as an "attitude," or "disposition." Obviously, there are particular dispositions that a community would like students to come away with as a result of attending school.

Trying to articulate the desired dispositions is not so difficult. School should inculcate a love of learning, a desire for continued learning, and a host of dispositions such as respect, cooperation, honesty, and so on. And measuring those dispositions is not so difficult either. The four basic approaches to assessment in an educational setting include selected-response (which includes the iconic "multiple-guess" format), essays (which can range from the "in a brief paragraph" variety to the master's thesis or doc-

---

Activity 8.4.
SHOULD DISPOSITIONS BE PART
OF THE EXPLICIT CURRICULUM?

You will likely find as many people in favor of this as you will opposed. Despite the fact that a person's attitude is the greatest contributor to *your* attitude toward that person, we still leave this area pretty much to chance. Are there, however, dispositions that the schools should be formally expected to inculcate in their students?

1. What dispositions do you feel that you learned as a function of attending school?
2. When you think of the classes you had, did the teachers respond differently to different student dispositions? Did they have an impact on grades and/or achievement?
3. Compile a list of the ten dispositions that the school could legitimately be expected to foster in students.
4. When you look at your list of ten items, would you say that students should receive grades for these dispositions, or should the school evaluate themselves based on the degree to which the students have or have not embraced the identified dispositions?

---

toral dissertation), performance (which is well suited to assessing the cognitive skills discussed previously), and personal communication (which could be a discussion between a student and teacher, an interview with particular questions and the opportunity to explore responses with follow-up questions, or a simple survey). The assessment of dispositions does require the very careful construction of assessment instruments, but it can be done and administered in a painless fashion. So, what's the problem?

The problem is in what is done with the assessment data. If students are *graded* on their dispositions, then the implication is that the school, which, on the one hand, is supposed to be broadening a student's mind and encouraging critical thinking, is, on the other hand, prescribing what that student is to think. This leads us down the slippery slope toward a sterilization of thinking that sanctions some views and penalizes others (we speak here in ideological terms, not in terms of the violation of law). Schools would also then be obligated to measure dispositions as a matter of degree and subsequently assign grades for how well a student has acquired a particular attitude. The whole notion, of course, is abhorrent to our cultural perspective of prizing individuality and the value of an individual's thinking. Yet, dispositions are, as we have suggested, an inevitable result of human experience.

One approach to the consideration of dispositions is to do what we have done for so long: to consider dispositions as part of the implicit curriculum of school. Interestingly, in a society that values innovation and originality of thinking, you may well recall that school was an experience all about conformity; the wiggle room for contradictory thinking was very limited. The result is that the implicit curriculum approach carries with it a high level of hypocrisy and "do as I say, not as I do."

The other possibility is that curriculum designers—and you should be seeing yourself as one of those folks by now—should identify the essential dispositions that students should acquire as a function of attending school (notice that this is phrased in terms of what we have said about dispositions; they result from human experience rather than being prescribed by someone). Having been identified as an expectation of the educational experience—openly, explicitly—educational activities should aim toward achieving those goals, and they should be assessed. However, and this is where assessment intentions often run amok, the assessment data should be used as a *formative assessment*, not as a summative assessment. Formative assessments inform educators of the progress of students, the effectiveness of their own teaching, and the efficacy of the programs that are provided to students. Summative assessments assign grades to student work and then use those grades to make decisions about the student's readiness to proceed. The formative use of such data is what would make the assessment of dispositions viable.

If the assessment data were to be used in this way, and if that data were to be communicated to parents and the community at large, *program improvement would be the result*. Not a single student's name need ever be mentioned. No student would ever receive a passing or failing grade (or anything in between) based upon his or her attitudes. But the schools and the community at large would be able to determine whether the program they are offering is accomplishing what they want it to accomplish and whether they might need to question (1) the program that is being presented to students, and/or (2) whether or not it is time to make changes in their own perspectives and attitudes. And while it would be naïve to say that the data would not be disaggregated by gender, ethnicity, and socioeconomic background, this information can indeed be informative and useful in the design of a curriculum that reflects the eruditionist perspective we spoke of previously.

Extracurricular Activities

Providing students with opportunities for extracurricular activities is an example of how the schools have slowly taken on responsibilities far beyond what should have been expected. Though some argument can be made that such activities serve an educational purpose, it would nonetheless have to be conceded that the purpose lies outside of the explicit curriculum for which students and schools are held accountable. As we reconceptualize school so that it might be a more effective learning experience, it will be necessary to question the purpose, breadth, and extent of these activities. This is not to say that the extracurriculum cannot exist in the new institution, but if it does, it should either contribute directly to the articulated goals of the school (and thus be required of all students) or be openly acknowledged for what it is (e.g., an extension of the time during which the school is expected to serve in loco parentis).

There are, of course, many activities that fall under the "extracurricular" heading. School clubs range from academic groups, to those with a religious basis, to those such as student government organizations. For the most part, activities such as these can be related back to academic expectations, though they must be seen as enrichment activities due to the fact that not all students are required to participate. If the activities are held *after* the school day has concluded, then the choice to engage in an enrichment activity can be voluntary. Still, designers of the new curriculum will have to ask themselves why the school is using its funds to sponsor activities that are neither required of all students nor assessed as an indicator of student progress.

Clubs and other organizations (which would have to include activities such as drama, band, and choir) that meet *during* the school day, however, pose a different problem. As has been suggested, if there is a public outcry with what our schools are

failing to accomplish, it is then unreasonable to allow nonrequired activities to occupy portions of the school day. Though band and choir, for example, may be opportunities open to all, it is a simple fact that there will be those who are capable of
taking advantage of the opportunity (for instance, in terms of skill or ability) and
those who are not.

A simple solution is that if the schools are going to include an extracurriculum, then
all students should be required to participate in *some* activity, and *all* activities must be
clearly allied with identified goals. This does not necessarily mean that the activity has
to be graded, but progress does have to be assessed in a manner that, at the very least,
indicates whether or not the activity is bringing students any closer to achieving the
goals set for the school.

You have probably suspected that this discussion is building up to another sacrilege
with regard to our contemporary perspective on the institution of education. Well, you
were right, and here it is. Perhaps the most egregious offender with regard to extracurricular activities is that of interscholastic athletics. *There is no academically defensible outcome of interscholastic athletic programs that could not just as easily and more cost-effectively
be accomplished with an outstanding intramural athletic program.* Lost, of course, would be
the use of students, currently at virtually all grade levels, for community entertainment,
but it should never have come to that point in the first place. And the argument that
says extracurricular athletics are what keep some students in school is an indictment of
the academic curriculum and its delivery systems; yet, parents and educators alike offer this as justification for a bloated, out-of-control use of school funding.

In 2007, communities in Massachusetts (e.g., Northbridge and Stoneham) voted
down tax overrides that would have funded extracurricular activities, primarily the athletic programs (Sacchetti, 2007), though music and art programs felt the crunch as
well. The result was that in the Northbridge community, parents collectively took out
a loan to support the activities in the fall. In Stoneham (Moskowitz, 2007), when the
$3-million override failed, the entire high school athletic program was terminated,
which included *fifty-four* coaching positions.

The interesting situations in these two communities, and in many other communities around the country as well, could be the beginning of a new era in public education. Turning back tax overrides that support what has become the extravagant use of
public funds for athletic programs (which also serve as community entertainment) is
a positive step. Whether or not parents would have taken out a loan to support academic programs in a fiscal shortfall is another matter, but in cases such as these, there
exists the possibility of reconceptualizing the function of school, extracurricular programs, and, in particular, athletic programs.

This perspective is not intended to say that athletics and other extracurricular activities are completely without merit. Rather, it is simply meant to indicate that many of
these programs have exceeded the responsibilities of an effective school system. Intramural athletic programs that are tied to the development of all students are viable options for schools. Extracurricular programs in music (e.g., band, drama, choir) are also
worthwhile but should be after-school programs. Schools should, on the other hand,
be offering true physical education, as well as programs in art and music appreciation
(some of it interactive, some of it knowledge based).

Pop Warner football, Little League baseball, and the many community soccer programs around the country are examples of where organized athletic competition
should occur: in the community. That the schools have somehow come to offer such

comprehensive programs that are not required for graduation is a clear matter of parents transferring their responsibilities to the schools. Again, this perspective is not an indictment of extracurricular experiences (though many schools use time during the school day for "extracurricular" programs); it is simply an indictment of using the schools as the vehicle for such experiences. The result is that schools are less effective than they should be at the tasks that represent their primary responsibility.

Vocational Education

Vocational education, which is certainly skills oriented, is an aspect of the curriculum that is very much affected by prevailing social attitudes. The dialogue over vocational training as part of public schooling has been hotly debated for decades and will likely continue in that manner for some time to come.

Two newer variations of the vocational theme have appeared on the educational scene. One is a concerted effort at what might be called "prevocational education" directed at middle school students. Most typical of districts with strong vocational or career education centers, these programs are intended to start middle school students thinking about the possibilities of vocational training in the high school and the coursework that would lead to successful completion of such programs. The other variation is the national movement toward "tech-prep" or "school-to-work" programs. Targeted most specifically for the non-college-bound student, these programs prepare students to transition into the workforce by spending time during their final two years of high school working with local businesses and industries. Alternatively, they prepare students to enter two-year postsecondary training programs.

Once again, the critical question to be answered is that of determining the purpose of school: Is it to prepare all students to enter productive citizenship with the ability to learn or is it to prepare students to take positions in the workforce with skills learned at school? As has already been suggested, we would favor an educational system that prepares students in terms of cognitive skills and knowledge to enter post–high school technical training or employer-based training programs rather than expecting the public schools to serve as the training forum for industry.

Building a New Institution

Sacrificing a Generation

We briefly alluded to this notion in chapter 6. Now is the time to discuss it further. It would be nice if, on the first day of school in a year not too far off, all students showed up to a new and improved educational system where everything from the old system was gone and the new had somehow seamlessly been put in its place. But that's not realistic. In fact, one of the fatal flaws in the reform model in education is the belief that piecemeal changes can be made that will eventually pervade all of education. Make a little change here, add in a little more there, and ultimately it will all tie together as a new system. That doesn't, and really cannot, happen. There are too many intervening and competing influences. That is why this book has repeatedly called for a revolution in education: the design and implementation of a new system that will replace the old. Even so, there will be a point in that implementation when it will be necessary for some students to be part of an old system while others are part of a new one, even if it is just a matter of those who are enrolled during a "transition period."

For that reason, we suggest that it is necessary to understand that some K–12-age children will be, at the very least, either the last to complete an old system or among the first to experience part of the old and part of the new. That's what we mean by sacrificing a generation, though as you can see, "sacrifice" is not such a bad notion. No child will be deprived of an education. No generation will be branded as inferior or tossed aside as unworthy. We simply must face the fact that to replace one system with another, there will be an apparent difference at some point. There will be no time when such a change can be made without this being the case. Whether or not we, as a nation, can accept this condition and maintain a visionary approach toward a truly effective education program remains to be seen. Realistically, our nation has faced more daunting tasks. This is ultimately a question simply of who (perhaps one person, perhaps many) will say that it is time and then lead the way.

The Old Cannot Be Replaced in a Day

Writing plans, in the greater scheme of things, is the easy part. What takes some real tenacity is the implementation. We have already suggested the following:

- Local control of education should continue.
- States should continue to remain sovereign in their responsibility to provide an exemplary educational experience for their constituents.
- The federal government should be constitutionally bound to the enterprise.
- The business model and reliance on the influence of business should be removed.
- An Education Congress of the States composed of educators should be the national curriculum design and administrative body for public education.

Now the question is how to go about the implementation. Devising restructuring plans, restructuring teacher-education programs, and reeducating current teachers is something that must be done before any change in curriculum and school operations is put into place. Many a reform effort has failed because the new system was installed before anybody within the system was instructed about what to do. But our discussion can be based on the assumption that an organization such as the Education Congress of the States has taken on these tasks and is now at the point of making things happen for children in the schools.

One approach, of course, would be to simply implement an entirely new system all at once. One day school ends using an old system, and then, whenever the new school year is set to begin, the doors open with a brand-new approach: K–G. ("G" stands for graduation. We use it in place of "12" because we suggest movement away from the traditional grade-level perspective). That would be nice, but in all honesty, it is very unlikely. The turmoil associated with such a radical change throughout the entire system would no doubt unravel the entire effort.

Another possibility would be to phase the system in over a thirteen-year period. In such a situation, it could be just the kindergarten that is changed in the first year. The students entering the traditional first grade would be those who would complete their entire education under the old system. With each succeeding year, another level of the program would be added. It might be the case that the first teachers to implement the program could be educated to lead those kindergarteners through the first several levels of the program (e.g., through what is now K–3). By the time those students were ready to progress beyond a given level, the new teachers would have been educated to take them through the next several levels.

Under this system, a new cohort of students would be added each year, and new cohorts of teachers could be added along with them. The downside, of course, is that it would take a full thirteen years to replace the old system with the new. Thirteen years means, at a minimum, two different presidential administrations, likely many changes of governors and legislators, and many changes in school personnel. This is without even mentioning the millions of parents that would be involved as their children, perhaps some under the current system and others under the new system, proceed through their formal education. It is disappointing to have to admit that we might not have that much vision and commitment as a nation. But it is also probably realistic to acknowledge that over such an extended period of time, there will be objections and calls for returning to the way it was "when I was in school."

As a means for addressing the decade-plus time issue, it could be possible to take an innovative approach to implementation by starting at the middle and working out in both directions. Under such a plan (and using the current grade-level structure as an example), implementation could begin at grade six. In the following year, grades five and seven would be added. In the next year, grades four and eight would be added. In this manner the entire system could be implemented in seven years, virtually cutting the implementation time in half.

A benefit of this "middle-out" approach would be that students who entered grades six or below after the first year of implementation would always encounter experienced teachers as they progressed. Students who began with the sixth grade in year one of implementation would always encounter the most currently educated teachers as the program was put in place. Similarly, if we think in terms of the current bulk grouping of grade levels, the sixth-grade teachers could mentor the new fifth- and seventh-grade teachers in year two (all of whom would be in the middle school setting). As implementation proceeded, the fifth- and seventh-grade teachers would mentor the new fourth- and eighth-grade teachers, and so on.

As an added bonus for those of you who are still feeling queasy about the "sacrifice a generation" idea, this approach would mean that only those students in grades seven to twelve when implementation began would finish all of their schooling under the old system. It is true that some students would begin under an old system and would have to transition to the new, but the number of years under the old system would decrease with each year of implementation (so, for instance, a child entering kindergarten in the sixth year of implementation would spend only one year in the old system). In addition, part of the preparation of teachers for the new institution would be in transitioning students from one system to the next.

FINAL THOUGHTS

The eruditionist perspective that we have been offering for a child's education, the expectation of developing the well-educated child, has emphasized the identification of curricular goals across the four basic curricula that characterize schools, a philosophical perspective to guide the development of content within the curriculum, and categories for the content of the curriculum as cognitive skills, knowledge, and dispositions. The intent in all cases has been to make the curriculum presented to students as open and clear as possible. We look for a minimizing of the implicit curriculum and the development of a common curriculum that makes the null curriculum something that can be critically and creatively considered by students in keeping with their developmental sophistication.

A greater emphasis on acquiring literacy with reading and writing the official language of the nation is part of the recommendation as we look to reconceptualizing public education. However, we also advocate the teaching of additional languages from the very beginning of school.

A focus of the new curriculum is on the use of language, mathematics, and scientific inquiry as tools to foster creative and critical problem-solving skills. When students can appreciate that the subjects they study will be useful and fruitful as they live their lives, the relevance of school itself will be enhanced.

Though developing an entire curriculum around the theme of problem solving and making the basic subjects relevant as tools for that task are exciting propositions, we see "Knowledge of the Wider World" in the knowledge portion of the curriculum as holding tremendous potential for exciting developments in curriculum design. In particular, the possibilities for students to find the connections between and among cultures and to bring their cognitive skills to bear on problems and issues that affect people throughout the world are very exciting.

We have also addressed a sacred cow in this chapter: extracurricular activities in general and interscholastic athletics in particular. Without a doubt, there are many people who will have a difficult time embracing a call for replacing such activities with others that are more in keeping with the goals and mission of public education. Yet, the perspective offered here does not minimize the value of athletics, only the emphasis that it has received as a function of the public school system. As the schools should not be the vocational training facility for business, they certainly should not be the field of broken dreams for the many thousands of students who expect that athletic prowess will result in a lucrative professional career as an athlete. And most importantly of all, if extracurricular activities are what keep students in school, then school has a problem with curriculum and delivery that cannot be ignored.

Sacrificing a generation: It need not be as ominous as it sounds, but it is a fact of making substantive change. Keep in mind that no child is being denied less of an education than is currently offered. Instead, it simply means that we must have the vision to understand that there will have to be people on either side of the line that marks the change in systems. That same point was made about revolution in general many chapters ago: It's not so much a matter (for us) of being on one side or the other of the revolution; it's a matter of staring the need for change in the eye and being willing to make the change. It is so easy to find reasons to maintain the status quo, even as we know that our children could be doing better, that we could be offering them more. But that inertia should not be sufficient reason in and of itself to prevent us from doing those things that demonstrate our uniquely human abilities.

III

AS THE CHANGE INCUBATES: WORKING WITH THE SYSTEM TO YOUR CHILD'S BEST ADVANTAGE

9

Educating Our Children
Means Educating Ourselves

To teach our children to innovate, to create, and to actualize, we must do the same.
—Steven Harrison

Up to this point, we have pondered the seemingly unknowable American culture. We have examined institutions brick by brick. We have disassembled the structures of reform and intervention and learned how to identify and improve those that have merit. We are beginning to understand what schools want and need. We are learning to ask the tough questions that will shape our future, and the future looks bright. Before we arrive, however, there is work to be done in the present. This next task will help you define what you want for your children *now*.

Everybody has an opinion on the subject of education. Mayors want to take over school systems. Charter schools and vouchers are regarded as either the saviors or the destroyers of public confidence. Your neighbors tell you that this school is excellent and that one is an unqualified disaster. Some of your friends bypass the whole situation and homeschool their children. Other families choose innovative private schools, but that may not be your inclination. Yet, you are raising a child who deserves to love learning: With all the negative press about public education, how do you ensure that happens?

We believe that a meaningful education begins with a parent who respects his child for who she is and provides an environment that challenges her to grow into who she can become. But you may need to educate yourself as well to make a coherent decision. While the change happens, what options does the American educational system have to offer? This chapter will provide a road map for navigating the systems already in place around you. There are, indeed, excellent schools out there, schools that can make learning an adventure for your child. You need to find them, you need to visit them, and you need to know what to ask.

SURVEYING THE TERRITORY

This chapter offers a series of activities to help clarify your thinking on the subject of schools. We begin with an exercise for which there are no right or wrong answers, just the starting place for a discussion about what's happening in your own backyard.

Activity 9.1.
THE LANDSCAPE SURVEY

Please jot down your first impressions when you read the following words. It's best if you respond to them from a local perspective, whether you live in a small town or a big city. They are common terms that you hear everyday: no trick questions!

1. Schools	
2. Teachers	
3. Students	
4. Programs	
5. Parents	
6. Community	
7. Other	

What kind of feedback are we looking for? It can be as general or specific as you wish. The "Schools" category could include entries for type (e.g., high school, parochial, charter, etc.), grade level (preschool, K–12), and philosophy (traditional, developmental, etc.). The "Teachers" section might address issues having to do with unions, or could be anything that comes to mind about the teachers you know or remember from childhood. "Students" could refer to demographics or any particular observations you make when you drive by a school facility, such as the quick take you get from the kids you see on the yard. "Programs" can identify any noteworthy extras you can recall (arts programs, healthy lunch, special education). The section for "Parents" can pertain to parental involvement. Or maybe it will refer to experiences with your own children at their school. "Other" is a place for you to take note of any random images that come to mind about education. Maybe it's a place for concerns, a place for goals.

You are taking your own pulse, if you will. And your notes offer us a starting place from which to examine the foundation of the current system. The revolution begins at home, but the change will not happen overnight. So, what can we make out of what we've got? Where will your child go to school?

It Starts with the Schools

Let's see what we know about school in broad terms. One hundred and fifty years after the Industrial Revolution, the one-size-fits all "factory" model still leaves a deep impression on American public education. A range of approaches characterize individual schools, but the majority can be classified into what Koetzsch (1997) describes as the public school "mainstream": boxy structures bathed in fluorescent lighting, teacher-centered classrooms conforming to a district-determined curriculum, the administration of standardized tests considered to be the norm, children grouped by ability, physical education and the arts ranked as low priorities, and religion and spirituality essentially "outlawed." Did your perceptions include anything similar? Yet, despite this rather dismal picture, some public schools succeed brilliantly, especially when you consider that they are charged with the almost impossible task of educating every child who enrolls.

Not all schools fit into the "box" described above; many alternatives exist today for educating a child in the United States. Magnets and charters, as well as intra- and interdistrict transfers, provide choices within the public school system. A wide variety of nonsectarian private schools offers a range of philosophical approaches, and parochial schools present the religious-traditionalist viewpoint. Homeschooling is yet another option.

Schools, like people, come with strengths and weaknesses. In exploring each of these categories, we'll present both perspectives so that you have an opportunity to digest facts and contemplate what works for your family. And you'll have the use of a handy school comparison chart to gather your thoughts and help you differentiate. If sending your child to a neighborhood school is a foregone conclusion, we'll help you to learn how to build a successful relationship with it. But let's not get ahead of ourselves; first, we need to talk philosophy.

A Question of Philosophy

When you start looking at the schools that are out there, you'll mainly find variations of two main educational philosophies: *traditional* or *humanistic-progressive*. It's important to grasp just how these differences manifest themselves. As we've mentioned in earlier chapters, neither of these terms has been well defined, so interpretations of their meanings abound.

Traditional schools revolve around methods such as *direct instruction*, where the teacher does most of the talking, asks most of the questions, and seeks to moderate the attention of a large group of students. Most traditional schools follow a rigorous curriculum and teach children to produce their work independently. The day is divided into segments, with children generally expected to sit quietly and participate as directed by their instructor. The teacher is responsible for classroom management and setting up systems that maintain order and discipline tends to be structured around rewards and punishment.

Humanistic-progressive schools, on the other hand, may adhere to any number of ideologies, but their classrooms embody certain similarities. Informal *child-centered* environments often feature experiential (hands-on) and cooperative learning, where students are encouraged to work together in small groups to achieve their goals. This kind of interaction involves discussion, and discussion can get noisy! The curriculum may still be rigorous, but the attitude is usually one of collaboration. The humanistic-progressive philosophy is often assumed to be synonymous with the *developmental* approach (in which a child is encouraged to progress based on his own unique, internal timetable, according to stages as suggested by Jean Piaget), but this is actually a subset of the humanistic-progressive philosophy. There are many other such subsets, such as Montessori, Foxfire, and Friends' schools, each with its own particular orientation and methods. The approach to discipline will often be the problem-solving, discussion model, which involves the student in deciding the course of action following an infraction.

As you begin to consider schools, we strongly urge you to relax your assumptions about these educational philosophies. Traditional doesn't necessarily mean old fashioned and outmoded; these schools don't automatically favor "drill-and-kill" strategies that take the life out of learning. And progressive schools are not necessarily any less academic than schools that flaunt their test scores. Both approaches have their own goals for building success in children.

Regardless of the direction in which your school search takes you—public, private, or into the home—it is important to grasp these major ideological differences because this is where most educational institutions find their roots. That said, you may encounter schools that do not fit neatly into either category, such as Waldorf education, which stresses the developmental and the experiential, but within a structured, teacher-centered classroom! As you will discover, mainstream public education dominates our present-day system, but there are still alternatives to be found, both within and outside the system, that reflect the diverse needs of our diverse culture. It's time to start scanning your options.

The Local Public School(s)

A free and academically sound public education that promotes a sense of community is fundamental to the principles of American democracy. The National Center for Education Statistics (NCES) defines a public school as "a school or institution controlled or operated by publicly elected or appointed officials and deriving its primary support from public funds" (National Center for Education Statistics, 2004, appendix

B). The 2000 U.S. census tells us that the nation has fifty-three million school-age children. NCES figures for the 2003 school year show that some forty-eight million of them attended public schools. This means that approximately 90 percent of this country's school-aged children attend one of the ninety-five thousand plus public schools in the United States!

You probably have one of those schools near you. Is it a viable alternative? If so, you are very fortunate. If not, it's hardly a surprise. Our national preoccupation with accountability and raising academic achievement may have made you aware that your local school could be underperforming. If so, don't make the mistake of dismissing it on reputation alone. If you are absolutely certain that this is the school your child will attend, now is the perfect time to get involved. If you have a choice to make, you definitely need to visit this school while you consider other options in your area.

Opportunities might exist for your child to attend another public school in a different neighborhood through *open enrollment*. Under this scenario (and if space is available), a school may fill seats with students from outside its boundaries. This usually takes place once a year through a lottery, but regulations vary, so check with your district for the specifics.

Magnet Schools

Magnet schools may also be worth exploring. Magnets are public schools dedicated either to a certain curricular theme or organizational structure and designed to "attract" families interested in their philosophy. Organized in the 1970s to remedy racial segregation in school enrollment, magnets pull their students from all over the district, not just specific neighborhoods. Twenty-five years later, magnet schools continue to proliferate, with over four thousand such institutions serving the needs of two million U.S. students (Friedman, 2000).

There are, of course, downsides to the magnet approach. Because of limited seats, and in some cases because the ethnic balance must be strictly maintained, gaining admission to a magnet program can be difficult. Some stipulate entrance requirements that make them semiselective; others accept students through a lottery process and waiting list. Another stumbling block is travel time; not only can a commute (or a lengthy bus ride) be troublesome, but it can also be difficult for your child to socialize easily when friends live far apart from one another.

Charter Schools

Since the early 1990s, charter schools have become another high-profile alternative in public education. In such a school, parents, administrators, community members, and other stakeholders exercise their right to create a free, nonexclusive, nonsectarian school organized around coherent educational philosophy. By signing a contract promising to maintain accountability and deliver student achievement, such a school is released from many of the typical bureaucratic restraints. After preparing a detailed proposal establishing goals and the plans for meeting them, plus demonstrating that it can attract a student body, the charter school is licensed by the state to operate. It is funded with taxpayer dollars according to enrollment and attendance. The proposal, the contract, and the license are all known as the "charter."

Charter schools make their own operational decisions (everything from personnel to curriculum) and afford great opportunity for parental input. They are largely exempted from district bureaucracy but not from accountability. Charter contracts are usually given for a three- to five-year period, at the end of which they may be renewed or withdrawn if the students are not performing acceptably on standardized tests or other designated forms of assessment.

Since the first charter law passed in Minnesota in 1991, these schools have become one of the most visible examples of school reform and one of the fastest-growing trends in education. Fifteen years later, approximately one million students are enrolled in close to thirty-six hundred schools nationwide (CER, 2006). U.S. Education Department research (2001) indicates that small school and class sizes are creating this demand and that other public schools are improving because of the competition. But other reports cite mixed success rates in student achievement and a variety of charter school failures due to either financial mismanagement or poor attendance. In any case, like the magnets, charter schools are open to all, but gaining admission can be difficult due to size and available space.

Secular and Parochial Private Schools

The focus of this book is obviously on public education, but you may also wish to consider alternatives outside of what your local public schools have to offer. In 2003, some twenty-eight thousand private schools educated six million American children (NCES, 2006), or about 10 percent of our student population in this country. One out of every four American schools is private, and they tout their limited enrollment, small class sizes, individualized attention, and variety of academic, athletic, and enrichment programs, as well as a climate where safety and security are paramount.

Parents consider a private school for its specialized focus, which can range from religious, to philosophical, to military/preparatory, to addressing learning differences (or other handicaps) and behavior issues. The spectrum of private parochial schools extends far beyond the better-known Jewish, Catholic, and other Christian varieties to offer vigorous moral and character development, a strong sense of community, and a relatively smaller price tag for those who may already be contemplating secular private schools. Whether parochial or nonsectarian, private schools pride themselves on their uniqueness, attract families in tune with their philosophies and vision, and depend upon those families to fund their programs and pay their bills.

Because private schools rely on those tuition checks, they are exempt from many of the laws steering public education. In 2007, our federal government remains loath to interfere with the rights of states to regulate the education code, and the states are loath to interfere with the Fourteenth Amendment constitutional rights of parents to direct the education of their children (U.S. Department of Public Education, 2000). Each state does retain certain rights to regulate private school, in categories that include curriculum, length of the school year, record keeping/reporting, health, safety, and special education, among others; a look at the statutes of four sample states (New York, Florida, Texas, and California) reveals great disparities in the legal detail among them. For example, in terms of curriculum, states provide few guidelines, leaving those decisions largely up to the control of the individual school. New York and California both assert that instruction given in a nonpublic school must be "substantially equivalent" to the course of study given at a local public school (N.Y. Educ. 3204.2, Ca. Educ. Code

48222). Texas will exempt a child from compulsory attendance in a public school if his or her private or parochial school includes a study of "good citizenship" (Texas Educ. Code Ann. 25.086 [a] [1]). And all that Florida indicates about private school curriculum is a regulation on biological experiments: "No dissection may be performed on any living mammalian vertebrate or bird" (Fla. Stat. Ch. 233.0674 [2] [a] [h])!

Private schools also do not uniformly require that their teachers be certified, although many do receive credentials. These schools set their own curricula and standards, and many administer their own tests. If you're considering private school, keep in mind that interviews (with both the prospective student and family) are usually required, along with admissions exams that assess how well a student might adapt to this academic program.

You can expect all private school constituencies to be geographically mixed, so organizing play dates with your child's friends may present logistical challenges. And along with the cost, most private schools, with their small sizes and exclusive natures, can't really help but contribute to an atmosphere of elitism in this country.

Homeschooling

In mid-1800s America, parents determined what their children needed to know to succeed in their lives. One hundred fifty years later, growing numbers of parents are still making such decisions. In the year 2001, somewhere in the range of one million American school-aged children were educated at home. Why? Why homeschooling?

The answers to that question are philosophical, political, economic, and religious. Some parents see homeschooling as an antidote to the failures of society and the public schools or the needless expense of private school. Some parents believe that they can offer their child the highest quality of education; some prefer to impart their own values, character, and morals. In any case, if you read recent headlines, it would appear that homeschooled students stand head and shoulders above their public-schooled counterparts.

Dr. Bryan Ray's 1997 study of over fifty-four hundred homeschooled students showed academic-achievement levels ranging, on average, in the eighty-second percentile in math and the eighty-seventh percentile in reading (NHERI, 1999), significantly higher than average public school scores, which hover around the fiftieth percentile. Dr. Lawrence Rudner, the former director of the Educational Resources Information Center Clearinghouse on Assessment and Evaluation, a U.S. Department of Education information service, conducted research in 1998 that evaluated 20,760 K–12 homeschooled students and found equally impressive results: Almost 25 percent of these students were on an academic level one or more grades above their age-level peers in public and private schools (Rudner, 1999).

But the glowing reports must be read for what they represent: studies reflecting a segment of the homeschooling population that is predominantly white and Christian. Even Rudner (1999) acknowledges that these findings "must be interpreted with a great deal of caution" and that "it was not possible to evaluate whether this sample is truly representative of the entire population of home school students" (25). In fact, Welner and Welner (1999), in response to Rudner's article, advise that the current homeschooling population is not so easily categorized: All class and ethnic groups are represented, along with a variety of political and intellectual values. What Rudner emphatically does assert in his study is that the parents who choose the homeschooling approach are highly motivated to provide an academic environment in which their children can succeed.

Homeschooling does deliver a customized, flexible, interest-driven education, with a teacher-student ratio of one to one. To teach children at home may not require a formal credential, but it does demand compliance with state laws and an interface with the local school district. Even though curriculum design rests solidly with the parents, the child may still have to take standardized achievement tests. Then again, there is an additional segment of the homeschooling population that embraces "unschooling," a philosophy that views the whole world as its classroom and allows a child's interests to set the pace of his education, even if it defies grade-level standards. Unschoolers feel that testing and curriculum demands are part of a misguided educational system and do what they can to avoid such unnecessary restrictions (Welner & Welner, 1999).

In addition to unschooling, there are probably as many homeschooling perspectives as there are families and a similarly wide range of curriculum materials available for purchase. This option gives a parent almost complete control over his or her child's education, which is a huge responsibility and an enormous commitment. It should also be noted that homeschooling is not a "one size fits all" way of thinking; it may not be the best choice for every child in a family and also may not work for one child over the course of his entire academic life. But if you do choose to embark on this path, there is a great deal of support available, especially on the Internet, from curriculum choices to locating homeschooling groups. Contact your state legislator's office or department of education for the legal requirements.

Summary

Public or private, magnet or charter, or doing it yourself: Which way do you turn? There's a great deal to sort out when considering your child's schooling! Each category encompasses alternatives, and each alternative has positives and negatives, strengths and weaknesses, if you will, that demand evaluation for an informed decision to be made. Neighborhood schools offer a convenient location and provide the chance to strengthen community ties. Magnet schools can be farther away and tougher to get into but offer thematic curricula that may appeal to some families. Charter schools have similar issues to those of magnets but trade some of the district bureaucracy for greater hands-on participation by the stakeholders.

Whether parochial or nonsectarian, private schools theoretically provide smaller class sizes and favorable teacher-student ratios, more individualized attention, and enrichment, but they are often quite a distance from home and frequently carry a hefty price tag. Homeschooling allows for a truly customized curriculum and enviable teacher-student ratio, but it demands a huge commitment from parents in terms of time and energy, not just for teaching but also to stay aligned with a school district's policies and procedures.

We've distilled this information for you into the School Comparison Chart presented in table 9.1. This format organizes the options so they can be compared, while advising you of the input you will need to make your own decision.

Every learning environment has its own personality; its strengths and weaknesses must be explored and seen for themselves. The *only* way to make that truly informed decision is by visiting a sampling of schools and sitting in classrooms, observing teachers, meeting with principals, chatting with parents, and asking your questions. And

Table 9.1. School Comparison Chart

	Location	Availability	Financials	Parent Involvement	Varies by Site
Neighborhood School	Geographically convenient; promotes peer socialization, friendships, and community involvement	Space is always available	Tuition-free, but expect fund-raising; expect to raise even more funds with state and district budget cuts	Type of involvement determined at school site; may be mandated by state and federal funds	School philosophy, reputation, class size, teacher attitude and motivation, teacher-student ratio, enrichment programs, and other extras
Magnet School	Unknown length of commute, although transportation may be provided; unknown logistics for convenient peer socialization	Limited space can promote a sense of competition for available spots; admissions lottery; sometimes admission testing required	Tuition-free, but expect fund-raising	Types of involvement determined at school site; may be mandated by state and federal funds	Focus of thematic curriculum, school philosophy, reputation, class size, enrichment programs, teacher attitude and motivation, teacher-student ratio
Charter School	Unknown length of commute; unknown logistics for convenient peer socialization	Limited space can promote a sense of competition for available spots; enrollment criteria vary: could be first-come, first-served neighborhood or perhaps lottery	Tuition-free, but expect fund-raising; charter schools are often underfunded (especially initially)	Parent involvement mandated by charter	School philosophy, reputation, class size, enrichment programs, teacher attitude and motivation, teacher-student ratio; sufficient state/local controls may be lacking to fully protect students

(continues)

Table 9.1. School Comparison Chart (*continued*)

	Location	Availability	Financials	Parent Involvement	Varies by Site
Private School: Parochial	Unknown length of commute; unknown logistics for convenient peer socialization; may not be an integrated community	Limited space; competition for available spots; application process; interviews/admissions testing	Tuition plus fund-raising; may be considered elitist	Types of involvement determined at school site	School philosophy, reputation, morals/ character and religious values, class size, teacher attitude and motivation, teacher-student ratio, enrichment programs, and other "extras"
Private School: Nonsectarian	Unknown length of commute; unknown logistics for convenient peer socialization; may not be an integrated community	Limited space; competition for available spots; application process; interviews/admissions testing	Tuition plus fund-raising; may be considered elitist	Types of involvement determined at school site	School philosophy, reputation, moral/ character values, class size, teacher attitude and motivation, teacher-student ratio, enrichment programs, and other "extras"
Home-Schooling	Geographically convenient, but raises socialization question	N/A	Technically, "tuition-free," but expect costs for materials and curriculum, if purchased	Requires enormous parental commitment, including need to interface with local school district	Educational philosophy; curriculum

when you go, please take along your School Tour Companion; you'll have in hand a concise checklist of questions to help narrow the field. Once you have made your site visits, refresh your memory with the School Comparison Chart.

The School Tour Companion: Questions to Ask of Any School

It's time to get out into the field for hands-on research. The School Tour Companion is a guide to help you understand the way educational facilities are run. Whether your child will attend the school down the street or you have the option of considering a vast array of choices, the questions are the same. We've assembled a collection of thirty-six categories to guide your exploration, help you compare approaches, and motivate questions you can ask. Informed parents serve their family and their community.

The school visit is an important first step in the relationship. Begin by scheduling an appointment. You may be able to drop by unannounced to observe classes in session, but some schools establish certain visitation days and times, so save yourself a trip by making the phone call. If there's an upcoming prospective-parent open house on the agenda, by all means attend it, but remember that an open house is still a sales tool; if you find yourself interested, plan a return trip. If you are already certain that your child will attend the neighborhood school, you'll want to return frequently! It's not too soon to begin laying the groundwork for what will be a major relationship in your foreseeable future.

When you arrive for the tour, be prepared to take notes as these will help you sort out your thoughts after the visit is long past. But do it discreetly; you don't want to spend a lot of time writing when you should be listening. This is why we've created the School Tour Companion. It's easy to use: Either fill in the blanks or check off answers to your satisfaction for the concrete information and utilize the spaces provided to record other details. (For now please ignore the column to the right marked "CYL." We'll get there at the end.) Because every school tour is organized differently, you may need to flip pages as you cover the following areas and all they encompass:

- First Impressions
- School Basics
- Philosophy and Attitude
- Teaching and Learning
- Facts and Formulas

The purpose of the tour is essentially quite scientific; looking, listening, and feeling will be very valuable commodities. This is your opportunity to record data and impressions; however, it is not the time to make decisions. For one of your authors, who has made dozens of such visits, there have been more than a few surprises: Sometimes the "popular" school that all your friends rave about is completely wrong for your particular child, and that unassuming place with lower test scores is a gem waiting to be discovered. These realizations would never have occurred if a variety of schools weren't on the list. So, be open to all your options, and keep in mind that your quest is just beginning. The true value of your school tour(s) will not be known until you can synthesize all the input, make comparisons, and begin evaluating in earnest.

Activity 9.2. SCHOOL TOUR COMPANION 1: FIRST IMPRESSIONS		
School:	Date:	
First Impressions	**Comments**	**CYL/___**
External appearance/state of repair	Attractive ____ Pleasant ____ Needs attention ____	
Grounds and location	Asphalt ____ Grassy areas ____ Gardens ____	
Safety and security	One main entrance ____ Multiple entrances ____ Doors locked at set time ____	
Interior atmosphere	Attractive ____ Pleasant ____ Dreary ____ Natural light ____	
Facilities	Library ____ Auditorium ____ Cafeteria ____ Comments _____ _____	
Student work displayed	Yes ____ No ____	
Type/quality of work displayed	Exceptional ____ Average ____	

First Impressions: Time to Take It All In

It's the day of your school visit, your first chance to record those important observations. Bring your School Tour Companion and a pen and, if at all possible, arrive at the site a few minutes early to begin noting external factors and conditions. A school situated near a busy thoroughfare has a very different feeling from one that is tucked away and secluded. Write down what you notice. Pay attention to the physical building and its state of repair, as well as the grounds, be they asphalt, lawn, or gardens. Is the location acceptable? What about the commute? And consider physical security: How easy is it to get onto the campus when class is in session (this will be clearer if you're there as an individual and not part of a tour, when gates initially stand open to welcome a group).

Once you're inside, look at the big picture: How is the atmosphere? How is the lighting? Look at the library, auditorium, gymnasium, parent center, and the like, if they exist. (Some schools in converted facilities lack those dedicated spaces. How do you feel about that?) Is current student art displayed on the walls? Does it smack of uniformity or creativity? What does that tell you about the school philosophy? We'll get into that a little later.

School Basics

This is a small, but essential, piece of the puzzle to which you will return repeatedly to make note of details provided during your visit. Jot down contact names, from those of the principal, to the office staff, to parent representatives.

How is the size factor: Comfortable? Overwhelming? A school may not be able to change its size, but it can manage it effectively. When student population reaches into the thousands and the calendar is year-round, students are sometimes assigned to different *tracks*, or fixed schedules. One way to personalize a large environment is to establish manageable units of operation known as "schools within a school," families, and so forth. If it's a middle or high school, sixth or ninth graders may be intentionally separated from the rest of the campus to ease their transition from lower to upper grades. Humble High School in Houston, Texas, with its twenty-five hundred students, actually maintains a separate campus for its ninth graders. According to Associate Principal Joyce Olson (1999, personal communication), here students "get to know each other, connect and find a place to 'plug in.'" If such a system exists, you'll want to know how it operates. How the school gets to know each child and manages its size tells you a great deal about its outlook on learning.

Pay attention to the demographics, and make note of the school's population percentages. Does it draw students from the surrounding area, or is there busing? If this is a public school, you will want to indicate (or summarize) the geographic boundaries so that you'll know on what basis your child stands to be admitted. If it's not your local school, you may need to apply for a permit. Or you may find yourself part of a lottery system for magnets or charters. For private schools, there will likely be applications, interviews, and other procedures. All of these require that you respect certain dates and procedures. Make note of hours (especially if you have more than one child, whether they are in pre-K, kindergarten, or secondary schools). As we've said before, you may find yourself flipping back to this section frequently to apply facts accumulated during the course of your tour.

Philosophy and Attitude

You've already recorded the main logistical information; now it's time to tackle philosophy. Does your visit begin with an overview of the school's educational approach, or do you plunge right into the day's proceedings? Neither one is necessarily better, but make sure to collect the philosophical data you need if the latter is the case. The

Activity 9.3.
SCHOOL TOUR COMPANION 2: SCHOOL BASICS

School:	Date:	
School Basics	**Comments**	**CYL/___**
Principal/other contacts		
Size/enrollment	Too big —— (If yes, are there other learning communities?) —— Too small —— Just right ——	
Demographics (approximately)		
Borders/boundaries	_____ _____ Neighborhood population ____ Busing ____	
Admission requirements	Neighborhood school ____ Application process ____ Permit/other requirements ____ Lottery ____	
Enrollment/other important dates		
Hours/days of operation	Preschool _____ Lower grades _____ Upper grades _____ Regular early dismissal days? ____	
Before-/after-school program		

school's *mission* lays out broad goals, while the *vision* details the way in which those goals will be accomplished. Mission and vision statements are frequently posted on bulletin boards or in classrooms, but if you don't see them, ask. A school with a clearly articulated mission and vision reveals a great deal about its administrative style. Chaos or order can be perceived very quickly, as can that elusive thing called "school pride." And while we're on the subject, attitude spills over everywhere, so how's the attitude of the front office staff? Is the principal available and approachable? Note your reactions: Maybe you feel welcomed, maybe ill at ease.

You'll want to understand if this is a traditional or progressive school. Maybe it's a hybrid, combining elements of both. How does its approach manifest itself? Maybe it strictly adheres to the teachings of a founder, such as a Montessori or Rudolph Steiner (Waldorf) school. Is there a dress code? Uniforms? What about homework? When does it start, how much is given, and how much should a parent help?

You can get a good sense of philosophy by looking at rules posted on classroom walls, but also inquire about a code of conduct. You'll definitely want to know in advance about the approach to discipline, which can range from the rewards-and-consequences model all the way to noncoercive problem solving. Finding out how students are disciplined will give you a quick and realistic peek at the school's philosophy.

Teaching and Learning

Philosophy leads us directly to curriculum and how it is experienced. Curriculum matters are impacted most profoundly on the local level in some fifteen thousand school districts across the country. In California, for example, districts have the freedom and the authority to decide which instructional materials best meet the needs of their students as long as their choices comply with the education code (Goddess, 1998). If you haven't done so already, take a look at your state and/or district standards, frameworks, and education code (see compendium for your state department of education's contact information).

In public education, the states shape legislation, deliver most of the budget, and appoint their own curriculum commissions (teachers, administrators, and other specialists) to create *content standards*. These standards are benchmarks for student learning, prescribing what a child should know and be able to demonstrate at the completion of a designated certain grade level. Curriculum *frameworks* then reiterate the specific goals and provide teachers with the details needed to implement them.

Private schools, funded primarily through tuition and donations, do not have to rely upon the government and are therefore less tied to rigorous compliance with the state's educational benchmarks (unless they are accredited). They develop curricula related to their educational philosophies. Even if you are not seriously considering private school, it could be worth your time to attend a school tour strictly for purposes of comparison.

Now that we have an idea of "what" is going to be taught, "how" is it going to be delivered? Curriculum can be *subject driven*, meaning that a certain subject is taught at a certain time: Language arts takes place first thing after morning business; math is from 11:00 a.m. to 12:00 p.m., and so on. Or maybe you hear the terms *integrated* and *thematic* curricula. An integrated curriculum will utilize a lesson to teach several subjects within a particular grade level: Following a recipe, for example, could teach math (amounts, measuring), science (cooking principles), and language arts (reading the

Activity 9.4. SCHOOL TOUR COMPANION 3: PHILOSOPHY AND ATTITUDE		
School:	Date:	
Philosophy and Attitude	**Comments**	**CYL/___**
Clear philosophy articulated Mission Vision	Yes ____ No ____ Yes ____ No ____ Yes ____ No ____	
Front-office attitude	Welcoming ____ Accessible ____ Indifferent ____	
Approachability of principal	Welcoming ____ Accessible ____ Indifferent ____	
School philosophy	Traditional ____ Progressive ____ Other ____	
Classroom style	Traditional ____ Open/collaborative ____	
Homework	How much _____ How often _____	
Uniforms	Yes ____ No ____	
Code of conduct	Rules/consequences ____ Develops student's self-control, collaboration as to appropriate measures ____	

recipe). It might also involve social studies by relating the cooking lesson to a particular culture. A thematic curriculum will relate more to a schoolwide instructional focus, with each grade assigned its particular area. The overall theme could be humanities, for example, and each grade level would then have a focus like identity, community, diversity, and the like. Of course, there are many variations on this concept.

Merrow (2001) says that teachers truly are the heart and soul of a school, and we wholeheartedly agree. You'll want to see as many teachers in action as possible. Consider instructional methods: Do you notice children sitting quietly at desks listening to a teacher ("traditional") or the busy, noisy "open classroom" in which students frequently work in groups to do their problem solving? Imagine your child in this context; think about how he might adapt to the situation. Neither one is necessarily better, but one is probably better for him.

Regardless of the teacher's approach, the classroom should be a place that is comfortable, inviting, and stimulating. Are the children actively engaged in learning? What about class sizes? Observe the teacher-student ratio; you may even want to count the desks yourself. Are the children all at one grade level, or are there mixed-age groupings? How many teachers are in the room? Are there instructional aides (*paraprofessionals*) assisting and for how many hours a day?

You may want to inquire as to how children are placed: Age, gender, and ability are three common groupings. Are textbooks fundamental to the curriculum or treated as references? How important are projects? Find out about grading too: Is it letters, numbers, or no grades at all?

Many schools include units teaching conflict-resolution and productive-citizenship skills; they might train students in *peer mediation.* They might offer *service-learning* courses in which students volunteer in their community as part of the curriculum. Now is the time to ask about similar programs at this school.

Beyond the core subjects (math, language arts, science, social studies), you would do well to investigate what other classes round out the school day. At the elementary level, are the arts, physical education, and foreign languages represented? In middle and high schools, electives will become very important. If your son is musical, you will probably be interested in schools with chorus or band. If your daughter is athletic, having sports activities on campus can save a lot of afternoon chauffeuring. Interest-based clubs, tutoring, and other after-school options can be very appealing. Many on-site programs keep children supervised and away from negative influences, providing a convenient and affordable service for busy parents while offering stimulating enrichment programs. In addition to receiving help with homework or tutoring in a specific subject area, children might have the chance to sign up for drama, dance, cooking, a variety of sports, woodworking, and so forth. At a time when certain programs (especially the arts) have been all but eliminated in public schools, this can be an excellent way to augment your child's general education. There's space to collect all of this data on the "Teaching and Learning" page.

Facts and Formulas

You've just about made it through your tour, and yet, there are still some fundamental pieces of information to pursue. Page five of the School Tour Companion, "Facts and Formulas," provides the space to notate the final details that may be crucial to your decision.

Testing and Accountability   Test scores and accountability are certainly at the top of that list. The federal government has enacted laws establishing general educational goals (like Goals 2000 and the No Child Left Behind Act of 2001) and detailing specific programs that, these days, are frequently tied to *accountability.* Accountability is addressed by assessing student performance on *standardized achievement tests.* You've seen

Activity 9.5. SCHOOL TOUR COMPANION 4: TEACHING AND LEARNING		
School:	Date:	
Teaching and Learning	**Comments**	**CYL/___**
Curriculum	Subject-driven ____ Standards-based ____ Thematic ____ Integrated ____	
Class sizes Mixed-age groupings? Number of teachers/aides?	_____ _____ _____	
How are children placed?	By age ____ By ability ____ By gender ____ Other _____	
Instructional methods	Teacher-driven ____ Student-centered ____	
Textbooks Projects?	Instrumental ____ Used as references ____ Yes ____ No ____	
Electives/enrichment classes or special features After school activities	List meaningful selections:	

these scores, but do you know how to interpret them? And do you understand how they are designed and scored? Cox and Puleo (2002) explain the procedure: After studying content standards from every state, test publishers devise questions intended to determine whether or not students are working at grade level. Such national tests are *norm referenced*: They compare results from each grade level at each school to those of a national *norm group* of students who have been selected to represent certain demographics and have already taken the test. Scores tell how children rank, but those numbers can be quite misleading. Percentiles don't reflect how many questions a child answered correctly; nor do they compare one child's results with those of the other students in his class. Instead, his scores compare with those of the norm group. For example, if your child scored in the seventy-second percentile, then 72 percent of the students who set the standard for the test scored the same or lower than he did, and 28 percent scored higher. If he ranked in the fiftieth percentile, it means half the students in the norm group for your child's grade level scored the same as your child or below, and the other 50 percent scored higher.

But there's a bigger picture to testing. It is not just the children whose test scores are ranked; the schools are also being rated by these results. Are they doing what they're supposed to be doing? Teachers and administrators may find that their careers depend upon the outcome of these instruments. Rewards (mainly financial) can be handed out for success, and consequences meted out for failure, ranging from job dismissal to the school's being put into receivership, that is, under state control.

Test scores, therefore, can make or break the reputation of a school, and this is where the standards movement is responsible for focusing parents unwisely on sheer numbers. For parents, a quick look at the numbers is not sufficient, and it's often completely confusing! It is critical to read the data correctly and understand it in context. If, at a school you visit, the scores are not immediately impressive, or you're unclear about what they represent, be sure to have them explained to your satisfaction by the principal or an administrator. It's not fair to hear a number and react subjectively to it; comparatively lower scores at a particular school may still reflect a year-to-year improvement within a grade level or subject area. And please remember that test scores—the "proof" of such a heavy reliance upon standards—should not be the only method used to judge a child's or a school's abilities. Consider them as one factor in your overall assessment.

While we're on the subject of scores, there are some more relatively tough questions you need to ask. At secondary schools, inquire about attendance, suspension, and dropout figures. If it's strictly high schools you're considering, how many students go on to four-year colleges?

Special Education   If you have a child with special needs, you will be particularly interested in the services offered under the category of "special education." The Individuals with Disabilities Education Act provides such children with the right to receive support in the "least restrictive environment" possible. Each such child has his or her own individualized education program, which is discussed in a joint meeting with parents, administrators, and any specialists who have been asked to evaluate and/or work with the child. Depending on the nature of the disability, maybe he will participate in a *pullout* program to work on academic and other skills with the *resource specialist teacher.* He might be *included* or *mainstreamed* in a "regular" classroom (sometimes with a one-on-one aide assigned solely to him) to help prepare him for the "real world." Or a group of children may be taught in their own separate class. In some states, *gifted* programs fall under the "special education" heading, and the manner in which they are conducted varies from school to school. In any case, special education services are frequently managed as much by the district as they are by an individual school, so ask for a meeting with the principal if you need more information on the subject.

School Culture and Parent Involvement   The last major area we're going to cover involves parents and school culture. In chapter 2, we spoke of the American culture and attempted to describe it. Now think in terms of describing school culture as well, for it's unique to every institution and evident as soon as you walk in the door. It is an atmosphere quickly perceived from the faces that greet (or don't greet) you and the attitudes of the parents and the students in attendance. New York principal Roberta Kirshbaum (1998) explains that "every system has its own culture, defined as 'because that's the way we do things'" (10).

If you have a chance on this tour or at another point, talk to the children. Sit in on Parent Teacher Association (PTA), booster club, or site council meetings. Ask parents about the ways in which they are involved; you'll very quickly see how they feel about the school. You'll also learn about current projects and priorities and be able to determine if they fit well with your own talents and values. There's no better way to get a true sense of this community than by talking to its constituents.

Among the questions you can ask is if there is an explicit or implicit expectation of parent participation. In some schools, an actual contract details how many hours per month or semester are to be dedicated; others may have less binding arrangements but still require a certain level of participation. The kind of involvement varies from site to site, but classroom volunteering, PTAs, booster (fund-raising) clubs, school- (or site-) based management, and advisory councils all generally offer ways for parents to contribute ideas, leadership, time, and/or financial support. Some schools reach out to their families with parenting classes; some offer tutoring and mentoring programs that depend upon community cooperation for their success. Some schools clearly do not want parents in the classroom! You will learn a great deal about a prospective school by investigating its outlook on parental involvement. If your child enrolls in this school, it's not just his life that will be spent here. Make sure you're comfortable too.

Summary

Your tour is complete. So then, how do you feel about this school? Beyond the checklists and fill-in-the-blank answers, and despite your best efforts to keep a neutral mind, you probably have formed an opinion. When you have a few minutes to yourself, either now or later on in the day, sum up your reaction in your own words.

A thorough school tour requires patience, diligence, and sensitivity; there's so much to see, to hear, to experience, and to record. Each time you visit a school, you observe how the facility appears from the outside, taking in everything from its physical state of repair to its grounds, buildings, and location. You study day-to-day routines and see the philosophy in action through classroom visits and conversations. During those conversations, you talk to a variety of people, from the principal, to staff, to parents and students. You inquire about test scores and teacher backgrounds; you study the art on the walls and attend parent meetings. If you're interested in this school, you visit more than once.

If there is no real decision to make—if you are sending your child to your neighborhood school—your evaluation is complete right now. Congratulations on laying the foundation for a constructive relationship. If you have learned about areas that could use your expertise and involvement, move right on to chapter 10.

If you are still considering which school is right for your child, keep looking at your options because comparison can only strengthen your commitment. Besides, you may have to deal with enrollment and acceptance issues if this is not your neighborhood school. The better informed you are, the better equipped you will be to come to a satisfactory conclusion about the array of choices before you. Take a copy of the School Tour Companion and fill it out on each of your subsequent trips. And please keep reading so we can help you navigate these waters.

Activity 9.6. SCHOOL TOUR COMPANION 5: FACTS AND FORMULAS		
School:	Date:	
Facts and Formulas	**Comments**	**CYL/___**
Test scores	Explained ____ Issues factored in ____	
For middle/high schools	Attendance rate ____ Suspension rate ____ Dropout rate ____	
For high schools	Percentage of students that go on to a four-year college ____	
Fully credentialed teachers Teachers in credentialing process	Percentage ____ Percentage ____	
Parent involvement	PTA/PTO ____ Booster club ____ Site council ____ Parenting classes ____ Classroom participation ____ Number of volunteer hours required ____	
Special needs	Special education classrooms ____ Mainstreaming ____ Resource ____ Gifted and talented ____	
Technology	In classroom ____ Computer lab ____ Internet ____	

Activity 9.7.
SCHOOL SUMMARY REFLECTION

Your tour is complete. So then, how do you feel about this school? When you have a few minutes to yourself, either now or later on in the day, sum up your reaction in your own words.

School	Visit Date:
Summary Reflection:	

Narrowing the Field

Having visited a variety of schools, you're getting closer to decision time. Choosing a school can be one of the most stressful events in your family's life. You may also find something curious happening to you: After weeks or months of research, interviews, and school tours, your expectations may have changed. Maybe you were determined to seek out a rigorous, traditional environment for your child, only to be struck by the excitement of an inquiry-based classroom. Or you were sure you wanted a developmental kindergarten for her, only to find that a bit more structure is an even better challenge. Luckily, this confusion can actually be managed with the summary activities.

When it comes to the school decision, there's a very basic bottom line here: You should not tacitly accept what others think, no matter how worthy they are of your respect. First of all, their information may not be up to date. Secondly, school dynamics can vary greatly from year to year, dramatically so when that change includes a new administration. And thirdly, nobody else really knows what's right for your situation. That school with the "great" reputation won't necessarily be the best environment to satisfy your child's needs or your own criteria. If she is in the upper elementary grades or older, get her involved in the decision because, after all, she's the one who will be attending every day. Once you've narrowed the field, take her along for a site visit. The right choice will be the one that's the best fit for your child *and* your family.

Can You Live with It?

It's time now to refer back to the School Tour Companion. You've noticed the letters "CYL" on the right side of the comments section on each page of your tour companion? They abbreviate the phrase "Can You Live with It?" Let's use that tool by revisiting the tour companion pages and, for each category, asking yourself, can I live with it? Now, you may be saying to yourself, "I don't want to live with it. I want to love it!" Hang on: This is just the first step in the process. If loving your school is a priority, we'll get there too.

But for the moment, let us remind you that there is no "perfect" school. It's like buying a house; there are certain factors you must have, but there will inevitably be others that require compromise. The question for us right now is, *can you live with it?*

If you can live with the data in that category, give it one point in the "CYL" section. If you love what you see in that category, give it two points. If you cannot live with the data in that category, give it a zero in the "CYL" section. Total up the points for each page and write them on the line next to "CYL/_____." Next, take the points for each page and copy them onto the "Decision Maker Table" below.

Let's see how this school did. Remember, we're not grading you; *you're* grading the school visit on that particular day. There are a maximum of seventy-two points possible here. If the school scored between zero and twenty-four, it's safe to say that you can't live with this school. A number between twenty-four and forty-eight means you should definitely include it in your ongoing comparisons with others. A score of between forty-nine and seventy-two means this is a strong candidate. We recommend you keep "shopping" and then visit again; you can tour a school multiple times and get very different impressions. You want to be sure your decision bears the test of scrutiny.

Activity 9.8.
DECISION-MAKER TABLE

Look at forms 9.2–9.6 for each school you are considering. Enter the point "CYL/___." box of each form in the appropriate category of the table below. Total all the points and compare the result with the scale below the table.

School Name	First Impressions Score	School Basics Score	Philosophy/ Attitudes Score	Teaching/ Learning Score	Facts/ Formulas Score	Total

Scoring: 0–24: This school doesn't meet enough of your needs; move on.
25–48: This school has potential; move to the next round.
49–72: This school fits your needs well; definitely move to the next round.

Activity 9.9.
THE LANDSCAPE SURVEY REVISITED

Some forty pages ago we invited you to climb down from the precipice and look around at the local educational landscape. We asked for some immediate reactions to the words "school," "teachers," "students," "programs," "parents," "community," and "other." Take a look at the original Landscape Survey again. How would you do it differently now? We encourage you to take the survey again. There's another form here just for that purpose so that you can have tangible proof of all you've learned from your fieldwork.

1. Schools	
2. Teachers	
3. Students	
4. Programs	
5. Parents	
6. Community	
7. Other	

Activity 9.10.
NEEDS AND VALUES SUMMARY

Ask yourself, *what am I looking for in a school?* As you write, feel free to consider the following categories:

Academic rigor	Atmosphere/school pride
Arts or other programs	Dress code/uniforms
Established versus emerging school	Ethics/citizenship/community involvement
Friends attending	Involved parent community
Location	Motivated teachers
Philosophy	Sports and after-school opportunities
Strong/visionary administration	Welcoming environment/culture

---

Along the way, we suspect you have developed a clear notion of what you are looking for in a school. Academics and a certain educational philosophy may do the trick; student uniforms and an easy two-minute walk from your house may seal the deal. What has become important for you? Take a moment now (yes, another little evaluation), and write out a statement of your emerging beliefs.

Decision Time

You've done your school research. You've gained specific knowledge of your local educational scene and become an informed parent. You have crystallized what you want for your child's education, maybe even developed your own educational philosophy. That's pretty impressive! You're just about at the finish line. If you have School Tour Companion pages for a variety of schools, with your "CYL" designations, collect them now. Plug all that information into the "Decision Maker Comparison Table" and see what happens.

Was your choice clear? Do you feel good about that decision? Then congratulations! If the choice isn't clear yet, compare your written summaries for each facility and refer to the "Needs and Values" summary—what you're looking for in a school. That should bring the focus back to what's most important for your family. Having a good choice or two is actually an excellent position to be in so that you have options as you proceed to applications, enrollment, and so forth. Good luck with these next steps!

Summary

We've examined a broad range of educational alternatives in this chapter. Whether you are planning to enroll at your neighborhood school or are entertaining other public, private, magnet, charter, or homeschooling options, it all comes down to what you can live with and what you can't live without. Maybe you didn't realize at the outset of

Activity 9.11.
DECISION-MAKER COMPARISON TABLE

School Name	First Impressions Score	School Basics Score	Philosophy/ Attitudes Score	Teaching/ Learning Score	Facts/ Formulas Score	Total

this chapter that you'd end up developing your own educational philosophy! But that's just what you've done as you looked at, listened to, questioned, and experienced different styles of schooling. We have endeavored to provide background thinking in all of these areas, plus topics like curriculum, standards, testing, and teaching. Hopefully the School Tour Companion, the "Decision Maker" tables, and the summary statements have articulated focal points, prompted you with checklists, and helped you to formulate your own opinions and goals.

Where are you now? We hope that by taking the time to do this mental and physical legwork, you have zeroed in on the educational experience you want for your child. We trust that you have identified at least one optimal school situation. And we hope that it points the way to a culture that welcomes the gifts you have to give.

FINAL THOUGHTS

In this chapter, we have carefully considered a variety of schooling options practiced in the United States at the start of the twenty-first century. We hope that by evaluating these resources, you have not only honed your skills as an educational consumer but also developed a philosophy to guide your family's instructional choices. The well-informed change agent is a diplomat who does the research, asks the tough questions, and comes up with innovative solutions. Change isn't the business of someone else; it starts with us.

10

Making an Impact on Education: What You Can Do

> It is time that the average citizen has his/her voice heard when it comes to what we do in our schools. We have relied only on industry boards, consultants, foundations and university experts to tell us what our graduates should be able to know and do. But that is not how a democracy should operate. Messy, and at times uncomfortable, conversations that include parents, students, and taxpayers about the aims of education are long overdue.
>
> —George Wood

We've stood on the precipice and envisioned the new institution. We've climbed back down the hill to find a consensus that education is broken: A steady drumbeat of surveys, reports, and opinion pieces feeds what's wrong with the system to a disenchanted public. Frankly, we're not interested in fixing education, past tense; we are, however, deeply committed to framing its future. And this will require an engaged citizenry that is ready to stop sitting in judgment. In redesigning a role for education on both the state and federal levels, we seek to craft an institution that remembers its purpose. In a community of learners, everyone can cultivate skills that nurture collaboration and develop leadership. Whether you are a parent, educator, legislator, or community member, no single demographic group can quiet the "fix-it" frenzy alone. Instead, shared responsibility becomes foundational as we create a vision, hold on to it, and forge ahead.

In this chapter, we'll reflect on each of the player's individual roles; we'll brainstorm as to how they fit together to move our collective consciousness forward. Rather than exploring every subsection exhaustively, we'll fill your mind with possibilities for further contemplation. And finally, we'll move from the general to the specific, altering the tone from generic talk of parents, educators, legislators, and citizens to the more specific "you." Right now, the revolution gets personal.

AS A PARENT

Parenting is a lifelong process of letting go. Every step of the way, you are preparing your children to be independent. During those sleepless nights with a newborn, the frantic days of keeping up with a toddler, the tearful hours of teen (and these days, even preteen) angst, time seems to stretch out and challenges you to make it through the day. But then, time cruelly and suddenly warps, the kids go off to school, and you're wondering how they got this *grown up*.

Easing the Transition

Your child is moving on: maybe it's to kindergarten, or the next year of elementary school, or perhaps to middle or high school. You've done your research. You've made your decision (if there was a decision to be made), and he's enrolled. Opportunities and challenges are on their way. And as with any new situation, you should expect a period of transition. What can be done to ensure it proceeds as smoothly as possible?

Consider visiting the school before the semester begins. Introduce yourself to the office staff. Remembering names and faces will help establish your positive identity on campus. If you haven't spoken with the principal, send an e-mail or a note or make an appointment to let him or her know how much you are looking forward to being a part of this community. Stop by the classroom(s) and say hello to the teacher(s); cordial relationships offer a promising start to a successful year.

Perhaps there will also be an orientation, a summer-camp program for the kids, or social events to welcome new families. If you can attend these outings, you'll meet some folks who are feeling just as awkward and excited as you are, and a few friendly faces will make the adjustment period easier for your whole family. All of these suggestions are intended simply to underscore the fact that this is your team now; you've gone from investigator to stakeholder. And once you're a stakeholder, collaboration follows right behind.

Collaboration at School

Collaboration happens when people share a goal and work together to achieve it. Conzemius and O'Neill (2001) explain that a collaborative environment has certain qualities too: Ideas are shared freely, team members feel that their contributions are valued and respected, and when problems arise, they are discussed openly. For many parents, collaboration with the school community begins with volunteering. Whether your child is in kindergarten or tenth grade, you should be prepared to contribute your time, your expertise, and/or your financial commitment.

Support for the School: On-site Volunteering

If you can make the time to volunteer on-site, you may be faced with an array of options. How will you choose? Attending Parent Teacher Association (PTA) or booster club meetings is one way to start: You'll gain an overview of involvement opportunities and then can identify a program or committee that needs your particular talents. Schools that don't have those sorts of organizational bodies still manage to bring you into the fold via e-mail, telephone, website, flyers, newsletters, or events.

There are many ways in which families can contribute time and talents to benefit their school. Three significant examples for such involvement would include working directly with a teacher, organizing projects, or serving on a schoolwide governing body.

Volunteers can *assist teachers* by duplicating worksheets and other handouts, prepping materials, reading to the class, tutoring, mentoring children, or chaperoning field trips. Another way to get involved is *by planning a special event or project*. Maybe it will be a talent show or silent auction; perhaps you'll choose to serve on or chair a specific committee, assist in the library, monitor the playground at recess or lunch, or coordinate the book fairs and gift wrap drives. These jobs may also offer behind-the-scenes opportunities for parents who cannot regularly take time off from work to participate on campus. The third type of volunteering is *the schoolwide approach*, which encompasses participation in various aspects of governance, such as school-based management, advisory councils and/or the board of the PTA, Parent Teacher Organization (PTO), Parent Teacher Student Association (PTSA), or booster club(s). These organizations can offer a voice in school procedure and policy.

Obviously, each school has its own priorities for the year, which may not relate to our sample suggestions. But whatever the specific form it takes, your expertise is needed in your new community. By getting involved, you gain understanding of the tasks at hand as well as the school culture. When you know how to effectively work within the system, both you and your child can benefit enormously. According to Dr. Joyce Epstein (1997), "When parents, teachers, students and others view one another as partners in education, a caring community forms around students and begins its work" (2).

Many of the above suggestions are, more or less, skewed toward the elementary years, when having a parent with a visible presence on campus is still a matter of pride for the children. While there certainly is some carryover to secondary schools in this list we've provided, the rules of the game do change by the time your child has entered adolescence. What kind of a role will you play then?

Support in Secondary Schools

Your middle or high school–aged child is testing the waters of independence. Your relationship is changing, but you still need a presence in your child's life, and you want to support the school. What do you do when the homework assigned is over your head, and your child doesn't want to be seen in public with you?

There actually are ways for parents to maintain a profile on campus in these challenging academic years. Many schools educate adults about curriculum, offer classes to help with the challenges of parenting adolescents, or teach English as a second language. Some parents are empowered to initiate programs of their own, perhaps gardening, theater, and the like. And, of course, there are always the fund-raising committees and governing bodies that need your involvement to exist.

Your main area of focus, however, will still be your child. With larger class sizes for him and less on-campus involvement for you, how do you stay keyed in to his learning? Marlyn J. Pino-Jones (2002), former principal of Bella Vista High School in Fair Oaks, California, suggests that parents stay aware of how their child is doing by keeping track of such items as dates for report cards (in case they don't make it home) and attendance printouts. She also advocates staying in touch directly with teachers. "A high school teacher sees 165 students a day. Let's face it, when a parent makes a connection with a teacher, he makes a better connection with the student or is more cognizant of the parents' involvement." And making that connection with the teacher is a very effective link to school activities.

Taking Part in School Activities

Apart from volunteering, and no matter what grade your child is in, your attendance will be requested at events like open houses, back-to-school nights, science fairs, and special performances. Of all of these, the parent-teacher conference is still the most significant "official" vehicle for communication. Since this occurs only a few times a year, it is quite vital that you attend. In some schools (charters especially, which have a significant amount of freedom to construct policies), attending these conferences may be mandatory. Your relationship with the teacher (or lack thereof) will inform the way you approach the meeting. If you have no relationship as of yet, the tone of the meeting takes on even more importance. Since you will, no doubt, have a limited amount of conversation time, it can be helpful to keep in mind these suggestions.

The Parent-Teacher Conference

Parents are well-advised to start their conference with a positive comment about either the teacher or the classroom. Even if your child is having difficulties, you can always find something to praise, so praise it genuinely. The teacher will guide the discussion to school and classroom performance, and it is your job to listen carefully. But feel free to ask questions, too, and to offer other pertinent information about your home life. If there's been a recent change in your family (illness, death, relocation, divorce, etc.), the teacher needs to know about it. Don't rely on your child to communicate these details. Very often, teachers sense a change in a child without knowing the details to explain it, and this kind of clarification can put the family and the teacher on the same page.

Are there areas in which you believe your child needs special help? Share any other insights that you think may be useful. It's always a good practice to relate aspects of home life that reinforce what's being done at school: Maybe he likes Sudoku, or your family is taking a trip to Tokyo and the class will be studying Japan next semester. And if he is having difficulty with a social situation, this is a good time to get the teacher's perspective and involvement, if necessary. Having a pleasant and positive parent-teacher conference sends good feelings in both directions. It can reinforce appreciation and respect, or build a bridge over shaky ground.

Student-Led Conferencing

Some schools adopt student-led conferencing for one or more of their scheduled parent-teacher meetings. In this case, the student, rather than the teacher, initiates the discussion with parents as he walks them through a portfolio of his work from the current reporting period. Student-led conferencing can be a powerful learning tool for all concerned. By discussing his goals, his strengths, areas that need improvement, and strategies to accomplish that intention, he demonstrates ownership of his learning.

Whether your conference is teacher or student led, please show up for an essential school activity. Your child needs to see your commitment to his development as a student, but even more so as a person. Now let's explore how parents can collaborate with their children at home to further facilitate that growth.

Collaboration at Home

Using the term *collaboration* in a parent-child context may be perplexing if you're used to the authoritarian actions of many parents of the previous generation. You have doubtless heard about your role as your child's first teacher, and you have certainly passed along many of your own values to him. But you have a unique opportunity to learn from him too. If we always make children conform to our rigid notions of how things should be done, we handicap them from developing their best selves. When we engage our children as our partners, they ultimately develop enough confidence to assume responsibility for their own learning.

Whatever the age of your child, you may already use these parenting techniques suggested by the National Association for the Education of Young Children (Center for CSRI, 2006):

- Reinforce family routines involving homework, meals, and a regular bedtime.
- Encourage dinner conversation—it develops kids' language abilities.
- Limit "screen time" (television, computer, and video); help your child choose what to watch and discuss it afterwards.
- Offer kind words, praise, and constructive criticism.

These worthy tools give children much-needed structure. And yet, families have an even larger obligation: They are instrumental in helping their children feel secure in themselves and their abilities. Veteran elementary educator Lynette Turman (1999, personal communication), who trains and supports new teachers in the Los Angeles area, identifies two key ways that parents can best be involved: by modeling the kind of behavior they want for their child and by simply being there—giving undivided attention—when needed. Joyce Olson, associate principal at Humble High School in the Houston, Texas, area, concurs: "It's really being present for them and knowing what their needs are, not just academically, but as a person." It sounds so simple, but how do you do it when you are late to a meeting, fielding phone calls, or rushing through the supermarket to get dinner on the table?

It begins with looking and listening. When parents slow down their busy lives long enough to give a child undivided attention, the payoff for both can be tremendous. And as important as this process is for a kindergartner, it is absolutely essential for the high schooler whose peer influence is apparently more relevant to him than you are. Where do you stand right now when it comes to being there for your child? Let's establish a point of reference.

As a culture, we Americans are working our children very hard, and although we may be preparing them for a lifestyle that demands persistence, organization, and multitasking, we are also teaching them to carry tremendous anxiety. Anxiety unmanaged shuts down our ability to learn. According to Chenfeld (2001), "Education is a journey we embark on together. It's not a race! We have our maps to guide us, but sometimes

---

Activity 10.1.
PARENTING REFLECTION

1. What do you know about your child's academic needs?
2. What do you know about your child's personal needs?
3. What is your favorite way to give your child undivided attention?
4. What is your child's favorite way to receive undivided attention?

Activity 10.2.
PARENTING REFLECTION

1. Could you be more available to your child?
2. What would you be willing to change to be more fully present for your child?

---

we hit detours, construction areas, and traffic jams. We reroute, make new connections. Don't we want to . . . take some time to talk about the journey? (181)"

With this in mind, is there anything you would change about the attention you typically give your child?

Children's learning is influenced by their attitudes about themselves and everything in their worlds, including school, friends, and teachers. So, what if you, as a parent, could help your child to feel good about learning? Students who know how to learn understand that it is a process that begins with a question and makes meaningful connections to prior knowledge. Krzysztof Grabarek (2005) goes on to explain how parents can help their child complete schoolwork by asking what he calls "trigger questions." This technique engages the student by using explanation, comparison, and summary to connect the assignment to the "big ideas" being taught in the classroom. In this model, parents can learn right alongside their children and have a way to engage effectively with the teacher. When parents take an active interest in the child's academic life, it sends the message that school is important.

So, let's assume that you are taking the time to listen to your child, to observe what is going on with him, and learning along with him. Congratulations; you're laying the foundation for his further growth and development. Your work continues as you stay aware of your child's needs and goals and how they are being met within the context of the classroom.

Remaining Diligent

Hopefully your child is doing well in school, and everything is proceeding smoothly. But perhaps something causes his grades or behavior to slip. We urge you to contact the teacher immediately. If you haven't had an in-depth conversation about your child, this is the time. You know him best, and the school needs your insights. You already have the experience; the chart below can help organize your thoughts before the meeting. As you consider the following categories, feel free to use these questions to spark your thinking:

- Does he need to sit in a certain part of the classroom to stay focused, either visually or auditorily? Is he easily distracted?
- Is he sensitive to certain materials, fabrics, or touch?
- Are there any recurring emotional issues or patterns that get in the way of class work?
- How about the attention factor? Does he have a hard time staying in his seat?
- What about the way he processes information: Does he need the overall concept first, or is it easier for him to connect the dots to see where he's going?

Activity 10.3. ASSESSING YOUR CHILD'S NEEDS				
Vision	Hearing	Tactile	Other Sensory Issues	Emotional
Attention	Movement	Big-Picture Thinker	Sequential Thinker	Other

Many of these details, if previously unknown to the teacher, can inform your conversation to help you arrive at a workable plan of action. The teacher will surely have his or her own insights to add, and you may also need to involve others who know your child. As appropriate, include your child in these conversations. Parents sometimes (and quite reflexively) wish to "protect" their son or daughter from such discussions, but it can actually be reassuring for the child to "demystify" a situation and learn to manage it (Levine, 2002). In any case, once you have come up with a feasible solution, look for changes in the first week or two after implementation.

Acting as a Change Agent

Respectful relationships open the door to listening, and listening allows new ideas to flourish. But you must be open to hearing them. And being able to hear what is *not* being said will be another invaluable asset, both in relating to your child and continuing to dialogue with school personnel.

Do you have a great idea that you are excited to share with this community or a concern that needs attention? Start by doing your homework on the subject. Has something like this been attempted in the past? If so, how did it go? How would your plan be different? Or is this a totally new concept? If so, what would be the benefit to the school? A reasonable, researched presentation spiced up with your passion for the project goes a long way toward getting your idea accepted. Staying open to receiving feedback and being willing to act upon it will make your case even stronger, especially if you then invite others to participate with you. In a collaborative community, there's a good chance that you will find a receptive audience for such a proposal.

Being Aware

When things are going well, it's easy to think they'll always stay that way. Suppose you find yourself in sync with the teacher now, and your child's grades and behavior have stabilized. You relax a bit and let days and weeks pass by, lulled into a false sense of comfort that he is keeping up, and everything is just fine. And then here comes a surprise: the "D" on a quiz. You need to be on top of it straightaway. And you may need to use your parental radar to detect just what is wrong. It could be a problem with vision, friends, or boredom. It may entail finding a new approach to study skills. Whatever the cause, attention and awareness will help you find solutions.

Changes in the school environment could also be having an effect. Budget crunches suddenly restrict services, a staff member leaves, and rumors abound. Staying in touch with your community can keep you aware of new developments. And, as unpleasant as this may be, you may choose to reevaluate the school's operation in the context of your family's needs. Serving as an agent for change means promoting it when it's your brain-child, but it also includes managing it when it's not of your making.

Being Heard

Because we don't live in a perfect world, it's conceivable that you might have some fundamental problems with attitudes or policies at your new school. Perhaps you've asked a question and not received a satisfactory response or made a suggestion to which the administration has been less than receptive. How will you handle that?

Effective two-way communication is actually mandated by the No Child Left Behind Act (Sec. 9101 [32], Center for CSRI, 2006, 1). But if this is not happening, it may be time to organize a larger group to address the issue. There is strength in numbers: Forming an alliance with like-minded individuals who are willing to present their concerns along with yours, either in writing or in person, can be an extremely effective, democratic tool for being heard.

In *A Primer on America's Schools* (Moe, 2001), Paul Hill writes about the ideas of Hirschman, who identifies three ways that customers (including school parents) can influence the quality of goods and services from businesses and government agencies (including schools):

- *Exit*: find another provider when you're dissatisfied.
- *Voice*: demand improvements.
- *Loyalty*: stay with a provider and work toward improvements together.

Although we don't advocate the business model as a way of changing education, we do like the clarity with which Hirschman structures his theory. He argues that these three modes of influence fit together very nicely, particularly because the effectiveness of voice and loyalty are enhanced by the ever-present possibility of exit. Hill informs us that Hirschman makes a special case for schools: When parents choose voice and loyalty over exit, those demands for improvements can benefit all students. We would modify Hirschman's use of the word "demand," calling instead for the need to *identify* areas requiring improvement as long-term relationships flower when requests, as opposed to "demands," are made.

This approach helps to clarify strategic steps to take when there is a problem that isn't finding a quick and easy resolution: Identify areas that need improvement, speak up, and, depending on the response, become a part of the resolution or find another option. After a series of unsuccessful attempts to resolve issues, if the time comes when you're convinced that this school is not the right fit for your child, there's nothing wrong with considering your alternatives. As Lawrence Kohn (1999, personal communication), program specialist at Quest High School in Houston, Texas, says, "It's our duty as educators to make sure that kids get educated. If this is not the proper place, there's no shame in saying that." No one school or way of schooling is right for every single child. As unfortunate as that situation may be, we are confident that you already have the skills to begin another school search.

Summary

As a loving parent, you make the best possible decisions you can when your children are small; you do your utmost to guide them as they mature. Your influence is particularly felt in the choice of a schooling environment and continues after they are enrolled. By collaborating at home or school, you'll be contributing your time and energy to make this experience a great success for all concerned. When your child sees your commitment, he will get the message that school is important. When he sees you resolving differences in a reasonable manner, he will learn that it's okay to voice his feelings. When he sees you engaged in discovery, he will understand that learning never stops. What more could you want for him?

AS AN EDUCATOR

If you volunteer at your child's school, you no doubt have a sense of the goodwill generated by such an effort. Substantial research further confirms the benefits of parental involvement, which include improved student attendance, more positive attitudes and behavior, and higher academic achievement (National PTA, 1997). It has a reciprocal effect on teachers by helping them feel that their work is appreciated. When teachers are valued, trust begins to grow. In this section, we will examine the role of educators as we move toward a new institution in which everyone has a significant responsibility for student learning.

Recognizing the Needs of Your Students

Teachers know that students in a classroom differ physically, emotionally, socially, and cognitively (Gould, 2004). Teachers are trained to differentiate instruction to meet a variety of academic needs within the context of one lesson. They are familiar with using multisensory techniques to engage visual, auditory, and kinesthetic learners. All of that is of considerable value. But the quickest way to gain the trust of parents may simply be to let them know that you "get" their child. When you speak to a child's talents or share observations as to his learning preferences and challenges, parents feel supported by knowing that their child's uniqueness is respected.

Activity 10.4.
TEACHER'S REFLECTION

1. What tools do you use in recognizing your students' needs?
2. Where could you use more support?

And often it's the smallest touches of human kindness that make the most lasting impressions. Associate Principal Olson (1999) speaks again: "It's the little things you do every day that make a difference. It's one brick in the wall, one step at a time. It's taking time. If someone needs to see me, do I have time to see that person? No. Can I take ten minutes? Of course I can. It's about always staying focused on what I can do at this moment. Maybe taking fifteen minutes to listen to a kid who wants to visit with me is the most important thing I can do that day."

Another tangible way to recognize and evaluate your students' needs is by goal setting with them. A goal, when achieved, organically leads to the next one. So, you may choose to have the children create individual goals for a set period of time, then reevaluate and reframe them and continue to the next. This approach could be modified to work on a daily basis with an entire class or a weekly or monthly basis with individuals. Maybe it's a contract between home, school, and child, as Bonnie McReynolds explains in her Partners in Education, or PIE, program in Phoenix, Arizona: The group agrees on a simple, general goal (helping a child to learn), each partner has certain responsibilities, and everyone signs off on the plan. Then, an individualized page can be created for the child's specific intentions (Hopkings, 2004). Empathy, insight, and specific teaching techniques, along with goal setting, can all enhance the teacher's ability to connect with the students and recognize their needs.

Recognizing the Attributes of Your Students' Parents

Educators have to be exquisitely sensitive to the subtle messages being sent by children, but they need to respond to their families as well. Frequently, they can guide or encourage parent involvement. On the one hand, you will have family members with time (or money) to spend at school and who want to give of themselves. This kind of parent can offer tremendous support when utilized effectively. There are also those parents who want to help so much or so aggressively (especially with a first-year teacher) that remaining diplomatic and establishing boundaries can be a real challenge. At the other end of the spectrum are parents who don't respond to messages, don't show up at conferences, and don't seem to care.

Schools often feel like they can't reach those parents, when, in reality, the parents may not know how to reach out themselves. As the Center for Comprehensive School Reform and Improvement's August 2005 newsletter points out, they might not feel welcome, they might not speak English, or they might work long hours and do not have the freedom to volunteer. Or perhaps their own negative memories of school lead them to feel that involvement will not be a positive experience (Center for CSRI, 2005). The parent may not even consciously be aware of this, and although teachers can't change the past for the adult, their calm persistence could show another perspective on school. Other parents may just feel great discomfort in knowing *how* to be involved. Therein lies a prime opportunity for educators to reach out to students' families.

Recruiting Meaningful Parent Participation

In a survey called "Playing Their Parts," Public Agenda (1999) found that both parents and teachers agreed that a parent's most important job is to raise a well-behaved child who comes to school ready to learn. They also discovered a powerful ambivalence on the part of parents who vacillate between wanting to enhance their children's self-esteem while at the same time pushing their independence. This presents a unique challenge for educators, who must deal with these mixed messages showing up in children's motivation levels. On the other hand, it allows potential for building trust with parents who appreciate reflection and discussion.

Working with Their Child

When parents don't really know how to help their kids, we appreciate the way that Columbia, South Carolina, elementary teacher Sharon Williams schedules time after school to explain subject matter being covered in class (1999, personal communication). Her colleague, Melissa Klosterman, prepares parents to ask children about their day by creating a class calendar of lessons. Both Williams and Klosterman also do home visits, which underscores a commitment to showing parents how important they are to their child's success.

Parents feel empowered to help with schoolwork when they have a good grasp of what's going on in the classroom. Homework hotlines, assignments updated on websites, and teacher contact can all help provide that information. Parenting classes, workshops, and a program like that discussed earlier by Grabarek with trigger questions and big ideas can be very useful in bringing parents up to speed with the curriculum. At the National Network of Partnership Schools at Johns Hopkins University, a program called Teachers Involve Parents in Schoolwork, or TIPS (see compendium), allows students to connect with their families and their school through engaging, interactive homework that relates to current units of study. By involving family members in surveys and interviews, students have a tool for sharing concepts and skills with their parents, who then provide feedback to the teacher. This takes the responsibility of explaining homework off of the parents' shoulders and gives them exciting catalysts for conversation!

You, no doubt, have your own suggestions for ways to bring home and school more closely into alignment. Many parents would be very receptive to your ideas if they knew they were available. We encourage the communication that would make this sharing possible. As we've indicated, sometimes parents just don't know how to ask. How might you broach such a subject?

Activity 10.5.
TEACHER-PARENT COMMUNICATION QUERY

How could you diplomatically let parents know that your help is available to them?

Working with You and the School

For many parents, teachers are the link that connects their child with school. Open communication is paramount here, and, again, we emphasize the need for contact to flow in both directions. Especially at the beginning of a new year, parents want to know how they can be involved at school as well as support their child at home. They want to be able to contact the teacher(s). They are interested in what their children will be learning. They appreciate guidance, but they also need an opportunity to give feedback. Some parents want to share expertise if it's a good fit for the classroom. Others may want to help in school policy and decision making. You won't know about any of this unless you initiate conversations with your parents.

Parent-teacher dialogue should ideally begin early in the school year, before any concerns arise. According to Robinson and Fine (1994), "The value of an ongoing connection is that it affords opportunities for parents and teachers to form collaborative relationships. This in turn means that a cushion of goodwill has been established that allows parents and teachers to meet as needed to problem-solve and work through their concerns without the situation escalating to a conflict" (12). Robinson and Fine go on to detail the myriad of relationships that then stand to benefit: student learning, parental appreciation of teacher skills, and parental feelings of effectiveness through their actions, which in turn raises their involvement, which heightens the teacher's feelings of efficacy. What a self-fulfilling prophecy, and potentially so easy to achieve.

Summary

Educators stand to gain so much from positive communication with parents, students, and the community. Parents who seem unreachable may simply need to be invited to participate. Teachers who make the extra effort with families open up possibilities for children to thrive, whether it's by explaining curriculum, encouraging parent involvement, or just showing kind consideration. But all members of the school community have a responsibility to seek such an opening for dialogue and growth.

Collaboration opens doors. It gets people to the table so that ideas can be generated. We need leadership and language that unite toward a common purpose, as well as the climate of respect and trust that invites solutions. In the words of former Los Angeles principal Sylvia Rogers (2001, personal communication), "If you have happy kids, you can really do something in a school. The way to have happy kids is to have parents who want to be there. If kids see their parents involved in school, they want to be involved in school." And then they can own their education.

AS A LEGISLATOR

Education reform has become a focal point for policy makers since *A Nation at Risk* made its grim warnings in 1983. Since that time, the United States has been submerged by wave after wave of efforts to change the system. As we know, the American public is obsessed with such efforts as well. "How can America get off the treadmill of perpetual reform and succeed in improving its schools? There is no easy answer. But one requirement is surely fundamental: policymakers must know what to do. They must have good ideas that are well supported by theory and evidence, and they must know how to put these ideas into action" (Moe, 2001, xvii).

Our understanding of collaboration resonates anew when we investigate the role of the lawmaker in education. We know that a legislator represents constituents and is involved in the enactment of laws, but for those of us who need a quick refresher course on our American history, let's recall what we know about the legislative branch of government.

Each state (except Nebraska—more on this in a moment) is divided into districts, which elect representatives to their state assemblies. Each state also elects senators. Both branches of the legislature meet in regular session to create state budgets and laws (with the exception of Nebraska, which under the "unicameral," or single-house, system, fulfills its legislative responsibilities solely by virtue of a state senate [Nebraska State Legislature, 2007, www.unicam.state.ne.us/web/public/unicameralism]).

A piece of legislation begins with an idea or an issue that is pertinent to one or more of the communities represented by the lawmaker. Senators and assembly members both introduce bills, which are reviewed by committees through discussion and debate. Part of this review process can include meetings at which members of the public ask questions and share their views. Many of the bills never make it past committee review, and those that do succeed by virtue of a vote. The bill is then brought to the house or senate floor to be voted on again. If it passes in the house, for example, it must also pass the senate. If it passes both, then it goes to the governor for approval or veto. This same process is echoed nationally with senators and congressmen who represent their constituents by introducing bills, debating them, working to get the support of other legislators, voting, and sometimes passing bills, which then go on to the president for signature or veto.

As a lawmaker, we appreciate that you carry a considerable burden to ensure that your region's children have safe schools with qualified teachers and sufficient resources. No doubt you spend a great deal of time talking with and listening to people from your state in order to understand their concerns and represent them effectively. Let's take a look at your process of collaboration and see how it can impact education policy.

Finding the Right Information

As former House speaker Tip O'Neill famously stated, "All politics is local" (Association for Supervision and Curriculum Development, 2006, 5). Your citizens certainly want to inform you about their priorities, and you already use a variety of techniques to entertain their viewpoints, including meetings, study circles, and community forums. We imagine that the experiences you hear recounted can be quite motivating. It's also important to balance that input with quality education research. You'll want to know whose report you are reading and understand the bias behind it. It's even more critical to understand *what* you are reading: Raw facts and figures can be used to support any position. Our own research has uncovered a useful online resource for analyzing this kind of data, called "A Policy Maker's Primer on Education Research" (see compendium). By posing questions and disaggregating facts, this tool helps to determine the reliability of the material and to see how it can be used to inform policy.

Once you have your data, it is time to seek or review that input from your constituents. The research fine-tunes the issue; the anecdotal evidence gives it a human face and can make it more compelling for you to pursue. As you identify issues that have weight and meaning for you, we hope you will also consider new ways of evaluating public education and disseminating your findings to the public. As Lagemann

(2007) discusses, the narrow focus on test scores, the product, causes society to over-look the bigger concern, the process, which is how children learn.

Avoiding the Assumption of Expertise

Just because you are in a leadership role doesn't mean you have stopped learning. You make education a high priority when you commit with words and then back them up with actions. Perhaps it is time to go beyond the surveys and the forums for some hands-on experience in the classroom. We urge you to make some time in your busy schedule to visit schools all over your constituency. We are not suggesting an hour-long meet and greet but a full day at each site. Schedule discussions with the superintendent, the principal, students, teachers, and parents. Ask them about their successes, their concerns, and their ideas for improvement (Barkley, 2005). Educators frequently feel that their opinions are disregarded, despite the fact that they work with children all day long. What would you ask them? Where would you start? Here's a place to record your notes.

We don't pretend that this kind of an approach will be easy and quick, but it will certainly be enriching, and maybe even illuminating. Can you imagine living your life, over a period of weeks, thinking like an educator? By looking at the individual schools, you will begin to see inside the system and take away knowledge to serve you during the reinvention process.

We know that you have a full plate and that education is just one item on it. But public education is so essential to our democracy that it demands your focused attention. If you took one week of your life and conducted research in five different cities across the state, conversations across your territory would be mightily informed. Think of the possibilities if you took two weeks and visited ten schools. You would come away with an array of data and personal impressions, as well as a network of relationships with stakeholders statewide. You would have an intimate understanding of what children and educators really need.

Education is hugely influenced by politics, and the individual states still bear the major fiscal and curricular responsibilities for the ways in which it is carried out. Your thoughtful and knowledgeable leadership can keep it in the forefront of public awareness. So many people, in all walks of life, consider themselves to be experts on school because they attended one. Please don't make that same mistake: Do your homework, get comfortable with the jargon, make sense of your research, and put a human face to it. Your communities are relying on your vision and your partnership-oriented solutions. How can you completely comprehend the facts (like test scores) without a living, breathing larger context?

Activity 10.6.
LEGISLATOR STARTER QUESTIONS

1. What would you ask teachers about their work?
2. What would you like to know from the principal?
3. Where would you start your conversation with the superintendent?
4. What would you want to know from parents?
5. What would you ask the children about school?

AS AN AMERICAN CITIZEN

As we've seen throughout this chapter, learning is not just for children. It's also for the legislator newly immersed in day-to-day school life, the teacher finding creative ways to support a student in need, a parent seizing the moment to compassionately honor his or her child's feelings, and the lightbulb going on in that child's mind. Learning is not just about school, but our nation was created with principles that assure the perpetuation of certain educational values. Our founding fathers envisioned that this country would produce citizens prepared to govern themselves and to make informed decisions; public education and a free press were designed to facilitate those experiences. Taxes paid by everyone, not just parents, would go to the schools to turn out productive citizens whose contributions would benefit us all (Graham, 2004). But decades of mixed results have left us with lingering doubts about our ability as a nation to fulfill this obligation. Report after report ranks our American students as struggling to compete with the best and the brightest from other countries: Our ingenuity factor has been eclipsed.

With this sort of recent past, it's no wonder that many people resist the notion of becoming invested in public education. It looks bad out there. And then there are the challenges that come from those parents who seek alternatives to public education and from the people without school-aged children. According to veteran Houston, Texas, educator Lynn Parsons,

> There seems to be this philosophy that if I don't have children that are school-aged, then I have no responsibility for public education, and specifically for taxes. Why should I pay taxes when my kids aren't going to school? As if taxes were a tuition. . . . The homeschool parents say it: if my kids don't go to your school, why should I pay taxes? The retired people say it: my kids are already grown, why should I pay taxes? And there's this lack of understanding that public education benefits society as a whole, not just my kids. . . . I think that schools and districts everywhere struggle with this: How do we get our entire community to see the value of public education?

It's easier to heap scorn on a seemingly rugged situation than to strike out on your own and be in the minority with the vision to see the potential hidden underneath. But our American educational system deserves just this sort of commitment. The public depends on public education. It is a national priority, and schools are ranked as the most important public community institution (Voke, 2002). While the changeover to the new system incubates, there is plenty that can be done right now to support education by the American citizen who enjoys the many freedoms of democracy.

Considering Our Cultural Responsibility

One of easiest and most profound ways to participate in democracy is by exercising your right to vote. Begin by educating yourself on the issues and the candidates in your own community. The school board offers a concise framework for local concerns. Attend one of their meetings. If there's an agenda item that particularly speaks to you, address your concerns at the microphone. This is another aspect of the democratic process that many of us take for granted. But you have a format for expressing your opinions. "The reality is that good ideas can generate political power. And when they do, policymakers will listen" (Moe, 2001, xx). They will listen more closely if you take action and support your beliefs with a track record of activism. If you can't get to a meeting, then do your own research and vote for the board member who most closely shares your values. And since these elections are notorious for eliciting low turnouts, this would be an excellent way to contribute to society in general and education in particular.

But what if you don't know how you feel on the issues? What if you don't have a point of view to express or don't even know where to begin constructing one?

Sharing a Vision

Find out what you believe. As we have stated repeatedly in this work, our country suffers from a perilous lack of vision, dominated by an "I-me-mine" individuality that keeps us isolated in our own solitary concerns. This disregard for the greater good is severely threatening our national identity. If you are an American citizen without children in the public schools system, there are still compelling reasons to join this community of learners and doers, even if it's just to find out what you believe. Reading is an excellent way to uncover your opinions. Look at our references and compendium for a host of titles and websites to jump-start your thinking. We compiled this information for you and hope you will avail yourselves of it.

Do your homework. If we adopt the 622 Curriculum, then states will be collaborating with their regional partners, as well as with the federal government. The delegates to the Education Congress of the States (ECS) will need to seek opinions from stakeholders throughout the community. With the research you have done on the issues, you could make yourself available to be interviewed for the American culture definition project. Being immersed in regional issues and concerns could even prepare you for a career in local politics, but first grab an Education 101 textbook and start studying for your credentialed role as a local policy maker!

Engage with your neighborhood school. Once you have developed your specific interests, you can engage with your neighborhood school in a number of ways. You might want to sponsor informative meetings on campus or participate in building and grounds beautification projects. You could attend PTA, PTO, PTSA, or site council gatherings to become familiar with current concerns and eventually run for a seat on one of those boards to have a say in school governance. You could support the children or teenagers by mentoring them and sharing your talents.

Put your inventive mind to use. If you are in the information technology field, you might consider developing computer programming to support and interconnect the new educational market in which collaboration will take place within and between schools, districts, states, and the ECS. The electronic wall, holographic displays, and other tools for teachers will need to be designed. As a scientist or engineer, you might tackle one of the systems needed to generate wind, solar, or "foot" power. Maybe you're the architect or interior designer to work up our modular schools.

Reach out. As a businessperson, you could offer internships or partnerships for service learning. Under such a scenario, you could collaborate with a school (or schools) to offer a program in which students apply their academic abilities in a business setting, thereby providing valuable services and attending to real-world needs within the community. Service learning is more than a charitable effort; it's a method of teaching whose life-enriching, larger themes include civic responsibility and the opportunity to reflect on the nature of learning through giving (Huseman, 1999, personal communication; McPherson, 2005).

Speak up. An impassioned citizen who has done his homework could use his voice to compose letters to the editor or to policy makers. And do not underestimate the value of your written communications! Putting your ideas in writing, thereby documenting them, supports concerns in a way that verbal communication just cannot match. This is a basic tool of both democracy and bureaucracy, so use it.

Talk to others. Study circles, which foster community change through focused and fair-minded regular discussion, can be an exceptional facility for creating reasoned change. The citizens' forum is a tool that could bring the dialogue to a wider audience. Aligning yourself with others who share the same concerns increases the amplitude of your message, particularly when the group represents a cross section of local perspectives. Policy makers listen with greater interest to an issue if it affects more than one individual viewpoint. All of these techniques can help focus the citizenry on matters of public urgency and keep education issues in the forefront of legislators' awareness.

Schools will need more than just themselves to effect this transformation from the old system to the new. We need a system in which shared responsibility invests the larger community with a sense of purpose that allows it to rise above the problems. We cannot focus on what we want while remaining bogged down in thoughts of what we don't want. A shared vision will sustain us through the years leading up to the new institution. It will be impossible to succeed without one.

Understanding Time

We are actually lucky to have this transitional period before the new institution is fully operational. It will take time to ask the questions and hold the discussions that will ultimately solidify our cultural identity as Americans. It will take time to engage the public as our vested partners through the various idea-sharing forums. It will take time to build relationships with legislators and other policy makers as we work together to propose education laws with vision and depth. Effective collaboration relies upon trust, and this is the period in which to nurture it; indeed, it is the only foundation on which we can structure all other endeavors. These intervening years are ripe for goal setting and thoughtful action.

And more than schools will benefit from this concentrated effort. When the public responds to legislators' call for opinions, it feels empowered, and policy makers gain much-needed input. When the school community feels supported by a broad spectrum of family involvement, then teachers, administrators, and students are encouraged to strive for even greater success (Voke, 2002). This brings us back to what must be the paramount focus of our efforts in education: the children. We must do our parts to nurture their growth, but ultimately, they have to pick up the reins themselves.

We return to the words of Epstein (1997): "The inarguable fact is that students are the main actors in their education, development and success in school. School, family and community partnerships cannot simply produce successful students. Rather, partnership activities may be designed to engage, guide, energize and motivate students to produce their own successes. The assumption is that if children feel cared for and encouraged to work hard in the role of student, they are more likely to do their best to learn to read, write, calculate, and learn other skills and talents and to remain in school" (4).

As an American citizen motivated to play an essential part in education, your role in informing the new system will have an impact that's even bigger than your efforts at the local school today. As valuable as those contributions are, you have the chance to help millions of children embrace their cultural inheritance tomorrow.

FINAL THOUGHTS

Our vision for a new educational institution is out there gleaming on the horizon. But maybe you have a better idea! *A School by Every Other Name* is meant to encourage just that sort of reflection. Instead of despairing over what's wrong with the system, we all have the same window of opportunity to make the dream a plan and the plan a reality. It's not about what *he* should do and what *she* should do; it's about what *we* can do together.

The school is not the enemy; the enemy is thinking your opinion doesn't matter or assuming someone else can do it better. As Kleinz (2000) so eloquently points out, "Educators have long understood the value of involving parents and the community in the schools. But if we are to realize the improvements we desire in education, we need to do more than ask them to support school-related projects—we need to engage the public in thinking through the challenges schools face and helping them to make decisions on how to solve them" (1).

We have a huge opportunity here for that public engagement, especially if the groups addressed in this chapter listen to, and learn from, one another. In an ideal world, parents will find a way to give each of their children blocks of undivided attention. Educators will discover new approaches to connect with families and deepen the two-way communication exchange. Children will become independent learners because discovery is fun when they know their strengths and have the tools to move beyond their weaknesses. Legislators will reach out to their broad-based constituencies in small groups to encourage open sharing. And citizens will feel that they have been heard.

The answer to our national educational obsession will not be found in higher test scores. It won't be found in the business model. No single effort is going to take us where we need to be. In your city, in your county, in your state, and in our nation, we no longer need a roster of one-off interventions, however well intentioned. We need a spirit of possibility that gives our stakeholders a vested interest in the success of *all* children. More than just sound practice, collaboration becomes a vehicle for change.

Epilogue

As the final entry in *A School by Every Other Name*, we refer to this section as the "epilogue." However, we hope you can appreciate that, as is the case with graduation ceremonies, completing this book and considering the issues, topics, and possibilities discussed constitutes a beginning rather than an end. And so, perhaps we should think of this as a "commencement." We can summarize what the book has been about, but what happens next is up to you.

Two issues contribute to both the academic and social confusion in our schools: the myth of educational reform and our cultural identity crisis. Reform is a myth because people tend to believe that substantive changes actually occur. But how much really changes? School today is substantively what it was literally centuries ago. The basic approach of having one teacher with two dozen or so students in a large room, the grade-level emphasis, time-dependent schedules for learning material, and even the administrative structure of schools have remained intact despite the ongoing calls for reform in education. Many "sensitive" issues facing curriculum designers today are the same issues that have bottlenecked curricular progress for generations. In view of all of this, we must ask why reform efforts fail.

They fail because the fundamental problem with education is that education is *fundamentally an institution* and is therefore resistant to change. Inherent in the structure of any institution is an inclination toward self-preservation. Substantive change threatens to redefine the institution, in which case the old institution would cease to exist. Reforms, however, can come and go, convincing their proponents that change has occurred though the greater institution remains intact. It is because of this survival mechanism that the *institution* of education cannot be reformed; it must be rebuilt. It must be *revolutionized*. So, when you hear someone say (perhaps in response to the ideas presented in this book), "We've got to work within the system to make changes in education," you will know that what you are listening to is the institution speaking out loud.

Yet, even in a revolution, we can be advocates for the more than four million teachers and administrators in the United States because *the school is not the enemy*. It is our society that is not clear about its own desires, which brings us to the imperative for change: a fading cultural identity.

Indeed, what does it mean to be American? We hope that you have seriously asked yourself that question by now and perhaps asked others as well. Though the answers or lack of answers may have surprised you, the important point to consider is whether the inability to clearly describe who we are as a culture is a good thing. We would argue that it is not. We will not go into a lengthy discussion of what that ambiguity means on the world stage, but it definitely confounds the efforts of any school system when trying to design a curriculum that serves our society. The result is that the students subjected to that curriculum become even further alienated from their cultural heritage. Eventually, we find ourselves trying to educate Culture X, generations of citizens who have abdicated their responsibility to take part in defining their own cultural identity.

The program of education discussed in this book does not try to prescribe what our culture should be or the specific content that students should be taught. It would be presumptuous for a couple of authors to do so. However, what has been presented recognizes that, as a culture, we have responsibilities to each other, and there are consequences for the decisions we make.

What issues should we make decisions about? There are many. In the chapters of this book, we have asked that you consider what it means to be American and why institutions resist change. We have discussed the groundwork plans for revolutionizing the institution but have also offered mechanisms for more critically considering reform efforts and for working with the system to the advantage of a child that you have, or will have, in the system as it is. So, as you close this book, you have several directions that can be taken, whether or not you accept the primary premise of systemically reconceptualizing the institution of education.

The philosopher Immanuel Kant referred to education as the greatest concern to which we can devote our energies. Though we adamantly argue about including less political and business involvement in the design and administration of schools, we do call for greater participation from all constituencies as our nation builds a school system that develops the well-educated child, a child who can grow into adulthood with the intellectual skills and breadth of knowledge to follow any career path he or she might choose. *A School by Every Other Name* has been about providing students with the skills, knowledge, and dispositions that make "you can be anything you want to be" a realistic statement rather than a mere platitude. The question that remains is whether we, as a nation, have the vision and the commitment to make it happen.

Compendium

INFORMATION ABOUT EDUCATION

Academic Benchmarks

123 South 2nd Street
Loveland, OH 45140
Phone: (513) 898-0534
Fax: (513) 697-6118
Website: www.statestandards.com

Academic Benchmarks focuses on providing state standards and the tools to align them with curriculum, assessments, and reporting. A no-nonsense website geared toward educators and the businesses that work in conjunction with them, this database of standards by state is nonetheless quite easy to browse. However, there is a limit to the number of free searches you may do, at which point you are asked to submit an e-mail to explain your needs.

Center on Education Policy

1001 Connecticut Avenue NW
Suite 522
Washington, D.C. 20036
Phone: (202) 822-8065
Fax: (202) 822-6008
Website: www.cep-dc.org

The Center on Education Policy is a nonpartisan site devoted to public education and effective public schools. It is devoted almost entirely to articles on an extensive array of topics to help citizens make sense of the conflicting viewpoints on the subject. The site is straightforward and businesslike.

Education Week

Editorial Projects in Education, Inc. (EPE)
6935 Arlington Road
Suite 100
Bethesda, MD 20814-5233
Phone: (301) 280-3100
Website: www.edweek.org

EPE publishes *Education Week*, "American education's newspaper of record." If you want to find out what happened this week on a national, state, or local level, from prekindergarten through the twelfth grade, this is the place to look. The nonprofit parent company's mission is to help raise the level of awareness about education issues among professionals and the public. Although their archived articles only cover a two-year period, the sheer mass of information makes this website the go-to place for education news.

Educational Resources Information Center (ERIC)

ERIC Project
c/o Computer Sciences Corporation
655 15th Street NW
Suite 500
Washington, D.C. 20005
Phone: (800) LET-ERIC (538-3742)
Website: www.eric.ed.gov

If you need education literature, you need to know about ERIC. This site (a division of the Department of Education and the Institute of Education Sciences) offers access to over one million journal articles and other materials. It is easy to navigate and search; check out the thesaurus feature to help zero in on your topic. Unfortunately, not all of the articles are available from ERIC in their full-text version—sometimes you have to order them from another publisher—but the scope of what ERIC makes available to the public is extremely impressive.

The National Center for Education Statistics

1990 K Street NW
Washington, D.C. 20006
Phone: (202) 502-7300
Website: www.nces.ed.gov

The National Center for Education Statistics, a division of the U.S. Department of Education and the Institute of Education Sciences, is the primary federal agency for collecting and analyzing educational data. There is a wealth of facts and figures to be found on this site, but it can be rather overwhelming if you are not comfortable with graphs, charts, and tables. If you are a statistician, this is the site for you.

A Policy Maker's Primer on Education Research: How to Understand, Evaluate and Use It

Websites: www.ecs.org/html/educationIssues/Research/primer/index.asp or http://www.mcrel.org/primer

This online tool is designed to assist lawmakers in crafting policy through research analysis; it also stands alone as a reference for anyone who wants to better understand how education research is conducted. The site is very user-friendly and seeks to help answer three main questions: What does the research say, is it trustworthy, and how can it guide policy? The material is also available to download as a PDF file.

The primer is a joint effort of Mid-continent Research for Education and Learning (McREL) and the Education Commission of the States (ECS). McREL is a private, non-profit organization dedicated to improving education for all students through applied research, product development, and service. The ECS is a nonprofit, nonpartisan organization focused on improving public education by enabling the exchange of ideas and information among state lawmakers and education leaders.

ECS
700 Broadway, #1200
Denver, CO 80203-3460
Phone: (303) 299-3600
Fax: (303) 296-8332
Website: www.ecs.org

McREL
2550 South Parker Road
Suite 500
Aurora, CO 80014
Phone: (303) 337-0990
Fax: (303) 337-3005
Website: www.mcrel.org

U.S. Department of Education (ED)

400 Maryland Avenue SW
Washington, D.C. 20202
Phone: (800) USA-LEARN (872-5327)
Website: www.ed.gov

ED was designed to promote educational excellence and to provide equal access to education throughout the nation. It is not surprising that this site offers considerable policy information. Clicking the "Parents" tab directs you to checklists and articles (frequently in both English and Spanish) that can help you (among other things) evaluate schools, offer homework tips, and find a tutor, frequently in reference to No Child Left Behind.

STATE DEPARTMENTS OF EDUCATION

Alabama

Alabama Department of Education
Gordon Persons Office Building
50 North Ripley Street
P.O. Box 302101
Montgomery, AL 36104-3833
Phone: (334) 242-9700
Fax: (334) 242-9708
Website: www.alsde.edu/html/home.asp

Alaska

Alaska Department of Education and Early Development
Suite 200
801 West 10th Street
Juneau, AK 99801-1894
Phone: (907) 465-2800
Fax: (907) 465-4156
Website: www.eed.state.ak.us

Arizona

Arizona Department of Education
1535 West Jefferson
Phoenix, AZ 85007
Phone: (602) 542-4361
Toll-free: (800) 352-4558
Fax: (602) 542-5440
Website: www.ade.state.az.us

Arkansas

Arkansas Department of Education
General Education Division Room 304A
Four State Capitol Mall
Little Rock, AR 72201-1071
Phone: (501) 682-4204
Fax: (501) 682-1079
Website: http://arkedu.state.ar.us

California

California Department of Education
P.O. Box 944272
1430 N Street
Sacramento, CA 95814
Phone: (916) 319-0791
Fax: (916) 319-0100
Website: www.cde.ca.gov

Colorado

Colorado Department of Education
201 East Colfax Avenue
Denver, CO 80203-1704
Phone: (303) 866-6600
Fax: (303) 830-0793
Website: www.cde.state.co.us

Connecticut

Connecticut Department of Education
State Office Building
165 Capitol Avenue
Hartford, CT 06106-1630
Phone: (860) 713-6548
Toll-free: (800) 465-4014
Fax: (860) 713-7017
Website: www.state.ct.us/sde

Delaware

Delaware Department of Education
John G. Townsend Building
P.O. Box 1402
Federal and Lockerman Streets
Dover, DE 19903-1402
Phone: (302) 739-4601
Fax: (302) 739-4654
Website: www.doe.state.de.us

District of Columbia

District of Columbia Public Schools
Union Square
825 North Capitol Street NE
Washington, D.C. 20002
Phone: (202) 724-4222
Fax: (202) 442-5026
Website: www.k12.dc.us/dcps/home.html.

Florida

Florida Department of Education
Turlington Building
Suite 1514
325 West Gaines Street
Tallahassee, FL 32399-0400
Phone: (850) 245-0505
Fax: (850) 245-9667
Website: www.fldoe.org

Georgia

Georgia Department of Education
2054 Twin Towers East
205 Jesse Hill Jr. Drive SE
Atlanta, GA 30334-5001

Phone: (404) 656-2800
Toll-free: (800) 311-3627
Fax: (404) 651-6867
Website: www.doe.k12.ga.us/index.asp

Hawaii

Hawaii Department of Education, Room 309
1390 Miller Street
Honolulu, HI 96813
Phone: (808) 586-3310
Fax: (808) 586-3320
Website: www.k12.hi.us

Idaho

Idaho Department of Education
Len B. Jordan Office Building
650 West State Street
P.O. Box 83720
Boise, ID 83720-0027
Phone: (208) 332-6800
Toll-free: (800) 432-4601
Fax: (208) 334-2228
Website: www.sde.state.id.us/Dept

Illinois

Illinois State Board of Education
100 North First Street
Springfield, IL 62777
Phone: (217) 782-4321
Toll-free: (866) 262-6663
Fax: (217) 524-4928
Website: www.isbe.net

Indiana

Indiana Department of Education
State House, Room 229
Indianapolis, IN 46204-2795
Phone: (317) 232-6610
Fax: (317) 233-6326
Website: www.doe.state.in.us

Iowa

Iowa Department of Education
Grimes State Office Building
East 14th and Grand Streets
Des Moines, IA 50319-0146

Phone: (515) 281-3436
Fax: (515) 281-4122
Website: www.state.ia.us/educate

Kansas

Kansas Department of Education
120 South East 10th Avenue
Topeka, KS 66612-1182
Phone: (785) 296-3201
Fax: (785) 296-7933
Website: www.ksde.org

Kentucky

Kentucky Department of Education
19th Floor
500 Mero Street
Frankfort, KY 40601
Phone: (502) 564-3421
Toll-free: (800) 533-5372
Fax: (502) 564-6470
Website: www.kentuckyschools.org

Louisiana

Louisiana Department of Education
1201 North Third
P.O. Box 94064
Baton Rouge, LA 70804-9064
Phone: (225) 342-4411
Toll-free: (877) 453-2721
Fax: (225) 342-7316
Website: www.louisianaschools.net/lde/index.html

Maine

Maine Department of Education
23 State House Station
Augusta, ME 04333-0023
Phone: (207) 624-6600
Fax: (207) 624-6601
Website: www.state.me.us/education/homepage.htm

Maryland

Maryland Department of Education
200 West Baltimore Street
Baltimore, MD 21201
Phone: (410) 767-0100
Fax: (410) 333-6033
Website: www.msde.state.md.us

Massachusetts

Massachusetts Department of Education
350 Main Street
Malden, MA 02148
Phone: (781) 338-3000
Fax: (781) 338-3395
Website: www.doe.mass.edu

Michigan

Michigan Department of Education
Hannah Building
Fourth Floor
608 West Allegan Street
Lansing, MI 48933
Phone: (517) 373-3324
Fax: (517) 335-4565
Website: www.michigan.gov/mde

Minnesota

Minnesota Department of Education
1500 Highway 36 West
Roseville, MN 55113-4266
Phone: (651) 582-8200
Fax: (651) 582-8727
Website: http://education.state.mn.us

Mississippi

Mississippi State Department of Education
Suite 365
359 North West Street
Jackson, MS 39201
Phone: (601) 359-3513
Fax: (601) 359-3242
Website: www.mde.k12.ms.us

Missouri

Missouri Department of Elementary and Secondary Education
P.O. Box 480
Jefferson City, MO 65102-0480
Phone: (573) 751-4212
Fax: (573) 751-8613
Website: http://dese.mo.gov

Montana

Montana Office of Public Instruction
P.O. Box 202501
Helena, MT 59620-2501
Phone: (406) 444-2082
Toll-free: (888) 231-9393
Website: www.opi.state.mt.us

Nebraska

Nebraska Department of Education
301 Centennial Mall South
P.O. Box 94987
Lincoln, NE 68509-4987
Phone: (402) 471-2295
Fax: (402) 471-0117
Website: www.nde.state.ne.us

Nevada

Nevada Department of Education
700 East Fifth Street
Carson City, NV 89701
Phone: (775) 687-9141
Fax: (775) 687-9111
Website: www.nde.state.nv.us

New Hampshire

New Hampshire Department of Education
101 Pleasant Street
State Office Park South
Concord, NH 03301
Phone: (603) 271-3495
Fax: (603) 271-1953
Website: www.ed.state.nh.us

New Jersey

New Jersey Department of Education
P.O. Box 500
100 Riverview Plaza
Trenton, NJ 08625-0500
Phone: (609) 292-4469
Fax: (609) 777-4099
Website: www.state.nj.us/education

New Mexico

New Mexico State Department of Education
Education Building
300 Don Gaspar
Santa Fe, NM 87501-2786
Phone: (505) 827-6516
Fax: (505) 827-6588
Website: www.sde.state.nm.us

New York

New York Education Department
Education Building, Room 111
89 Washington Avenue
Albany, NY 12234
Phone: (518) 474-5844
Fax: (518) 473-4909
Website: www.nysed.gov

North Carolina

North Carolina Department of Public Instruction
Education Building
6301 Mail Service Center
Raleigh, NC 27699-6301
Phone: (919) 807-3300
Fax: (919) 807-3445
Website: www.ncpublicschools.org

North Dakota

North Dakota Department of Public Instruction
11th Floor
Department 201
600 East Boulevard Avenue
Bismarck, ND 58505-0440
Phone: (701) 328-2260
Fax: (701) 328-2461
Website: www.dpi.state.nd.us

Ohio

Ohio Department of Education
25 South Front Street
Columbus, OH 43215-4183
Toll-free: (877) 644-6338
Fax: (614) 752-3956
Website: www.ode.state.oh.us

Oklahoma

Oklahoma State Department of Education
2500 North Lincoln Boulevard
Oklahoma City, OK 73105-4599
Phone: (405) 521-3301
Fax: (405) 521-6205
Website: http://sde.state.ok.us

Oregon

Oregon Department of Education
255 Capitol Street NE
Salem, OR 97310-0203
Phone: (503) 378-3600
Fax: (503) 378-5156
Website: www.ode.state.or.us

Pennsylvania

Pennsylvania Department of Education
333 Market Street
Harrisburg, PA 17126-0333
Phone: (717) 787-5820
Fax: (717) 787-7222
Website: www.pde.state.pa.us/pde_internet/site/default.asp

Rhode Island

Rhode Island Department of Elementary and Secondary Education
255 Westminster Street
Providence, RI 02903-3400
Phone: (401) 222-4600
Fax: (401) 222-2537
Website: www.ridoe.net

South Carolina

South Carolina Department of Education
1006 Rutledge Building
1429 Senate Street
Columbia, SC 29201
Phone: (803) 734-8492
Fax: (803) 734-3389
Website: http://myscschools.com

South Dakota

South Dakota Department of Education
700 Governors Drive
Pierre, SD 57501-2291

Phone: (605) 773-3553
Fax: (605) 773-6139
Website: www.state.sd.us/deca

Tennessee

Tennessee State Department of Education
Andrew Johnson Tower
Sixth Floor
710 James Robertson Parkway
Nashville, TN 37243-0375
Phone: (615) 741-2731
Fax: (615) 532-4791
Website: www.state.tn.us/education

Texas

Texas Education Agency
William B. Travis Building
1701 North Congress Avenue
Austin, TX 78701-1494
Phone: (512) 463-9050
Fax: (512) 475-3447
Website: www.tea.state.tx.us

Utah

Utah State Office of Education
250 East 500 South
P.O. Box 144200
Salt Lake City, UT 84114-4200
Phone: (801) 538-7500
Fax: (801) 538-7521
Website: www.usoe.k12.ut.us

Vermont

Vermont Department of Education
120 State Street
Montpelier, VT 05620-2501
Phone: (802) 828-3135
Fax: (802) 828-3140
Website: www.state.vt.us/educ

Virginia

Virginia Department of Education
P.O. Box 2120
101 North 14th Street
Richmond, VA 23218-2120

Phone: (804) 225-2020
Toll-free: (800) 292-3820
Fax: (804) 371-2455
Website: www.pen.k12.va.us/go/VDOE

Washington

Office of Superintendent of Public Instruction (Washington)
Old Capitol Building
600 South Washington
P.O. Box 47200
Olympia, WA 98504-7200
Phone: (360) 725-6000
Fax: (360) 753-6712
Website: www.k12.wa.us

West Virginia

West Virginia Department of Education
Building 6, Room 346
1900 Kanawha Boulevard East
Charleston, WV 25305-0330
Phone: (304) 558-0304
Fax: (304) 558-2584
Website: http://wvde.state.wv.us

Wisconsin

Wisconsin Department of Public Instruction
125 South Webster Street
P.O. Box 7841
Madison, WI 53702
Phone: (608) 266-3390
Toll-free: (800) 441-4563
Fax: (608) 267-1052
Website: www.dpi.state.wi.us

Wyoming

Wyoming Department of Education
Hathaway Building
Second Floor
2300 Capitol Avenue
Cheyenne, WY 82002-0050
Phone: (307) 777-7675
Fax: (307) 777-6234
Website: www.k12.wy.us

Territories

American Samoa

American Samoa Department of Education
Pago Pago, AS 96799
Phone: (684) 633-5237
Fax: (684) 633-4240
Website: www.doe.as

Commonwealth of the Northern Mariana Islands

Commonwealth of the Northern Mariana Islands Public School System
P.O. Box 501370
Saipan, MP 96950
Phone: (670) 664-3721
Fax: (670) 664-3796
Website: http://net.saipan.com/cftemplates/pss/index.cfm

Guam

Guam Department of Education
P.O. Box DE
Agana, GM 96932
Phone: (671) 475-0462
Fax: (671) 472-5003
Website: www.gdoe.net

Puerto Rico

Puerto Rico Department of Education
P.O. Box 190759
San Juan, PR 00919-0759
Phone: (787) 763-2171
Fax: (787) 250-0275
Website: http://de.gobierno.pr/dePortal/Inicio/Inicio.aspx

Virgin Islands

Virgin Islands Department of Education
44-46 Kongens Gade
St. Thomas, VI 00802
Phone: (340) 774-2810
Fax: (340) 779-7153
Website: www.doe.vi

TAKING ACTION FOR EDUCATION

Give Kids Good Schools

601 Thirteenth Street NW
Suite 710 South
Washington, D.C. 20005-3808
Phone: (202) 628-GKGS (4547)
Fax: (202) 628-1893
Website: www.givekidsgoodschools.org

The Give Kids Good Schools website is a subsidiary of Public Education Network (see below), which serves almost as a "PAC," or political action committee, by providing facts about public schools. This site is a tutorial for activism, with many easy-to-follow ways to get involved. One is a link to current national educational news articles. Another is a link to efficiently contact your elected officials and local newspapers; plugging in your zip code directs you to the appropriate address. Give Kids Good Schools even provides a template for a letter you can personalize. This site also prepares the layperson to question elected officials. Access is free, but donations are accepted.

Public Education Network (PEN)

601 Thirteenth Street NW
Suite 710 South
Washington, D.C. 20005-3808
Phone: (202) 628-7460
Fax: (202) 628-1893
Website: www.PublicEducation.org

PEN is a national association of local education funds and individuals working to mobilize community engagement and improvement in American public education. This is a well-designed and easily navigated website with clear opportunities for taking action to improve public schools. Highlight: The informative weekly e-newsletter (available free by subscription) contains links to the latest studies and education-themed articles and funding opportunities.

Rethinking Schools

1001 East Keefe Avenue
Milwaukee, WI 53212
Phone: (414) 964-9646
Toll-free: (800) 669-4192
Fax: (414) 964-7220
Website: www.rethinkingschools.org

This small nonprofit was started by a group of Milwaukee, Wisconsin, teachers who wanted not only to improve their local educational milieu but to impact education nationwide. Over twenty years, Rethinking Schools has become a prominent publisher of educational materials (including a quarterly journal by the same name) that primarily focus on issues affecting urban schools. The journal is available by subscription, and a portion of the articles can also be accessed online. Highlight: Their "Web Resources" tab contains links to a vast array of pertinent sites that will appeal to other activists.

ORGANIZATIONS FOR EDUCATORS AND PARENTS

American Association of School Administrators (AASA)

801 North Quincy Street
Suite 700
Arlington, VA 22203-1730
Phone: (703) 528-0700
Fax: (703) 841-1543
Website: www.aasa.org

The AASA site encompasses a wealth of information for a much broader audience than just school administrators. The association was founded in 1865, with a mission to prepare effective school leaders dedicated to providing high-quality public education. Publications, surveys, and presentations focus on topics such as childhood obesity, asthma, and healthy school environments. One high-profile initiative is the AASA's Stand Up for Public Education Campaign, which describes its priorities as "getting children ready for school, getting schools ready for children, and getting children ready for democracy." The layperson will be able to freely access substantial materials on this website. Even greater resources and research are available to AASA members (professional educators), who also enjoy discounts from publishers in the education field.

Association for Supervision and Curriculum Development (ASCD)

1703 North Beauregard Street
Alexandria, VA 22311-1714
Phone: (800) 933-2723, press 2 (toll-free from the United States and Canada)
(703) 578-9600, press 2 (local to the Washington, D.C., area)
Website: www.ascd.org

The ASCD prides itself on being a source for ideas, information, and professional development for educators. Non-Educators will find this site to be a valuable resource as well. It offers free access to research materials on teaching and learning; additional archived articles can be purchased. Members can access the complete library and are eligible for newsletters and the ASCD's flagship publication *Educational Leadership*. Highlight: The "Lexicon of Learning" section under "Publications" provides an "edu-speak" glossary.

Family Education Network

501 Boylston St
Suite 900
Boston, MA 02116
Phone: (617) 671-2000
Website: www.fen.com

This is a comprehensive learning/information resource and online consumer network for parents and teachers. Parents can benefit from advice and articles geared to children from infants to teenagers (www.FamilyEducation.com), teachers can receive classroom ideas and support through www.TeacherVision.com, and children can play educational games and even get help with homework at www.FEKids.com. Free newsletters are available and lead to some fee-based services.

GreatSchools

301 Howard Street
Suite 1440
San Francisco, CA 94105
Phone: (415) 977-0700
Fax: (415) 977-0704
Website: www.greatschools.net

GreatSchools is a savvy resource for choosing a school. Not only does it clarify the differences between types of schools (charter, magnet, etc.), but it takes families step-by-step through the process of how to make informed decisions. Check out the nationwide comparison feature that locates schools within a geographic area or school district. This site is also overflowing with helpful articles about children's development, academics, and special needs.

Home School Legal Defense Association (HSLDA)

P.O. Box 3000
Purcellville, VA 20134
Phone: (540) 338-5600
Fax: (540) 338-2733
Website: www.hslda.org

HSLDA is an organization that offers a wide variety of resources, including legal representation for homeschooling parents. Sample topics include a guide for parents in determining if homeschooling is right for them and extensive checklist queries about the struggling learner. This easy-to-use website has links to articles that support its Christian philosophy. Membership dues are paid yearly.

National Coalition for Parent Involvement in Education (NCPIE)

Sue Ferguson, Chair
1400 L Street NW
Suite 300
Washington, D.C. 20005
Phone (202) 289-6790
Fax (202) 289-6791
Website: www.ncpie.org

NCPIE seeks to enable families, schools, and communities to develop strong communication skills to work together successfully. It serves as part of a coalition to represent parent- and family-involvement initiatives and seeks to encourage family involvement and monitor legislation. This website is helpful as an initial introduction to the subject of parent involvement. Particularly useful are the extensive links to partner organizations and resources.

National Parent Teacher Association (PTA)

541 North Fairbanks Court
Suite 1300
Chicago, IL 60611-3396
Phone: (312) 670-6782
Toll-free: (800) 307-4PTA (4782)
Fax: (312) 670-6783
Website: www.pta.org

PTA is known as the largest volunteer advocacy group in the United States. It acts as a proponent for children and youth in communities and governmental forums, coordinates programs that encourage involvement in public education, and provides tools for successful parenting. Highlight: The article "National Standards for Parent/Family Involvement Programs" is quite helpful. This website discusses the benefits of membership, but the fee structure is unclear.

SITES OF EDUCATIONAL VALUE

Parent Academic Resources, Inc. (PARI)

Attn: Krzysztof Grabarek
16 Coventry Road
Grafton, MA 01519
Website: www.academicresources.org

PARI believes that parents can still be an essential part of student learning at home during the secondary school years. PARI creates and distributes print and training materials to offer specific academic support and adolescent guidance. Highlight: Mr. Grabarek's articles are intelligent, practical, and easy to apply, especially "Staying Involved: Approaches to Helping Our Middle School and High School Students Learn." The website is streamlined and economical, and the resources are first-rate.

Teachers Involve Parents in Schoolwork (TIPS)

Johns Hopkins University
National Network of Partnership Schools (NNPS)
Johns Hopkins University
3003 North Charles Street
Suite 200
Baltimore, MD 21218
Phone: (410) 516-8800
Fax: (410) 516-8890
Website: www.ncpie.org

NNPS collaborates with schools, districts, states, and organizations by using research-based approaches to organize family- and community-involvement programs for student success. TIPS is one such partnership process structured around interesting, interactive homework shared between family members. It even includes a teacher-feedback mechanism. The website is highly academic and can be a bit daunting for the layperson; however, the lesson plans themselves are innovative and worth exploring. Educators, schools, and districts will get the most out of this by adopting the TIPS program.

Connect for Kids

The Forum for Youth Investment
The Cady-Lee House
7064 Eastern Avenue NW
Washington, D.C. 20012
Phone: (202) 207-3333
Fax: (202) 207-3329
Website: www.connectforkids.org

Connect for Kids, managed by the Forum for Youth Investment, aims to link young people with concerned adults and accurate data on issues that affect children. This website suggests ways to take action, and it also gives youth-focused organizations a platform from which to reach a wider audience. The breadth of articles is quite impressive, and although they always center on issues that impact children's lives, the tones vary from the folksy to the academic. An interesting advocacy section supplies tools for interacting with elected officials.

Greater Good

The Center for the Development of Peace and Well-Being
University of California, Berkeley
2425 Atherton Street #6070
Berkeley, CA 94720-6070
Phone: (510) 643-8965
Fax: (510) 643-7350
Website: www.greatergood.berkeley.edu

Greater Good "advances the Center's mission to sponsor and disseminate leading scientific research into the roots of everyday altruism, healthy relationships, and happy children." This quarterly publication has addressed such issues as compassion in the classroom and motivating children to think ethically, behave empathetically, and take appropriate action when situations require it. *Greater Good* marries science with compassion and altruism to produce thought-provoking and inspiring articles aimed simultaneously at parents, educators, and community leaders. The magazine is available by subscription.

Koret Task Force on K–12 Education

Hoover Institution
434 Galvez Mall
Stanford University
Stanford, CA 94305-6010
Phone: (650) 723-1754
Toll-free: (877) 466-8374
Fax: (650) 723-1687
Website: www.hoover.org/research/ktf

The Koret Task Force on K–12 Education is a team of high-profile education experts brought together to gather, evaluate, and disseminate data in an analytical context and to analyze reform measures with the purpose of enhancing the quality of K–12 education. Click on the "In the News" tab to read articles by the likes of Diane Ravitch, Chester Finn, and Caroline Hoxby, among others.

New Horizons for Learning

Website: www.newhorizons.org

New Horizons was established in 1980 as a voice for educational change and a launching pad for educational practices that had not yet found the mainstream. Although the founder of New Horizons has retired, the site is still up and running, and the archived journal articles (of surprising range and depth) remain available. This is one of those websites to spend hours on, reading one fascinating article after another with titles like "A Brain Compatible Approach to Studio Dance" and "Training Kids to Think Like Olympians."

Study Circles Resource Center

P.O. Box 203
697 Pomfret Street
Pomfret, CT 06258
Phone: (860) 928-2616
Fax: (860) 928-3713
Website: www.studycircles.org

The Study Circles Resource Center helps communities organize and develop frameworks for structured dialogue that welcomes diverse viewpoints and supports change. In working with groups of all sizes, the center attends especially to the racial and ethnic dimensions of problems. The website offers extensive education in just what a study circle is, how to organize one, various issues that lend themselves to the format, and news articles that share past experiences. This is an informative and well-structured website; you can sense that the creators truly desire to educate the public.

What Kids Can Do, Inc.

P.O. Box 603252
Providence, RI
Phone and fax: (401) 247-7665
Website: http://ww.whatkidscando.org

The mission of What Kids Can Do is to provide a forum for the views of adolescents related to their lives, their learning, their work, and their partnerships with adults. This website is limited in size but a rich provider of stories, articles, and books inspiring to children, teens, and adults alike.

Glossary

accommodation: A major change in a schema or the construction of an entirely new schema.

accountability: A characteristic of an educational system where a designated entity (a school, a district, or governmental body) is held responsible for student achievement.

acculturation: Cultural adjustment on the part of an individual, group, or people as a result of adaptation to or the borrowing of another culture's characteristics. Prolonged contact resulting in a merging of cultures also constitutes acculturation.

advisory councils: In school-based management, committees are established to attend to the needs of certain sectors of the school population (e.g., Title 1, bilingual, etc.), and these committees or councils bring their findings to the general meetings, but they do not have voting rights.

assessment: A tool used to document performance in a given subject or area; another word for "test."

assimilation: What we do when small changes to an existing schema become necessary.

benchmarks: The hierarchy of knowledge and skills for which students are responsible at each grade level.

block scheduling: A method of organizing instructional time (primarily in secondary schools) by creating longer class periods (blocks) of usually an hour or more.

charter schools: Independent public schools designed and run by stakeholders (e.g., parents, teachers, administrators, foundations) and often tailored to community needs. Charter schools receive public funding, but are free from many local district regulations in return for promising a certain level of student achievement. These schools are licensed and monitored for their effectiveness; they risk losing funding if they cannot deliver on their promises of achievement.

child-centered: A method of teaching attuned to the interests and individual needs of the child.

cognitive: Pertaining to the acquisition of knowledge through thought, perception, belief, and memory.

cognitive processing: The way in which input is sorted and organized by the brain.

consumables: Expendable supplies (e.g., paper, pencils, etc.) used in the course of a school or work day.

conventions: Accepted techniques.

criterion-referenced: Compared to a standard for mastery of certain skills.

culture: The totality of behaviors, thoughts, and beliefs common to a particular community.

curricular program: "What" is taught in school.

curriculum: The means and materials with which students will interact for the purpose of achieving identified educational outcomes.

developmental: Focusing on the naturally unfolding, best pace for each child to acquire different skills.

direct instruction: "Teacher-centered" teaching. The instructor endeavors to maintain control of students' attention to tasks instead of allowing students to pace and control their own learning rates, behaviors, and styles.

disaggregated: This term usually refers to segments of data, separated from the whole, so that various subcategories (usually test scores) can be analyzed.

dyslexic: A cognitive dysfunction manifested by a difficulty with reading and writing.

enrichment: Enhanced educational opportunities that supplement and add value to the regular academic curriculum.

equilibration: Cognitive balance.

essentialism: The perspective that suggests there are core skills and knowledge that all students should acquire, skills that are essential for sustaining our social order.

evaluation: A report assigning value to collected information.

explicit curriculum: Facet of the school curriculum concerned with the subjects that will be taught, the identified "mission" of the school, and the knowledge and skills that the school expects successful students to acquire.

extracurriculum (or *cocurriculum*): All of those school-sponsored programs that are intended to supplement the academic aspect of the school experience.

formative assessment: Assessment of student progress used for making instructional decisions as opposed to assigning grades.

frameworks: Specific goals explained by subject or grade level.

gain scores: An assessment of student progress that compares their preinstruction academic level to their postinstruction level rather than using the assumption that students enter a grade level having mastered the previous level.

gifted program (a.k.a. Gifted and Talented, GATE): A program designed to serve students deemed capable of succeeding beyond the norm, based either on IQ tests, psychological profiling, demonstrated academic motivation, or display of exceptional talent in a variety of designated areas (e.g., arts, etc.).

heuristics: Problem solving using rules of thumb methods.

humanistic-progressive education: A humanistic-social approach to education that aims to develop excellent citizens through child-centered activity.

ideological: Relating to the fundamental beliefs that illuminate a culture, community, or individual.

implicit curriculum: The lessons that arise from the culture of the school and the behaviors, attitudes, and expectations that characterize that culture.

individualized education program: A comprehensive written plan created by teachers, parents, administrators, and other specialists to formalize an educational approach for a student with learning disabilities.

institutions: Organizations that arise from *the ideas that people hold in common*. Institutions are the dynamic manifestations of a culture that has found an *identity* through its shared ideals and so wishes to sustain itself through time.

instructional program: "How" students will be taught.

integrated curriculum: Two or more subjects (like math and science or English and social studies) combined in the teaching of a lesson.

intervention: An education effort that supplements usual procedure.

learning styles: Consistent habits or preferences that characterize how an individual takes in, sorts out, remembers, and utilizes new information.

local education agency: Administrative body at the local level (e.g., a school district) responsible for the public school.

magnet schools: Schools originally designed to achieve racial balance and built around a theme that "attracts" students from a wide geographic area.

mainstreaming: The practice of including an educationally disabled student in a general education classroom.

mentoring: Providing particular wisdom or expertise in a guiding, facilitating manner.

multiculturalism: A philosophy that looks beyond the white, Western European tradition to honor a variety of cultures.

myth: A widely held but false belief.

norm group: A sample of test takers representing a particular age, grade, background, and so forth.

norm-referenced: Compared to the performance of others in a group with certain defining characteristics.

null curriculum: Topics that are intentionally left out of the explicit curriculum.

open classroom: A multiage classroom in which children can receive individualized attention and learn at their own pace.

open enrollment: A period in which a school may admit applicants from outside its normal geographic boundaries.

pedagogy: The study of the teaching of children.

peer mediation: A program in which students are trained to provide conflict resolution or similar services to fellow students.

perennialism: The notion that there are ideas, or truths, that have transcended time and remain as vital today as they ever were.

performance assessments: Evaluations where the participants are required to produce something or demonstrate a hands-on skill.

perpetuation: The process by which something's existence is prolonged.

phonics: The study of the relationship between letters (written language) and sounds (spoken language); an instructional strategy used to teach beginning readers to sound out words.

progressivism: A philosophy that focuses on the positive change that individuals with a particular educational background could provide. Change was based on "doing" more than on "knowing" and on solving problems more than on passing on the culture as it existed. Within the schools, this would mean a shift from the subject-centered perspective of the traditional curriculum to a child-centered approach.

pullout program: A special learning opportunity for students, individually or in small groups, who are "pulled out" from their regular classroom.

random processing: Organizing data in sections without the appearance of a master plan.

reform: A program that seeks to replace some aspect of the current educational operation.

remediation: An instructional strategy whose goal is to bring students with deficient skills up to a standard level.

resource specialist: A specially credentialed teacher who provides extra help to students in the classroom or in a pullout program.

revolution: The process through which, by virtue of some imperative for change, one thing is replaced with something significantly different from that which previously existed.

rigorous: Precise, accurate, strict.

schemas: General representations of how something is done or what one expects to happen based upon accumulated experiences.

school within a school: A trend designed to personalize large schools by creating smaller learning communities within them.

school-based management: Aspects of decision making are shifted from school districts to individual school sites.

sequential processing: Proceeding in a linear fashion through a series of logical steps.

service learning: Programs that recognize citizenship as an intrinsic educational value through students' participation in community-service projects.

site council: An active decision-making council (comprising teachers, administrators, parents, and community members) that collaborates on developing a school plan.

social reconstructionism: A perspective that specifically sees the schools as the agency for solving the problems of society. Schools provide the future leaders for the community, state, and nation and therefore must present a curriculum that prepares students to meet the very real challenges that lie ahead.

standardized tests: Selected-response exams designed to generate reliable scores by containing questions of recognized validity.

standards: Minimum learning expectations for all children that serve as benchmarks in a particular subject.

summative assessments: Assessments of student progress that are used for the assigning of grades.

systematic: Methodical.

systemic: Occurring throughout an entire system or body.

thematic curriculum: A schoolwide instructional focus where each grade may be assigned a different aspect.

tracks: The manner in which students are grouped by their abilities.

unschooling: A homeschooling philosophy which regards the whole world as a classroom and where curriculum content and pacing is driven by the child's interests.

whole language: A method of reading instruction where language is learned by meaning in context as opposed to being segmented into drills.

References

Adler, M. J. (1982). *Paideia proposal: An educational manifesto.* New York: Macmillan.

Adler, M. J. (1983). *Paideia problems and possibilities.* New York: Macmillan.

American Association for the Advancement of Science. (1989). *Science for all Americans* (Project 2061). Washington, D.C.: Author.

American Association of Colleges for Teacher Education, Bicentennial Commission on Education for the Profession of Teaching. (1976). *Educating a profession.* Washington, D.C.: Author, 6–12.

Amschler, D. H. (January 2002). The alarming increase of type 2 diabetes in children. *Journal of School Health, 72,* 39–41.

Anderson, L. W., and Krathwohl, O. R. (2001). *A taxonomy for learning, teaching, and assessing.* New York: Longman.

Association for Supervision and Curriculum Development. (2006). *Advocacy guide.* Alexandria, VA: Author.

Barba, R. (1995). *Science in the multicultural classroom: A guide to teaching and learning.* Boston: Allyn & Bacon.

Barkley, R., Jr. (2005). *Leadership in education: A handbook for school superintendents and teacher union presidents.* Cincinnati, OH: Knowledge Works Foundation.

Benefits of small class sizes found to last years. (April 30, 1999). *Charlotte (NC) Observer.* (From Cox News Service).

Bloom, B. (1976). *Human characteristics and school learning.* New York: McGraw-Hill.

Bode, B. H. (1938). *Progressive education at the crossroads.* New York: Newson.

Brown, B. (1988). The vital agenda for research on extracurricular influences: A reply to Holland and Andre. *Review of Educational Research, 58*(1), 107–11.

Bruner, J. (1960). *The process of education.* Cambridge, MA: Harvard University Press.

Buchanan, B. (October 2005). Getting to wellness. Supplement to *American School Board Journal, 192,* 4–7.

Buchen, I. (2004). *The future of the American school system.* Lanham, MD: Scarecrow Education.

Burns, R. (1984). How time is used in elementary schools: The activity structure of classrooms. In L. W. Anderson (Ed.), *Time and school learning: Theory, research, practice.* London: Croom Helm.

Center for Comprehensive School Reform and Improvement (CSRI). (August 2005). Newsletter. Available at www.centerforcsri.org/index.php?option=com_content&task=view&id=130&Itemid=5.

Center for Comprehensive School Reform and Improvement (CSRI). (September 2006). Newsletter. Available at www.centerforcsri.org/index.php?option=com_content&task=view&id=367&Itemid=5.

Center for Education Reform (CER). (2001). Charter school highlights and statistics. Available at www.edreform.com/pubs/chglance.htm.

Chenfeld, M. (November 2001). Oy! Education! *Kappan Professional Journal, Phi Delta Kappa International, 83*(3), 181.

Committee for Economic Development. (1985). College Board, Academic preparation for the world of work; Investing in our children: Business and the public schools.

Conzemius, A., and O'Neill, J. (2001). *Building shared responsibility for student learning.* Alexandria, VA: Association for Supervision and Curriculum Development.

Cox, J., and Puleo, P. (2002). Measuring up: A parent's guide to testing, grades and assessments. Ask an Expert. School Wise Press. Available at www.schoolwisepress.com/expert/test.1html.

Curriculum standards for the social studies. (1994). Silver Spring, MD: National Council for the Social Studies.

Darling, S., and Westberg, S. (May 2004). Parent involvement in children's acquisition of reading. *Reading Teacher, 57*(8), 774–76.

Ebert, C., and Ebert, E. (1998). *The inventive mind in science.* Englewood, CO: Teacher Ideas Press.

Ebert, E. (1994). The cognitive spiral: Creative thinking and cognitive processing. *Journal of Creative Behavior, 28*(4), 275–90.

Ebert, E., and Culyer, R. (2008). *School: An introduction to education.* Belmont, CA: Wadsworth/Thomson Learning.

Eisner, E. (1994). *The educational imagination: On the design and evaluation of school programs.* (3rd ed.). New York: Macmillan.

Elkind, D. (1981). *The hurried child: Growing up too fast.* New York: Addison-Wesley.

Epstein, J. L., et al. (1997). *School, family and community partnerships: Your handbook for action.* Thousand Oaks, CA: Corwin Press, Inc.

Finn, J. (March 2002). Small classes in American schools: Research, practice, and politics. *Phi Delta Kappan, 83*(7), 551–60.

Friedman, R. (September 2000). Magnet schools: Creative choices within the public schools. *Parenting Magazine.*

Gifford, V., and Dean, M. (1990). Differences in extracurricular activity participation, achievement, and attitudes toward school between ninth-grade students attending junior high school and those attending senior high school. *Adolescence, 25*(100), 799–802.

Goddess, J. (1998). *California school rules.* San Francisco, CA: School Wise Press.

Gould, H. C. (2004). Can novice teachers differentiate instruction? Yes, they can! *New Horizons for Learning Online Journal, 11*(1), *Winter 2005.* Available on the New Horizons website at www.newhorizons.org/strategies/differentiated/gould.htm.

Grabarek, K. (2005). Staying involved: Approaches to helping our middle school and high school students learn. Parent Academic Resources, Inc. Available at www.academicresources.org/learning.html.

Graham, P. A. (May 2004). Whom should our schools serve? *School Administrator.* American Association of School Administrators. Available at www.aasa.org/publications/saarticledetail.cfm?ItemNumber=1379&snItemNumber=950&tnItemNumber=1995.

Henkoff, R. (October 21, 1991). Four states: Reform turns radical. *Fortune Magazine,* 137–44.

Hirsch, E. D., Jr. (1988). *Cultural literacy.* New York: Vintage Books.

Holland, A., and Andre, T. (1987). Participation in extracurricular activities in secondary school: What is known, what needs to be known? *Review of Educational Research, 57*(4), 437–66.

Hopkings, G. (2004). Parental involvement is as easy as PIE! *Education World.* Available at www.educationworld.com/a_curr/curr030.shtml.

Hymowitz, K. (Spring 2001). Parenting: The lost art. *American Educator,* 4–6.

Illustration digest. (January 1996). *Reader's Digest,* 82.

King-Sears, M. (2001). Three steps for gaining access to the general education curriculum for learners with disabilities. *Intervention in School and Clinic, 37*(2), 67–76.

Kirshbaum, R. (1998). *Parent power.* New York: Hyperion.

Kleinz, K. (Spring 2000). Engaging the public in the public schools. *Focus on Study Circles, 11*(2), 1, 8. Available on the Study Circles Resource Center website at www.studycircles.org/en/Resource.62.aspx.

Koetzsch, R. E. (1997). *The parents' guide to alternatives in education.* Boston: Shambhala.

Lagemann, E. C. (May 16, 2007). Public rhetoric, public responsibility and the public schools. *Education Week, 26*(37), 30, 40. Available on the *Education Week* website at www.edweek.org/ew/articles/2007/05/16/37lagemann.h26.html?print=1.

Lauer, P. (2004). A policy maker's primer on education research. Education Commission of the States. Available at www.ecs.org.html/educationIssues/Research/primer.

Levine, M. (2002). *A mind at a time.* New York: Simon and Schuster.

Lickona, T. (October 2000). Character-based sexuality education: Bringing parents into the picture. *Educational Leadership, 58*(2), 60–64.

McEwan, E. (1998). *Angry parents and failing schools: What's wrong with the public schools and what you can do about it.* Wheaton, IL: Harold Shaw.

McPherson, K. (2005). Service learning: Introduction. New Horizons for Learning. Available at www.newhorizons.org/strategies/service_learning/front_service.htm.

Merrow, John. (2001). *Choosing excellence*. Lanham, MD: Scarecrow Press.

Moe, T. M. (Ed.). (2001). *A primer on America's schools*. Stanford, CA: Hoover Institution Press.

Moskowitz, E. (June 23, 2007). Stoneham cuts all sports at high school. *Boston (MA) Globe*, 1A.

National Center for Education Statistics (NCES). (1999). *Digest of education statistics, 1998*. Washington, D.C.: U.S. Department of Education.

National Center for Education Statistics. (2000). *Digest of education statistics, 1999*. Washington, D.C.: U.S. Department of Education.

National Center for Education Statistics. (September 2001). Overview of public elementary and secondary schools and districts: School year 1999–2000. Statistical Analysis Report. Available at http://nces.ed.gov/pubs2001/overview/table09.asp.

National Center for Education Statistics. (2003). *Digest of education statistics, 2002*. Washington, D.C.: U.S. Department of Education.

National Center for Education Statistics. (2004). *Digest of education statistics, 2003*. Washington, D.C.: U.S. Department of Education.

National Center for Education Statistics. (2005). *Digest of education statistics, 2004*. Washington, D.C.: U.S. Department of Education.

National Center for Education Statistics. (2006). *Characteristics of private schools in the United States: Results from the 2003–2004 Private School Universe Survey*. Washington, D.C.: U.S. Department of Education.

National Health and Nutrition Examination Survey. (1999). Washington, D.C.: National Center for Health Statistics.

National Home Education Research Unit (NHERI). (1999). Facts on home schooling. Available at www.nheri.org/98/research/general.html.

National Parent Teacher Association. (1997). *National standards for parent-involvement programs*. Chicago, IL: Author.

National Research Council. (1996). *National science education standards*. Washington, D.C.: National Academy Press.

Newman, R. (Winter 1997–1998). Parent conferences: A conversation between you and your child's teacher. *Childhood Education*, 74(2), 100–101.

Northwest Regional Educational Laboratory. (1998). *Catalog of school reform models*. (1st ed.). Washington, D.C.: U.S. Department of Education, ch. 12, p. 12.

Oppenheimer, T. (2004). *The flickering mind: Saving education from the false promise of technology*. New York: Random House.

Orange, C. (2002). *The quick reference guide to educational innovations: Practices, programs, policies, and philosophies*. Thousand Oaks, CA: Corwin Press.

Piaget, J. (1926). *The language and thought of the child*. New York: Harcourt, Brace & World.

Piaget, J. (1985). *The equilibration of cognitive structures: The central problem of intellectual development*. Chicago: University of Chicago Press.

Public Agenda Online. (1999). Playing their parts: What parents and teachers really mean by parental involvement. Available at www.publicagenda.org/issues/angles.cfm?issue_type=education.

Ravitch, D. (2000). *Left back: A century of failed school reforms*. New York: Simon & Schuster.

Robinson, E., and Fine, M. (1994). Developing collaborative home-school relationships. *Preventing School Failure*, 39(1), 9–15.

Rose and Gallup. (September 1998). Thirtieth annual Phi Delta Kappa/Gallup poll of the public's attitudes toward the public schools. *Phi Delta Kappan*, 80(1), 41–58.

Rudner, L. (March 1999). Scholastic achievement and demographic characteristics of home-school students in 1998. *Education Policy Analysis Archives*, 7(8).

Rutherford F. J., and Ahlgren, A. (1990). *Science for all Americans*. New York: Oxford University Press.

Sacchetti, M. (June 22, 2007). For schools, parents crack open bank book. *Boston (MA) Globe*, 1A.

Sadker, D., and Sadker, M. (2000). *Teachers, schools, and society*. Boston: McGraw-Hill.

Scott-Little, C., Kagan, S., and Frelow, V. (November 2005). *Inside the content; the breadth and depth of early learning standards: Creating the conditions for success with early learning standards*. Greensboro, NC: SERVE.

Senge, P. (1990). *The fifth discipline: The art and practice of the learning organization*. New York: Doubleday.

Sheurer, D., and Parkay, F. (1992). The new Christian Right and the public school curriculum: The Florida report. In J. B. Smith, and J. G. Coleman Jr. (Eds.). *School library media annual*, vol. 10. Englewood, CO: Libraries Unlimited.

Sizer, T. (1985). *Horace's compromise: The dilemma of the American high school*. Boston: Houghton Mifflin.

Small class sizes produce long-term benefits. (September 1999). *National Education Association*, 16(1), 33.

Stiggins, R. (2001). *Student-involved classroom assessment.* (3rd ed.). Upper Saddle River, NJ: Prentice Hall.

Sweeney, J. (1990). Classroom practice and educational research. *Social Studies, 81,* 278–82.

Tanner, L. (April 9, 2003). Obese kids' suffering profound. *Charlotte (NC) Observer,* 12A.

U.S. Department of Public Education. (June 2000). State regulation of private schools (CA, FL, NY, TX). U.S. Dept of Public Education, Office of Non-Public Education. Available at http://www.ed.gov/pubs/RegPrivSchl/intro.html.

Vail, K. (January 2004). Raising the (salad) bar on obesity. *American School Board Journal, 191,* 22–25.

Voke, Heather. (2002). Engaging the public in its schools. Association for Supervision and Curriculum Development, July Info Brief, No. 30.

Washburne, C. (1926). The philosophy of the Winnetka curriculum. In Harold Rugg (Ed.), *The foundations and technique for the study of education.* National Society for the Study of Education. Bloomington, IN: Public School Publishing.

Welner, K. M., and Welner, K. G. (March 1999). Conceptualizing homeschooling data: A response to Rudner. *Education Policy Analysis Archives 7*(13), 3.

White, L. (1975). *The concept of cultural systems: A key to understanding tribes and nations.* New York: Columbia University Press.

Wong, H., and Wong, R. (2005). *The first days of school.* Sunnyvale, CA: Harry K. Wong Publications.